Finance
Policies and Procedures Manual

Easily Create Your Financial Policy Manual to
Manage Risk and Establish Effective Internal Controls

Bizmanualz, Inc.

St. Louis, MO, USA

TRADEMARKS

Bizmanualz® is a Trademark of Bizmanualz, Inc.

This publication is sold with the understanding that the publisher is not engaged in rendering legal, accounting, or other professional services. If legal advice or other expert assistance is required, the services of a competent professional should be sought. The Publisher cannot in any way guarantee the forms, agreements, and statements in this manual are being used for the purpose intended and therefore assumes no responsibility for their proper and correct use.

Other Products from Bizmanualz, Inc.

ABR31M	Accounting Policies and Procedures Manual	ISBN 978-1-9315-9102-7
A490	Business Policies and Procedures Sampler	ISBN 978-1-9315-9114-0
ABR34M	Computer & IT Policies and Procedures Manual	ISBN 978-1-9315-9109-6
ABR33M	Disaster Recovery Policies and Procedures Manual	ISBN 978-1-9315-9113-3
ABR41M	Human Resources Policies and Procedures Manual	ISBN 978-1-9315-9110-2
ABR211M	ISO 9001 QMS Policies and Procedures Manual	ISBN 978-1-9315-9141-6
ABR213M	ISO 22000 FSMS Policies and Procedures Manual	ISBN 978-1-9315-9143-0
ABR44M	Sales & Marketing Policies and Procedures Manual	ISBN 978-1-9315-9111-9
ABR32M	Security Planning Policies and Procedures Manual	ISBN 978-1-9315-9112-6

Finance Policies and Procedures
Table of Contents

    1. Introduction
    2. Usage Instructions
    3. The Policy Manual
    4. Effective Communication
    5. Procedures

    1.0 Purpose
    2.0 Scope
    3.0 Management Responsibility
    4.0 Financial Management System
    5.0 Processes and Controls
    6.0 Resource Management

    1.0 Financial Objectives Plan
    2.0 Creating Specific Financial Objectives
    3.0 Balancing Financial Objectives
    4.0 Approval and Monitoring of Financial Objectives
    5.0 Improving Financial Objectives
       Forms/Records
  FA1000-1 Financial Objectives

    1.0 Management Commitment to the Financial Management System
    2.0 Financial Policy
    3.0 Financial Objectives Planning
    4.0 Responsibilities, Authority, and Communication
    5.0 Management Review
       Forms/Records
  FA1010-1 Sample Management Review Agenda

[This page intentionally left blank]

PROCEDURES

Finance Administration

FA1000 Financial Objectives
FA1010 Management Responsibility
FA1020 Continuity Planning
FA1030 Document Control
FA1040 Record Control
FA1050 Annual Stockholders' Meetings
FA1060 Board of Directors' Meetings

Raising Capital

RC1000 Business Plan
RC1010 Capital Plan
RC1020 Valuation
RC1030 Bank Loans
RC1040 Stock Offerings
RC1050 Debt and Investment
RC1060 Asset Acquisition
RC1070 Leasing

Treasury Management

TM1000 Working Capital
TM1010 Cash Management
TM1020 Inventory Management
TM1030 Related Party Transactions
TM1040 Foreign Exchange Management
TM1050 Managing Bank Relationships
TM1060 Merchant Accounts
TM1070 Letters of Credit

Financial Statements

FS1000 Financial Forecasting
FS1010 Financial Reporting
FS1020 Financial Statement Analysis
FS1030 Financial Management Review
FS1040 Financial Restatements
FS1050 Financial Information Release

Internal Controls

FORMS

Finance Administration

Raising Capital

Treasury Management

TM1000-1 Working Capital Plan
TM1010-1 Cash Management Plan
TM1020-1 Inventory Management Plan
TM1020-2 Inventory Management Results
TM1030-1 Related Party Transaction Policy & Conflict Of Interest Questionnaire
TM1030-2 Related Party Transaction Questionnaire Log
TM1040-1 Foreign Exchange Management Plan
TM1040-2 Foreign Exchange Results
TM1050-1 Banking Relationship Contact Management Log
TM1050-2 Banking Relationship Meeting Agenda/Minutes
TM1060-1 Merchant Account Review
TM1070-1 Letter of Credit Checklist

Financial Statements

FS1000-1 Financial Forecasting Checklist
FS1010-1 Financial Report Checklist
FS1010-2 CEO/CFO Certification Checklist
FS1020-1 Financial Analysis Plan
FS1030-1 Financial Management Plan
FS1030-2 Financial Management Meeting Agenda
FS1040-1 Financial Restatement Checklist
FS1050-1 Financial Information Request
FS1050-2 Financial Information Release Log

Internal Controls

AC1000-1 Sarbanes-Oxley Compliance Checklist
AC1010-1 SSAE 16 Compliance Checklist
AC1020-1 Risk Assessment / Management Worksheet
AC1020-2 Sample Chart of Accounts
AC1020-3 Internal Control Checklist
AC1040-1 Corrective Action Plan
AC1050-1 Audit Schedule
AC1050-2 Audit Plan
AC1050-3 Audit Checklist
AC1050-4 Audit Opinion
AC1050-5 Audit Report
AC1060-1 Nonconformity Report
AC1060-2 Corrective Action Request
AC1060-3 Corrective Action Log

[This page intentionally left blank]

Finance Policies and Procedures

Section 100

Introduction

Section 100
Introduction

Introduction

This section provides an introduction and overview of the basic concepts of Finance.

The Finance field is broad, complex, and dynamic, so that no document can claim to be absolute in capturing every possible issue, policy, or procedure and remain current. The concepts discussed in this manual cover the common, basic elements of a Finance Management System.

Please read this whole section <u>before you begin editing</u> your manual.

[This page intentionally left blank]

Finance Manual Introduction

Table of Contents

- 21 -

[This page intentionally left blank]

Contributors

Christopher J. Anderson, MBA, CQA, CQPA, CQIA

Christopher Anderson is the Managing Director of Bizmanualz, Inc., responsible for leading services engagements and directing the development of all manual products and training materials. He has over twenty years of business management and quality process consulting experience, working with small to large software and technology corporations.

As founder, CEO, and President of Investorsoftware.com, an Internet catalog and e-commerce company, Chris oversaw the construction of the e-commerce website, LAN & WAN networks, firewalls, Internet marketing, and other IT systems that supported the company, including multiple Linux web, mail and e-commerce servers, Microsoft Windows 2000/NT domain controllers, PC and MAC systems, and digital copiers, faxes, and printers connected over a LAN. The LAN is connected to a dedicated high-speed internet line behind a firewall.

Mr. Anderson served as Vice President at Arc Tangent, a software publisher where he managed all operations, technical support, sales, accounting and administration. Software development was performed over a Novell LAN.

Prior to Arc Tangent, Mr. Anderson managed North American distribution sales for Interactive Systems, a UNIX operating system developer, publisher and services firm. Interactive Systems supported or developed UNIX multi-user systems, TCP/IP networking and X11 workstation solutions including VP/ix, Novell Ported Netware, Norton Utilities, Lotus 1-2-3, OSF Motif, Visix Looking Glass and variants of UNIX System releases for computer companies.

He has worked as a marketing analyst as Nixdorf Computer Corporation that provided integrated custom solutions for retail department stores, fire and police dispatch, large-scale data entry, and other markets.

As an electrical and computer engineer for McDonnell-Douglas Corporation (now Boeing), Mr. Anderson developed Tomahawk anti-ship missile simulation and analysis software on a high-end line of HP Unix workstations. He developed custom interfaces using FORTRAN and C, color graphics routines, and full screen edit and color windowing capabilities similar to Unix curses routines. He designed and implemented an automated source code management system using Unix's SCCS and INFORMIX SQL relational database and he was responsible for basic system administration, installation, and configuration of all systems.

He served as a Lieutenant and Aeronautical Engineering Duty Officer for the U.S. Navy, working for the Naval Air System Command. He is currently the Managing Director of Bizmanualz, Inc., and lead business process consultant and instructor for his company's "How to Create Well-Defined Processes" and "How to Align a System of People and Processes for Results" course.

Mr. Anderson holds a Master of Business Administration degree from Pepperdine University and a Bachelor of Science degree in Electrical Engineering from Southern Illinois University-Carbondale. He also holds American Society for Quality (ASQ) certifications in quality analysis (CQA), process analysis (CQPA), and quality improvement (CQIA).

John E. Oeltjen, CPA

John is a widely known and respected professional, offering more than 30 years of business leadership and consulting experience. He began his 33-year business career with a "Big 4" firm, where he served as lead regional partner for the middle market practice, leading its rapid revenue growth and expansion.

John also has experience in the private sector, where his titles included President, Chief Operating Officer, and part owner in various manufacturing and distribution businesses that saw significant increases in operational profitability under his watch. His contributions included areas of finance, operations, distribution, logistics, corporate governance, regulatory compliance, and information technology areas, all with an emphasis on process improvement and infrastructure. John is currently Director of Risk Advisory Services for MPP& W, P.C., located in St. Louis, Missouri.

Today, John's areas of concentration include risk assurance and attestation services, corporate strategic and financial planning, operational efficiency, cost accounting, operational controls, and information technology. John's professional expertise also includes merger and acquisition activities, information systems, corporate expansion and personnel related issues.

John is an active member of numerous professional, civic and charitable organizations. He is a graduate of Southern Illinois University-Edwardsville (SIU-E) with a degree in Business Administration-Accounting. He received the Silver Medal for the 1975 Uniform CPA Examination.

Stephen Flick, MBA, MIM, CQA, CMQ/OE, CSSBB

Steve was the Product Director of Bizmanualz, Inc., and from 2005 to 2011 was responsible for developing new products and updating inventory. He has over twenty years of information technology experience as a data analyst, programmer, systems analyst, process analyst, data warehouse subject matter expert, and business consultant. His experience was primarily with large corporations in the manufacturing and service sectors.

Steve is an independent quality consultant, experienced in ISO 9001 auditing, quality training, and content design and development (technical writing).

Steve holds a Master of Business Administration degree in marketing from Webster University, a Master of Information Management from Washington University of St. Louis, and a Bachelor of Arts in biology from St. Louis University. Steve is certified by ASQ as a Quality Auditor (CQA) and a Manager of Quality and Organizational Excellence (CMQ/OE). He also holds IRCA certification as an ISO 9001 auditor.

Don Reed, MA, CQA

Don Reed was with Bizmanualz from 2006 to 2009. Don has extensive technical and informative writing experience. He taught Technical Communication and Advanced Technical Writing at Saint Louis University for over six years and continues to teach English Composition and Basic Writing Workshops at Southwestern Illinois College. He has taught Professional and Business Writing Seminars for numerous organizations in the St. Louis area.

Don also served as the Managing Editor of the *Journal of Policy History*, a peer-reviewed, scholarly journal published through the cooperation of the History Department at Saint Louis University and Penn State University Press.

He has twelve years of experience as a Research & Development Project Engineer, designing and building automated production equipment for a Fortune 500 manufacturer. He was intricately involved with the manufacturing processes including implementing Just-In-Time methods and achieving ISO 9001 certification. He played leadership roles in Statistical Process Control, Continual Process Improvement, Corrective Action Teams, and in creating compliance-driven documentation to achieve and maintain agency certifications.

Don has a Master of Arts in Communication from Saint Louis University and a Bachelor of Science in Electrical Engineering from Southern Illinois University in Carbondale. He is also an ASQ-certified Quality Auditor (CQA).

[This page intentionally left blank]

An Introduction to Financial Processes and Procedures

How important are good financial strategies and processes for your business? Of course they are very important. The goal of this manual is to assist you with key aspects of financial operations that include regulatory compliance, improving performance (through well-defined processes) and implementing best practices into operational areas like Raising Capital and Treasury Management.

While some larger public companies pay attention almost exclusively to financial results, conversely many small and medium businesses do not pay much attention to their overall financial strategies and structures. The goal is to strike some kind of balance between paying attention to financial matters and other aspects of the business such as operations.

Figure 1 below shows the operational sections in which financial processes are divided for the purposes of this Finance Policies and Procedures Manual, and the procedures included in each section. Each procedure is guided by a stated policy, as well as defined objectives stated as the purpose of the procedure. Each procedure includes forms typically used to collect information and data as part of executing the procedure. Each procedure and the associated forms are included on CD in Microsoft Word format so that you can customize all procedures and forms to meet your individual organization's needs, or use them as templates to create additional procedures you feel are important to you financial operations.

The manual describes, in procedure form, best practice activities needed to manage financial processes to achieve regulatory compliance and improve financial performance.

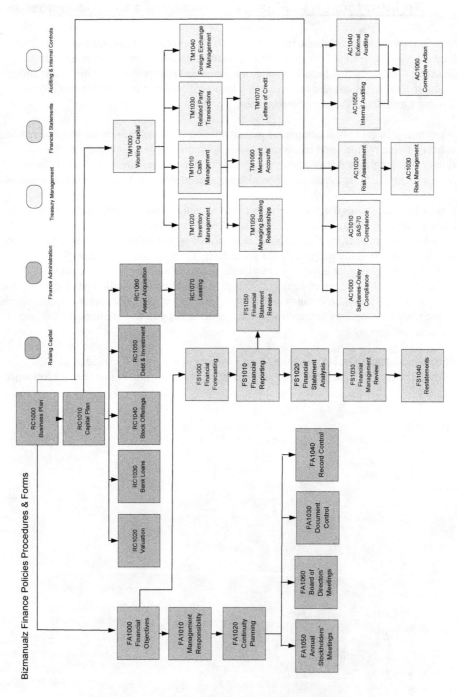

Figure 1: Procedures of the Bizmanualz Finance Manual

The Balanced Scorecard

Before discussing aspects of finance management and finance processes in detail, let's review the concept of a Balanced Scorecard.

Different segments of the business must each operate effectively in their own right for a business to be truly successful. Some businesses survive in spite of poor performance in some segment(s), and that performance is being masked by the performance of another segment. In other words, when one segment is not productive, other segments must be even more productive to compensate for it.

While this condition certainly exists in many businesses, it is far from ideal. When all segments are not functioning it leaves the business vulnerable. When sales fall or production drops can your business survive if it does not have a solid financial structure and practices?

In their important work *The Balanced Scorecard,* Kaplan and Norton discuss four business segments that require focus in some balanced way. (Note: The idea of balance should not be taken too literally – that there has to be perfect balance in all areas of business. Some areas may take priority. The point is that to be successful a business needs to be pay attention to, and work to improve in, all key business areas.) The four segments presented for a balanced scorecard include:

- Customer
- Learning & Growth
- Internal Processes
- Financial

This should be viewed as a minimal list; your organization might identify other areas that require attention in a balanced way. Success in financial areas alone can not translate into overall success if the business does not have good products that are delivered in a timely way that satisfies customers. While financial operations are important, they should never be the exclusive focus of management, no matter how large or small the business.

That Finance is listed as one of the pillars needed for business success in the Balanced Scorecard does indicate its importance in the over-arching view of what in required for businesses to be successful. Surprisingly, however, studies show a large number of medium and small businesses do not proactively manage financial processes such as developing financial strategy or conducting financial analysis. If you are one of these business owners, we hope this manual helps you take positive steps in this direction. If you do already make such financial efforts, we hope this manual will help you incorporate best practices and systematic approaches.

Finance and Regulatory Basics

Regulatory compliance and accuracy for financial reporting is an on-going concern for all public and private companies. History has taught us that the regulatory burden on companies in all types of areas, including finance, will only increase. Therefore, compliance is something that companies must master. If compliance is difficult, then that may be a hint that management may not be setting the right tone or agenda in an organization, because compliance to laws and regulations should be the most basic function of any business.

Concerning regulations, the government has primarily addressed financial operations by regulating information provided to investors thru the Securities Act of 1933 and the Securities and Exchange Act of 1934, and even more recently through the Sarbanes-Oxley Act of 2002.

While the next section focuses on U.S. regulations, similar regulations or requirements exist in most countries. For example, similar versions of the Sarbanes-Oxley Act are in place in Japan and Canada.

Securities Legislation of the 1930's

The Securities Act of 1933 was the first major U. S. federal regulation over the offering of business shares for sale to the public. It attempted to address the fraud and misrepresentation in the markets that was a contributing factor in the market crash of 1929 and its poor performance afterward as the country entered into the depression of the 1930s. The goal of the measure was to increase investor confidence by requiring companies that offer to sell shares to the public to make periodical financial statements that report financial information to the government and to the public (or at least to interested investors). The Act also created penalties for fraud, deceit, and misrepresentation.

It was through this legislation that disclosure requirements were established for companies initially offering stock for sale to the public, and that Annual and Quarterly reporting requirements were created for companies who offered sales for trade in the stock markets.

The Securities Exchange Act of 1934 enhanced the requirements of the 1933 legislation and extended securities regulation into the markets themselves, as well as brokers and agents. It also created the Securities and Exchange Commission (SEC) to enforce the new regulations. Both acts had similar goals: To shed light on how public company financial information is collected and reported and upon how markets selling share based on this information using detailed regulatory requirements.

While companies may find complying with the reporting requirements of these acts cumbersome, the integrity and fairness that these regulations brought to the U. S. markets has made it strong and attractive to investors over an extended period of time, which in turn has provided broad benefits to the U.S. economy.

The Sarbanes-Oxley Act

Most recently, partly in response to several high profile corporate ethical failures where cooked books and inaccurate/incomplete reporting created a financial house of cards, Congress crafted legislation to address corporate accountability - the Sarbanes-Oxley Act of 2002, commonly referred to as "SOX." Most of the compliance requirements created by SOX for public companies are very straightforward. For example:

- Form an Audit Committee from the Board of Directors (including at least one member with financial expertise) to oversee auditing functions.
- Create limits to auditor-auditee relationships to prevent conflicts of interest.
- Create clear channels for employees to report fraud and abuse without fear of retribution.
- CEO and CFO must sign, and be accountable for, financial statements.
- Create rules concerning executive performance pay bonuses, loans, and disclosure.

Besides these requirements, SOX also created a Public Company Accounting Oversight Board (PCAOB), defined criminal penalties for violations, and created commissions to study the topic of corporate accountability and fraud.

Not so straightforward, however, are the two sections that refer to a required internal control system. SOX Section 302 states that the financial statement signing officers are responsible for designing, establishing, and maintaining internal controls to ensure all material information is presented, and that the officers evaluate and report on the effectiveness of the internal controls. SOX Section 404 requires that the annual report contain an internal control report that states the responsibilities of management maintaining an internal control structure and procedures for financial reporting.

The systems that create accurate and complete financial reporting is important for all business – whether they are public companies with regulatory reporting requirements or a private business with few financial reporting regulations. Complete and accurate information is the foundation to managing any business segment, and it is hard to set strategies, form objectives, and produce action plans effectively with knowing where you have been and where you stand know. This is true for operations, sales and marketing, and finance.

So while compliance with regulations are important, it is not the only reason for creating timely and accurate financial statements. As shown in the discussion of the Balanced Scorecard, managing financial operations is a crucial factor in business success, and having the proper information, including financial statements, is a key to successful management.

Finance and Internal Control

The perceived nebulous requirements about internal controls in SOX have created a lot of attention for the topic. What are internal controls? How can they be evaluated as effective? As SOX became law, the topic of internal controls was preeminent in expressed concern by corporate and business leaders about being able to comply. While the SEC and the PCAOB did not want to provide detailed internal control system requirements in their published interpretations of SOX, both did point to publications by the Committee of Sponsoring Organizations of the Treadway Commission (COSO) that provided examples of effective internal control systems.

COSO and Internal Control

COSO has produced two notable publications on internal controls. The first was "Internal Control – Integrated Framework" published in 1992, followed by "Enterprise Risk Management – Integrated Framework" in 2004, expanding on the Risk Assessment section of the 1992 report. Since the first publication dealt with internal control in a more broad and general way (while the 2004 report emphasized Risk Management), this section will explore the 1992 published description of an internal control system framework.

In "Internal Control – Integrated Framework," COSO describes internal control as a process that provides reasonable assurance of organizational achievement in three areas:

- Effectiveness and efficiency of operations
- Reliability of financial reporting
- Compliance with applicable laws and regulations

COSO lists five components that create a framework for internal control all which must be in place to some degree for an internal control system to be effective.

Control Environment – The control environment sets the tone of the organization in which control activities take place. It includes the organizational culture that informs integrity, ethics, competence, and management style.

Risk Assessment – Identifying internal and external risks that can prevent an organization from reaching important goals. Risks can involve inability to perform internally, or external risks that involve the market place, the environment, etc… COSO reemphasized the importance of understanding risk for organizations by expanding on the discusson provided in this section through producing an entire work devoted to the topic. In "Enterprise Risk Management – Integrated Framework", Risk Assessment in itself is not considered sufficient to address organizational risks, so it is expanded to include the following:

- Objective Setting;
- Event Identification;
- Risk Assessment; and
- Risk Response.

Control Activities – The policies and procedures that an organization develops to ensure that processes carry out management directives. These activities are diverse and range from setting and monitoring approvals and authorizations to reviewing and correcting operating performance.

Communication and Information – Information that helps organization members understand and carry out their responsibilities must be communicated in meaningful and timely ways. This includes clear information concerning strategic direction, expectations, and roles and responsibilities at every level of the organization. Communication and Information also involves internal events and external factors and parties such as customers, suppliers, regulators, and shareholders.

Monitoring – Ongoing assessment and evaluation of internal control is an important component of ensuring the control system remains effective and is accomplishing its goals. Through monitoring, problems or deficiencies in the internal control system can be discovered and corrected.

Why Internal Control?

While the COSO publications were directed specifically at *financial* processes, discussions of process improvement have been historically relegated to the *production* floor. The importance of understanding and developing office processes has gained traction, of late. Is it any less important for your office processes to function effectively and efficiently? How well your company manages financial processes (e.g., working capital, debt and investments, leasing) is as important as managing other organizational processes, as the Balanced Scorecard shows. Yet even today, many companies do not attempt to understand and improve finance processes or other office processes to the same degree as production processes.

In fact, a lack of focus on financial processes is common especially among privately owned small and medium sized businesses (SMBs). Research shows that a majority of SMBs unfortunately do not create capital plans, do not actively manage working capital, and do not conduct ratio analyses of their financial statements.

What really represents the biggest threat to the success of your business – minor pilfering from petty cash, or having no thought-out, consistent methods for managing high level financial processes like financial analysis? Many companies have strict control over handling cash, while control over high level financial processes is ignored.

Internal control as defined by COSO is not just about appropriate levels of approvals and implementing checks upon the system like requiring double signature, although these are important aspects. Notice the first reason for internal control listed by COSO is "effectiveness and efficiency of operations." How do required approvals and signatures help an organization with effectiveness (achieving goals) and efficiency (resources needed to reach goals)? The short answer is – they don't. A control system is more than checks and balances.

A Control System that Focuses on Improvement and Success

Of course, we are not saying that businesses should ignore prudent controls over cash. The point is that focusing on small components while not knowing how much cash is tied up in receivables does not represent a control system that recognizes priorities and risk. Focusing solely on the rote and mundane does little to improve your overall financial performance. Plus, financial control systems shouldn't just be about "procedurizing" practices – it should be about continually improving key aspects of the financial operation, such as:

How are you making financial decisions?

- Regularly reviewing and improving the overall capital structure;
- Using a capital plan to minimize cost of capital while strengthening the Debt/Equity position;
- Managing working capital so excessive inventories and receivables do not sap financial resources;
- To ensure proper calculations and scenarios are explored while making debt/investment or leasing decisions; and
- To maximize return while minimizing costs of cash accounts, merchant accounts, and so on.

A control system of well-defined processes is not only about control, it is about consistently striving to be a little better. Control systems that are designed only to achieve compliance are doing the bare minimum, and they are a missed opportunity to gain improvement and a competitive edge. That should be enough reason for any size and type of company to think about using a well-defined, continual improving process approach to creating a financial internal control system.

The Bizmanualz philosophy applies the well-defined process model for internal control. The well defined process approach involves reflectively determining all process elements and desired results, and then dividing process activities into four key stages: Plan, Do, Check, and Act.

The Plan-Do-Check-Act Approach to Well-Defined Processes

The Plan-Do-Check-Act (PDCA) as shown in Figure 2 is a proven method of developing well-defined processes. Under this method, processes are appropriately thought of as recurring or continuing cycles that should not only describe activities, but uses phases for planning and carrying out activities as well as reviewing results. The phases of a process defined by the PDCA approach can be described as follows:

- **Plan** – Understanding goals and requirement of the process (including required resources), as well as researching and incorporating best practices and industry benchmarks, and setting clear objectives.

- **Do** – Execute the plan (carry out activities) while capturing data related to goals and objectives.
- **Check** – Regularly review process results: are objectives being achieved? are resources sufficient? How can improvements be implemented (i.e. change the plan, altering the execution steps, modifying forms or data collection methods).
- **Act** – Implement improvements identified during the review (check) step; modify policy, procedures, objectives, forms, or training materials as necessary.

Using the PDCA process approach is the foundation of Quality Management Systems such as the ISO Standards, and of defect reduction/ continual improvement programs such as

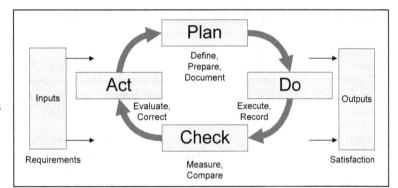

Figure 2: The PDCA Process Approach

Six Sigma. This philosophy of understanding the process then taking a disciplined approach to planning, executing, measuring and improving has been successfully applied to business functions like product design, manufacturing, fulfillment, and accounting. This same disciplined process philosophy can be used to improve finance operations. That is certainly the goal of this Finance manual, as well as all the Bizmanualz Policies, Procedures & Forms product line.

Besides using the PDCA to create well-defined process, other key facets of creating well-defined processes include:

- Understand process inputs and outputs and their requirements.
- Identifying suppliers and customers (external and internal).
- Learning and incorporating industry standards and benchmarks into the Plan; set meaningful goals.
- Monitor (Check) process measurements for discrepancies between goals and results.
- Identify root causes of discrepancies and make corrections (Act) to improve the process.

Another important reason for employing well-defined processes is continual improvement. While continual improvement will be discussed in more detail later, we will note now that continual improvement is the understanding of how you are doing relative to goals and objectives, and what needs to be done to improve performance relative to goals and objectives.

Successful businesses aren't static; neither is the environment they are operating in. Competitors get better and new competitors enter the marketplace. If there isn't a culture of reflection and improvement, then there is a good chance the business will not remain competitive. In fact, it is claimed that there is no such thing as a static business. If you aren't moving forward, you're probably falling behind.

An Internal Control System Can Drive Improvement

With the implementation of the Sarbanes-Oxley Act (SOX), finance and accounting departments have scrambled in recent years to put in place internal control systems as required by SOX section 404. Compliance with SOX and SEC regulations are certainly good reasons for companies to create an internal control system. Small and medium size business owners might wonder, though, how this applies to them or helps their business. They might have a few investors or creditors and need to produce financial statements, but they don't have to worry about complying with SEC or SOX regulations.

Internal control systems at public or private companies can provide a mechanism for improvement. If any company is taking the time and effort to develop a procedure based, financial control system, then it seems worth the small amount of additional effort it would take to:

- Understand major financial processes.
- Establish key finance polices and goals (including performance goals as well as producing accurate financial statements).
- Determine which process provides a level of risk or materiality in reaching financial goals.
- Prioritize development of the control system according to materiality, risk, and other important goals.
- Incorporate best practices and a continual improvement philosophy to build effective processes and nurture a culture of improvement.

Is there a better indicator of an effective control system than clear goals and key performance metrics that are consistently measured and regularly improving?

So the question that applies to companies of all sizes, shapes, and types: Are you taking advantage of a financial control system to improve process results and drive your financial performance upward?

A Disciplined Approach

As previously noted, taking a more disciplined approach to business processes began decades ago with a focus on manufacturing and production operations. This is where waste in the form of work-in-process, rejects, rework, and inventory were obvious and easily observed. It was also where results of improvement efforts could be easily recognized. While not always as easy to recognize, waste exists at all levels and all areas of business in forms such as duplicated efforts, delays, and non value-added activities. Activities to identify and eliminate waste can be designed into a well-defined process. But it takes effort, commitment, and discipline to achieve improvement goals.

While a disciplined approach to designing and managing processes is important for all segments of a business operation, it can be particularly important to Finance. Poor financial management can spell disaster for a business, no matter how great the product or service may be, or how efficiently other segments of the business operate. A disciplined approach to Finance means a relentless, yet reflective, pursuit of improving key facets of finance performance (i.e. Cost of Capital, Working Capital, Cash Management) while ensuring operational needs are being met. Applying a disciplined process approach to Finance means that performance is not left to chance; it is executing a well thought-out strategy that is continually monitored, controlled, and improved.

It is important to add a note here about the terms control and continual improvement. In the context of managing a process, control does not mean micro-management or having unrealistic expectations. Control means understanding what value a process brings to a product or service, and ultimately to a customer, and then ensuring that the process adds the maximum value possible using available knowledge and resources. Continual improvement means documenting what is done, then adding key measurements that demonstrate the success of a process. By using measurements and reflection, small incremental steps can be taken to add the value more efficiently, or to improve the added value.

Frequently organizations delay implementing a best practice, well-defined process approach because they want to design and document a "perfect process" for implementation. Delays are inevitable and stretch on indefinitely because of the high level of difficulty in achieving such a lofty goal. In the meantime, processes run on as is, out of control and operating through reaction and intuition.

Using an intuitive feel to manage business finances may be effective enough to keep a business afloat, or even appear successful. How well, however, does that approach align with your overall business strategy? Is using intuition good enough for the operating the manufacturing line or handling invoices in accounting? Just like manufacturing, fulfillment, and other aspects of business operation, the finance functions can also be quantified and specific structures put in place that aid in effective operation, measurement, and improvement.

Understanding Key Financial Processes

Is your organization guilty of using a common form of capital management known as "checkbook accounting." In other words, if you have money in the checking account then you can write a check to cover the expenses. When the money runs out then some payable is going to be put off. While this might be how many small organizations execute financial, it is not an effective way to manage business finances.

The opposite can also be true. Cash can pile up in a checking account faster than it can be spent. At some point, to be effective, planning a capital strategy is needed. This begs the obvious question: How much capital do you need?

Capital is a critical component that provides fuel for your organization. Without it, organizations can't grow, and both having too little or too much can be detrimental. How much capital do you need? There are two main facets to determining your capital needs: medium/long term capital planning and working capital management.

Capital Needs Analysis

Capital needs are based on projected revenue growth and projected cash flow. The likely source of revenue growth will be from increasing sales, which in turn will require increases in expenditures, replacement and expansion of assets, and increased working capital needed to fulfill those sales. Healthy growth, however, is limited to your growth in equity.

Equity increases either through retained earnings (from profits), or through selling shares in the business to investors. If revenue is growing faster than equity, then assets and working capital may increase faster than the capacity to pay for liabilities (assets = liabilities + equity). If equity doesn't grow in line with revenue then it is very likely the business will be short on cash and forced to raise capital. A common way to raise capital is to take on debt, but the debt load is bounded by the "debt-equity ratio" and "earnings before interest, taxes, depreciation, and amortization" (EBITDA) or cash flow. Therefore, equity creates a ceiling for growth.

Since profits are taxable, reporting as little profit as possible will reduce taxes. Profit, however, through retained earnings, creates equity growth and increases debt capacity via your debt-to-equity ratio (explained below). Profits fuel future revenue growth, and profit is what is demanded by investors.

The debt-to-equity ratio is calculated by dividing your debt by your equity. A ratio of one or less is considered good, whereas ratios greater than one increases the lenders perception of risk. Risk tolerances vary by industry, however, so there are no absolutes.

Operating Cash Flow or EBITDA

A business can borrow only up to its ability to make debt payments. So debt is bounded by EBITDA, which is a measure of operating cash before expenses like interest, taxes, and depreciation. Since depreciation and amortization are non-cash expenses for tax purposes, EBITDA represents the amount of actual cash produced. (Note that interest is typically deductible, so increasing debt will subsequently increase interest expense, which lowers taxes paid.)

Making Investment Decisions

Excess cash should be managed as part of the capital plan. It can be used to purchase assets, pay expenses, invest/hold it, pay debt, or disburse it to shareholders. Choices about how to use retained earnings or excess cash is really making choices about investing. Investment choices should be understood using analysis methods like Return On Investment. Various choices using various scenarios should be calculated in determining where to invest money.

Of course, the business needs should be considered as well. Perhaps holding retained earnings in an investment account would not create as much return as increasing capacity for a particular product line. However, an acquisition opportunity may be on the horizon that will require a significant amount of cash on hand. Blindly chasing returns may prevent you from taking advantage of important opportunities.

Generally speaking, though, the best return on investment is usually found by investing in the business. While a money market account may make 4%, and in a good year the stock market may return 12%, investing internally usually has goals of retuning 30-100%. If a company cannot find worthy investments to make in itself, then perhaps the best use of the excess cash (beyond emergency reserves and earmarked funds) is to return it to investors in the form of dividends, and allow them to reinvest it elsewhere.

Paying down debt is another consideration, but usually this only a good option if the debt load is excessive or high interest rates are being charged.

Return on Invested Capital (ROIC)

ROIC is used to determine the effectiveness of the investments into the business. It is calculated by dividing net profit by total assets less cash and outside investments

$$ROIC = Net\ Profit\ /\ (Assets - Cash)$$

As mentioned above, most new businesses are considered risky investments, so the ROIC should be 20-30% in order for a new business to interest investors. (Even for a closely held company or for a single shareholder – there should still be a competitive return). If ROIC is low then shareholders are not being compensated for the risk they are taking. As discussed above, selecting investment options requires calculation and considerations.

Purchasing assets should be the first choice for spending money but only to a point. We want performing assets that can be productively used to make more profit. Returns vary by industry but a reasonable target is a 15-30% ROA (Return on Assets).

Paying off debt is an investment consideration. Currently interest rates are around 6%. Paying down debt might be better than holding it in a money market account.

Holding cash is not an effective use of cash. Typically safe investments produce a very low return of 2-5%. This may be considered, however, if you have specific plans (i.e. expansion, acquisition) that will require large amounts of cash in the future.

Returning cash to shareholders should be the last option, however, but with many mature companies it is the only option available. It basically means there are no good assets to purchase, debt and expenses are at reasonable levels, and as noted above investing usually produces poor returns. In this case, with no better options left, you should give the cash to your shareholders to invest somewhere else.

As noted above, spending cash is like making an investment into the business, and understanding the Return On Investment is one critical factor in making decisions. Returns typically have a direct correlation to risk; the higher the return the greater the risk. Thirty-year government bonds are low risk with 3-5% returns. The stock market is more risky but produces an 8-13% return. Small or new businesses are considered the most risky, which is one reason why venture capitalists require average returns of 25-30%.

Investment	Rate of Return	Risk
Government Bonds	3 - 5%	Low
Stock Market	8 - 13%	Moderate
Small/New Business	20-30%	High

Cost of Capital

A decent Return on Invested Capital is needed to attract capital, but the cost of capital (i.e. debt interest) must be lower than the Return on Invested Capital. The goal is to find capital for as little cost as possible and then invest it on projects within your business that will return as much as possible.

To do this we need to determine the cost of capital from debt and equity using the Weighted Average Cost of Capital or WACC. This weighs the contribution of each piece of debt or equity using the capital's cost factor times the percentage of capital used from each source to produce the weighting factor.

$$WACC = \frac{E}{V} * Re + \frac{D}{V} * Rd * (1 - Tc)$$

Where:
Re = cost of equity (investor's expectations of risk)
Rd = cost of debt (interest rate)
E = market value of the firm's equity

D = market value of the firm's debt
V = E + D (or total assets)
E/V = percentage of financing that is equity
D/V = percentage of financing that is debt
Tc = corporate tax rate
(Note how the cost of debt is reduced by the company's tax rate because interest is tax deductible.)

It is easy to determine the cost of debt used for capital because the lender provides that straightforward information. If borrowing from the bank at 6% or from credit cards at 15%, then the cost of capital is 6% and 15% respectively. Determining the cost of equity capital can be less straightforward.

For large public companies it is not difficult. Add dividends (per share) divided by the current stocks market value to your dividend's growth rate.

Cost of equity capital = (Dividends / market value) + dividend growth rate

If you don't have dividends then this becomes the expected growth in your stock's value. The earlier table shows this appreciation at 20-30% for small companies. Therefore, equity is the most expensive form of capital and using (less expensive) debt can reduce our cost of capital. Debt provides leverage, which increases both positive growth and negative downturns. Debt keeps management focused on managing better, and reduces the cost of capital.

We have discussed Return on Investment both in how capital is deployed and in how capital is raised. We have looked at the cost of capital for both equity and debt. What implications does this have for capital planning?

First, determine revenue growth and compare it to equity growth. If revenue growth is less than equity growth then capital should come from internal financing. It may still be desirable to raise cash to decrease the weighted average cost of capital and lower the threshold return needed for investment projects. Use cash for assets first, followed by increasing expenses, paying down debt, holding cash, and finally returning excess cash to shareholders as the last resort.

Managing Working Capital

Besides planning to ensure the business has the resources to grow the business in healthy and proportional ways, another key facet to financial management is working capital. Working capital is the money it takes to run the business on a daily, weekly, and monthly basis. It is the money used to pay suppliers, pay employees, pay for facilities and utilities, pay for services provided, and for debt payments. Usually a business has to pay for all of these and more before being paid by the end customer. Working capital describes the capital needed to make the business run while it waits to be paid by the customer. In managing working capital, there are three important areas (as stated by the formula below) that companies should actively manage in order to get the most from their working capital.

Working Capital = Accounts Receivable + Inventory – Accounts Payable

Accounts Payable

Accounts payable is perhaps the easiest process to control because it simply involves paying the bills. But paying bills shouldn't just be left to chance; there should be clear policies and goals that direct these activities. Generally, when it comes to paying bills, The Golden Rule should apply. Treat others' invoices as you wish others would treat your invoice. Basically, that means pay it on time according to the terms. There may be no advantage in paying early, but purposely paying late as a working capital management tool is unprofessional and can negatively impact a business.

You may think you are getting away with paying your bills late, but in reality, if the organization being paid late has proactive receivables processes, then delayed payment may eventually result in increased prices or reduced service levels. Plus, building such a negative reputation can have long term detrimental repercussions.

Ensure your policy states that payment will be made according to terms, with a goal of mailing payment five business days prior to the due date, or funds are transferred on the due date for electronic payments (and a supporting measurement that indicates performance in relationship to the objective).

The accounts payable policy should also describe the terms in which invoices should be paid early. Is a 2% reduction in the invoice amount enough of an incentive to pay within 10 days? Typically it is. By some measures paying early for a 2% reduction can result in a 37% return.

$$\text{Return} = (\text{Discount}/100\% - \text{Discount }\%) \times (\text{Total Period}/\text{Days Saved})$$
$$(2\%/(100\% - 2\%)) \times (365/(30-10)) = 37.2\%$$

The important issue is that accounts payable policies are well thought-out and followed through with objectives and measurements.

Accounts Receivable

The cash flowing into the business as a result of customers paying invoices is crucial in managing your business' working capital. Organizations should actively measure receivable metrics such as Days Sales Outstanding (DSO); the average number of days it takes to collect payment after the sale was made. Typically calculated as [(Accounts Receivable / Sales) X (Days)]. Days would be determined by the period for which you are calculating DSO; for example 30 if you calculate it monthly and 90 if you calculate it quarterly.

One key to managing Accounts Receivable is to remove the delay in invoicing customers after shipment of an order or delivery of a service. Delays in invoicing is a form of waste that literally consumes cash in the form of working capital. Set a goal to invoice customers immediately after fulfillment. If it currently takes 10 days to invoice a customer, then the goal should be to do it in 5. If it currently takes 5, then the goal should be 2 days. Finding ways to reduce the DSO frees cash tied up in receivables that the business can use in more productive ways.

Prompt invoicing is the most important method to reduce cash tied up in receivables, and more importantly it is something the business has direct control over. Other processes also help in reducing funds tied up in receivables. Conducting proper credit/qualification reviews, good communication with the sales department (why sell more to delinquent accounts?), and immediate collection activities can all improve (lower) the amount of working capital consumed by accounts receivable.

Inventory Management

Including inventory as a finance function (as opposed to operations) can cause confusion and skepticism. While inventory does have important operational relationships, there is no doubt, however, that inventory consumes financial resources. Inventory consumes working capital whether in the form of purchased materials/parts, work-in-process, or finished goods. Those responsible for managing the company's financial resources and performance should have information and input regarding inventory practices.

The purchasing representative might believe they are getting a good deal by buying one year's worth of parts, and perhaps they are. But making such decisions impacts the overall financial resources consumed by inventory, especially when you include the total cost of ownership.

The financial manager should stay informed of inventory performance, and in response, set clear policies and goals for reducing and managing inventory levels through metrics such as:

- Inventory Turns (the number of times that a company's inventory cycles or turns over per year)
- Days Inventory (the average number of days of inventory on hand per accounting period)
- Average Inventory (the starting inventory number at the start of a period minus the ending period inventory number divided by 2)
- Cost of Ownership (the total cost of maintaining inventory such as warehouse space including utilities and maintenance, finance costs, personnel, equipment, shrinkage, obsolescence, and insurance).

The overarching goal should be to find ways to reduce all types of inventory (and their associated cost of ownership) while ensuring operational needs are being met (i.e. on-time shipping). This, as with accounts receivable, releases cash tied up in non-productive means so it can be used to gain return or grow the business.

Other Financial Processes

Besides raising capital (as required by capital planning efforts) and Treasury Management (managing the working capital and available cash in the business), other important financial processes addressed in this manual include Financial Statements, Financial Administration, and Auditing and Internal Controls.

Financial Statements

Financial statements, particularly in terms of meeting regulatory requirements, were discussed earlier in this introduction. But as was also mentioned, creating clear and complete financial statements is not only done for compliance, but also to accomplish the following:

- To track performance over time;
- Conduct financial analysis (using analysis ratios);
- Guide strategy and tactic decision making; and
- Provide information to investors and creditors.

Creating regular and accurate financial statements (e.g., Balance Sheet, Statement of Cash Flows, Income Statement) provides an important information and measures for performance. They are also used by management to determine where to direct resources, directions and strategies, and setting priorities.

While producing financial statements in order to analyze and guide performance should be reason enough to view producing statements as a key financial process, as the list above demonstrates, there are other important reasons as well. Creditors expect to see financial statements before lending money. Investors (even in private companies) expect to see regular financial statements. Frequently incorporated private businesses must provide financial statements to state and local governments.

Administration and Auditing

Administrative functions such as conducting Shareholder and Board meetings (associated with SEC compliance). Conducting regular shareholder and board meetings are required by SEC regulations, and they are frequently required by state law for any incorporated organization, public or private. Other activities such as document control and record control are important activities that demonstrate a control environment (as noted by COSO).

There is a misconception about internal auditing functions in many organization. Auditing is perceived by individuals as an examination to determine what they are doing wrong. The phrase, "I am here to audit you," can strike fear in most of us, thanks in part to our good friends at the IRS. In the business world as well, those five words can send a chill down the spine of everyone from the Finance VP to the shipping department clerk. But it shouldn't. If your organization has an aggressive and well run Internal Audit system, when an external auditor shows up (whether from a customer, a regulator, or third party registrar), then nothing they do or find will be a surprise to you. In fact, if the Internal Audit system has already identified non-compliances and areas for improvement, and plans and activities for corrections are in place (or even better – completed), then most external auditors will view your proactive management very positively.

Internal audits should be viewed not only as a way to prepare for external audits, but as a business improvement process.

Using the Bizmanualz Finance Manual

Now that we have emphasized the importance of managing your financial processes through employing policies and procedures, we hope you are ready to start using your Finance Manual.

After this introduction section, the Manual Preparation Section provides information about procedure and documentation design. The CFO Manual Section combines organizational information with a manual overview and the financial policies that are part of each procedure. This is followed by the sections of procedures as illustrated in Figure 1 at the start of this Introduction (Financial Administration, Raising Capital, Treasury Management, Financial Statements, and Auditing & Internal Controls).

We hope this product assists your business or organization in complying with financial regulations, improving financial performance, and fulfilling over-arching organizational goals.

[This page intentionally left blank]

Finance Policies and Procedures

Section 150

Glossary

Section 150

Glossary

Finance Glossary

TERM	DEFINITION
Aggregation	Process by which data values are collected with the intent to manage the collection as a single unit.
AICPA	American Institute of Certified Professional Accountants - National, professional organization for all Certified Public Accountants in the USA. The AICPA provides members with resources, information, and leadership that enable them to provide services in the highest professional manner to benefit the public, employers, and clients. The AICPA had over 330,000 members as of August, 2007.
Asset acquisition	A buyout strategy in which key assets of the target company are purchased, rather than its shares. This strategy is generally applied to bankrupt companies that might have valuable assets which could be of use to other companies, but whose financing situation makes them unattractive to buyers.
Attestation	Something (e.g., documentation, records, statements) presented in support of the truth or accuracy of a claim; specifically, a CPA expressing a conclusion about the reliability of a written statement someone else has made. An attestation is usually the result of an "attestation engagement."
Audit committee	Body formed by a company's Board of Directors to oversee audit operations and circumstances; in accordance with SEC regulation (USA), the Committee must be composed of outside directors.
	Selects and appraises the performance of external auditors. Besides evaluating external audit reports, the Committee may evaluate internal audit reports as well. Management representations under the Foreign Corrupt Practices Act (USA) are also reviewed. The Committee may also get involved with public disclosure of corporate activities.
Audit risk	Risk of material misstatement in the audited financial statements or an audited financial statement item. (In particular, SAS #104-111 address audit risk.)
Audited financial statements	Financial statements which have been prepared and certified by a certified public accountant (the auditor). In the USA, an auditor certifies that the financial statements meet the requirements of the US GAAP. An auditor can have an unqualified opinion, in which he or she agrees with how the company prepared the statements, or a qualified opinion, in which he or she states which aspects of the company's statements he or she does not agree with. In extreme cases, the auditor may express no opinion on financial statements at all, in the case that the scope of the audit was insufficient.
Balanced scorecard	An analysis technique (developed by Robert Kaplan and David Norton) designed to translate an organization's mission statement and overall business strategy into specific, quantifiable goals and to monitor the organization's performance in terms of achieving these goals.

TERM	**DEFINITION**
Beta	Measure of a fund's *relative volatility*. A beta value greater than 1.0 indicates the fund is more volatile than the market in general, 1.0 means the fund is less volatile, and 1.0 means the fund and the market are equally volatile.
Burn rate	Rate at which a start-up uses its capital funding before it begins earning revenue. The burn rate is extremely critical to the investor, as it dictates how long the business or project can survive on available cash resources. The burn rate should be established in advance and closely monitored.
Capital	Any asset or stock of assets, financial or physical, capable of producing income; money or wealth needed to produce goods and services.
Capital asset	Asset expected to be in use for one year or longer. Examples include land, buildings, and machinery.
Capital asset pricing model (CAPM)	Model describing the relationship between expected risk and expected return for financial assets; a linear relationship:

$$Rj = rf + ßj\ (Rm - rf)$$

where

- Rj = Expected return;
- ßj = Security's beta;
- Rm = Expected market return; and
- rf = Return on riskless assets.

Capital budget	Plan of proposed capital fund expenditures and the means of financing them from the current fiscal period and over a longer term planning horizon (i.e., more than one year).
Capital budgeting	See "capital planning."
Capital expenditure	Outlay of cash for a project that is expected to produce a cash inflow over a period of time greater than one year.
Capital planning	Process of identifying, evaluating, and implementing investment opportunities. The primary goal of capital planning is to identify investments (in plant, materials, etc.) that enhance the organization's competitive advantage while providing acceptable cash flows and rates of return. A secondary goal is to enable the Company to meet regulatory and other requirements (e.g., environmental directives).

TERM	DEFINITION
Capital project	Project that typically involves construction, purchase, or renovation of fixed assets in order to increase or improve production, achieve a specific level of economic return, add value to the Company's physical assets or significantly increase their useful life, and/or comply with regulations. A capital project is relatively large – the dollar amount is set by the Company (e.g., $25,000 and over) – and the result of the project (a building, new equipment, etc.) has a useful life of more than one year. Some organizations categorize capital projects as "major" and "minor" (e.g., $25,000-100,000 is a minor capital project and a project over $100,000 is major).
Collateralization	Securing a debt in part or in full by a pledge of *collateral* (an asset pledged as security to ensure payment or performance of an obligation).
CAFR	Comprehensive Annual Financial Report; annual financial report issued by state and local governments, consisting of three sections: an introduction, a financial section, and a statistical section.
Continuity plan	Plan to ensure that the effects of an extended disruption (such as a natural disaster or cyberattack) are minimized and the organization maintains or quickly resumes mission-critical functions.
Control deficiency	Design or operation of a control does not allow management or employees to prevent or detect misstatements on a timely basis while in the normal course of performing assigned functions. A *deficiency in design* exists when a control necessary to meet the control objective is *missing* or an existing control is *not properly designed*. A *deficiency in operation* exists when a properly designed control does not operate as designed or when the person performing the control does not possess the necessary authority or competence to perform the control effectively.
Control objective	Specific target against which effectiveness of a control is evaluated; generally relates to a relevant assertion and states criteria for evaluating whether the control provides a reasonable assurance that a misstatement or omission in that relevant assertion is prevented or detected by controls on a timely basis.
Conventional cash flow	Cash outflow followed by a series of inflows, or an inflow followed by a series of outflows; the cash flow changes direction only *once*. Compare with "non-conventional cash flow."

TERM	DEFINITION
COSO	Committee of Sponsoring Organizations - Treadway Commission; voluntary private sector organization dedicated to improving the quality of financial reporting through business ethics, effective internal controls, and corporate governance (see http://www.coso.org). COSO was formed in 1985 to sponsor the U.S. National Commission on Fraudulent Financial Reporting, a private sector initiative which studied the causes of fraudulent financial reporting and developed recommendations for public companies, their independent auditors, the SEC and other regulators, and educational institutions.
	The Commission was jointly sponsored by the American Accounting Association, the AICPA, Financial Executives International, the IIA, and the National Association of Accountants (now the Institute of Management Accountants, or IMA). The Commission represented industry, public accounting, investment firms, and the New York Stock Exchange (NYSE).
	The original chairman of the National Commission was James C. Treadway, Jr., a former SEC commissioner (hence, the "Treadway Commission").
Cost of capital	Return on investment needed to make a capital budgeting project, such as building a new factory, worthwhile; includes cost of debt and cost of equity. The cost of capital determines how a company can raise money (through a stock issue, borrowing, or a mix of the two). This is the rate of return that a firm would receive if it invested in a different vehicle with similar risk.
Country risk	Risk that a country will not be able to honor its financial commitments. When a country defaults on its obligations, this can harm the performance of all other financial instruments in that country as well as other countries it has relations with. Country risk applies to stocks, bonds, mutual funds, options and futures that are issued within a particular country. This type of risk is most often seen in emerging markets or countries that have a severe deficit.
Covenant	Condition that a borrower must comply with according to the terms of the loan agreement; if the borrower does not act in accordance with covenants, the loan can be considered "in default" and the lender has the right to demand payment, usually in full.
Credit risk	Risk that a borrower will be unable to repay its debt obligations in full when they are due. Also known as "default risk."
Critical success factor (CSF)	Factor so important to the Company's success that if objectives associated with that factor are not achieved, the Company will fail – perhaps catastrophically.
Currency risk	Risk that currency movements alone may affect the value of an investment; also called "foreign exchange risk."

TERM	DEFINITION
Debt-equity ratio	Measure of the Company's financial leverage:

$$Total\ liabilities \div Owners'\ equity = Debt\text{-}equity\ ratio$$

A high debt-equity ratio *generally* means that a company has been aggressive in financing its growth with debt. This can result in volatile earnings as a result of the additional interest expense. The "right" debt-equity ratio for a company depends on its line(s) of business (e.g., a manufacturers typically have higher debt-equity ratio than a service business).

Default risk	See "credit risk."
Deficiency	Gap in internal control that by itself does not affect the validity or integrity of the financial process or reporting (e.g., control designed incorrectly or not working properly). Deficiencies are generally not reportable in a final audit but warrant a follow-up plan immediately after the audit. See "significant deficiency."
Derivative	Financial contract whose value depends upon the value of an underlying instrument or asset (typically a commodity, bond, equity or currency, or a combination of these); financial instrument whose value is based on, or derived from, another security or index. Examples include warrants, futures, and options contracts.
Detective control	Control designed to detect errors or fraud that *have occurred* which could result in a misstatement (e.g., reviewing monthly Statement of Accounts for activity in the general ledger). See "preventive control," "directive control."
Directive control	Control designed to encourage a desirable event (e.g., written policies and training seminars to help accomplish area goals and objectives). See "detective control," "preventive control."
Disclosure document	Statement that must be provided to prospective customers that describes trading strategy, fees, performance, etc.; material information (e.g. management practices, financial statements and legal involvements) made public by an issuer as required by the Securities and Exchange Commission. The purpose is to put investors on notice of information pertinent to their making initial and continued investment decisions about the issuer.
Discounted cash flow (DCF)	Method of assessing value of an investment based on predicted cash flows, discounted to account for the reduction in value of money over time; uses future free cash flow projections and discounts them (most often using the *weighted average cost of capital*) to arrive at a *present value*, which is used to evaluate the potential for investment. If the value arrived at through DCF analysis is higher than the current cost of the investment, the opportunity *may be* a good one.
Downtime (or "down time")	Duration of equipment or system stoppage, scheduled or unscheduled, measured from the moment of failure to the moment at which normal operations resume.

TERM	DEFINITION
Drawdown	Magnitude of decline in account value, either in percentage or dollar terms, measured from peak to trough.
EBITDA	Earnings before interest, taxes, depreciations, and amortization; the Company's raw operating cash flow before tax or debt effects.
Enterprise risk management	Process effected by an organization's board of directors, management, and other personnel, applied in strategy settings and across the enterprise, designed to identify potential events that may affect the entity and manage risks to be within its risk appetite, to provide reasonable assurance regarding the achievement of the entity's objectives.[1]
FASB	Financial Accounting Standards Board; private, non-profit organization, the primary purpose of which is to develop generally accepted accounting principles in the public interest. The SEC has designated the FASB as the organization responsible for setting accounting standards for public companies in the USA.
Financial risk	Risk that there may be a disruption in the internal financial affairs of the investment (offering company), thereby causing a loss of value.
Financial risk management	Practices by which a firm optimizes the manner in which it takes financial risk.
Foreign exchange risk	See "currency risk."
Fraud	Intentional perversion of truth for the purpose of inducing another in reliance upon it to part with some valuable thing belonging to him/her or to surrender a legal right. (Black's Law Dictionary)
Funding risk	See "liquidity risk."
GAAP	Generally Accepted Accounting Principles; a widely accepted set of rules, conventions, standards, and procedures for reporting financial information, as established by the FASB.
GAAS	Generally Accepted Auditing Standards; set of guidelines developed by the AICPA, used by auditors when auditing companies' finances to ensure accuracy, consistency, and verifiability of their actions and reports. Auditors relying on GAAS can *minimize the probability of missing material information*. GAAS's three sections are:

1) General standards;
2) Standards of fieldwork; and
3) Standards of reporting.

Each has requirements that the auditor and the company being audited must meet. An auditor must adequately plan the audit in advance, be independent, and always obtain reliable evidence. The auditee must present its financial statements in accordance with GAAP, report consistently, and explicitly disclose all pertinent information.

---

[1] From "COSO Enterprise Risk Management Framework"

TERM	DEFINITION
Hedging	The purchase or sale of a derivative security (such as options or futures) to minimize all or some of the risk of holding another security; purchase or sale of a commodity, security or other financial instrument for the purpose of offsetting the profit or loss of another security or investment.
Hurdle rate	In a discounted cash flow analysis, the required rate of return. Where the rate of return exceeds the hurdle rate, an investment is acceptable; where the rate of return is less than the hurdle rate, investment is unacceptable.
Inherent risk	Risk to the organization if *nothing* would be done to alter the likelihood or impact of an event. See "residual risk."
Initial public offering (IPO)	The first time a company offers shares of stock to the public for purchase.
Institute of Internal Auditors (IIA)	Established in 1941, the Institute of Internal Auditors is an international professional association of more than 150,000 members, headquartered in Altamonte Springs, FL, USA. The IIA is recognized around the world as the internal audit profession's leader in certification, education, research, and technological guidance. More information may be found at the IIA web site, http://na.theiia.org/pages/iiahome.aspx .
Interest rate risk	Risk that an investment's value will change as a result of a change in interest rates. Interest rate risk affects the value of bonds more directly than it affects stocks because bonds are issued at a set interest rate.
Internal audit	Independent, objective assurance and consulting activity designed to add value and improve the Company's operations, helping the Company accomplish its objectives by bringing a systematic, disciplined approach to *evaluate and improve the effectiveness of* risk management, control, and governance processes. (IIA, 1999)
Internal control	Process performed by an entity's board of directors, management, *and* other personnel, designed to provide *reasonable assurance* regarding achievement of objectives in (a) the effectiveness and efficiency of operations, (b) reliability of financial reporting, and (c) compliance with applicable laws and regulations. According to COSO, internal control:

- Is a *process* – a means to an end and not an end in itself;
- Is carried out by *people* – not just policy manuals and forms, but people at every level of the organization;
- Can be expected to provide *reasonable* – not absolute – *assurance* to an entity's management and board; and
- Is geared to the achievement of *objectives* in one or more separate but overlapping categories.

TERM	DEFINITION

Internal control over financial reporting (ICFR)

Process designed by or under supervision of the Company's CEO and CFO (or persons performing similar functions) and performed by the Company's board of directors, management, and other personnel *to provide reasonable assurance regarding the reliability of financial reporting and the preparation of financial statements for external purposes*, in accordance with GAAP; includes policies and procedures that:

- Pertain to maintenance of records that, in *reasonable* detail, *accurately* and *fairly* reflect the transactions and dispositions of the assets of the Company;
- Provide *reasonable* assurance that transactions are recorded as needed to permit preparation of financial statements in accordance with GAAP and that receipts and expenditures of the Company are being made *only in accordance with authorizations of management and directors* of the Company; and
- Provide *reasonable* assurance regarding prevention or timely detection of *unauthorized* acquisition, use, or disposition of the Company's assets that *could have a material effect* on Company financial statements.

Internal rate of return (IRR)

Discount rate at which present value of future cash flows of an investment equals the cost of investment. When an IRR is greater than the required return (the "hurdle rate"), the investment is acceptable.

IASB

In March 2001, the International Accounting Standards Committee (IASC) Foundation was formed; the Foundation is the parent entity of the International Accounting Standards Board, or IASB. The IASB is committed to developing - in the public interest - a set of high quality, understandable, and *enforceable* global accounting standards that require transparent and comparable information in general purpose financial statements. The IASB also cooperates with national accounting standards bodies (e.g., AICPA) to achieve convergence in accounting standards around the world.

More information on IASB may be found at http://www.iasb.org.

TERM	DEFINITION
IOSCO	International Organization of Securities Commissions; began in 1983 as a group of eleven securities regulatory agencies from North and South America. In 1984, they were joined by securities regulators from France, Indonesia, Korea and the United Kingdom. In 2007, IOSCO is made up of 109 Ordinary, 11 Associate, and 69 Affiliate member agencies worldwide. These agencies have resolved to:

- Cooperate in the promotion of high standards of regulation in order to maintain just, efficient, and sound markets;

- Exchange information on their respective experiences in order to promote the development of domestic markets;

- Unite their efforts to establish standards and an effective surveillance of international securities transactions; and

- Provide mutual assistance to promote the integrity of the markets by rigorously applying standards and effectively enforcing against offenses.

More information on IOSCO can be found at http://www.iosco.org.

TERM	DEFINITION
Liquidity	Ability to convert an asset into cash quickly and without any price discount.
Liquidity risk	Risk that a borrower will not make payments when they are due because of liquidity problems (i.e., insufficient cash plus an inability to readily convert assets to cash). Also known as "funding risk."
Market risk	Risk of large losses from adverse changes in the price of assets (securities); also known as "volatility risk."
Material	Of real importance or great consequence; highly significant.
Material misstatement	Misstatement in an organization's financial statements that may materially affect their *completeness*, *validity*, or *accuracy*. A financial statement item (or underlying account balance or class of transaction) of an entity may be misstated:

- By *not including* in a financial statement (or underlying account balance or class of transaction) an item that *should be included* (completeness);

- By *including* in a financial statement (or underlying account balance or class of transaction) an item that *should not be included* (validity); and

- By including in a financial statement (or underlying account balance or class of transaction) an item that *should* be included *but not including it accurately* (accuracy).

TERM	DEFINITION
Material weakness	When one or more of a company's internal controls - put in place to prevent significant irregularities in financial statements - is considered ineffective. To say a deficiency in an internal control is a material weakness means it *could lead to a material misstatement* in the Company's financial statements.
Materiality	Quality of having real importance or great consequence; relevance. According to the FASB, an omission or misstatement of an item in a financial report is *material* if, in light of the surrounding circumstances, the *magnitude* of the item is such that *the judgment of a reasonable person relying on the report probably would have been changed or influenced* by including or correcting that item.
Misstatement	Untrue financial statement information.
Modified Accelerated Cost Recovery System (MACRS)	Current method of accelerated asset depreciation required by the U.S. Income Tax Code, where assets are divided into *classes* that dictate the number of years over which an asset's cost is recovered. See IRS Publication 946, "How to Depreciate Property," for details.
Net present value (NPV)	Future stream of benefits and costs converted into equivalent values today, done by assigning monetary values to benefits and costs, discounting future benefits and costs using an appropriate discount rate, and subtracting the sum total of discounted costs from the sum total of discounted benefits.
Non-conventional cash flow	Cash flow that changes direction more than once (e.g., inflow, then outflow, then inflow); see "conventional cash flow."
Operational risk	Risk of monetary loss resulting from an organization's inadequate or failed internal processes, people, or systems (e.g., system breakdowns, employee fraud or misconduct), natural or man-made catastrophes, incomplete or incorrect documentation of trades, etc.
Political risk	Risk that a country's government will suddenly change its policies; a major reason why developing countries lack foreign investment.
Preventive control	Control designed to prevent errors or fraud that *could result* in a misstatement from occurring (e.g., processing a requisition only after it has been properly approved by appropriate personnel.). See "detective control," "directive control."
Prospectus	Formal written offer to sell securities that sets forth an enterprise plan; in the USA, a company must file a prospectus with the SEC prior to selling securities.
Recovery point objective (RPO)	Amount of time between a system failure and the last full backup of data. RPO is one way of gauging risk in the case of computer system failures.

TERM	DEFINITION
Related-party transaction	Business deal or arrangement between two parties who are joined by a special relationship prior to the deal (e.g., business transaction between a major shareholder and the corporation). Note: American public companies are required to disclose all transactions with related parties such as executives, associates, and their family members in their annual 10-K report.
Relevant assertion	Financial statement assertion that has a reasonable possibility of containing a misstatement or misstatements that would cause the Company's financial statements to be materially misstated.
Residual risk	Risk remaining *after* action is taken to alter the likelihood and/or impact of an event. See "inherent risk."
Risk	(n.) Possibility of loss or injury; dangerous element or factor; a specified hazard. (v.) Expose to hazard or danger; incur danger of.
Risk appetite	Degree of risk an entity is willing to accept in the pursuit of its goals.
Risk exposure	Simple calculation that assigns a numeric value to a risk, enabling comparison of different risks:

> ***Probability of a threat occurring***
> **x *Probability of total loss if the threat occurs***
>   ***Risk exposure***

Note this calculation can result in high-probability/low loss risks and low-probability/high loss risks being equivalent (e.g., $0.9 \times 0.2 = 0.2 \times 0.9 = .18$), so it should be used in conjunction with other risk measures. See "risk matrix."

Risk matrix   Matrix used to illustrate and prioritize risk in terms of its impact (columns) and likelihood (rows), as shown below:

Impact	Low	Medium	High
High	Low or Medium (2 or 3)	High (4)	Very High (5)
Medium	Low (2)	Medium (3)	High (4)
Low	Very Low (1)	Low (2)	Low or Medium (2 or 3)

(rows labeled **Likelihood**)

In the risk matrix, a low likelihood of an event plus a low impact, should the event occur, suggests a very low risk to the organization. Conversely, high likelihood plus high impact signals a very high risk. The risk matrix can help an organization *concentrate its resources* where they are most needed (i.e., where the greatest benefit may be realized).

TERM	DEFINITION
Risk modeling	Using econometric techniques to determine the *aggregate risk* in a financial portfolio, help portfolio managers assess the amount of capital reserves to maintain, and help guide purchases and sales of various classes of financial assets. Risk modeling uses a variety of techniques (e.g., market risk, Value-at-Risk (VaR), Historical Simulation (HS), Extreme Value Theory (EVT)) to aid portfolio analysis and forecast likely losses that would be incurred for a variety of risks.
Risk response	How management responds to relevant risks, having assessed them. An organization will generally respond to risk in one of four ways: • Avoidance; • Reduction (mitigation); • Sharing (transferring); and • Acceptance. In considering its response, management should consider costs and benefits and select a response that brings expected likelihood and impact within the organization's desired risk tolerances.
Risk tolerance	Investor's comfort level with fluctuations in the value of investments and the potential for loss; investor's willingness to accept short-term declines in the value of investments in exchange for long-term rewards.
Securities and Exchange Commission (SEC)	Independent, nonpartisan, quasi-judicial regulatory agency, responsible for administering US federal securities laws designed to protect investors in securities markets and ensure that investors have access to all material information concerning publicly traded securities. Additionally, the SEC regulates firms that trade securities, people who provide investment advice, and investment companies.
Settlement risk	Risk that a party will default on clearing obligations to one or more counterparties; may contain elements of credit risk and/or liquidity risk.
Significant account	Account in which a reasonable possibility exists that a misstatement could be contained – a misstatement that, individually or aggregated with others, has a material effect (overstatement or understatement) on the Company's financial statements.
Significant deficiency	Internal control deficiency or aggregation of related deficiencies that could result in a misstatement of the financial statements that is more than inconsequential. Significant deficiencies are reportable in a final audit.
Significant process	Process or activity required to initiate, authorize, process, and record a major class (or classes) of transactions.

TERM	DEFINITION
Statement on Auditing Standards (SAS)	Statement promulgated by the Auditing Standards Board of the American Institute of Certified Public Accountants (AICPA) to provide guidance to auditors on generally accepted auditing standards (GAAS). Also see "SSAE."
Statements on Standards for Attestation Engagements (SSAE)	Statements issued by the Auditing Standards Board of the AICPA on matters of attestation; they are guidelines for CPAs who provide attestation services. Such guidelines include but are not limited to: professional requirements; compliance; procedures; documentation; reporting on internal control; and financial forecasts and projections.
Swap	Contract in which two parties agree to exchange their interest payment liabilities on an agreed amount of each other's debt for a fixed time period.
Sweep account	An account that automatically transfers excess balances out of a cash account and into interest bearing accounts, or vice versa (e.g., from a money market account into a checking account, to prevent a shortfall/overdraft).
System (systemic) risk	Risk that the inability of one participant in a payment system (or financial market) to meet its obligations when due will cause *other* participants in the system to fail to meet *their* obligations.
Third-party audit	Audit of an organization performed by independent auditors who are not employees of either the organization being audited ("auditee") or the auditee's subcontractors. Third-party auditors are generally required to be certified by a recognized, authoritative body (e.g., AICPA, ACCA) and be impartial and free from potential conflicts of interest.
Total equity	Total liabilities + owners' equity.
Value at risk (VaR)	Method of measuring how the value of an asset or portfolio of assets could *decrease* over a certain time period (e.g., 1-10 days) under *normal* conditions. VaR is typically used by security houses and investment banks to measure market risk of their asset portfolios. Models for estimating VaR include "variance-covariance," "historical simulation," and "Monte Carlo simulation."
Volatility	Measure of the amount by which an asset price is expected to fluctuate over a given period; rate of change in the price of a security over a given time.
Volatility risk	See "market risk."

TERM	**DEFINITION**
WACC	Weighted average cost of capital, or the overall return in annual percentage that a corporation must earn on its existing assets and business operations in order to increase or maintain its current value. WACC is calculated by multiplying the cost of each capital component by its proportional weight and then summing:

$$WACC = \frac{E}{V} * Re \; + \; \frac{D}{V} * Rd * (1 - Tc)$$

Where:

Re = cost of equity
Rd = cost of debt
E = market value of the firm's equity
D = market value of the firm's debt
V = E + D
E/V = percentage of financing that is equity
D/V = percentage of financing that is debt
Tc = corporate tax rate

Working capital   Amount of capital needed to run the business; calculated as

(Accounts receivable + Inventory) – Accounts payable

Finance Policies and Procedures

Section 200

Manual Preparation

Section 200
Manual Preparation

Manual Preparation

For the Company Policies and Procedures Manual to be effective, it should be easily understood by all employees. Therefore, it has to be written clearly and concisely. The objectives of this Manual are to enable and encourage continual improvement within the organization, improve communication within the Company and with the Company's target market and channel partners, and increase customer satisfaction.

This section, "Manual Preparation", provides an introduction and guidance to help you develop and implement your Company's Policies and Procedures manual. *Please read this entire section **BEFORE** you begin to modify your Manual*.

[This page intentionally left blank]

Manual Preparation
Table of Contents

SECTION 1 - INTRODUCTION

This prototype *Policies and Procedures Manual* was developed to assist organizations like yours in preparing their own policy and procedure manuals. As it is written in general terms, this document needs to be tailored to your Company's specific needs, requirements, and operations.

Bizmanualz Policies and Procedures manuals generally consist of eight sections:

100 – the Introduction

150 – a Glossary

200 – a Manual Preparation document (what you're now reading)

300 – a master Policy Manual

400 – a set of Procedures

500 – a Business or Departmental Guide

550 – Job Descriptions

600 – Index

The *Policy Manual* (section 300) is a policy manual template and is designed to work as a guide to the accompanying procedures (sections 400-4*nn*[1]). Note that Bizmanualz does not intend to imply that these are "best practices" or recommended for your Company's unique circumstances. They are designed to be used as a minimum documentation set for you to use in your effort to introduce controls to your Company's core functions – or improve existing ones – and thereby promote the concept of ***continual improvement***.

The language style and usage is generally representative of that practiced by companies based in the United States of America. In some cases, information presented in this manual will not apply to your business.

When you edit and construct a policy, it should be easy to read, to the point, and convey a message that is readily understood by both non-management and management employees.

When you have completed your Policy Manual and the Procedures, it is best that you have a team of managers from various departments review the entire set of

---

[1] In Bizmanualz Policies and Procedures manuals, Procedures are often broken into subsets (e.g., "400 Strategy procedures," "410 Tactics procedures").

documents, identify opportunities for improvement, and agree on changes needed before "finalizing" the documents.

This publication is sold and/or distributed with the understanding that the publisher is not engaged in rendering legal, accounting, or other professional services. Always seek the assistance of a qualified, competent legal advisor to review your "final" manual before you publish, even if it's only intended for internal use.

The corrected and finished product is then ready for distribution. However, it should never be considered final and complete. Building a Management System, described in your policies and procedures, is not a one-time event. The one constant in the business world is change. Therefore, your Company must look at its management systems as fluid. Revisions will be required from time to time if you are to keep your management systems current.

Top 10 Management Mistakes

As a busy executive, you face some extremely difficult challenges, like creating and dominating new markets and finding and keeping the best people. But do you find yourself spending too much time solving everyday problems and not enough time on strategy and growing your business?

If so, you may be making some of these mistakes:

1. You have a compelling *vision* for your company that projects a remarkable future but few of your employees have heard of it or can explain it in their own words.

2. You have a company *mission* that addresses your goals yet your operations fail to measure their progress towards your goals.

3. Your objectives focus on increasing *revenue* and *profitability* while your assets are performing poorly, generating negative cash flows, or encumbered by debt and unable to create a profit.

4. You talk a lot about your employees' *performance* (positive or negative) without noting what employee turnover or performance metrics are for your industry.

5. You spend a lot of time working IN your business on *tactics*, yet you fail to spend an adequate amount of time working ON your business, defining your *strategy*, performance metrics, and real resource needs.

6. You have regular *interactions with employees*, yet you fail to communicate the status of objectives, financials, or metrics.

7. You make resources available for *training*, yet you don't measure training in terms of achieving individual or Company goals.

8. You continually strive to improve your Company's performance, yet you don't compare your performance against external benchmarks for success.

9. You *believe* your customers, employees, and vendors all love your company, yet you don't have a process for monitoring and measuring their satisfaction.

10. You produce annual *forecasts* and **budgets**, <u>yet</u> you fail to achieve agreed-upon goals or learn from the experience to improve in the future.

Daily operational issues eat up much of a manager's time – too much for most managers. But with the purchase and use of this manual, you have the opportunity to correct all that and build a superior organization that keeps your best people, increases revenue, and increases margins.

You now have an opportunity to provide your organization with the methods, tools, and training to achieve superior results. Bizmanualz has helped companies all over the world build superior organizations with increased compliance, control, and customer satisfaction.

Manual Development Process

The manual development process consists of four phases: Discovery, Planning, Development, and Implementation. W. Edwards Deming, Ph.D., one of the leading experts on process improvement, called this the "Plan-Do-Study-Act" cycle. The Deming cycle is more commonly known as Plan-Do-Check-Act, or "PDCA."

The PDCA cycle consists of four main phases of continual process improvement. You should develop your manual in this manner to avoid mistakes that could occur later when you skip these steps. In other words, spending a little time on getting things right now is far better than spending a lot of time correcting mistakes later on.

Many people incorrectly believe they can save a lot of money by eliminating the Discovery and Planning steps and going directly into Development. If you start writing procedures without proper Discovery and Planning, though, you could find yourself in a lot of trouble before long. Without Discovery and Planning, expect project delays, cost overruns, scope creep, and a lot of rewrites.

The lack of prior organization and planning leads to a lack of cooperation, which then leads to frustration, anger, and indifference. Spend time in discovery and planning, and development and implementation will run a lot smoother. What you're trying to do is anticipate the future.

<u>Discovery</u>

Discovery starts by clearly identifying the project vision, mission, objectives and the action plan. It is considered part of the "Plan" phase in the PDCA cycle. In Discovery you are probably interpreting the results of a previous "Check" phase of some kind. You may have been dissatisfied with the results and, therefore, you are "Acting" on those results and preparing to "Plan" for the future.

You should include clear business objectives that include how customer needs are satisfied with agreed upon effectiveness criteria beyond compliance. Otherwise, the procedures look like administrative overhead and a waste of time to others, making it more difficult to get their buy-in and participation during implementation and training.

Once everyone agrees to the objectives and action plan then you can start management planning. The Discover phase takes about 2-4 weeks depending on how organized the executive management team is regarding mission, vision and objectives.

Does your project need a vision? You bet! Every project requires a vision of the future. All the employees involved will want to know how all of this work will improve their lives. You need to communicate a picture of "what's in it for them." If you can't explain it to them, all you have is a big wish that it turns out the way you planned. And it won't.

Planning

Planning starts with a "gap analysis" – a method of determining the difference between reality and your objectives. A Gap Analysis consists of an audit of your current processes, capabilities, and constraints, comparing them with the "ideal" state, and identifying the "gaps" that need to be filled.

You use the gap results, along with the objectives and action plans from Discovery to produce the management materials needed to control the project and set the budget/expectations. Other functions include creating a development team, assigning process owners for each process and deploying your effectiveness criteria to each process. This may take about 2-4 weeks.

This includes producing a:

- Project plan (activities, resources, dates, etc.);
- Project roles and responsibilities;
- Organization chart;
- Change & approval review structure;
- Status reports;
- Document control and format;
- Process maps identifying all process inputs and outputs;
- Compliance requirements; and
- Training, implementation, testing, and audit plans.

You should now be 1-2 months into the project. At this point, you should not yet have written a single procedure. Before that, everyone should understand the scope of the project, its relationship to the company objectives, what the future will look like, and what their roles are in development.

Development

Development starts by identifying a group of related processes and completing just that group. Follow the document control format, use the review structure, perform a walk through of the related processes, test for compliance and effectiveness, and move on to the next group until finished. It represents the "Do" phase of the PDCA cycle.

This takes two to four months, depending on the number of processes, compliance requirements, resource constraints, and the skill and knowledge of the project managers, leaders, writers and reviewers. If you have not done this before, plan on four months.

Development also includes creating all supporting documents such as job descriptions, forms, the training plan, and the collection of technical manuals, references, etc, for document and record control and later implementation.

Using a rule of thumb, you should plan on the Discovery, Planning, and Development phases taking as much as 50% of the total project time but consuming 80% of the project cost. You should try to include the time of all personnel working on the project in your project plan so you have a real picture of the costs involved. Frequently, it is a lot more than you imagine, at first.

You are now three to six months into the project and should have completed the procedure writing. You are now ready for a complete document review. You should not implement processes before the entire system is documented and reviewed; otherwise, you may find yourself rewriting and reimplementing and it will take longer to complete the development. Once you implement the system, you implement the concept of continual improvement.

Implementation

Implementation includes skills assessment, training to improve competencies, and auditing of the entire system against the objectives and compliance requirements. It represents the "Check" phase of the PDCA cycle. The length of time depends on number of employees, locations, and processes. It should take 3-6 months, or about 50% of the project time, to complete. You are working toward a stable system of processes and this takes time.

Training

Implementation starts with an assessment of employee skills and competencies to determine training gaps. Then training begins introducing the job descriptions, processes, procedures, and the relationship of people and tasks to objectives and effectiveness.

Once training is complete, you should use execute the processes as documented for 1-3 months. Procedure forms, logs, and other records should be used to collect data for measurement and analysis. All personnel should become accustomed to using the processes recently created. In fact, it is the collection of data which now becomes the most important part.

Collected data are used to:

- Determine if processes are in control;
- Identifying if a process can be improved; and
- Demonstrating to auditors and management that the organization is progressing towards achieving the objectives.

Auditing

Auditing is one of the most important steps in building business processes. Auditing provides management visibility into the ongoing progress towards objectives and the capabilities of the organization. Without auditing, management limits its predictive knowledge of the systems potential.

Management Review

You are now 6-12 months into the project and almost finished. The last step consists of analyzing what's been done, reviewing lessons learned, and looking for ways to improve performance, compliance, and effectiveness. This is typically done within a Management Review meeting held after the audit cycle has been completed.

Management holds the review meeting to discuss:

- The audit report documenting the findings of the audit team;
- Progress towards objectives;
- Results of customer satisfaction processes;
- Corrective actions to be taken to resolve "common cause" errors;
- Preventive action to be taken to resolve "special cause" errors; and
- Follow-up from previous meetings.

Rediscovery

The actions from the Management Review meeting lead into Rediscovery or the Discovery process for the next cycle. Rediscovery starts the process of continuous improvement all over again. It represents the "Act" phase of the PDCA cycle. The result is a new set of objectives and action plans for the next period and you now begin again. This phase overlaps with the discovery phase of the next year to chain together each period in a constant cause-effect cycle of improvement.

Using these four phases, you should complete the project in 6-12 months; spending less than six months or more than twelve indicates problems in scoping the project. If the organization is big and complex, the problem should be broken into smaller projects and focused on core processes, or outside contractors should be used to deploy the experience and bandwidth required to meet your schedule.

Staffing the project depends on the number of employees, locations, compliance requirements, and processes involved. You should consider at least one full-time project leader that drives the project, manages document controls, leads the audits, and reports to management on the overall effectiveness.

The project leader should be experienced in control methodologies and auditing. If your project leader is not experienced in these areas, you should look for training. Training is available to learn how to use quality tools, acquire auditing skills, and lead audit teams and programs.

Others are needed to create documents or perform audits. Obviously, there are a lot of variables to staffing requirements. It is difficult for one person to know everything about your business, build the system and then be responsible for auditing the processes. A solo person will lose their objectivity and they can not audit their own processes either.

Bizmanualz Training

Bizmanualz training courses are available for In-house training as well as on a customizable basis. A tailored in-house training program is one of the best options to meet your business objectives. Tailored programs are designed to specifically fit your organization's culture and circumstances, targeting the training to meet your specific needs.

A Training Advisor is available to discuss your organizational needs and plan a course designed around the outcomes you want to achieve. Stop by http://www.bizmanualz.com/ for a current schedule or call for more information.

Benefits of In-House Training

- Save on Training Costs – In-house training is more cost effective than public training if you have 5 of more delegates that require training.

- Plan Around Your Schedule – Training can be done at your convenience (i.e., dates and times that suit your organization).

- Save on Travel Costs – Training can be done at your location.

- Customized to Your Needs – Training courses can be tailored to the various roles within your organization.

- Focused on Your Organization – The trainer's time is dedicated to your organization.

Onsite Training Classes for Your Place of Business

Business Process Design
– Process Design & Consulting (2-4 days)
– Creating Well-Defined Processes (2 days)
– Aligning a System of People and Processes (3 days)

Quality Tools & Techniques
– Implementing Lean Thinking (2 days)
– Leading Lean Thinking in Your Organization (10 days)
– Statistical Process Control Workshop (2 days)
– Quality Tools Workshop (2 days)

ISO 9001 Quality Management
– ISO 9000 Series Internal QMS Auditor (2-3 days)
– ISO 9000 Series Auditor/Lead Auditor (5 days)
– Creating a Lean ISO 9000 QMS (1-2 days)

Technical Support

Thank you for your interest in our product. Please let us know how else we may be of service. We provide telephone support for the initial installation of the software without charge. Additional support is available for assistance on Microsoft Word usage, policies and procedures development, and other manual development questions.

Hours of Operation:	9am to 6 pm, Central US time
Phone:	314-863-5079
Fax:	314-863-6571
Sales:	800-466-9953
Web:	http://www.bizmanualz.com/
E-mail:	support@bizmanualz.com

Consulting and Advisory Services

We implement a full system approach to creating strategic growth for your company. We understand you want to increase sales, but our process goes a step further to ensure your revenue growth is built on quality management.

Whether you are trying to evaluate your business opportunities, implement strategic growth, or position your company for sale, our expert consultants can help you succeed. Contact us to find out more.

Value Proposition

Understanding the way your customers perceive your value is essential. We work with you to define your customer so you can tell your unique value story.

Lead Generation

Sell more! We help you create a visually compelling marketing plan that will bring customers to you who are ready to buy now.

Quality Management Planning

You could be saving hundreds of thousands of dollars. We work with you to cut the waste out of your organization and maximize your capacity.

Quality Training

An educated workforce is an efficient and empowered workforce. We create customized training classes for your staff to provide continual improvement.

Bizmanualz Consultants

A variety of in-house technical writers and consultants, as well as specialized professionals, are used to produce all of the policy and procedures content. These very same resources are also available on a project basis to utilize their business expertise to provide process implementation for your company.

Bizmanualz Engagements

A typical project consists of a full system engagement to create and maintain strategic growth. Projects of this type consist of identifying, developing and implementing management systems of business controls; increasing revenue through designing and testing a strategic or tactical value proposition and implementing lead-generation marketing techniques; as well as in-house or onsite training in many of these same industry standard techniques.

Implementation assistance, training, coaching, and/or mentoring are available to complete your project – call Bizmanualz today! Typical projects range from strategic marketing and sales planning, development, and support to more tactical ISO 9000 quality or Lean/Six-Sigma operations implementation to ensure you're delivering on your strategy.

Potential training, consulting and implementation engagements include:

- Strategic Planning, Goals and Objectives Implementation

- Sales and Marketing System Implementation and Support Through Value Proposition and Lead Generation Services
- ISO 9000 Quality Management Systems Certification, Business Process Design and Continuous Process Improvement
- General Policy and Procedure Development, Training, and Assistance

For a full explanation and examples of our consulting engagements, visit our consulting Web pages: http://www.Bizmanualz.com/consulting.

Benefits of Consulting

Over the past ten years thousands of CEOs, CFOs, and other executives worldwide have realized increased profits, compliance, and operating efficiencies from their business by using one of Bizmanualz® Policies and Procedures products or services.

Our consulting clients receive:

- A quality process designed to comply with accepted standards and regulations (e.g., ISO 9001, Sarbanes-Oxley);
- Demonstrable changes in quality improvement;
- An opportunity to compete for customers that require ISO certification; and
- An improved understanding of ISO and the quality process.

Why?

1. Using an <u>objective third party</u> such as Bizmanualz, Inc., to lead the process assists the Client in sidestepping internal political battles and power struggles resulting in keeping the focus on what's best for the organization.

2. Using an <u>experienced third party</u> such as Bizmanualz, Inc., to lead the process provides exposure to business process methodologies that allow the Client to keep the project on schedule, on budget, and on alignment with the project objectives.

3. Using a <u>focused third party</u> such as Bizmanualz, Inc., to lead the process ensures the result is not clouded with legal, accounting, or technical jargon; instead, it provides a foundation for real improvements in effectiveness, efficiency, and the bottom line.

Gap Analysis

The first step is a Gap Analysis, to determine gaps in performance or compliance. Bizmanualz, Inc., will arrange a mutually convenient date for your **Bizmanualz® Gap Analysis**.

During this assignment, Bizmanualz proposes two review meetings: one at the outset and the other at completion of the assignment, to review the effectiveness of the project and deliverables.

The analysis itself consists of five primary activities:

Activity 1   Pre-planning activity between the organization and Principal Consultant. The Principal Consultant will contact you to obtain background information used to become familiar with the engagement. Pre-planning occurs prior to the onsite visit and includes the collection of:

- An organization profile describing the business activities, locations, and number of employees at each location;
- Organization structure (chart) and employee data by functioi
- Current Quality Manual, if available; and
- Contact details identifying the employees available to support the gap analysis within the organization.

Activity 2   An introductory meeting with top management, facilitated by the Principal Consultant, outlining the methodology and deliverables. The introductory meeting will occur on the first morning of the engagement.

The aim of this meeting is to agree on the overall delivery plan and to review and determine the full requirements and scope of the project, allocate tasks and analyze and mitigate any project risks. There will also be an opportunity for questions and answers.

Activity 3   Data gathering activity involving interviews, data analysis, and observation with a cross-section of the organization's personnel. After the introductory meeting is concluded, the Principal Consultant will spend the rest of the first day collecting the data needed for the Gap Analysis Report.

NOTE: It is vitally important that the Client agrees to make available the data and/or personnel identified to support the engagement. Any delay caused by the Client may also cause a revaluation of the engagement sum, subject to client acceptance.

Activity 4   Production and distribution of the Gap Analysis Report and MS Project Plan. The Principal Consultant will produce a detailed report (see "Gap Analysis Product Specifications," below) that will be delivered to you, the Client, within five business days following Activity 3.

Activity 5   A concluding meeting with top management and the Principal Consultant. The Principal Consultant will lead a presentation and discussion of the Gap Analysis Report findings and recommendations.

The rest of the afternoon will be spent presenting the findings, answering questions about the findings, and discussing project implementation issues including agreement and finalization of the MS Project Plan.

Gap Analysis Product Specification

The primary purpose of the **Bizmanualz® Gap Analysis** is to identify, in practical and specific terms, the gaps that exist between your current management system and an ideal ("target") system.

You will receive a detailed report upon completion of the analysis, providing:

- A Management System Plan that identifies the strengths and weaknesses of the existing system and includes recommendations on how to proceed and address or close the identified gaps.
- A Position Statement on the degree to which the Client's management system meets the needs of the business and customers.
- A Training Plan that identifies the gaps, if any, in the Client's technical skills and knowledge that may prevent the Client from successfully transitioning to the ideal system. This Training Plan will also include recommendations on how to address training and development requirements.
- An MS-Project Plan outlining the phases, activities, and tasks the the Client must undertake in order to close the gaps and successfully implement a management system. This will also include generic timelines required to successfully implement the improved Management System.

New Requirements Resolution

Inevitably, during the development of proposed solutions, new requirements evolve. These requirements can either be listed and considered as part of a separate follow-on project or discussed and treated by an 'exception' mechanism, outlining the work involved, the timing, and any changes to the overall schedules and the costs involved.

Client Resource Requirements

In order to ensure that all activities are conducted in a timely fashion, the Client agrees to supply the following information and/or personnel prior to the start of and during the engagement:

- An organization profile describing the business activities, locations, and number of employees at each location;
- Current Scope and Objectives;
- The Client structure (chart), job descriptions, and employee data;
- Current policy and procedure manuals, if they exist; and
- Contact details identifying the Client's employees available to provide information required to support the gap analysis.

Engagement Process Description

Just like building a house, the best way to manage a development process is with well-thought-out and well-documented iterative phases. The ***Bizmanualz Management Architectural Process*** is Bizmanualz methodology for implementing the planning, design, development and optimization of your management system.

The process incorporates an objective appraisal of your management system to identify key performance metrics while incorporating a solid system of: project status reporting, appropriate delegation to less experienced personnel, and holding everyone accountable for their assigned tasks.

These are the primary elements behind any form of management conversion designed to get the right things done right.

The process incorporates critical features for success including:

- A simple-to-follow project management and monitoring methodology;
- A solid foundation based on business "best practices";
- Prompting and facilitating non-experts to create effective systems; and
- The ability to maximize the strengths and minimize the weaknesses of both technical and business people involved.

Management Architecture Process

The ***Bizmanualz Management Architectural Process*** has four phases:

1. Client Discovery & Assessment
   - Research Industry (research client)
   - Identify Needs (client objectives)
   - Industry Analysis (benchmarks)
   - Needs Analysis (standards, regulations, objectives)
   - Gap Analysis (objective appraisal, project definition)
   - Engagement Proposal (project scope, schedules, costs)

2. Project Management
   - Working Engagement Plan (actual schedules, costs)
   - Resource Staffing (work breakdown structure)
   - Process Communication (status reports, meetings, software)
   - Configuration Management (management controls)
   - Testing Sensitivity (test plan)

3. Process Design & Development
   - Process Requirements (constraints)
   - Process Definition (effectiveness criteria)
   - Process Mapping (inputs, outputs, action steps)
   - Draft individual processes
   - Test, discuss and review processes

4. Process Implementation & Conclusion
   - Publish Processes and Train Employees

- o Test and Optimize processes until objectives are achieved
- o Lessons learned and Recommendations
- o Project Performance Appraisal

Principal Consultants

A Principal Consultant (PC) provides experience in business process design, quality methodologies, communication, implementation, and training. Typical consultants have over 20 years of either accounting, sales, marketing, quality, and or business management experience working with small to large corporations.

It is standard company policy that all Managers/Consultants/Trainers shall be experienced professionals with advanced degrees, certification and training, and familiarity with business process design and the compliance standard for the projects implemented. A brief resumé or curriculum vitae (CV) of the consultants/trainers can be provided upon request, following order acceptance.

Subject Matter Experts

Subject matter experts (SMEs) provide the detailed technical knowledge that is often required to establish, implement, and continually improve the Management System. Their experience ranges from front-line to support to management to serving as adjunct professors, professors, and/or researchers at the college and university level.

Project Managers

Project Managers (PM) provide experience in project management, communication, implementation, and training. Bizmanualz PMs usually have an MBA and over 10 years of experience working with a variety of business projects from ISO quality and Sarbanes-Oxley to continuous process improvement. Project Managers use MS-Project for scheduling, MS-Word for engagement communication, and MS-Visio for process mapping.

Technical Writers

A Technical Writer provides the written communication expertise required to translate the SME and PC content into clear policy statements, procedure actions and understandable forms. A Technical Writer is utilized, as needed, to develop materials or train Client staff.

Technical writers usually have backgrounds in English, journalism, or quality or business communications. More experienced writers may have technical knowledge and experience in computer and software design, accounting, law, medical devices, chemistry, engineering, or other fields.

Bizmanualz Quality Management

The objective of Bizmanualz is to provide the highest quality services to its clients. In order to ensure this, we utilize an ISO 9001 Quality Management System, or QMS. The scope of the QMS covers all activities we will carry out during the life cycle of the projects. It has been designed to comply with the requirements of ISO 9001 and integrates techniques from Six-Sigma, Theory of Constraints, Lean Thinking, and other quality methodologies.

Project Management Methodology

The project management methodology's particular strengths are:

- A simple-to-follow project management and monitoring methodology with definition of the roles that are needed in a project.
- Involvement of The Client at all levels and in all aspects of the project from beginning to end including allowing non-technical business people to lead and manage the development of the project.
- A comprehensive set of plans, controls, and reviews relevant to the size and risk involved in the project.
- A solid foundation based on business "best practices" that facilitates non-experts to create effective systems.
- The ability to maximize the strengths and minimize the weaknesses of both technical and business people involved.

Meetings and Presentations

It is Bizmanualz philosophy to conserve the Client's time, communicate necessary information frequently, and use documentation to keep the process moving.

To accomplish this every meeting shall include:

- An agenda prepared and distributed before the meeting that contain a summary with action items and responsibilities for follow-up tasks from the previous meeting.
- A Principal Consultant responsible for moving the meeting along.
- Meetings notes prepared and distributed after the meeting that contain a summary with action items and responsibilities for follow-up tasks.

Progress Reports

Progress reports are generated at regular intervals throughout the engagement by the Project Manager to advise management and other personnel on the current status of the engagement.

Progress reports include:

- Key activities starting and project activities recently completed.
- Open items requiring resolution and Possible conflicts.
- Current project short term goals and new requirements identified.
- Comments, news and other information updates.
- Budget vs. Actual cost and activity summary.

References

A. American Marketing Association, 311 South Wacker Drive, Suite 5800, Chicago, IL 60606 (phone 800.262.1150) – ama.org/pages/default.aspx

B. National Association of Sales Professionals, 555 Friendly St., Bloomfield Hills, MI 48341 – http://www.nasp.com

SECTION 2 - USAGE INSTRUCTIONS

Once you have copied all the files into your computer, you are ready to edit or enter data into the included WORD files.

Editing Files

Word Processing (Text) Files

All files are written in Microsoft Word and stored as Word documents (".doc" or ".docx" files). Graphics come from a variety of sources – there are picture files (in ".bmp", ".jpg", etc., format), screen captures, and MS-Visio. If you want to manipulate Visio files, you will need MS-Visio; you may, however, substitute with the file format of your choice. WordPerfect or Mac users should be able to load and use the Word files – consult your word processor's documentation for conversion instructions.

> **NOTE:** There may be compatibility issues if your copy of MS-Word predates Word 2000.

When you have loaded your word processing program, edit the manual's text files as you would any text file. Consider saving them under a new name immediately by changing the procedure number (from "MPnnnn", "MTnnnn", etc.) to one that conforms to your own numbering (indexing) system.

We also suggest you immediately create a new directory for your working files and preserve the original files that came with the CD-ROM.

File Properties and Style Formats

File Folders (Directories):
- Files are organized into various folders that are named by the groups that they represent. [ex. "200 Manual Preparation"].

Page Setup:
- Paper: Letter, 8-1/2 x 11" page size, portrait. (Use landscape as needed).
- Printer defaults: HP LaserJet 4 compatible.
- Mirror margins: One (1) inch inside, outside, left, and right. One-half (0.5) inch left/right gutter, to allow for binder holes. One-half (0.5) inch header and footer.

Header Settings:

- Manual name, left justified; Company name (in place of "Bizmanualz.com"), right justified.
- Font: Times New Roman, 10pt, normal, line below.

Footer Settings
- Filename, left justified; "page # of #", right justified.
- Font: Times New Roman, 10pt, normal, line above.

Section Headings
- Section # (soft return) then section name, set in a black bar with reversed type.
- Font: Arial, 24pt, bold, white on black fill.
- NOTE: Sections begin on odd-numbered (right hand) pages. Insert a spacing page with the words "[This page intentionally left blank]" (font: Times New Roman, 12pt, centered) at the end of any section ending on an odd page number.

Default Style Format Usage

Format	Used for	Font	Paragraph Setting
Normal	most manual-procedure text	Times New Roman, 12pt, regular	"0 pt" before, "6 pt" after, line=single
Heading 1	tab title pages	**Arial, 24pt, bold**	"18 pt" before, "6 pt" after, single line
Heading 2	procedure titles	**Arial, 12pt, bold, UPPERCASE**	"12 pt" before, "6 pt" after, single line
Heading 3	primary procedure components	**Arial, 12pt, bold, UPPERCASE**	"6 pt" before, "6 pt" after, single line

Other:
- Page breaks occur throughout the text to minimize orphan/widow occurrences, etc.
- Section breaks are inserted when, for instance, the document's layout is changed from "portrait" to "landscape", and vice versa (e.g., to accommodate certain forms).

SECTION 3 - THE POLICY MANUAL

This first step in building your Management System is the creation of a Policy Manual. This is a separate, distinct step from developing procedures. The purpose of the Policy Manual is to concisely state the Company's overall policies that drive its strategic and operational objectives.

More than likely, the input for your Policy Manual will come from your customers (and, to a lesser extent, from statutes, regulations, industry benchmarks, and guidelines, etc.). Concern for your customers' satisfaction will ultimately drive your business processes. Their requirements, needs, and future desires are the basis for implementing a management system in the first place.

At a minimum, your Policy Manual should address the products and services the Company provides and their associated Sales/Marketing processes. You may, however, wish to expand the scope of your manual to include other industry or sector specific requirements.

Each area covered by your Policy Manual should include, at a minimum, three parts – scope, policy, and responsibilities:

- The "Scope" portion should simply state the purpose of the functional area and indicate under what conditions the Manual applies;

- The "Policy" portion should state the company policy regarding the functional area; and

- The "Responsibility" portion should state who (by title or position, not by name) is responsible for the policy.

Nowhere is a format requirement specified for the Policy Manual. A sample manual is provided in this guide for your use as a template to create your own Policy Manual (see Tab 3). The Policy Manual's Table of Contents ensures that commonly-used elements are addressed and it provides an excellent starting point for building your management system.

Style and Format

1. Use a cover or title page.
2. Include a table of contents.
3. Put policy statements on a 8 1/2" x 11" page and print only on one side to make revisions easier.
4. Organize material by major headings, for easy reference.
5. Include an alphabetized index if your manual is lengthy and/or complex.
6. Avoid a detailed paragraph identification system of numbers and letters, as this will detract from your manual's readability and the message will be lost.
7. Write in simple, easy-to-understand statements to avoid confusion.

Sample administrative forms and instructions for their completion are included with many of the procedures in this manual. It is expected that you will use your existing forms instead of the forms we provide, where appropriate. Note that the forms included with this product are not designed to be all inclusive or to apply to every situation; rather, they are meant to be guidelines.

Considerations In Writing Your Manual

1. It is now common practice to use pronouns that are applicable to either sex or to use his or her, or the more personal and direct, "you." Social changes influence policies on topics concerning smoking, physical fitness, etc.

2. Have your manual reviewed by a qualified attorney, to ensure that your manual complies with applicable federal, state, and local laws, regulations, and statutes.

3. Define terms specific to your (type of) business in your manual. Definitions should be placed in each procedure, as appropriate; some terms are defined in individual procedures of this product. A glossary of terms (section 150) is included with some Policies and Procedures manuals, as well. We certainly recommend that you add a Glossary to your P&P manual, as it's especially helpful to new employees and contractors.

Revisions

Every organization is dynamic – in some state of change. This necessarily leads to changes to your policies from time to time. Revisions should be completed and sent to all personnel who hold a copy of the manual. The revision should have an effective date and should be distributed in advance of the effective date. When making a change to your manual, be cognizant of the impact that language might have on other policies. Finally, make sure there is a clear record of revisions made and that all employees have current information in a timely manner.

The Policy Manual includes a "Revision" section at the end, as does each procedure. It is important to keep this section – the revision log – up to date. It is the only way to ensure that distributed copies of your manual are current and approved.

Some companies, due to their size and specific business application, require expanded information. For this reason, Bizmanualz, Inc., offers additional business publications that include detailed, topic-specific manuals.

Each manual is intended to be a simple, "top-to-bottom" guide, addressing the minimum set of procedures for the administration and creation of a Management System. Most guidelines presented have immediate use and importance. However, by using the MS-Word documents, you can edit the samples and customize them to your company's individual needs.

- **ISO 9001 Quality Management System Policies and Procedures** – Includes a sample Quality Manual and easily editable quality policies and procedures. Also, it contains a guide to the ISO 9000 set of standards.

- **Accounting Policies and Procedures** – Includes sections on General and Administrative, Cash Management, Inventory & Asset Control, Revenue, and Purchasing.
- **Computer & Network (IT) Policies and Procedures** – Includes sections on Management Information Systems, Software Development, and Network Security.
- **ISO 22000 Food Safety Management System Policies and Procedures** - Includes a sample Food Safety Manual and easily adaptable policies and procedures, including guidance for developing a HACCP plan, standard operating procedures, and Good Practices.
- **Disaster Recovery Policies and Procedures** – Includes your Disaster Manual Preparation, Recovery Procedures, and a section on Coping with Workplace Violence.
- **Human Resources Policies and Procedures** – Includes Employee Handbook Preparation, sample HR policies and procedures, a Human Resources Legal Guide, a sample Employee Handbook, sample Job Descriptions, and sample Reports and Forms.
- **Security Planning Policies and Procedures** – This includes sample procedures for Security Operations and a special section on Embezzlement Prevention.

Bizmanualz, Inc., is committed to providing professional publications for those business owners and managers dedicated to the development and success of their companies. To this end, we will continue to publish useful business guides to assist you in your endeavors. To obtain the latest information on each of our products and services, visit our website, http://www.bizmanualz.com/.

Sources of Additional Information

With the help of the prewritten documentation in this publication, you should be able to produce an effective Management System. You may also wish to draw from other sources of information to develop a truly comprehensive program that meets the needs of your organization and your customers. Sources may include:

1. Industry or trade association publications;
2. Industry/sector consultants;
3. Your Company's legal, financial, and accounting counsel;
4. Other related company manuals and procedures;
5. Internal memos and records;
6. Equipment user manuals;
7. Customer surveys (formal or informal), proposals, or requirements;
8. Regulatory agencies or standards organizations (e.g., FDA, ISO); and
9. Small business advisory centers.

[This page intentionally left blank]

SECTION 4 - EFFECTIVE COMMUNICATION

Communication – Addressing Your Audience

In order for your manual to be effective, it must be clearly written and easily understood by all employees in your organization. Remember – the objective of your Policies and Procedures Manual is to improve the efficiency and effectiveness of your Company. Therefore, the most important rule is that clarity and readability are more important than style, perfect grammar, and a large vocabulary.

While developing policy and procedure statements, you, the writer, must try to put yourself in the position of the user at all times. Some general guidelines for you to keep in mind are:

1. Explain new or unusual terms the first time they are used or in the "definitions" section of the procedure.
2. Avoid jargon wherever possible, especially when training new employees.
3. Avoid unneeded verbiage.
4. Avoid complex writing. If the writer's vocabulary is unusually large or if they write using complex sentence structures, the writing may be at too high a level for many of the users. Understanding is far more important than the correctness of the language.
5. Use active verbs instead of passive phrases.
6. Write the way you speak. Use words and phrases you would normally use in expressing the same thought orally.

Sexism in Writing

Webster's New Collegiate Dictionary defines "he" as used in the generic sense or when the sex of the person is unspecified. However, many people will not accept "he" being used when referring to people in general. There have been suggestions that the generic "he" be replaced with "he or she" and "him" with "him or her."

Another recent method that is gaining acceptance is the switch to a plural pronoun with a singular subject, such as "When someone orders their supplies, they will have to complete a ..."

Often it is more practical for the writer to use generic nouns or by recasting sentences to include positions or titles (i.e., Applicant, Manager, Accountant, Driver, etc.) to eliminate the need for most sexism in writing of policy and procedures.

Number Usage

Writing and development of procedures may often include the frequent usage of numbers in the writing. The following rules cover how numbers should be used in print.

1. Never begin a sentence with numbers. Write "Fifty states have been admitted to the union", not "50 states have been admitted..."
2. Spell numbers one through nine in word form; use the numeric form for 10 or greater.
3. Write compound numbers, such as fractions, in numeric form (e.g., 8-1/2 x 11").
4. When showing odds (ratios), use hyphens (e.g., "4-to-1").
5. For a number less than one in decimal format, place a zero to the left of the decimal point (e.g., "0.5 percent", not ".5 percent").
6. Write the year, decade, etc., in numeric form (e.g., "the 1990's"), rather than spell it out.
7. Spell out the percent sign ("%" as "percent" when embedding it in text; when listing several in a table, use the "%".
8. Indicate the time of day in numeric format (e.g., "12:00"), including "a.m." or "p.m."

Organizing Your Thoughts

To help the writer formulate and organize ideas for developing and writing policy and procedures, it may be useful to outline the material to be covered. Outlining is a fast and effective way to show a great amount of information in a concise, efficient manner with a minimum of writing.

To achieve well-written and easily understood policy and procedure statements that flow in a cohesive and logical form, your personnel should first outline their thoughts before beginning to write a procedure.

When outlining a policy and procedure, the following areas should be defined:

- What is the objective that the procedure is going to accomplish?
- What is the Company's policy on this matter?
- Who is affected?
- When is the policy/procedure appropriate?
- How is the objective to be accomplished? This should include outlining major areas in a step-by-step fashion in chronological order.

Outlining Technique

There are some basic standard rules for effective and consistent outlining. It may be helpful to briefly review a few of these that deal primarily with formatting. These rules concern indentation and numbering.

Standard outline formatting is as follows:

I.
    A.
        1.
        2.
            a.
            b.
    B.
II.

There should always be at least two of each type of character. For example, there should not be an I without a II, an A without a B, etc.

The four characters to mark each section level, Roman numerals, capital letters, Arabic numerals and lower case letters are followed by a period. Line up the periods vertically for each type of character. Thus, Roman numerals are shown:

I.

II.

Arabic numerals are lined up as follows:

5.

39.

By aligning the periods, the text is more visually pleasing. Indentation of section text should be uniform; two to five spaces (or 1/4 to 1/2 inch) for each change in type of line is common. The part of a single line carried to a second line should be indented the same number of spaces as the original part of the line (a "hanging indent").

Defining the Format and Organization of Your Manual

After reviewing the preliminary listing of procedures to be included in the manual and discussing with the personnel assigned to each section, you should be able to determine the estimated length and usage of your manual. With the guidelines presented in this publication and from your own organization's needs determine the format of your policy and procedures and how you will organize the manual into sections.

The format and appearance of your policy and procedures are just as important as the organization and content of the manual. A manual that is appealing to the eye and that emphasizes the importance of the procedures is more likely to be taken seriously and used on a regular basis by employees.

However, it is important to remember that the true objective of the manual is to disseminate information in a timely and efficient manner and <u>not</u> to "impress" the reader with intricate headings or fancy printing techniques.

The simplest format is often the best. A simple format also allows for the most time and cost effective manner for production and maintenance of the manual. Therefore, it may be best to avoid temptations such as, detailed corporate logos in headings, two sided copies, odd sized paper patterns, expensive and restrictive binding techniques, etc.

Design Features

No Manual or procedure within it should ever be regarded as "complete." The best manual is one that is geared to continual improvement over time and incorporates design features that make this kind of change possible. In this regard, the use of standard 8-1/2 x 11" paper, housed in a three-ring binder, is ideal.

The three-ring binder provides the benefits of allowing a place for procedures to be inserted while the manual is being developed and provides for easy updating through simple replacement of pages or superseded procedures. Further, as the organization grows, the use of standard three-ring binders allows additional copies of the manual to be produced on an as needed basis instead of having to be concerned with minimum production runs required for hard bound versions.

Production of procedures on a single-side, standard size paper medium provides for easy reproduction of the manual by high-speed copiers. Use of single-side printing also provides for easy updating of the manual with changes by allowing for one or two pages to be replaced without affecting the order or sequence of the manual. However, if the manual becomes too voluminous for ease of handling, it may be necessary to bind the manual by different sections or utilize two-sided printing to reduce paper volume.

A window type binder should be used to allow you to describe the contents of the manual on the spine, for locating sections quickly from a bookcase. The outside of the binder (front and spine) may be imprinted with the company's name and logo, to give the manual a more professional and authoritative appearance.

Divider tabs on heavy stock should be used to separate functional areas or departmental sections for ease in finding a specific procedure.

Style and Mechanics

The style and mechanics of writing include the paper, typestyle, and print quality.

Paper - Some organizations use color to differentiate manuals, forms, memos, etc. While color can create a pleasing appearance, it can complicate photocopying or printing. Some colors do not provide adequate contrast from the ink color for ease in reading. Nothing is better than black ink on white paper.

The grade of paper is not important, since the manual is designed for internal use only. Regular 20-pound paper is adequate for single-sided printing. A heavier weight (for greater opacity) may be necessary for two-sided printing.

Typestyle - Avoid unusual artwork or type styles that are difficult to read and/or reproduce over a long period of time. Strive for consistency in the overall appearance of the entire manual, regardless of what area or department originates the procedures, by selecting a common typewriter element or word processing typestyle font. 12-point Times New Roman and Arial are common typefaces in word processing software.

Avoid using small print, photocopy reductions, all-capital print, or fancy script styles whenever possible, as these are tiresome and difficult to read and, therefore, make it harder for the reader to comprehend the message.

Provide adequate margins on the printed page. Recommended margins are a one-inch (1") top and bottom margin with one-inch left and right mirror margins and a half-inch (1/2") gutter margin for punching holes.

Additional Sources

There are many excellent references available to technical writers, editors, and others developing policies and procedures. A sample of these is listed below:

- Alred, Gerald, Brusaw, Charles, and Oliu, Walter, Handbook of Technical Writing, 8th Edition, St. Martin's Press, 2006 (ISBN 0-312-35267-0)
- Campbell, Nancy, Writing Effective Policies and Procedures: A Step-by-Step Resource for Clear Communication, American Management Assn., 1998 (ISBN 0-814-47960-X)
- Hartman, Peter, Starting a Documentation Group: A Hands-On Guide, Clear Point Consultants Press, 1999 (ISBN 0-967-41790-2)
- Hackos, JoAnne, Managing Your Documentation Projects, Wiley Publishing, 1994 (ISBN 0-471-59099-1)
- Microsoft Corp. Editorial Style Board, Microsoft Manual of Style for Technical Publications, 3rd Edition, 2004 (ISBN 0-735-61746-5)
- Page, Stephen, Establishing a System of Policies and Procedures, Project Management Institute, 2002 (ISBN 1-929-06500-0)
- Page, Stephen, Achieving 100% Compliance of Policies and Procedures, Process Improvement Publications, 2002 (ISBN 1-929-06549-3)

[This page intentionally left blank]

SECTION 5 - PROCEDURES

Format

Procedures address the primary steps or tasks of an activity for a department or function and the personnel (generic titles or positions) responsible for accomplishing the procedure(s). These procedures can be organized on a departmental basis.

The procedures in this manual start with various designations (e.g., "AD," "PD") and may be used as a template to create your own procedures. The exact format, field names, and titles in this manual are not prescribed by any industry standard – consider much of the information in this manual recommendations, not requirements.

Heading Information

The following heading format is a compromise between simplicity and completeness. Heading information should be kept to the minimum necessary to accurately describe the procedure, identify the revision level, demonstrate authorization and be easy to produce. If you don't need all of the information called for in this format, simplify it. If you need more, add it.

A sample heading follows:

Document ID **HR1040**	Title **JOB DESCRIPTIONS**	Print Date **mm/dd/yyyy**
Revision **1.0**	Prepared By **Preparer's Name / Title**	Date Prepared **mm/dd/yyyy**
Effective Date **mm/dd/yyyy**	Reviewed By **Reviewer's Name / Title**	Date Reviewed **mm/dd/yyyy**
	Approved By **Final Approver's Name / Title**	Date Approved **mm/dd/yyyy**
Applicable standard: **ISO 9001, clause 6.2.2**		

The heading above provides the following information:

Document Number – For small manuals, an ID/numbering system may be unnecessary; the title alone may suffice for identification purposes. With larger manuals, however, it is best to use a simple alphanumeric numbering system to identify procedures for ordered storage and easy retrieval in electronic document management systems.

The first two or three character(s) of the ID are alphabetical characters that represent the subject matter covered in the section (e.g., "MP" for marketing planning, "AD" for administration). You are not obliged to use the Bizmanualz ID format – this is supposed to be your company's policies and procedures manual, after all.

The numbering system employed here is sequential, within sections. The purpose of initially assigning numbers by tens is that if a new procedure belongs between existing procedures, for whatever reason, the new procedure number can fall between existing procedure IDs, so existing procedures don't have to be renumbered *and* references to existing procedures within other procedures don't have to be changed, either.

Title – Keep document titles concise and descriptive. Titles are usually incorporated as part of the filename for the electronic version of the file.

Print Date – This is a "field function" feature of MS-Word. It is useful in quickly assessing the degree to which documents used in the operation are kept up to date.

Revision Level – Once a procedure is issued, it will be subject to changes and updates as the operation matures and improves. A revision code should be used to distinguish the current document from all previous versions and assist with purging obsolete procedures. Initial procedures are often issued with a revision level of zero (0 or 0.0). If a new procedure supersedes this prior procedure, the revision number will be incremented upward by one (1 or .1).

Prepared By – It is useful to identify the primary individual or department that developed the procedure, in the event questions arise during the approval process or subsequent to the issuance (implementation) of the procedure.

Date Prepared – Accompanies "Prepared By."

Effective Date - The actual date the procedure or revision will be implemented. Note the effective date is not the issue date of the original procedure. Dates should be *consistently* formatted throughout the Manual (e.g., "mm/dd/yyyy," "dd mm yyyy").

Reviewed By – Multiple review levels may not be needed for some simple procedures but in the majority of cases, a procedure can only be improved by having additional persons evaluate it. This field provides a record, if necessary, of additional review.

Date Reviewed – See "Reviewed By."

Approved By - After the procedure has been properly reviewed and authorized, the title page is initialed by an authorized individual (typically, this is someone in top management, like the chief financial officer or the product vice president). It is best to initial the approval section by hand rather than type it in; this clearly indicates the PROCEDURE has been authorized and distinguishes the final version from any draft versions that may still be in circulation. The "Approved by" identification should be placed directly underneath the "Prepared by" section.

Page Numbering - All pages should be numbered in "Page # of #" format, to quickly identify the order or placement of pages within a procedure. It is also useful when updating an existing procedure where only one or two pages will be replaced. In this product, the page number is placed in the footer of each page.

In addition to the page number, the footer of all Bizmanualz products includes the *document name*.

Introduction

Located directly below the title block, the ***introduction*** section provides information the reader needs to determine the Company policy covering this area, the purpose of the procedure, who is affected in what situation(s), and the definition of any new or unusual terms.

A sample Introduction section can appear as follows:

Policy:	It is the policy of Sample Company that all departments will prepare and maintain standardized operating policies and procedures that cover the performance of all major functions within their department.
Purpose:	This procedure outlines the steps involved in preparing, maintaining and approving standard operating policies and procedures in order to provide consistent, informative and effective procedures to the employees of Sample Company.
Scope:	This procedure applies to all policies and procedures used or written by all departments and individuals of Sample Company.
Responsibilities:	All Personnel are required to understand and use this procedure.
	Management is responsible for approving and/or maintaining the procedure.
Definitions:	Policy – Definite course or method of action to guide and determine present and future decisions; guide to decision making under a given set of circumstances within the framework of corporate objectives, goals, and management philosophies.
	Procedure – Particular way of accomplishing something; established way of doing things; series of steps followed in a definite regular order to ensure consistent and repetitive approach to actions.

A general description of the Introduction follows:

Policy - The policy should clearly indicate the company's or top management's requirements, beliefs, and/or protocol affecting this area.

Purpose - A brief description of the objective of the procedure, it should expand and clarify the Policy statement.

Scope - Describes the areas, functions, individuals, or departments affected by the procedure and in what situations the procedure applies.

Responsibilities - Identify who is responsible for implementing or maintaining the procedure or parts of the procedure, in generic titles or positions. For example, write "The Department Manager is responsible for...", *not* "John Doe is responsible for...".

Definitions - Describes any terms contained in the procedure that may be new or unusual to the reader.

The Body Of The Procedure

The body of the procedure includes a complete description of the policy and/or the procedure, the methods to be used, form names, cross references to other procedures related to it, etc.

Although the narrative information in the body can vary considerably in format, it is imperative that it clearly explains to the reader in an orderly fashion exactly how to accomplish the objective of the procedure.

For lengthy procedures, it may be useful to identify and segregate the steps or areas by a numbering system. For example, each procedural category would be identified with a step number, starting with "1.0" and a heading. All steps within the category would then be numbered sequentially (For example, "1.1," "1.2," "1.3"). The step number should be located at the left margin with the narrative indented.

In addition to the detailed steps for implementing the procedure, a well written procedure will include the following items:

Effectiveness Criteria - Describe any thresholds or standards that are used to evaluate the work product or results of the procedure. How will an employee know that the procedure was executed correctly?

References - List applicable documents, procedures, manuals, laws and regulations, validation studies, or other sources that were used to develop, refine, or influence the policy/procedure statement.

Records - Describe the records, minutes, reports, notes, forms, or other documents that are generated or used when implementing the procedure.

Revision History - Describe all revisions made to the procedure. Include a revision number, date of the revision, a short description of the changes made, and the source of the change request.[2]

Attachments

Any forms, diagrams, illustrations or other documents referenced in the body of the procedure should be attached and referenced as exhibits in the Records section using a sequential numbering system, (e.g., "Exhibit 1"). It may be useful to use copies of actual completed forms or documents partially or completely filled in, to illustrate to the reader how they are completed.

Once all comments have been received and a final version approved, the procedure should be printed in its final form. The procedure should then be authorized by the appropriate individual and released for production and distribution.

---

[2] By name or initials

Authorization

Origination of policies and procedures usually begins at the unit level by employees or department managers. Once a draft copy of a proposed procedure is developed it should be reviewed, corrected if necessary, and approved before being released as a corporate policy and procedure. The approval process generally consists of review for consistency and accuracy, compatibility/conflict with corporate policy or other procedures, and general readability.

The approval process can vary widely between companies, but it is recommended to keep approvals to a minimum. If too many people or managers of equal ranking are required to authorize a procedure, it can turn procedure development into a bureaucratic nightmare – considerably slowing release of policies and procedures, while adding little of value to the final version.

A method for gaining the input of others while streamlining the process and keeping authority at the functional or departmental level is to release draft copies of proposed procedures to a select number of individuals for comment. It should be made clear to these individuals that they should confine their suggestions to what they feel is really essential to the procedure's accuracy, readability, and usefulness.

Who should receive a draft copy depends mainly on the nature and content of the procedure. Sensitive issues or areas that deal with corporate exposure (such as personnel, intellectual property, or trade secrets) should be reviewed by top management including the president and possibly the Company's legal counsel.

Review of rudimentary procedures – ones that affect only a small unit within the company and are not likely to affect others on a day-to-day basis – should be a minimal process; however, it is advisable to have someone familiar with the area but separate or outside of the unit or department review the proposed procedure (e.g., the chief financial officer might review a proposed accounting SOP). This type of review serves three purposes:

First, what makes sense to the preparer directly involved in enforcing the policy or conformance to a procedure may not be understood when read for the first time by someone not as closely or frequently involved;

Second, a review by multiple department managers may prevent a conflict with a policy/procedure document still in the formative or discussion stage elsewhere in the Company of which the original preparer was unaware; and

Third, it allows the input of multiple individuals while allowing the department manager to maintain control of the integrity of the procedure and drive its completion and release in a timely manner.

Production And Distribution

Once a policy and procedure statement is authorized, it may be duplicated on standard white copy paper and three-hole-punched on the left margin. Multiple page procedures may be corner stapled to prevent losing pages until it is included in the manual.

The number of copies of the procedure should correlate to the number of manuals that have been distributed. It is generally advisable to designate one individual in the company to develop procedures, keep track of the number of manuals issued, and ensure that new or revised procedures are distributed to the appropriate personnel.

The Company's top management should decide which departments or positions will receive copies of the manual or, as an alternative, which sections of the manual may be distributed to specific functions or departments. However, if the manual is to serve as a communication tool, enough copies of the manual should be available to employees.

Since the manual contains many operating procedures that are vital to the company's business practices and methods, there should be some accountability for the manuals. Generally, one individual will maintain a list of the number of copies in circulation and the names of those to whom they have been assigned. When a supervisor or manager leaves the company, there should be a strong incentive to return their copy of the manual; some companies withhold final compensation until the manual has been returned.

However, one should avoid numbering each copy of a manual, unless absolutely necessary. Numbering implies confidentiality and some degree of importance, which may not be the case. Besides, the issuer must maintain a permanent record of the numbers cross-referenced to the recipients that can make personnel changes a tedious record-keeping task.

The Company may elect to produce, distribute, and control copies of its manual electronically. According to the laws of most countries, electronic production, distribution, and control of Company documents is allowed and even encouraged (see various Paperwork Reduction Acts, for instance). In all cases, a clear audit trail is required. The question of "Paper or electronic?" is one your Company has to resolve on its own.

Revising and Updating Procedures

As we've already pointed out, your policy and procedure manual is never complete. It should never stop changing or evolving, because the needs of the business, its customers' needs, the legal landscape, and the business climate *are continually changing*.

Encourage all your employees to initiate changes or revisions to existing policies and procedures, especially those that affect their area of responsibility. Such encouragement will greatly assist the Company in keeping its Policies and Procedures manual accurate, comprehensive, and up-to-date, because it gives employees a sense of purpose and a stake in the Company's well-being.

In addition to an ongoing review process for all policies and procedures, the entire manual should periodically undergo a complete audit. This audit might occur every six months, annually, or every other year, depending on the Company and the business environment. Your policies and procedures should also reflect changing conditions within and outside the company, so you should also strongly consider revising them on an "as needed" basis.

A new procedure should be issued if an existing one is to be modified in any way. The revised procedure should undergo the same approval process as the initial release and should be assigned a new revision number level to indicate that it supersedes the prior procedure. Superseded procedures should be purged from the manual immediately and discarded.

[This page intentionally left blank]

Finance Policies and Procedures

Section 300

Finance Policy Manual

Section 300
Finance Policy Manual

\<Company Logo\>

\<Company Name\>

Finance Policy Manual

mm dd yyyy

Approved By_____   Date:_____

President/CEO

The following document contains a sample Finance Policy Manual, covering common requirements and best practices.

It is intended only to provide an example of wording that might be used in a Manual of this type.

This sample wording can be helpful in generating ideas for developing a manual for your own company. However, finance policies should be drafted as appropriate and necessary to accurately reflect your company's internal financial policies and standards.

Finance Policy Manual

Table of Contents

List of Referenced Procedures

Finance Administration (Section 400)

1. FA1000 – Financial Objectives
2. FA1010 – Management Responsibility
3. FA1020 – Continuity Planning
4. FA1030 – Document Control
5. FA1040 – Record Control
6. FA1050 – Annual Stockholders' Meetings
7. FA1060 – Board of Directors' Meetings

Raising Capital (Section 410)

8. RC1000 – Business Plan
9. RC1010 – Capital Plan
10. RC1020 – Valuation
11. RC1030 – Bank Loans
12. RC1040 – Stock Offerings
13. RC1050 – Debt and Investment
14. RC1060 – Asset Acquisition
15. RC1070 – Leasing

Treasury Management (Section 420)

16. TM1000 – Working Capital
17. TM1010 – Cash Management
18. TM1020 – Inventory Management
19. TM1030 – Related Party Transactions
20. TM1040 – Foreign Exchange Management
21. TM1050 – Managing Banking Relationships
22. TM1060 – Merchant Accounts
23. TM1070 – Letters of Credit

Financial Statements (Section 430)

24. FS1000 – Financial Forecasting
25. FS1010 – Financial Reporting
26. FS1020 – Financial Statement Analysis
27. FS1030 – Financial Management Review
28. FS1040 – Financial Restatements
29. FS1050 – Financial Information Release

Internal Controls (Section 440)

30. AC1000 – SOX Compliance
31. AC1010 – SSAE 16 Compliance
32. AC1020 – Risk Assessment
33. AC1030 – Risk Management
34. AC1040 – External Auditing
35. AC1050 – Internal Auditing
36. AC1060 – Corrective Action

1.0   PURPOSE

The purpose of this Finance Policy Manual is to document the principles and policies governing the Company's financial practices.

The principles and policies provide:

- A foundation for an effective system of internal controls;
- Guidance in current financial activities;
- Criteria for decisions on appropriate financial treatment; and
- Financial management with direction and guidance with regard to policies, procedures, and reports that should be uniform throughout the Company.

When consistently applied throughout the Company, these principles and policies assure shareholders that financial statements issued by the Company accurately reflect the status of the Company's operations.

By developing and implementing this manual, the Company is declaring its intent to comply with standards and regulations governing internal controls and risk management. These issues have always been important, but they have recently received significant attention in the business environment, in the media, *and* in the courts. The Company's systems of internal controls and risk management are based, in part, on the recommendations of the Committee of Sponsoring Organizations (COSO) contained in two documents, "Internal Control – an Integrated Framework" and "Enterprise Risk Management Framework."

Properly designed, implemented, and maintained internal controls are a system of checks and balances, intended to:

- Ensure the effectiveness of the financial management system (FMS);
- Ensure that financial objectives are met;
- Identify irregularities;
- Prevent or minimize waste, fraud, and abuse; and
- Assist in resolving discrepancies that may be accidentally introduced into the operations of the business.

All additional departmental or functional policies and procedures written should conform to or parallel the policies in this Manual. All changes to policies and procedures must be reviewed to ensure that there are no conflicts with policies stated in this Manual.

2.0   SCOPE

The Finance Policy Manual is an official directive of the Company President (or chief executive officer (CEO)). It is published and maintained by the Company's chief financial officer (CFO), in line with general responsibility for Company financial policy assigned to the chief financial officer.

2.1   RESPONSIBILITY

The policies stated in this manual apply primarily to Company financial operations and activities. It is the responsibility of all Finance department managers to help implement and maintain the procedures comprising this manual and ensure that all financial processes conform to applicable requirements.

It is the responsibility of all Finance employees to follow procedures that implement these policies and to help strive for continual improvement in all Company financial activities and processes.

The goal is to make the Finance Policy Manual as clear and useful as possible. All users are encouraged to contact the Company's CFO with suggestions for improving the Manual.

2.2   EXCLUSIONS

2.2.1   Accounting

Accounting functions are included in Bizmanualz® ABR31, *Accounting Policies and Procedures Manual*.

2.2.2   Payroll

Payroll functions are included in Bizmanualz® ABR41, *Human Resources Policies and Procedures Manual*.

2.2.3   Information Systems

Information Systems functions are included in Bizmanualz® ABR34, *IT Policies and Procedures Manual*.

2.2.4   Security Planning

Specific physical security planning functions are included in Bizmanualz® ABR32, *Security Planning Policies and Procedures Manual*.

2.2.5   Disaster Recovery

Specific disaster recovery functions are included in Bizmanualz® ABR33, *Disaster Recovery Policies and Procedures Manual*.

3.0   MANAGEMENT RESPONSIBILITY

The Finance department is headed by the controller or chief financial officer (CFO); in a small organization, this may be the same person.

3.1   FINANCE ORGANIZATION

The Finance department is organized into five main areas of responsibility: (a) planning and budgeting; (b) investing and financing; (c) coordination and control; (d) accounting operations; and (e) money and capital markets.

3.1.1   Finance Department Organization Chart

The Company's organizational framework provides a foundation for administration and coordination of the financial management system. Descriptions of Finance roles and responsibilities are provided. Responsibilities specific to certain procedures or tasks are presented in related procedures.

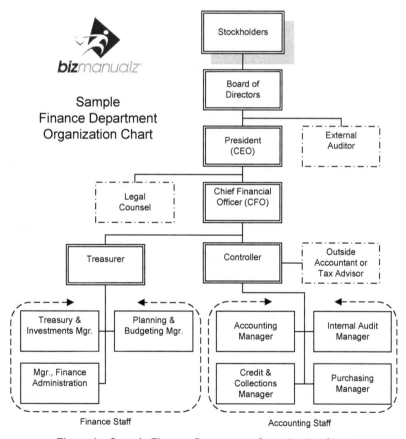

Figure 1 – Sample Finance Department Organization Chart

Figure 1 shows the reporting mechanism of a typical Finance department. The Company's actual organization chart will likely vary from this one.

3.1.2 Chief Financial Officer Responsibilities

The chief financial officer, or CFO, possesses exceptional leadership qualities, including strong communication skills and attention to planning, process, and detail. In addition to the CFO's responsibility for developing the Company's annual financial plan and ensuring internal and external financial reporting, the CFO's key responsibilities include overseeing/ensuring:

- Projections and forecasts;
- Due diligence;
- Budgeting;
- Capital planning; and
- Risk assessment and management.

3.1.3 Treasury Responsibilities

Finance & Treasury responsibilities are focused on raising capital, debt and or equity appropriations, cash management, Treasury investments, fund balances, and management activities.

The Treasurer is responsible to the President/CEO and CFO for all long-range financial matters (e.g., planning, budgeting) and company-wide financial and administrative objectives, policies, programs, and practices which assure the Company of a continuously sound financial structure.

The Treasurer controls the flow of cash through the organization and maintains the integrity of funds, securities and other valuable documents.

3.1.4 Controller Responsibilities

The Controller directs the accounting and control functions, reporting the results of operations and providing chronological systems. The Controller is accountable to the CFO and supervises the accounting and operations staff.

See Bizmanualz® #ABR31M, "Accounting Policies and Procedures," for a complete discussion of accounting activities.

3.2 MANAGEMENT COMMITMENT

Top Management at our Company shows its commitment to the finance management system in part through the development and implementation of this Finance Policy Manual. Management also demonstrates its commitment through the Company finance policies, specific objectives that are set and reviewed during Board of Directors and Management Review meetings, and by providing the resources necessary to meet our objectives for continually improving the effectiveness of our finance management system.

The management team – consisting of the Company President, chief financial officer, and department managers – is chartered with ensuring our financial management system enables the Company to meet customer, as well as statutory and regulatory, requirements.

3.3   FINANCE POLICY

Our Company has established a Finance Policy Manual that is judged to be appropriate to our organization and meets established standards and practices, as well as promotes our ability to comply with applicable regulations. This policy is communicated throughout Top Management and the Finance organization. Department managers and supervisors are responsible for ensuring that all employees understand the policy. To ensure our policy remains appropriate, it is reviewed at least annually at one of our Management Review meetings.

The Company Finance Policy:

❖ It is the policy of our Company to design and produce financial statements in compliance with such widely recognized standards as: Generally Accepted Accounting Principles (GAAP); Financial Accounting Standards Board (FASB) Statements of Financial Accounting Concepts; International Financial Reporting Standards (IFRS); and the Committee Of Sponsoring Organizations (COSO) Frameworks. Our policy is also to comply with applicable statutory/regulatory requirements. We accomplish this by development and implementation of our Financial Management System (FMS) and by using operational methods as documented in our Finance Policy Manual.

❖ We strive to continually improve the effectiveness of our Financial Management System by monitoring our performance against stated objectives and requirements and through leadership that promotes employee involvement. This concept represents our Company's commitment to quality financial management and the increasing need to better serve our customers, shareholders, and employees.

3.4   PLANNING

3.4.1   Finance Objectives

Our company shall establish financial objectives on an annual basis. These objectives shall be measurable and consistent with the Finance Policy and be reviewed at least annually at Management Review meetings.

3.4.2   Financial System Planning

As part of our annual Strategic Planning meetings, our Company establishes strategic objectives and goals for revenue, profit, and expenses and develops, implements, and updates the Business Plan. These objectives are supported by specific measures that track performance against those objectives using the budgeting process, which is supported by capital planning. Department managers in turn set departmental objectives with specific performance measures and targets that support the Company objectives.

Situations may arise from time to time that demand immediate changes to the Company's financial management system. Business conditions and rules also change naturally with the passage of time. The best FMS is one that evolves. The management team will review the FMS itself, as well as changes to the FMS, to ensure that the effectiveness and integrity of the financial management system is maintained.

3.5.4 Referenced Procedures

FA1000 – Financial Objectives
FS1000 – Financial Forecasting
RC1000 – Business Plan
RC1010 – Capital Planning

3.5 RESPONSIBILITY, AUTHORITY, AND COMMUNICATION

3.5.1 Responsibility and Authority

Responsibilities and authorities at our company are defined in each Job Description. Job Descriptions are posted on the company intranet and are also used during annual performance reviews.

3.5.2 Management Representative

The President has appointed the chief financial officer (CFO) as the financial management system's Management Representative, charging that person with the responsibility and authority to:

a) Ensure that processes needed for the FMS are established, implemented, and maintained;

b) Report to top management on the performance of the FMS and any need for improvement;

c) Ensure the promotion of awareness of financial policies and requirements throughout the organization; and

d) Serve as a liaison with external parties (e.g., financial institutions, examiners) on matters relating to the FMS.

3.5.3 Internal communication

In line with our Company's policy of leadership through employee involvement, our company's personnel policies have established open communication throughout the organization.

The effectiveness of our FMS is evident through Internal Audit results, Management Reports, and various performance measures. With the notable exception of confidential and/or sensitive information, financial performance measures should be shared with the organization (posted on bulletin boards throughout, published in a Company newsletter, etc.). Internal Audit results are shared at departmental and other meetings, as appropriate.

Referenced Procedures

FA1010 – Management Responsibility
AC1050 – Internal Auditing

3.6   MANAGEMENT REPORTING

3.6.1   General

The Management team (consisting of the President and CFO, at a minimum) shall periodically[1] review the Company's financial management system to ensure its continuing suitability, adequacy, and effectiveness. This review shall include assessing opportunities for improvement and the need for changing the FMS, including financial policy and objectives.

The CFO shall be responsible for maintaining management review records.

3.6.2   Review input

The CFO and Finance managers shall provide the following information for management review meetings:

a) Results of audits;

b) Employee feedback;

c) Process performance;

d) Follow-up actions from previous management reviews;

e) Changes that could affect the financial management system; and

f) Recommendations for improvement.

3.6.3   Review output

Records shall include the output from the management review and shall include decisions and actions related to:

a) Improving the effectiveness of the Financial Management System and its processes;

b) Improvement of processes related to accounting requirements; and

c) Resource needs.

3.6.4   Referenced Procedures

AC1040 – External Auditing
AC1050 – Internal Auditing
FA1010 – Management Responsibility
FS1010 – Financial Reporting

---

[1] This review should be conducted annually, at a minimum.

3.7   BUSINESS CONDUCT

Unethical business conduct or action – even the appearance, suggestion, or consideration of unethical behavior – is unacceptable *under any conditions*. The reputation of the Company depends on each employee applying common sense and sound judgment in situations where specific rules of conduct are insufficient to provide clear direction. A strong sense of personal ethics, which should extend *beyond* compliance with applicable statutes and regulations, is necessary to guide the behavior of all employees.

All employees should comply with the ethical standards of the Company set forth in this manual. If a situation feels awkward to the employee – if there is ever a doubt about whether what they're about to do is morally and ethically correct – they should take the time to ask themselves:

o   Is my action legal and ethically sound?

o   Does my action comply with Company policy?

o   Is my action appropriate, given the situation?

o   Would my action cause the Company embarrassment or loss if it was discovered?

o   Is the action I'm about to take consistent with my personal ethics or behavior?

An employee should be able to answer "yes" to *all* of these questions before taking action or compromising themselves in the situation. For instance, an action that saves the company money can be a positive...as long as the result of that action does not compromise someone's health and safety.

All Managers are responsible for the proper ethical business conduct and behavior of their employees. Managers should consider the appropriate course of action in terms of economic *and ethical* factors. Each decision should be based on the policy guidelines provided in this Finance Policy Manual, as well guided by the employee's own personal sense of what is right and wrong.

3.7.1   Related Party Disclosure

The Company's policy regarding related-party transactions is that they are thoroughly reviewed prior to approval, to ensure that the best interests of the Company are foremost. In addition, all related-party transactions are properly disclosed and are in compliance with applicable disclosure regulations.

3.7.2   Referenced Procedures

TM1030 – Related Party Transactions

4.0   FINANCIAL MANAGEMENT SYSTEM

4.1   OBJECTIVES

Through this manual and the associated procedures and documents, our Company has established, documented, and implemented a Financial Management System, or FMS. The FMS is designed to improve the effectiveness of our Finance operations and our ability to meet financial objectives while ensuring compliance with auditing and regulatory requirements.

4.2   REQUIREMENTS

Maintaining the FMS is the responsibility of the Company's chief financial officer (CFO), with the timely and capable assistance of the Finance and Accounting departments.

4.2.1   **Overview**

The CFO, in conjunction with Finance managers, ensures that all documents identifying the sequence and interaction of processes are maintained. Processes for management activities, provision of resources, and measurement reporting are included. Procedures shall include the methods needed to ensure that the accountability and control of processes are effective.

By regularly interacting with department managers and reviewing activities and reports at Management Review meetings, Top Management will ensure that resources needed to support the operation and monitoring of Finance processes are available.

Finance managers shall monitor, measure, and analyze processes and take any action necessary to ensure that results are in line with financial objectives and to ensure continual improvement of processes. The CFO shall monitor the results, which shall be reviewed at Management Review meetings.

Any outsourced process that may affect the Company's ability to conform to requirements shall be controlled. The CFO and appropriate Finance managers are responsible for defining the methods used to control outsourced processes and procedures.

4.2.2   **Internal Controls**

Internal controls, procedures, and practices are developed and implemented in order to ensure:

- The Company meets its financial objectives;
- Effectiveness and efficiency of financial operations;
- Reliability of financial controls and reporting; and
- Compliance with applicable statutes/regulations.

It is important to note that everyone in the Company affects internal control to some extent and, therefore, effective internal control is everyone's responsibility.

Effective internal controls help the Company achieve its operational, financial, reporting and compliance objectives. And, while a well designed system of internal controls *can help* the Company achieve its objectives, it cannot guarantee success all the time.

4.2.3 Audit Opinions

Auditing is crucial to effective financial systems management. Evaluating the Company's FMS for overall suitability and effectiveness, making sure, in particular, that internal controls are effective, corrective action is taken promptly, efficiently, and effectively, and ensuring compliance – these are among the many reasons why the Company routinely has its books audited.

Finance managers promptly evaluate audit opinions and recommendations – whether internal or third-party audit – and determine the appropriate response (e.g., corrective action). Managers should, within the time frame established by auditors, complete all actions that correct or otherwise resolve matters brought to management's attention.

The audit resolution process begins when the results of an audit are reported to management and is completed only after actions have been taken to correct identified deficiencies, produce improvements, or demonstrate audit findings and recommendations are either invalid or so insignificant that they do not warrant management action.

4.2.4 Referenced Procedures

AC1040 – External Auditing
AC1050 – Internal Auditing
AC1060 – Corrective Action

4.3 TRANSACTIONS

All transactions recorded or posted should be properly authorized and accurately represent the activity being documented. Both the timing and amount of the transaction should be in accordance with company accounting policies.

4.3.1 Authorization

Transactions and other significant events are to be authorized and executed only by persons acting within the scope of their authority. It is the principal means of assuring that the Company *only* enters into valid transactions and other events. The Company requires its employees to be properly authorized to modify or adjust previously recorded transactions.

4.3.2 Timing

All transaction dates recorded shall accurately reflect the dates on which those transactions occurred. Revenues shall be recognized when earned; expenses, when incurred. Processing, cutoff, and period-end closing schedules and procedures should be documented. Cash sales should be recorded at the time of sale and deposited.

4.3.3 Amounts

Prior or related transactions should be checked for conformity with the transaction being recorded (e.g., match invoice to purchase order). Amount of posted transactions should be checked against source documents. Balances with third parties (i.e., debtors, creditors, or custodians of investments) should be verified, as appropriate. Transactions shall be recorded in conformance with documented Finance and Accounting policies.

4.3.4 Accuracy

Transactions shall be accurately recorded. An approved set of general ledger and subsidiary accounts is maintained for assets, liabilities, revenues, expenses, budgetary accounts, and other accounts.

All transactions should be supported by documentary evidence, which becomes part of the accounting record. Error transactions should be reviewed, resolved, and cleared in a timely fashion. Manually determined control totals should be reconciled with recorded results.

The Financial Management System should utilize standard forms and provide control and accountability with respect to these forms. Supervisors should review posted accounting transactions with source documents and processing documents.

4.4 DOCUMENTATION

The Finance Policy Manual and its associated procedures are intended to satisfy applicable documentation and control requirements. Finance managers and supervisors are responsible for identifying additional documents needed to ensure the effective planning, operation and control of processes.

Procedures will vary in detail/complexity, depending on the size of the department or organization involved and the nature of the activity performed. Procedure developers should consider this, as well as the complexity of process interactions and the competence, awareness, and training of the personnel involved.

Documentation may take any form/medium, including software programs, electronic text files, hardcopy documents, and physical samples.

4.4.1 Finance Policy Manual

The Finance Policy Manual is the top-level organizational document for the Company's Financial Management System. The Finance Policy Manual defines the scope, policies, and processes of our Company's FMS, as well as Management's responsibility for the FMS.

4.4.2 Control of Documents

All Documents required by the Financial Management System shall be controlled. The Document Control procedure defines the controls needed to:

- Approve documents for adequacy/appropriateness prior to issue;

- Review and update, as necessary, and reapprove documents;

- Ensure that changes and the current revision status of documents are identified;

- Ensure that relevant versions of applicable documents are available at points of use;

- Ensure that documents remain legible and readily identifiable;

- Ensure that documents of external origin are identified and their distribution is controlled; and

- Prevent the unintended use of obsolete documents and apply suitable identification to them if they are retained for any purpose.

4.4.3   Control of Records

Procedures define the appropriate records to be maintained for the effective operation of the Financial Management System, including evidence of conformance to requirements. Records shall remain legible, readily identifiable, and retrievable. The Record Control procedure defines the controls needed for identification, storage, protection, retrieval, retention, and disposition of records.

4.4.4   Referenced Procedures

FA1030 – Document Control
FA1040 – Record Control

4.5   SECURITY

Access to resources and records should be limited to authorized personnel only. Accountability for the custody and use of resources should be assigned and maintained, as well. Periodically, resources and recorded accountability should be reviewed for accuracy and completeness; review frequency should correlate to the relative importance and vulnerability of the resource/record. Restricting access to resources and records likewise depends on the vulnerability of the resource as well as the perceived risk of loss, both of which shall be periodically assessed.

4.5.1   Continuity

The Company has a policy of anticipating and preparing for possible disruptions of normal Finance operations. The goal is to ensure the Finance department's ability to return to normal and the likelihood that it will resume normal operations with minimal loss and downtime. The Company better ensures its survival – its continuity – by maintaining effective functional capability, minimizing downtime, and reducing the potential for adverse results in the event of a major disruption.

4.5.2   Physical Security

Physical security measures should be adopted to protect the assets and employees of the Company from abuse, fraud, theft, or damage. Security procedures for the protection of assets and employees are addressed within the Company's Security Manual. See Bizmanualz® ABR32M, *Security Planning Policies and Procedures Manual*.

4.5.3   **Disaster Recovery**

Disaster security measures should be adopted to enable the company to continue the operations of the Accounting Management System with limited interruption. Disaster procedures for operations recovery are addressed within the company's Disaster Manual. See Bizmanualz® ABR33M, *Disaster Recovery Policies and Procedures Manual*.

4.5.4   **Information Security**

Information security measures should be adopted to protect the company's information assets from unauthorized access, abuse, tampering, theft, or use. Information security procedures for the protection and authorized use of computer and network assets are addressed within the Company's Information Systems Manual. See Bizmanualz® ABR34, *IT Policies and Procedures Manual*.

4.5.5   **Referenced Procedures**

FA1020 – Continuity Planning

[This page intentionally left blank]

5.0   PROCESSES AND CONTROLS

The Company has planned and developed processes needed to properly document, monitor, and control financial activities. The results are the processes and procedures defined in our Financial Management System documentation.

These processes and procedures include the finance objectives and requirements for our Company and the required verification, validation, and inspection activities specific to our Company. The records needed to provide evidence that these processes meet International Financial Reporting Standards (IFRS), Generally Accepted Accounting Practices (GAAP), the COSO Frameworks, and other applicable standards and regulations (e.g., Sarbanes-Oxley) defined in the procedures.

Finance
Management
System Processes
and Controls

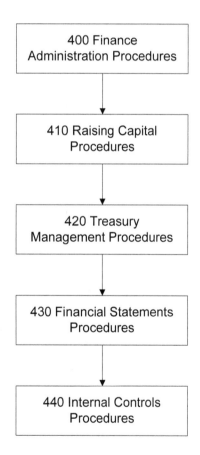

[This page intentionally left blank]

Administrative

The Administrative procedures section encompasses a range of activities, from continuity to accountability. The following Administrative procedures are designed to help the Company control miscellaneous activities not directly related to, but crucial to the efficiency and effectiveness of the Financial Management System.

Administrative
Procedures

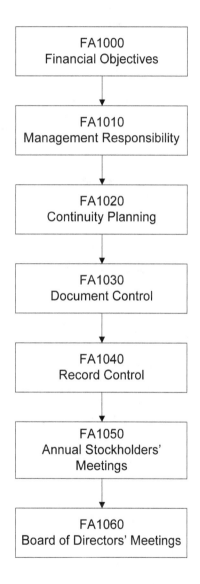

5.1.1 Financial Objectives

The Company's top management, in conjunction with the Board of Directors[2], creates and documents specific, balanced financial objectives that align with the Company's business strategies and objectives. Setting and approving measurable financial objectives is critical – make that *necessary* – for the Company to continually improve its financial performance. In addition, the Company's financial objectives are periodically evaluated and revised to reflect changing needs and requirements, as well as help the firm adapt to the ever-changing business climate.

5.1.2 Management Responsibility

The Company's top management – generally consisting of the chief executive officer, chief financial officer, and functional area managers (e.g., production, sales) – is committed to the development, implementation, and continuing improvement of the Company's Financial Management System (FMS). Top management shall effectively communicate and consistently demonstrate its commitment.

Management ensures that methods are spelled out which define the responsibility, authority, and interrelation of personnel who manage, perform, and verify work affecting Company finances. Management also defines how the FMS is to be reviewed to ensure its continuing suitability and effectiveness.

5.1.3 Continuity Planning

The Company shall anticipate and prepare for possible disruption of normal financial operations. The Company has a plan in place to ensure the Finance department's ability and likelihood to return to normal, effective function with minimal downtime and other adverse effects. The CFO is responsible for development, implementation, and review of the Finance department's continuity plan.

5.1.4 Document Control

All documents used to provide work direction or set policy should be reviewed, approved, distributed, and controlled by the office of the chief financial officer (CFO). The Company should define methods and responsibilities for controlling documents used to provide work direction or set policy and define methods for document revision, approval, and distribution. This applies to all documents required by the FMS and documents of internal and external origin are included.

5.1.5 Record Control

Financial records are established and maintained to contribute to and provide evidence of the effective operation of the Company's FMS and to demonstrate conformance to specified requirements (regulatory, etc.). The Company has implemented a documented system for the control of financial records; the CFO is responsible for ensuring that this system, described in the Record Control

---

[2] In the case of small businesses, an Advisory Board to the owner (consisting of legal and financial advisors and other interested parties) is recommended.

procedures, is effective. The CFO also helps ensure that this procedure and related policy is maintained and reviewed periodically for effectiveness.

5.1.6 Annual Stockholders' Meetings

Top Management is responsible for periodically informing shareholders (owners) of the state of the Company's business operations, especially with respect to its financial well being. Management is also responsible for informing shareholders of votes on important company actions and for compliance with regulatory requirements (e.g., "C" corporation shareholder meetings).

5.1.7 Board of Directors Meetings

The Company holds regular Board of Directors meetings to ensure proper oversight and management of the Company by its Board and to promote free and open communication between the Board and the Company's top management.

5.1.8 Referenced Procedures

FA1000 Financial Objectives
FA1010 Management Responsibility
FA1020 Continuity Planning
FA1030 Document Control
FA1040 Record Control
FA1050 Annual Stockholders' Meetings
FA1060 Board of Directors Meetings

5.2   RAISING CAPITAL

There are several ways to fund the Company's activities, ranging from retained earnings to government grants and loans to public offerings. The following procedures are designed to help the Company plan its capital needs, determine how much capital should be raised and the best means of raising it, and how to effectively manage capital.

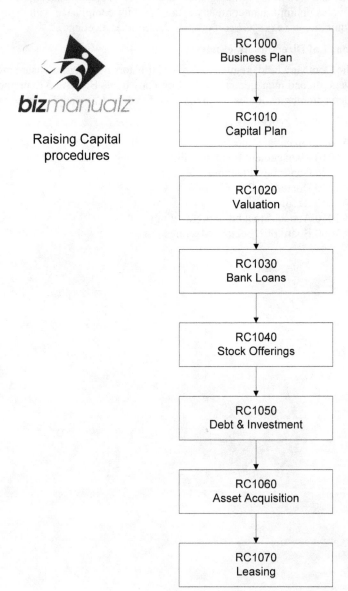

bizmanualz

Raising Capital
procedures

5.2.1   **Business Plan**

The Company develops a Business Plan prior to the start of each fiscal year to guide and enable its operations so that it is able to accomplish defined objectives. Among the purposes of the Business Plan are: (a) direct and manage the Company's growth; (b) define and prioritize short- and long-range business activities; (c) develop a planning and review document for reference; and (d) develop meaningful, attainable strategies and objectives.

Top Management is primarily responsible for developing and administering the Plan, as well as for ensuring that its progress is being measured and evaluated on an ongoing basis through the year.

The Board of Directors[3] reviews and approves the Company's Business Plan. A representative of Top Management – typically the President/CEO – periodically reports to the Board of Directors on the Company's performance against stated and implied objectives.

5.2.2   **Capital Plan**

The Company develops an annual capital budget to ensure the planned and orderly growth of the business, ensure proper use of investors' funds, and give the Company credibility with potential investors and/or lenders. The Capital Plan is designed to: (a) help Top Management make informed decisions with respect to long-term investment opportunities; (b) have a system for assessing capital needs, opportunities, and resources; (c) ensure conformance of projects to business priorities, investment strategies, and applicable regulations; and (d) establish priorities for project funding.

5.2.3   **Valuation**

The Company periodically conducts a valuation assessment, setting valuation targets and working toward them in order to monitor valuation and multipliers in relation to valuation and multiplier targets, provide general and industry economic information that affects the business, and provide information for business strategic planning.

Top Management sets valuation objectives and reviews the Company's progress toward them. In addition, Top Management monitors and adjusts the Business Plan to enable the Company to achieve those objectives.

The CFO executes the valuation process, records valuation plans, results, and improvement plans, and ensures that all necessary information for the valuation process is provided.

5.2.4   **Bank Loans**

The Company has developed and implemented a plan for financing its capital needs in order to: (a) expedite loan approval processes; (b) prepare for loan officer questions; and (c) aid in negotiating rates and other terms with the lending institution(s). The Bank Loan procedure provides guidelines for determining

---

[3] "Advisory Board" may be substituted for "Board of Directors" throughout this document.

suitable lending requirements and for formatting and preparation of loan proposals.

The Company's Board of Directors authorizes bank loans. The CFO directs development of bank loan proposals and serves as the primary Company interface with lending institutions.

5.2.5   Stock Offerings

Top Management plans and prepares stock offerings to ensure that capital goals are reached in a timely, efficient manner. Top Management is responsible for creating the stock offering plan, overseeing its implementation, and reviewing the stock offering process. The CFO, in particular, is responsible for advising Top Management with respect to offering stock (equity) to investors and for executing the stock offering process.

5.2.6   Debt and Investment

The Company has established guidelines for managing its surplus funds (e.g., invest, distribute to owners, pay off debt) and devised a set of criteria for evaluating and utilizing various investment vehicles. The goal is for the Company to receive the greatest possible return/benefit from its surplus funds while balancing benefits against costs and risks and reducing the overall cost of capital while implementing its business plan.

5.2.7   Asset Acquisition

The Company has established and implemented appropriate financial analysis methods and guidelines to better evaluate potential uses of its capital to acquire fixed assets. The Budget Committee reviews and gives final approval to acquisition requests, while the Company's CFO oversees the acquisition process.

5.2.8   Leasing

When purchasing capital equipment, as well as making other major expenditures, the Company considers and carefully evaluates lease and buy options, making decisions based on the overall benefit to the Company and alignment with financial strategies and objectives. The CFO shall ensure that "lease vs. buy" decisions are made only after comparing all lease options to ownership, accounting for *total* equipment costs over the life of the lease/asset.

5.2.9   Referenced Procedures

RC1000 Business Plan
RC1010 Capital Plan
RC1020 Valuation
RC1030 Bank Loans
RC1040 Stock Offerings
RC1050 Debt and Investment
RC1060 Asset Acquisition
RC1070 Leasing

5.3   TREASURY MANAGEMENT

Treasury management (or treasury operations) includes management of an enterprise's holdings in and trading in vehicles like: (a) government and corporate bonds; (b) currencies; (c) financial futures; (d) options and derivatives; and (e) payment systems. Only the largest corporations have an in-house treasury management function; most companies outsource those functions. Still, the CFO should have a working knowledge of some, if not all, of these functions to ensure that the contractor meets all requirements and that implemented controls are effective. The Company may also be required _by law_ to show outsourced functions, like cash management, are under control.

Treasury
Management
procedures

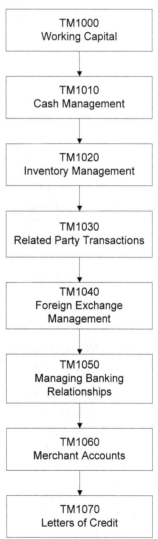

TM1000
Working Capital

TM1010
Cash Management

TM1020
Inventory Management

TM1030
Related Party Transactions

TM1040
Foreign Exchange
Management

TM1050
Managing Banking
Relationships

TM1060
Merchant Accounts

TM1070
Letters of Credit

5.3.1   **Working Capital**

The Company's CFO manages the working capital invested to operate the business, by keeping working capital at the minimum level needed to maintain ongoing operations. The goal is to make the best use of working capital by setting goals and monitoring, reviewing, and improving working capital performance.

5.3.2   **Cash Management**

The Company has established and implemented a plan to manage its cash on hand and cash deposits in short, medium, and long-term accounts in a way that best meet its cash and liquidity needs (e.g., preventing cash shortfalls) while managing risk. The CFO oversees the cash management process, reviews performance, makes recommendations, and ensures that the cash management plan is updated, as needed.

5.3.3   **Inventory Management**

The Company manages its inventory to minimize the cost of inventory ownership while meeting operational requirements and ensures that its inventory practices are aligned with its overall financial objectives. The CFO develops and maintains the inventory management plan and oversees the Company's investment in and management of inventories.

5.3.4   **Related Party Transactions**

The Company has established and implemented policies for review and approval of related-party transactions, to ensure that the Company's best interests are foremost, that transactions are properly disclosed, and such disclosures comply with regulations. Our policy is that all potential conflicts of interest are reviewed, addressed appropriately, and disclosed. This policy is communicated to all affected employees by the CFO.

The CFO reviews the Company's related-party transaction policy periodically with the Board of Directors ("the Board"), to ensure it is up to date and appropriate.

5.3.5   **Foreign Exchange Management**

The Company has implemented a foreign exchange management policy to guide its dealings in foreign currency. The Board analyzes risks and rewards associated with foreign currency exchange and sets policy. The CFO identifies risks/rewards and makes recommendations to the Board and carries out the policy.

The CFO and Board periodically review and, when needed, make changes to the foreign exchange management policy to keep it relevant.

5.3.6   **Managing Banking Relationships**

The Company CFO manages relationships with financial institutions with an eye to the long term, cultivating the relationship on a personal and professional level in a way that ensures favorable treatment and terms and enables the Company to maximize returns while minimizing the cost of doing business with those institutions.

Top Management periodically reviews the Company's relationship(s) with its financial institution(s) to ensure the Company is accruing the maximum benefit from the relationship. The CFO periodically meets with the financial institution's contact (account manager, etc.) to maintain the personal side of the relationship, keeping the lines of communication open, and makes sure the Company is aware of changes in the lending business that may impact the Company, among others.

5.3.7 **Merchant Accounts**

The Company's CFO plans, establishes, monitors, and reviews merchant accounts in a manner that allows the Company to receive the maximum value and best service while managing the risks (e.g., fraud) associated with credit card processing.

5.3.8 **Letters of Credit**

The Company processes letters of credit in a timely, efficient manner, avoiding unnecessary delays in payments or shipments while managing (mitigating) risks typically associated with foreign transactions.

The CFO establishes and manages the process of providing and receiving letters of credit and is responsible for related bank communication and transactions.

5.3.9 **Referenced Procedures**

TM1000 Working Capital
TM1010 Cash Management
TM1020 Inventory Management
TM1030 Related Party Transactions
TM1040 Foreign Exchange Management
TM1050 Managing Banking Relationships
TM1060 Merchant Accounts
TM1070 Letters of Credit

5.4   FINANCIAL STATEMENTS

Financial statements are formal records of the Company's financial activities, an overview of the firm's condition in the short and long term. There are four basic financial statements: (1) the *balance sheet*, reporting the Company's assets, liabilities, and net equity at a point in time; (2) the *income* (or *profit and loss*) *statement*, reporting on the Company's operational results over a specific period of time; (3) the *statement of retained earnings*, which explains the changes in the Company's retained earnings over a specific reporting period; and (4) the statement of cash flows, the record of the Company's cash flow activities; in particular, its operating, investing, and financing activities.

The CFO is primarily responsible for monitoring financial activities and reporting on them periodically. Timely and accurate financial statements are needed to effectively manage the business, required by lenders and investors, and often to demonstrate compliance with regulations.

Financial
Statements
procedures

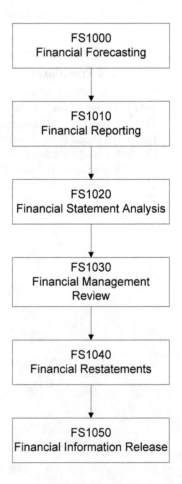

FS1000
Financial Forecasting

FS1010
Financial Reporting

FS1020
Financial Statement Analysis

FS1030
Financial Management
Review

FS1040
Financial Restatements

FS1050
Financial Information Release

5.4.1   **Financial Forecasting**

The Company conducts financial forecasting, creating *pro forma* financial statements for financial planning and management. Predictions that are well thought out regarding revenue and expenses that allow for capital planning, creating budgets, and financial management that aligns with overall Company objectives and strategies, and that help ensure the financial resources for operating the business are in place.

5.4.2   **Financial Reporting**

The Company's financial reports are prepared and submitted in a timely manner, in accordance with applicable regulatory requirements and ethical standards and guidelines.

The CFO is responsible for ensuring that financial reports accurately reflect the financial status of the Company at a given point in time (e.g., end of quarter, end of fiscal year). In addition, the CFO ensures that such reports conform to applicable legal requirements, standards, and accepted practices (e.g., Sarbanes-Oxley, IFRS, GAAP). The CEO/President and CFO review Company financial statements and, in accordance with accepted practices and regulatory requirements, attest to (a) the accuracy of those statements and (b) the implementation of a system of internal controls.

5.4.3   **Financial Statement Analysis**

The Company monitors financial activity and analyzes financial statements in order to better understand and manage – and improve – the Company's overall financial performance. Information contained in Company financial statements is made more understandable, meaningful, and useful by (a) ensuring consistency and ease of use; (b) presenting information in terms of financial objectives, forecasts, and historical performance; and (c) using commonly accepted analytical tools and standards (e.g., financial ratios).

The CFO analyzes and/or oversees analysis of financial statements, prepares reports and recommendations for the Board of Directors, and presents this information to the Board on a periodic basis.[4]

5.4.4   **Financial Management Review**

The Company has implemented a plan for communication between Top Management and the Board of Directors for the purpose of timely and effective financial management (establishing and monitoring progress toward financial goals and objectives, documenting and implementing strategies, communicating progress and results, etc.). Top Management and the Board are responsible for maintaining, reviewing, and updating this plan, as needed.

---

[4] Periodicity (monthly, quarterly, etc.) depends on the size and nature of the Company's business, financial standards and accepted practices, and applicable regulations.

5.4.5   **Financial Restatements**

The Company has established and implemented procedures for handling errors discovered in submitted or published financial statements. The CFO ensures that errors are thoroughly investigated and addressed appropriately. The CFO supervises the preparation and submission of corrected/revised financial statements accurately, in a timely manner, and in accordance with accepted practices, standards, and regulations.

The CFO ensures proper and timely communication of restatements and their effect to interested parties. Finally, the CFO ensures the implementation of effective safeguards against errors that would lead to restatements, as well as the continued effectiveness of those safeguards.

5.4.6   **Release of Financial Information**

The Company controls the release of its financial information to outside parties. The CFO reviews requests for financial information and approves the release of financial information to outside parties (e.g., creditors, customers) on a conditional, as-needed basis.

5.4.7   **Referenced Procedures**

FS1000 – Financial Forecasting
FS1010 – Financial Reporting
FS1020 – Financial Statement Analysis
FS1030 – Financial Management Review
FS1040 – Financial Restatements
FS1050 – Financial Information Release

5.5   INTERNAL CONTROLS

Internal controls are the measures the Company adopts to comply with internal and stockholder requirements (and, in some cases, regulatory requirements); promote operational efficiency and effectiveness; safeguard assets; and provide *reasonable* assurance of the accuracy and reliability of financial and accounting data to interested parties. Internal controls are an important part – arguably, the most important aspect – of the Company's risk management process. Developing and implementing a system of internal controls is crucial to ensuring and demonstrating compliance. Auditing, both internal and external, is considered the best method of verifying and ensuring the continued effectiveness of the Company's internal control system.

Internal
Controls
procedures

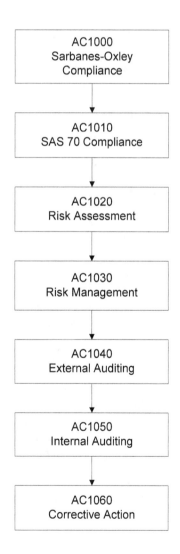

5.5.1 Sarbanes-Oxley Compliance

The Company complies with reporting and control requirements of the "Public Company Accounting Reform and Investor Protection Act of 2002" (USA), known commonly as "Sarbanes-Oxley" or just "SOX." The Company has identified compliance requirements as they relate to the firm and has developed and implemented a system of internal controls to help ensure its compliance. The Company ensures the effectiveness of internal controls by conducting internal reviews and internal auditing and by using third-party auditors, as required.

5.5.2 SSAE 16 Compliance

(Formerly "SAS 70 Compliance".) Before the Company enters into a formal agreement with another firm to provide financial services, the Chief Financial Officer shall request – and receive – written verification from that financial services provider that it has been audited in accordance with the Statement on Standards for Attestation Engagements #16, better known as "SSAE 16."

A Service Audit Report based on SSAE 16 signifies that the service provider's control objectives and control activities were examined by an independent (third-party) auditor. Without that report, the Company could incur the cost of auditing the service organization itself.

5.5.3 Risk Assessment

The Company periodically identifies, reviews, assesses, and prioritizes financial risks to manage them effectively and efficiently, substantially decrease the opportunity for *material* weaknesses to go undetected, and reduce the Company's risk exposure. The Board of Directors forms a Risk Management Committee to identify and assess risks.

5.5.4 Risk Management

The Company has developed and implemented a risk management system that enables, supports, and promotes: awareness and understanding of risks and their potential impact; demonstration of due diligence in decision making; exercising appropriate duty of care; innovation through calculated risk taking; and assurance that risks are managed according to exposure levels. The Risk Management Committee is responsible for execution of the risk management plan and reports periodically to Top Management on the adequacy of the plan and the need for improvement.

5.5.5 External Auditing

The Company periodically undergoes a third-party (external) audit of its financial operations to determine if they are in conformance and are achieving the desired results. Third-party auditing is done by independent, accredited auditors, whose job it is to determine if the Company is presenting financial information in accordance with established criteria, is in compliance with specified requirements, and has designed and implemented internal controls over financial reporting to achieve stated control objectives.

An Audit Committee is formed to select an external auditor and to review and evaluate the audit results.

5.5.6   **Internal Auditing**

Internal auditors (who may be Company employees) periodically evaluate financial and accounting processes – typically between third-party audits – identifying material weaknesses (deficiencies) and recommending improvements to the Financial Management System.

The scope of internal auditing may be narrow or broad and may involve issues such as the efficacy of Company operations, the reliability of financial reporting, fraud, safeguarding assets, and checking compliance with pertinent regulations and internal policies and procedures. Internal auditors are not responsible for executing company activities or changes to them: they merely advise Top Management and the Board of Directors on how they might better execute their responsibilities.

The Internal Audit process is designed to assure Top Management and the Board of Directors that the Company is in compliance with applicable standards and regulations pertaining to internal controls and financial reporting.

5.5.7   **Corrective Action**

The Company ensures the ongoing effectiveness and security of its financial management system by taking prompt corrective action when internal controls are found inadequate or have been compromised. All Finance employees are empowered to initiate corrective actions.

The CFO tracks corrective actions, ensures they are executed effectively and in a timely manner, and follows up on those actions to ensure they are preventing recurrence of nonconformities.

5.5.8   **Referenced Procedures**

AC1000 – Sarbanes-Oxley Compliance
AC1010 – SSAE 16 Compliance
AC1020 – Risk Assessment
AC1030 – Risk Management
AC1040 – External Auditing
AC1050 – Internal Auditing
AC1060 – Corrective Action

6.0   RESOURCE MANAGEMENT

6.1   PROVISION OF RESOURCES

During planning and budgeting for the coming fiscal year, and as needed throughout the year, the Company President, CFO, and the management team determine the resources needed to implement and maintain the Financial Management System and continually improve its effectiveness.

6.2   HUMAN RESOURCES

6.2.1   Finance Staff

Managers and employees are expected to have personal and professional integrity and maintain a level of competence that allows them to accomplish their assigned duties, as well as understand the importance of developing and implementing an effective system of internal controls.

This requires managers and their staff to maintain and demonstrate at all times:

- Personal and professional integrity;

- The level of knowledge and skills needed to effectively perform their duties; and

- A sufficient understanding of internal controls to enable them to effectively discharge their responsibilities.

6.2.2   Competence, Awareness, and Training

Finance personnel shall be competent based on appropriate education, training, skills and experience. The minimum competencies required for each position at our Company are defined in each position's Job Description. Human Resources, department managers and supervisors are responsible for ensuring job descriptions are current and adequate.

Where otherwise qualified personnel require additional training or other action to meet minimum competency requirements, these needs are identified. The Finance department provides task-specific training; general training or education is provided or coordinated by Human Resources. The Finance department should evaluate the effectiveness of training or other actions taken, as appropriate.

The Finance department maintains records of task-specific training. The Human Resources department maintains records of all training and education, skills, and experience in accordance with Human Resources policies and procedures.

Department managers are responsible for ensuring their employees are aware of the relevance and importance of their activities and how they contribute to the achievement of Finance objectives.

6.2.3   Separation and Supervision of Duties

Key duties and responsibilities should be clear and easy to understand and should be assigned to individuals. Duties and responsibilities should be assigned systematically to a number of individuals to ensure that effective checks and balances exist. Key duties include generating financial statements and reviewing or auditing statements, controls, and/or financial processes (procedures).

Qualified and continuing supervision is to be provided to ensure that internal control objectives are achieved. This standard requires supervisors to continually review and approve assigned work of their staffs, as well as provide the necessary guidance and training to ensure that errors, waste, and wrongful acts are minimized and that specific management directives are followed.

6.2.4   **Referenced Procedures**

Bizmanualz® publication #ABR41, ***Human Resources Policies and Procedures Manual.***

6.3   INFRASTRUCTURE

Our Company provides the infrastructure necessary to achieve conformity to applicable standards and requirements. During annual budgeting and strategic planning process, buildings, workspace, and associated utilities are evaluated and provided. When new personnel are added, Human Resources coordinates activities to ensure appropriate process equipment, including hardware, software, and support services are available based on information provided on the Personnel Requisition.

6.4   WORK ENVIRONMENT

The management team, the CFO, and the Office Manager determine and provide the appropriate work environment to ensure a safe, comfortable, and desirable place to work. They ensure the environment is appropriate for achieving conformity to requirements.

Finance Policy Manual - Revision History

Revision	Date	Description of Changes	Requested By
0.0	mm/dd/yyyy	Initial Release	

Finance Policies and Procedures

Section 400

Finance Administration Procedures

Section 400

Finance Administration Procedures

Document ID **FA1000**	Title **FINANCIAL OBJECTIVES**	Print Date **mm/dd/yyyy**
Revision **0.0**	Prepared By **Preparer's Name / Title**	Date Prepared **mm/dd/yyyy**
Effective Date **mm/dd/yyyy**	Reviewed By **Reviewer's Name / Title**	Date Reviewed **mm/dd/yyyy**
	Approved By **Final Approver's Name / Title**	Date Approved **mm/dd/yyyy**

Policy: The Company shall create and document clear financial objectives that align with the Company's RC1000-1 BUSINESS PLAN and the Company's strategic objectives.

Purpose: Setting and approving clear financial objectives assists the Company in achieving improved financial performance.

Scope: This procedure applies to the Finance and Accounting departments in creating specific and balanced financial objectives.

Responsibilities: The CFO (Chief Financial Officer) is responsible for completing and gaining the approval of FA1000-1 FINANCIAL OBJECTIVES, and is responsible for the overseeing the financial health and financial performance of the Company, as well as a fiduciary responsibility to shareholders.

Top Management and the Board of Directors are responsible for reviewing and approving FA1000-1 FINANCIAL OBJECTIVES.

Department Managers are responsible for providing information and feedback necessary for preparing FA1000-1 FINANCIAL OBJECTIVES.

Definitions: Financial Objectives – Clearly expressed and specific objectives (i.e. expressed in numbers, percentages, ratios) of the Company as they relate to its financial operations and financial structure.

Balanced Scorecard – A management system organized around four distinct business perspectives – financial, customer, internal, and innovation/learning – that seeks to balance short and long term objectives, financial and non-financial measures, lagging and leading indicators, and internal and external perspectives.

SMART Objectives – An acronym that describes important attributes for objectives: Specific, Measurable, Attainable, Relevant, and Time-Bound.

Leading Indicator – Indicator of future performance (e.g., an increase in interest rates is often a leading indicator of reduced consumer spending).

Lagging Indicator – Indicator of past performance, such as actual sales over a period.

Business Phase – The period or phase of a business usually defined by its potential for growth and profitability. For example, businesses are not typically profitable in their initial phase but have tremendous growth potential. On the other hand, while mature businesses may no longer be capable of rapid growth rates, they are often more profitable than when they were new.

Return on Investment (ROI) – Profit or loss resulting from an investment transaction, usually expressed as an annual percentage.

Procedure:

1.0   FINANCIAL OBJECTIVES PLAN

1.1   The CFO shall create clear financial objectives that account for and align with diverse and variable business considerations, such as:

- Overall business strategies and plans; segment/department plans

- The Capital Plan (see RC1010 CAPITAL PLAN);

- Business priorities for short and long term sustainability;

- Experience and history of Company performance;

- History of Company and Finance objective setting and achievements;

- Industry standards and benchmarks;

- Customer and marketplace needs and dynamics;

- Sustainability reports; and

- Audit reports and opinions (see AC1040 EXTERNAL AUDITING and AC1050 INTERNAL AUDITING).

1.2   The CFO shall select financial objectives that focus on areas critical to business success, such as:

- Revenue;

- Earnings;

- Profit margins;

- Total debt and debt expense;

- Return on investment;

- Cost of capital;

- Expenses;

- Investment Interest Return; and

- Cash on hand.

1.3   The CFO shall create financial objectives that adhere to the SMART Objectives philosophy, and shall create long and short term objectives (i.e. one year, three year, five year, ten year) as determined necessary by the CFO, Top Management, and the Board of Directors.

1.4   The CFO shall meet regularly with Top Management to discuss creating balanced objectives to meet various operational needs, financial and non-financial objectives, and long and short term goals.

1.5   The financial objectives for a coming fiscal year shall be approved by Top Management and the Board of Directors at least 30 days prior to the end of the current fiscal year.

2.0   CREATING SPECIFIC FINANCIAL OBJECTIVES

2.1   After reviewing materials and requirements listed in Sections 1.0, the CFO shall complete the FA1000-1 FINANCIAL OBJECTIVES form per steps in Section 2.2 (See Figure 1) with "SMART" financial objectives that include detailed actions required and measurement goals, including explicit figures.

FS1000-1 – FINANCIAL OBJECTIVES

Objectives for Year _____   Objectives for Period _____ to _____

Specific Objective	Measurement	Steps to Attain	Relevant	Time Frame	Notes
Increase Income from Investments by Increasing Avg APY from 4.0% to 4.5%	Cumulative APY from Investment Account Statements	Shift 25% from Short Term to Long Term Accounts. Move $10K from Cash on Hand to Investment Account to Improve APY	Relates Directly to Financial Dept. Responsibilities; Meets Industry Standards for Interest Income	For FY 2009	

Figure 1 – Example of Financial Objective Setting

2.2   To complete form FA1000-1, the CFO shall ensure each column is completed thoroughly and accurately. The columns should be completed as follows:

- Specific Objective – Avoid vague declarations (e.g., "fiscally sound"). State specific objectives; for example, dollar amounts or percentages.

- Measurement - Measurable objectives shall relate directly to regularly appearing line items on monthly, quarterly, and yearly accounting and financial statements, in other financial or operational reporting, or results of financial statement analysis, so that actual performance can be clearly compared with stated objectives.

- Steps to Attain – Objectives can be demonstrated as attainable by listing specific steps or concrete actions that can be taken to reach the objective (i.e., an objective for increased sales should list concrete steps needed such as hire 3 new sales people for 2 new markets).

- Relevant – Objectives listed should be described as clearly relevant to the financial performance of the Company and within the responsibilities of the Finance department. It should also include if and how the objective aligns with the business plan, industry standards, market dynamics, or customer needs.

- Time Frame – The specific time frame applicable for this objective should be included here (i.e. which fiscal year, which quarter of which fiscal year, what period or range of fiscal years).

- Notes – Any additional notes or information can be included in this column, including complete action items and actual performance results.

3.0 BALANCING FINANCIAL OBJECTIVES

3.1   The CFO fulfills their fiduciary obligation as trustee of stakeholder assets by ensuring Top Management gives due consideration to creating a balanced approach in allocating resources and management focus to all critical business areas and that areas necessary for the long term success of the business are not ignored in favor of short term financial gains.

3.2   The CFO shall meet with key organizational members such as Top Management, department managers, and the Company strategy committee in order to make decisions to apply the required emphasis necessary in terms of resources and focus to distinct business areas that contain the Company assets. Typically these business areas are divided into four distinct segments (but could be expanded up to six to include areas such as health and safety or security, according to business unit requirements). The four business areas usually used in the Balanced Scorecard approach are:

- **Customer** – satisfactorily identify and fulfill customer needs;

- **Internal Business Processes** – control and improve the internal processes needed to fulfill customer needs;

- **Learning and Growth** – develop infrastructure and employees, to ensure business processes continue to meet customer needs; and

- **Financial** – focus on financial performance and the financial assets needed to support customer requirements, internal business process, and learning needs.

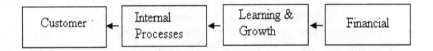

3.3   The CFO shall incorporate balanced objectives into the FA1000-1 FINANCIAL OBJECTIVES form in ways that account for the stage of the business cycle the Company is currently in, as well as other aspects of the business, such as:

- The current and desired capital structure;

- Proper focus on particular financial objectives (i.e., in the *growth* stage, a focus on percentage growth in revenue; in the *sustain* stage, a focus on profitability; in the *harvest* stage, a focus on cash flow and asset utilization);

- Relative investments into new products or new technologies versus cost reductions or investment into production capacity; and/or

- Balance investment risk and return in accordance with requirements from Top Management.

3.4   The CFO shall, as part of a balanced approach to setting objectives, create metrics that include *leading* and lagging indicators of financial performance.

4.0   APPROVAL AND MONITORING OF FINANCIAL OBJECTIVES

4.1   The CFO shall meet with Top Management within 90 days of the end of the fiscal year to review the FA1000-1 FINANCIAL OBJECTIVES, after which the CFO shall:

- Revise FA1000-1 as necessary and agreed upon by the CFO and Top Management; and

- Review all changes to FA1000-1 with Top Management and receive final approval within 60 days of the start of the fiscal year and prior to the Board of Directors review (Section 5.2).

4.2   The CFO shall meet with the Company Board of Directors within 60 days of the start of a new fiscal year to review the FA1000-1, after which the CFO shall:

- Revise FA1000-1 as necessary and agreed upon by the CFO, Top Management, and the Board of Directors; and

- Review all changes to FA1000-1 with Top Management and the Board of Directors and receive final approval within 30 days of the start of the fiscal year.

4.3   The CFO shall conduct regular meetings with Top Management to review progress in achieving financial objectives:

- The CFO shall confer with Top Management to decide the frequency of Financial Objectives review meetings (quarterly, at a minimum);

- The CFO shall discuss objectives that are not or will not be met and explain circumstances, suggest alternate strategies, or modify the objective(s); and

- The CFO shall report the results of financial objective review meetings to the Board of Directors.

5.0   IMPROVING FINANCIAL OBJECTIVES

5.1   The CFO shall review the Company's historical performance relative to financial objectives over a period of three to five (3-5) years and evaluate the relationship of historical trends to the financial objective setting process, such as:

- If very few objectives are actually achieved, what are the probable causes (e.g., unattainable objectives, lack of concrete actions)?

- If all objectives are achieved, are they set to improve performance in fundamental ways or just a rote exercise?

- Do the necessary steps to attain financial objectives need to be reviewed and altered in order to achieve financial objectives?

5.2   The CFO shall, through regular financial meetings (see section 4.0), review the overall process of setting and achieving financial objectives.

5.3   The CFO shall review the process for creating the FA1000-1 FINANCIAL
       OBJECTIVES after a period of setting and reviewing financial objectives and
       make necessary improvements to the financial objectives procedure and
       associated forms.

Effectiveness Criteria:

- Clearly stated, detailed, and communicated financial objectives

- Aligned and balanced financial objectives

Forms/Records:

- FA1000-1 FINANCIAL OBJECTIVES

- Meeting minutes and reports

References:

A. Finance Policy Manual

- Section 5.1.1 Financial Objectives

B. Finance procedures

- RC1000 BUSINESS PLAN

- RC1010 CAPITAL PLAN

Additional Resources:

A. "Rules to Setting Business Goals and Objectives: Why and How to be SMART",
    Ezine article at http://ezinearticles.com/?Rules-to-Setting-Business-Goals-
    and-Objectives:-Why-and-How-to-be-SMART&id=24276.

B. GAAP Handbook of Policies and Procedures, CCH, Inc.

C. *Balanced Scorecard: Translating Strategy into Action* - Kaplan, R. S. and
    Norton, D. P. (1996) Harvard Business School Press.

D. *The Practice of Management: A Study Of The Most Important Function In
    American Society* – Drucker, P. (1954)

Revision History:

Revision	Date	Description of Changes	Requested By
0.0	mm/dd/yyyy	Initial Release	

[This page intentionally left blank]

FA1000-1 FINANCIAL OBJECTIVES

Objectives for Year _____

Objectives for Period _____ to _____

Specific Objective	Measurement	Steps to Attain	Relevant	Time Frame	Notes

Comments:

Completed By:

_____ Date _____

Approval:

_____ Date _____

[This page intentionally left blank]

Document ID **FA1010**	Title **MANAGEMENT RESPONSIBILITY**	Print Date **mm/dd/yyyy**
Revision **0.0**	Prepared By **Preparer's Name / Title**	Date Prepared **mm/dd/yyyy**
Effective Date **mm/dd/yyyy**	Reviewed By **Reviewer's Name / Title**	Date Reviewed **mm/dd/yyyy**
	Approved By **Final Approver's Name / Title**	Date Approved **mm/dd/yyyy**

Policy: Top Management is committed to the development, implementation, and continuing improvement of the Company's financial management system and shall effectively communicate and support that commitment.

Purpose: To outline the methods for ensuring that the responsibility, authority, and interrelation of all personnel who manage, perform, and verify work affecting quality is defined and how the financial management system is to be reviewed to ensure its continuing suitability and effectiveness.

Scope: This procedure applies to Top Management and all managers involved with the financial management system.

Responsibilities: Top Management is responsible for implementation of this procedure and, ultimately, for the entire financial management system.

Financial Management, as part of the Management Team, is responsible for supporting Top Management in implementing this procedure.

The CFO (Chief Financial Officer) is responsible for ensuring that processes needed for the financial management system are established, implemented, and maintained. The CFO is also responsible for reporting to the CEO and Board of Directors (or Advisory Board) on the performance of the financial management system and reporting any need for its improvement.

Definitions: Management Team – Consists of the CEO, CFO, and Financial Management, at a minimum.

Top Management – Generally, a group of Company officers (e.g., CEO, CFO) with primary responsibility for decisions and activities affecting the Company in the long term (e.g., strategic planning); may also be referred to as "senior level management."

Financial management system (FMS) – System of managing the Company's financial resources, including accounting and financial reporting, internal controls, budgeting, collecting accounts receivable, risk management, and insurance. The FMS for a small business includes how you are financing the business and how you manage its money.

Procedure:

1.0   MANAGEMENT COMMITMENT TO THE FINANCIAL MANAGEMENT SYSTEM

Top Management shall demonstrate ongoing commitment to the development and implementation of the Company's financial management system and the continual improvement of its effectiveness by:

- Communicating the importance of meeting internal as well as statutory regulatory, and other requirements throughout the Company;
- Establishing financial policy;
- Ensuring that financial objectives are established;
- Conducting management reviews; and
- Ensuring that sufficient resources (people, materials, training, technology, etc.) are available.

2.0   FINANCIAL POLICY

2.1   Top Management shall establish a set of financial policies that applies to the entire Company (section 1.0) and supports the Company's financial management system.

2.2   Top Management shall ensure that the Company's financial policy:

- Is compatible with the Company's purpose, both stated and implied;
- Includes a commitment to comply with requirements (section 1.0);
- Includes management's commitment to continually improving the effectiveness of the financial management system;
- Provides a framework and/or set of guidelines for establishing and reviewing the Company's financial objectives;
- Is reviewed for its continuing suitability to the Company's purpose, goals, and objectives;
- Is communicated clearly and effectively; and
- Is understood, accepted, and put into practice throughout the Company.

3.0   FINANCIAL OBJECTIVES PLANNING

3.1   The Board of Directors shall ensure that financial objectives are established at relevant functions and levels within the Company in accordance with FS1000 FINANCIAL OBJECTIVES. Top Management shall determine which functions and levels are relevant in terms of financial objectives.

3.2   The Company's financial objectives shall be:

- Measurable; and
- Consistent (or aligned) with the Company's financial policies.

3.3   Top Management shall ensure that:

- The Company's financial management system is planned (designed) to meet federal, state, and local regulatory requirements and various financial standards, as well as the Company's own financial objectives; and
- The integrity of the Company's financial management system is maintained when changes to it are planned and implemented.

4.0   RESPONSIBILITIES, AUTHORITY, AND COMMUNICATION

4.1   The Board of Directors shall ensure that financial responsibilities and authorities are defined and communicated throughout the Company.

4.2   The Board of Directors shall establish an Audit Committee for the purpose of overseeing financial reporting processes and audits of the Company's financial management system. If the Board of Directors is not able to establish such a Committee, they shall serve as the Audit Committee.

4.3   The Company CFO's responsibilities and authorities shall include:

- Ensuring that the financial management system (including a system of internal controls) is established, implemented, maintained, and updated;
- Reporting to the CEO and Board of Directors on the performance of the financial management system and the need for improvement;
- Ensuring that awareness of requirements is promoted throughout the Company; and
- Freedom to resolve matters pertaining to quality of Company goods/services.

The CFO's responsibilities *may include* performing a *liaison* function relative to the financial management system (i.e., communicating matters, issues, and information from top management to external parties and vice versa).

4.4   Top Management shall ensure the establishment of appropriate communication processes within the Company and communication of the effectiveness of the Company's financial management system.

4.5   Top Management shall ensure that an adequate internal control structure is established and in force, so that financial information contained in reports (in particular, annual reports to shareholders, lenders, and other interested parties) reasonably represents the Company's financial status at that point in time.

Top Management shall indicate, by their signatures, that the information contained in such reports is accurate and timely.

5.0   MANAGEMENT REVIEW

5.1   The CFO shall periodically coordinate a meeting of the Management Team, the purpose of which shall be:

- To review the Company's financial management system and ensure its continuing suitability, adequacy, and effectiveness; and
- To assess opportunities for improvement and the need for changes to the system, including financial policy and objectives.

5.2   The CFO shall ensure that a record of each management review is kept, in accordance with applicable federal, state, and local regulations. The CFO may have the minutes of all such meetings recorded and added to the management review record.

The management review record should, at a minimum, consist of:

- Time, date, and location of the meeting;
- An attendance log; and
- The meeting agenda (see FA1010-1SAMPLE MANAGEMENT REVIEW AGENDA for guidance).

5.3   *Inputs* to management review meetings shall include (but need not be limited to):

- Results of audits;
- Reports on the performance of the financial management system relative to stated objectives (see FS1000 FINANCIAL OBJECTIVES) and the need, if any, to improve it;
- Performance of financial processes (including process conformities and nonconformities);
- The status of preventive and corrective actions open at – or opened since – the close of the last management review meeting;
- Follow-up actions from previous management reviews;
- Changes to products, processes, contracts, regulations, etc., that could have an effect on the Company's financial management system; and
- Recommendations for improvement.

5.4   Output of the management review meeting shall include all decisions and actions relative to:

- Improving the effectiveness of the financial management system and system processes; and
- Resource needs.

Management review action items should clearly indicate:

- Who (name and title) is responsible;
- What action is to be taken; and
- When (a start and end date).

Effectiveness Criteria:

- Periodic management review meetings (at least one per year is recommended).

- Financial objectives are periodically reviewed and updated if necessary (at least once a year is recommended).

- Management Review record accurately represents meeting inputs, outputs, and proceedings.

Forms/Records:

- FA1010-1 SAMPLE MANAGEMENT REVIEW AGENDA
- Records of management reviews (e.g., meeting minutes)
- Financial policy
- Financial objectives
- Annual reports

References:

A. Finance Policy Manual

- Section 3.5 – Responsibility, Authority, and Communication
- Section 3.6 – Management Reporting

B. Finance procedures

- FS1000 FINANCIAL OBJECTIVES

Additional Resources:

A. American Institute of Certified Professional Accountants (AICPA) standards and guidelines – see http://www.aicpa.org/pages/default.aspx or write to AICPA, 1211 Avenue of the Americas, New York, NY 10036 USA.

B. International Accounting Standards Board (IASB) standards and guidelines – see IFRS website www.ifrs.org/pages/default.aspx or call "44 (0)20 7246 6410."

C. Legal/regulatory requirements

- **SARBANES-OXLEY ACT OF 2002** (USA). Section 404 of the Act requires that companies' annual reports contain internal control reports that (1) state the responsibility of management for establishing and maintaining an adequate internal control structure and procedures for financial reporting and (2) contain an assessment, as of the end of the most recent fiscal year of the issuer, of the effectiveness of the internal control structure and procedures of the issuer for financial reporting.

- **EUROPEAN UNION ACCOUNTING DIRECTIVES**. The EU's financial reporting strategy has been to ensure that all listed Community companies follow a uniform financial reporting system that guarantees a high level of transparency and comparability by requiring them to prepare their consolidated accounts in conformity with international accounting standards (IAS) by 2005, at the latest.

Revision History:

Revision	Date	Description of Changes	Requested By
0.0	mm/dd/yyyy	Initial Release	

FA1010-1 SAMPLE MANAGEMENT REVIEW AGENDA

Meeting Date/Time: _____

Location: _____

Attendance: _____

_____

_____

_____

_____

Agenda:

I.   Review minutes of previous Management Review (MR) meeting

II.   Review results of internal, external audits since last MR

III. Review continuity plan, tests

IV.   Review objectives, targets

V.   Review progress toward objectives/targets

VI.   Determine need to adjust existing objectives/targets and set new (additional)
      objectives/targets

VII. Review the Financial Management System's effectiveness and suitability (e.g.,
      were there any changes to the business/regulatory environment since the last MR?)

VIII. Other issues

IX.   Schedule next MR meeting

Notes

_____

_____

_____

_____

_____

_____

_____

_____

_____

_____

_____

Document ID **FA1020**	Title **CONTINUITY PLANNING**	Print Date **mm/dd/yyyy**
Revision **0.0**	Prepared By **Preparer's Name / Title**	Date Prepared **mm/dd/yyyy**
Effective Date **mm/dd/yyyy**	Reviewed By **Reviewer's Name / Title**	Date Reviewed **mm/dd/yyyy**
	Approved By **Approver Name / Title**	Date Approved **mm/dd/yyyy**

Policy: The Company should anticipate and prepare for possible disruption of normal Finance operations.

Purpose: In the event of Finance operations being disrupted, to ensure the Finance department's ability to return to normal functional capability with minimal downtime and minimal adverse effects.

Scope: This procedure applies to the Company's Financial Management System (FMS).[1]

Responsibilities: The CFO (Chief Financial Officer) is responsible for ensuring development and implementation of a continuity plan for Finance and for ensuring that the continuity plan is in force; this includes ensuring that the plan is tested and verified periodically.

The CFO is also responsible for reporting to the CEO and the Board of Directors (or Advisory Board) on continuity plan test results and recommending improvements to the plan. (If the Company is large enough, the CFO may assign responsibilities to a continuity manager.)

The Board of Directors is responsible for reviewing and approving the Finance department's continuity plan.

The Continuity Team Leader is responsible for implementing the plan and participating in plan testing.

Definitions: Continuity plan – Plan to ensure that the effects of an extended disruption (e.g., natural disaster) are minimized and the organization is able to maintain or quickly resume mission-critical functions.

Downtime (or "down time") – Duration of an equipment or system stoppage – scheduled or unscheduled – measured from the moment of failure to the moment at which normal operations resume.

---

[1] NOTE: It is strongly recommended that the Company have an overall continuity plan, of which the *financial* continuity plan should be just one aspect.

Procedure:

1.0   CONTINUITY PLANNING

1.1   The CFO should conduct or direct a *risk assessment* of the Finance Management System in accordance with AC1020 RISK ASSESSMENT, identifying:

- Specific threats and vulnerabilities;
- Their impact;
- The likelihood of threats materializing or vulnerabilities being exploited; and
- Controls needed to prevent, reduce, or mitigate vulnerabilities and threats.

1.2   Based on the impact analysis and risk assessment, the CFO should develop a *continuity plan*. The continuity plan should:

- Identify risks and how to deal with them;
- Specify the conditions that should trigger specific parts of the plan;
- Specify the steps to be taken in the event of a system disruption or failure;
- State the minimum system and data requirements;
- State the time frame in which the minimum system functionality and data must be available;
- Be flexible to allow appropriate response to unanticipated threats and/or evolving conditions;
- Focus on recovery and resumption rather than on the nature of the disruption;
- Minimize disruptions and financial losses; and
- Be communicated and understood so that it can be implemented by Finance personnel in a timely manner.

See next section.

1.3   The CFO should lay out the continuity plan, using FA1020-1 CONTINUITY PLAN WORKSHEET to describe the following:

- **Section I** – Who is going to be involved with execution of the plan and testing (i.e., the continuity team leader, or crisis management command structure);

- **Section II** – What continuity plan training each team member has received and how current that training is;

- **Section III** – Periodic backing up of critical data;

- **Section IV** – Inspection and testing of backup data, including testing of communication between the primary and secondary work sites, application software at the backup site, data replication methodology between primary and secondary sites, etc.; and

- **Section V** – The steps, in order, that the continuity team leader must take to restore Finance to a normal state of operations; and

- **Section VI** – A threat matrix (see previous section).

See AC1030 RISK MANAGEMENT for more information and further guidance.

1.4   The CFO shall present the continuity plan to the Board of Directors for discussion and approval.

1.5   Upon approval of the continuity plan by the Board of Directors, the CFO shall communicate the plan to the Finance department, assign responsibilities, and begin implementing the plan.

2.0   IMPLEMENTING THE CONTINUITY PLAN

2.1   The CFO shall identify key Finance *continuity personnel* (also known as the "continuity team leader") and assign roles and responsibilities. The CFO shall also ensure that a "call list" of continuity personnel, their roles and responsibilities, and key contact information is developed and distributed to all Finance personnel.

2.2   The CFO shall ensure that continuity team members are appropriately trained – and cross-trained – to implement the continuity plan. In addition, all personnel must receive crisis response training. Such training should be part of new employee orientation and all employees should receive refresher training at least annually.

        Members of the continuity team should be trained in their specific duties early in the original continuity plan implementation. As other personnel are moved into the continuity team, they should receive specialized training immediately. The continuity team leader should also receive periodic refresher training; see "Testing the Continuity Plan" (next section).

2.3   If it is feasible for the Company to do so, the CFO should identify and secure at least one secondary (backup) work site for Finance to use during response and recovery. Depending on the Company's needs (for a hot or cold site or even a mobile command center), the CFO should ensure that the secondary site is appropriately stocked and equipped.

        The secondary site should not be so close to the primary work site that it is subject to the same or similar threats (e.g., quakes, weather-related hazards).

2.4   The CFO shall ensure that financial data are periodically backed up (this should be done at least once a week) and stored offsite in such a way that they are secure, yet retrievable by authorized Company personnel at a moment's notice.

3.0   TESTING THE CONTINUITY PLAN

3.1   The CFO should ensure that the continuity plan is tested upon implementation and periodically thereafter (annually, at a minimum).

3.2   Continuity plan testing may take the form of a(n):

- *Actual (live) test*, using the secondary work site(s), alternate equipment, and data stored offsite to "restore normal operations"; or

- *Tabletop exercise*, where the strategy and logic of the continuity plan are validated using a realistic scenario. Key personnel walk through the plan and explain their responses/activities at various points in the scenario.

NOTE

While a tabletop exercise is OK as an occasional refresher, *it is not an acceptable substitute for a live test.* Tabletop exercises will not expose all weaknesses in the continuity plan. A live test is the only way to be sure equipment and personnel will perform as planned and normal operations can be resumed within an acceptable time frame.

3.3   The CFO should schedule continuity plan testing for the coming year; timeliness of testing, as well as test results, should be analyzed and reported on as soon as possible after any test.

3.4   The CFO shall maintain a file of continuity plan test results for reference.

4.0   MAINTAINING AND UPDATING THE CONTINUITY PLAN

4.1   The CFO should review the results of continuity plan testing with Finance managers, determine the areas of greatest risk exposure, make changes to reduce risk in those areas, and retest them in accordance with section 3.0 (previous section).

4.2   The CFO should periodically[2] review the continuity plan with other Finance managers to:

- Ensure that the plan is relevant and up to date;
- Compare test results with stated objectives;
- Ensure that equipment, facilities, and training are adequate; and
- Review the test schedule, to determine if it should be adjusted.

The CFO should present a report of this review to the Board of Directors for their commentary and recommendations.

4.3   Internal Auditing should review the continuity plan and test results on a regular basis. Corrective actions recommended by internal auditors should be reviewed, tested, and implemented in a timely manner, in accordance with AC1060 CORRECTIVE ACTION.

4.4   Any third-party audit of the finance management system should also include an audit of the continuity plan and test results.

---

[2] Annually, at a minimum

Effectiveness Criteria:

- The Company has a continuity plan in place.

- The continuity plan is periodically tested for effectiveness *and* test results are reviewed.

- Gaps in the continuity plan are found *during testing* and are resolved in a timely manner.

- Crises are managed quickly and effectively; downtime, losses are minimized.

Forms/Records:

- FA1020-1 CONTINUITY PLAN WORKSHEET

- AC1020-1 RISK ASSESSMENT/MANAGEMENT WORKSHEET

- Continuity plan test results file

References:

A. Finance Policy Manual

- Section 5.1.3 Continuity Planning

B. Finance procedures

- AC1020 RISK ASSESSMENT

- AC1030 RISK MANAGEMENT

- AC1060 CORRECTIVE ACTION

Additional Resources:

A. Disaster Recovery Policies and Procedures, Bizmanualz, Inc. (Bizmanualz #ABR33M, ISBN-10 1-931591-01-6), 2002.

B. Computer & Network Policies and Procedures, Bizmanualz, Inc. (Bizmanualz #ABR34M, ISBN-10 1-931591-06-7), 2005.

C. Enterprise Risk Management Framework - Executive Summary, Committee of Sponsoring Organizations of the Treadway Commission (COSO). See http://www.coso.org for information.

D. FFIEC Business Continuity Planning - IT Examination Handbook, Federal Financial Institutions Examining Council (FFIEC), March, 2003.

E. ISO/PAS 22399:2007, "Societal Security – Guideline for Incident Preparedness and Operational Continuity Management," Industrial Organization for Standardization (ISO), 2007. ISO 22399 provides general guidance for organizations of all types and sizes to develop specific performance criteria for incident preparedness and operational continuity and to design management systems. It provides a basis for understanding, developing, and implementing continuity of operations and services within the organization and can help provide confidence in business, community, customer, first responder, and organizational interactions. See http://www.iso.org for more information.

F. Wrobel, Leo, <u>Legal Requirements for Disaster Recovery Planning: Common Facts and Misconceptions</u>, InformIT.com, 3 Aug. 2007 – http://www.informit.com/articles/article.aspx?p=777896.

G. The Business Continuity Institute (BCI) was founded in 1994 to enable its members to obtain guidance and support from fellow business continuity practitioners. In addition, the BCI offers certification in the field of business continuity management. See http://www.thebci.org for more information on this organization.

H. Regulatory requirements

- The **US OCCUPATIONAL SAFETY AND HEALTH ACT** (29 USC 654) requires employers (a) to furnish employment and a place of employment free of recognized hazards that are causing or are likely to cause death or serious physical harm and (b) to comply with occupational safety and health standards promulgated under this Act. This *may be construed* to mean that businesses are required by law to develop and implement continuity plans, in general. The Company should seek the advice of qualified legal counsel.

- The **SARBANES-OXLEY ACT** (USA) does not spell out the need for a financial continuity plan. However, the requirement that financial data are available in a timely manner has been construed by many to mean that a continuity plan is necessary to ensure compliance. Again, the Company should seek the advice of qualified legal counsel.

Revision History:

Revision	Date	Description of Changes	Requested By
0.0	mm/dd/yyyy	Initial Release	

FA1020-1 CONTINUITY PLAN WORKSHEET

I. People

Name / Title	Plan Responsibilities	Name / Title	Plan Responsibilities
1.		4.	
2.		5.	
3.		6.	

II. Training

Name/Title	Training	Trained By	Completion Date

III. File Backup[3]

Backup Date	Description

IV. File Backup Inspection and Testing

File(s) Inspected/Tested	Inspected By	Description of Test/Inspection	Scheduled Date	Actual Date

---

[3] Backups and logging should be automatic. Backup logs should periodically be reviewed in conjunction with inspection & testing (section IV).

V. Continuity Plan
Secondary Site: _____

Step No.	Description	Assigned To	Scheduled Date	Actual Date	Start Time	End Time	Results

Test Notes:

VI. Threat Matrix[4]

(Put a check in the appropriate box and fill in details below; use additional sheets as needed.)

Have the following been identified / included?	THREAT #1 (name)	THREAT #2 (name)	THREAT #3 (name)	THREAT #4 (name)
1. Trigger(s)				
2. Steps to take if threat occurs				
3. Minimum system/data requirements identified				
4. How soon minimal system functionality & data must be available				
5. Flexibility, to allow appropriate response to evolving threats, etc.				
6. Focus on recovery and resumption				
7. Minimizing disruption, financial loss				
8. Communication of continuity plan				

Comments (attach additional sheets, if needed):

---

[4] Also see AC1020-1, "Risk Assessment/Management Worksheet".

Document ID FA1030	Title **DOCUMENT CONTROL**	Print Date mm/dd/yyyy
Revision **0.0**	Prepared By **Prepare's Name / Title**	Date Prepared mm/dd/yyyy
Effective Date mm/dd/yyyy	Reviewed By **Reviewer's Name / Title**	Date Reviewed mm/dd/yyyy
	Approved By **Final Approver's Name / Title**	Date Approved mm/dd/yyyy

Policy: The Company will control Financial Management System (FMS) documents to ensure that everyone is working according to identical (and the most up-to-date) procedures and guidelines.

Purpose: To define the methods and responsibilities for controlling documents used to provide work direction or set policy and to define methods for document revision, approval, and distribution.

Scope: This procedure applies to all documents required by the FMS. Documents of internal or external origin are included.

Responsibilities: Document Control is responsible for controlling all FMS procedures and instructions, as well as all internal and external documents required by the FMS. Document Control is also responsible for ensuring that documents conform to applicable standards.

Department Managers are responsible for ensuring that the latest versions of relevant documents are available at the point(s) of use, that these documents are legible, and that they are understood and followed. They are also responsible for reviewing and responding to document change requests in a timely manner.

Top Management is responsible for reviewing requests and giving final approval to FMS-related procedures.

Definitions: Controlled Document – Document that provides information or direction for performance of work within the scope of the FMS. Characteristics of control include such things as revision number (letter), signatures indicating review and approval, and controlled distribution.

Document – Information and its supporting medium (paper, magnetic, electronic, optical, photograph, *or a product sample.*)

External Document – Document originating outside the Company (e.g., customer drawings, industry and/or international standards, suppliers' equipment maintenance manuals, or references) that provides information or direction for performing activities within the scope of the FMS.

Finance Management System (FMS) – Ordered, well-documented

system of policies, processes, and procedures, designed to assure compliance, conformity, and security; demonstrate a system of internal controls; and promote continual improvement of financial processes.

Form – Printed, typed, or electronic document with blank spaces for insertion of required or requested information (e.g., tax form, order form).

Internal Document – Document of *internal* origin (developed entirely by or completed by the Company) that provides information or direction for the performance of activities within the scope of the FMS. Examples include, but are not limited to, FMS procedures.

Procedure – Process or series of acts involved in a particular form of work; detailed elements of a process used to produce a specified result.

Uncontrolled Document – Document that is not a part of the controlled document system. Uncontrolled documents may not be used to provide work direction or information necessary for the performance of work.

Work Instruction – For a step in a process, the instruction(s) on how to perform that step, sufficiently detailed to allow an inexperienced person to perform the work.

Procedure:

1.0   PROCEDURE FORMAT

1.1   Procedures should follow the "Plan-Do-Check-Act" (Deming Cycle) format whenever possible. Finance procedures may use this document as a template; however, if any heading in this procedure format is not applicable to the situation requiring a procedure, it may be deleted.

1.2   All Finance procedures shall have a(n):

- Procedure name;
- Revision number;
- Revision history;
- Effective date;
- Page numbers (e.g., "page x of y") *on each page of the document*;
- Cross-references to other documents, where applicable; and
- Clear indication of Management's approval (e.g., signature(s) in ink[1]).

1.3   All procedures in hardcopy form must show approval signatures on the first (cover) page of the document.

- *Electronic* versions of procedures may show approving parties' names *typed*.

---

[1] See Reference "C".

- *Electronic signatures* may be allowed, provided they meet customer and/or regulatory requirements (Reference "C").

1.4   Document Control shall keep the original signed *paper* copy (called the "master copy") of *all* required documents. Alternately, Document Control shall be responsible for the Company's electronic document management system.

1.5   Electronic files shall be named using the document number, title, and revision number (e.g., "FA1030 – Document Control .doc").

2.0   WORK INSTRUCTIONS (WI)

2.1   Work instructions, by definition, must be specific as to the work that is performed.

2.2   Work instructions may take the form of text, drawings, diagrams, charts, photographs, video, or any combination of these or other forms not mentioned here.

2.3   Work instructions must have a(n):

- Unique identifier (name and/or ID);
- Date of origin;
- Revision number and date;
- Effective date; and
- Indication of Management approval (i.e., signature).

3.0   FORMS

3.1   Forms should be as simple as possible, with ample space for recording the required information.

3.2   Forms may exist in print or electronic media.

3.3   Once a form is populated with data, it becomes a *record*.

3.4   In this FMS, forms are approved by Management as part of the associated procedure approval (see section 4.0).

3.5   Within this FMS manual, sample forms are included with their associated procedures. Form identifiers correspond to procedure ID's (e.g., "FA1030 – DOCUMENT CONTROL" shows a sample document control database, identified as "FA1030-2").

4.0   DOCUMENT APPROVAL

4.1   Designated Management personnel (at a minimum, the manager with direct responsibility for the area/department where the document is used) shall approve all documents.

- Approval shall be indicated by signature (in blue or black ink) where indicated on the print version of a document.

- For electronic documents, approval should be indicated by electronic signature. Electronic signatures, where provided, must conform to Company and statutory/regulatory requirements (see Reference "B").

4.2   Approved documents are considered *master* (original) documents. Master documents are managed by Document Control and are not circulated. Copies of Master documents are made by Document Control and circulated (distributed) as needed – these are "controlled documents."

4.3   Master documents are kept in a Master Document file in a physically (and electronically) secure environment, to prevent loss, tampering, or destruction.

5.0   TEMPORARY DOCUMENT CHANGES

5.1   When temporary changes to documents are needed for any reason (e.g., unplanned change in response to an urgent request or emergency situation), such changes must be defined and approved by Top Management.

5.2   Any employee may bring a temporary change to the attention of Department Management. If an employee of one department is requesting a temporary change to another Department's procedure or document, that employee shall submit the request to their/her Department manager, who shall communicate with the affected Department's management.

5.3   If a document (e.g., a procedure) does not exist – for example, a set of instructions is e-mailed by a manager to subordinates – Department management may develop a temporary document, which must bear the Manager's name, title, and current date. If an *existing* document needs changes, Department management must red-line, initial, and date changes on the existing document.

        Whether the document in question is new or altered, changes shall be legible *and* readily identifiable.

5.4   Temporary change documents shall include the range of dates in which the changes are valid and the scope of applicability. Temporary documents may not be used for more than two business days without being superseded, terminated, or made permanent.

5.5   Department management shall submit temporary changes to Document Control. Document Control shall initial and date the temporary (or temporarily changed) document.

5.6   If temporary changes bypass any part of the FMS, Document Control shall submit the changes to Top Management, who shall review the changes and indicate approval by initialing and dating the document *before* the temporary change is implemented.

6.0   DOCUMENT REVISIONS

6.1   All FMS documents are subject to revision.

6.2   To submit a *change*, the requestor should obtain a current copy of the document and "red-line" requested changes on the copy. All changes should be clearly identified, initialed, and dated. If changes are *extensive* or *complex*, the requestor may type a new document and submit this with a copy of the original.

        • To request a *new* document, the requestor should provide an explanation and detailed layout for the new document.

- In either case, the requestor shall fill out an FA1030-1 DOCUMENT REQUEST, attach the new/changed document, and submit this to his/her Department Manager for review.

6.3   After reviewing the request, the Department Manager should submit the FA1030-1 and any attachments to Document Control, who shall review the request to ensure the document conforms to the FMS:

- If Document Control finds the requested document (change) does not conform to the FMS, Document Control should return the FA1030-1 and attachments to the Department manager with an explanation (e.g., what is needed to make the document conform).

- If the requested document is determined to conform to the FMS, Document Control shall determine who else needs to review the new/changed document (e.g., the originator is not involved with the process the document pertains to) and submit the FA1030-1 form, with attachments, to those individuals for their review and approval.

6.4   Upon receiving the necessary approvals, Document Control shall update the document and generate a new Master document.

6.5   Document Control shall circulate the new Master document among designated Management personnel (see section 4.1) to obtain approval/signatures.

6.6   When the required signature(s) have been obtained, Document Control shall file the original document in the Master document file and distribute copies of the new (revised) document (see 4.2, 4.3).

7.0   EXTERNAL DOCUMENTS

7.1   Documents generated outside the Company (e.g., industry standards, hardware/ software user manuals) are to be submitted to Document Control with an FA1030-1DOCUMENT REQUEST form.

7.2   Document Control shall log external documents in FA1030-2 – DOCUMENT CONTROL DATABASE and distribute to approved/interested parties (section 8.0).

8.0   DOCUMENT DISTRIBUTION

8.1   Document Control shall maintain a database, or master list, of all controlled documents (see FA1030-2 DOCUMENT CONTROL DATABASE). The Document Control Database (list) should contain, at a minimum, the following information on each document:

- Document number;
- Document title;
- Current revision number/ID;
- Revision date;
- Effective date; and
- Distribution list.

8.2   Document Control shall distribute (or limit distribution of electronic) documents only to locations shown on the database.

8.3   Document Control shall remove any previous version of documents from work areas as revisions are released. In the case of electronic document distribution and control systems, access permission for any previous version must be withdrawn or denied.

8.4   Document Control should periodically review FA1030-2 for document currency and relevance (at least annually is recommended). If Document Control believes a document to be out of date and/or no longer relevant, Document Control shall alert the CFO and the process owner(s) who use the document – in writing, preferably – at a minimum.[2] The CFO or delegate should attest to the obsolescence in writing (see next section). Document Control shall record the date of obsolescence in FA1030-2.

8.5   Document Control shall maintain a file on each document, which shall contain current and previous (retired/obsolete) Master documents *only*. When previous versions of documents are no longer required, Document Control shall physically destroy or electronically purge them, in accordance with FA1030 –RECORD CONTROL.

Effectiveness Criteria:

- No obsolete documents in use or available for inadvertent use
- Average time to release document changes

Forms/Records:

- Master documents
- Master document file
- Signed copies of documents
- FA1030-1 DOCUMENT REQUEST
- FA1030-2 DOCUMENT CONTROL DATABASE

References:

A. Financy Policy Manual

   - Section 5.1.4 Document Control

B. Finance procedures

   - FA1040 RECORD CONTROL

C. Statutory/regulatory requirements

   - **SARBANES-OXLEY ACT** (USA).

     Regarding the Company's annual report, Section 404 of the Act requires it to contain an *internal control report* that (a) states Management's responsibility

---

[2] Process owners are responsible for contacting employees/contractors reporting to them.

for establishing and maintaining an adequate internal control structure and procedures for financial reporting and (b) contains an assessment, as of the end of the Company's fiscal year, of the effectiveness of the internal control structure and procedures of the issuer for financial reporting.

- **ELECTRONIC RECORDS; ELECTRONIC SIGNATURES**, Title 21, Code of Federal Regulations (21 CFR Part 11) – (USA).

  While Title 21 pertains specifically to the U.S. Food and Drug Administration, it was the first U.S. federal regulation to spell out requirements for electronic recordkeeping. It and associated documents provide valuable guidance to food *and non-food* industries with regard to electronic signatures.

- **ELECTRONIC SIGNATURES IN GLOBAL AND NATIONAL COMMERCE ACT**, Public Law #106-229 (USA).

  This law (commonly known as "E-Sign") was enacted in June, 2000, to promote the use of electronic contracts, signatures, and recordkeeping in private commerce by establishing equivalence between contracts on paper and in electronic form, ink and electronic signatures, and other legally required documents in paper and electronic form.

- **ELECTRONIC SIGNATURES REGULATIONS 2002**, Statutory Instrument 2002 No. 318 (UK).

Additional Resources:

A. Guidance on Implementing the Electronic Signatures in Global and National Commerce Act (USA) – http://www.whitehouse.gov/omb/memoranda/esign-guidance.pdf.

Revision History:

Revision	Date	Description of Changes	Requested By
0.0	mm/dd/yyyy	Initial Release	

FA1030-1 DOCUMENT REQUEST

Date: _____   Request # _____

Originator: _____

Existing ☐   New ☐ document

Internal ☐   External ☐ document

Document title / publication date: _____

Page / chapter / paragraph number: _____

Description of problem, opportunity, or reason for request (define in detail):

_____

_____

Solution recommended and action required by (date):_____

_____

_____

Comments:_____

_____

_____

Distribute document to (department/position):

Department manager approval: _____

Recommended solution to problem or postponement/dissolution of request
 (attach all necessary documentation to support response) _____

_____

_____

Approved By_____   Date:_____

PROCEDURE FOR COMPLETING FORM

1) Complete top section of this form.
2) Obtain Department manager's approval.
3) Forward original to Document Control.
   a) Document Control will give copy to originator
   b) If related process owner is not the originator, Document Control will forward copy to process owner for review and action; process owner will respond to Document Control.
4) Document Control will notify originator and/or process owner upon resolution of request.

Distribution: Original – Document Control
                   Copy 1 – Originator
                   Copy 2 – Process owner

[This page intentionally left blank]

FA1030-2 DOCUMENT CONTROL DATABASE

Document Number	Document Title	Rev Num	Rev Date	Eff Date	Distrib[3]	Obs Date[4]
FA1020	Document Control	0.0	mm/dd/yyy	mm/dd/yyyy		

[3] Distribution codes: 1=Finance Mgmt.; 2=Strategy; 3=Operations; 4=Accounting (NOTE: These are examples and your finance department need not be segmented in this manner.)

[4] If obsolete, enter date of obsolescence; if in use, leave blank.

[This page intentionally left blank]

Document ID **FA1040**	Title **RECORD CONTROL**	Print Date **mm/dd/yyyy**
Revision **0.0**	Prepared By **Preparer's Name / Title**	Date Prepared **mm/dd/yyyy**
Effective Date **mm/dd/yyyy**	Reviewed By **Reviewer's Name / Title**	Date Reviewed **mm/dd/yyyy**
	Approved By **Final Approver's Name / Title**	Date Approved **mm/dd/yyyy**

Policy: Records are established and maintained to contribute to – and provide evidence of – the effective operation of the Company's financial management systems (FMS).

Purpose: 1) Demonstrate conformance to specified customer, regulatory, and other requirements and demonstrate effective FMS operation.

2) Explain how records are maintained.

Scope: This procedure applies to all records – regardless of form – that pertain to the Company's finance-related activities and are required to demonstrate implementation of and conformance to the Company's FMS.

Responsibilities: Financial Management is responsible for maintaining a list of Finance records and for controlling record distribution.

All Finance personnel are responsible for ensuring that the financial records they generate are legible, accurate, and timely.

Definitions: Controlled document – Document that provides information or direction for performance of work and is part of a controlled document system. Characteristics of control include such things as revision number (or letter), signatures indicating review and approval, and controlled distribution.

Document – Information and its supporting medium; the medium may be paper, magnetic, electronic, optical, photograph, or a sample of the Company's product.

Form – Document or web form with spaces in which to write; business document that typically contains some predefined data and designated, labeled areas for filling in data.

Record – Anything retained to provide and preserve *permanent evidence of* or *information about* an event (e.g., document, photograph, nonconforming product sample).

Procedure:

1.0 IDENTIFICATION OF RECORDS

1.1   When a hard copy or electronic *form* is filled in, it becomes a *record*. Records are *controlled documents* and are, therefore, part of the Company's document control system (see FA1020 DOCUMENT CONTROL).

1.2   The Finance Department and functional groups within it shall be responsible for generating and maintaining adequate records to demonstrate:

- Effective operations (as defined within each FMS procedure); and

- Compliance with customer, regulatory, and other requirements.

1.3   Blank forms should be consistently formatted and grouped by department and/or function. (See FA1040-1 SAMPLE MASTER FILE GUIDE INDEX for guidance.) Blank forms may be centrally located or they may be distributed to departments, depending on the Company's needs.

- Forms may be paper-based or electronic.

- The Company may distribute blank electronic forms via its intranet, for standardization and control.

1.4   Finance records should contain the following, at a minimum:

- When the record was created (date and, if required, time);

- Information on the situation, event, or entity (a factual description, visual or physical evidence, data, etc.); and

- A *unique* record identifier.

1.5   Financial Management shall maintain an FA1040-2 – FINANCE RECORDS LIST, which should be a *complete* list of Finance records. The Record List, whether in hard copy or electronic form, should contain the following information on each record, at a minimum:

- A unique identifier (e.g., sequentially numbered alpha/numeric ID);

- A description of the record;

- The location of the record;

- Minimum retention time[1]; and

- Directions for record disposition.

2.0 RECORD GENERATION

2.1   Every Finance employee may generate records in the course of performing his/her normal duties (e.g., production monitoring logs, receiving logs). Such records should be identified within FMS procedures.

---

[1] See section 4.0 and FA1040-3, "Record Retention Guidelines."

Electronic records of Finance activity will typically be generated and logged automatically in their respective data files (databases/data warehouses). Reference (procedures in this manual); also see Reference "C."

2.2   All Finance Records must be accurate, timely, legible, and readily accessible for reference and verification purposes.

2.3   *Hardcopy* records should be completed in ink or generated using word processing software to help ensure legibility and protect them from unauthorized change.

2.4   *Electronic* records should be write-protected and access restricted to enforce change control Document Control should control access to electronic records.

2.5   Individual financial records shall not be altered or destroyed before the minimum retention period has passed. "Changes" shall take the form of *update* records.

- If necessary, changes or corrections to *hardcopy* records should be made to *copies* of originals, with a single line through each incorrect entry. The change/correction should be written in ink (on the copy or a separate piece of paper) and dated and initialed by the person making the change. Correction fluid or tape should not be used, even on the copy.

- *Electronic* records shall not be altered or deleted. Originals shall be superseded by and shall cross-reference update records. Electronic records shall

- Updates shall be kept with originals (in the same folder, database, etc.).

- In all cases, originals shall be retained in accordance with Company guidelines (see FA1040-2, "Finance Records List") and applicable laws/regulations (see "References" section).

- The department responsible for maintaining a given record shall maintain a separate log of "changes" for that record type.

3.0   RECORDKEEPING AND TRACEABILITY

3.1   To ensure efficient access, filing centers should be established in each department. To reduce the amount of duplicate and unnecessary record retention, individual desk files should be avoided unless they are used in daily operations. All other departmental or company records should be filed in the department's central filing area.

3.2   Unless necessary, records should only be kept by the originator or sender and not by the receiver, to avoid duplicate filing systems. Alternatively, records may be maintained in an electronic record management system, where the original record should be copy- and write-protected, to avoid duplication.

3.3   When an original record or update is generated, its originator should note the following in a record log (which should be kept with the record file):

- Record name/ID;

- Date (and time) of origin/update;

- Reference (pointer) to the original, in the case of a record update;

- Record originator; and

- Purpose.

  If an electronic record management system is used, it must *automatically* log all records – originals and updates – entered into the system.

3.4   The following filing guidelines should be adhered to optimize filing efficiency and records access (for paper records):

- All file cabinets and files should follow generally recognized rules of order (e.g., left-to-right, top-to-bottom, front-to-back) and, in the case of chronological records, newest to oldest (i.e., reverse chronological order).

- File markers or label headings should always be placed at the beginning or front of a file or group of files.

- Alphabetical files should always be filed under broad topical categories. Files should never be filed under individual employee names, to avoid confusion and re-filing in the event of turnover. Files should always be filed under the "proper" or company names whenever appropriate. In the case of individuals, files should be maintained according to the persons "Last name," then "First Name" and "Middle Initial."

- Alphanumeric codes should be attached to colored end tabs of all file sets to show type of file by subject area and sub-category; for instance:

  a. Fixed asset files may have a green end tab on the lateral file folder, with an alpha code of "FA" followed by a three-digit numeric code to designate the subcategory (e.g., Asset Planning = SL100, Asset Purchases = SL200).

  b. A sample chart of accounts is provided

- Extra care should be taken with regard to sensitive or private information. Company records that contain performance reviews, salary information, and any health related information should be kept in a secure area with limited access to only those that have a "need to know," such as the Director of Human Resources or the Controller.

4.0   RECORD RETENTION AND LONG-TERM STORAGE

4.1   Storage of archived records will be maintained in the locked storage area of the building. Access to this area will be limited to the Controller, officers of the Company and the File Manager.

4.2   Non-permanent files will be stored in cardboard file boxes. Each file box will be labeled on the front with the contents, dates covered, and destruction date if applicable. Permanent records will be maintained in metal fire-resistant file cabinets.

4.3   Files should be stored only in boxes with similar items, dates and retention periods. This will allow easier access and purging of records. A general rule to keep in mind is that it is better to only half-fill a file box than to file dissimilar types of files in the same box.

4.4   The file manager will be responsible for categorizing and maintaining a listing of records maintained and the location (i.e. by wall unit and shelf row number).

4.5   Maintain all files for as long as is necessary and only to the extent they serve a useful purpose or satisfy business or legal requirements. FA1040-2, "Record Retention Guidelines," provides a guide to the typical business life of financial documents. The retention periods provided are suggested with federal requirements in mind. Be sure to check with local and state authorities for specific record retention requirements.

4.6   Copies of critical records that are vital to the daily operations of the Company should be kept off site in case of possible disasters. This may include information needed to file insurance claims (assets lists, insurance contacts, policy numbers), financial data for tax purposes (wages paid, income, and expenses), contacts lists to inform or restart the business (vendors, customers, investors, and employees), and other data that would assist in rebuilding the business (business plans, intellectual property, or proprietary information).

5.0   RECORD MAINTENANCE

5.1   The authority associated with a particular Finance Record (should be the CFO in most, if not all, cases) shall ensure that records are maintained in an environment that prevents their damage, deterioration, alteration, or loss.

-   Document Control shall control access to hardcopy, electronic, and other records (see Reference "C").

-   Relative to their importance to the Company, records should be backed up periodically in accordance with business, customer, and statutory/regulatory requirements (see Reference "B").

5.2   Document Control shall ensure that Finance records are readily retrievable.

-   Records shall be made available for customer and/or regulatory review, in accordance with contractual and regulatory requirements.

-   Records shall be made available to auditors, as required by applicable statutes/ regulations.

-   Inactive records may be archived before minimum retention times are reached, if circumstances warrant. Archived records must be controlled and maintained and should be reasonably retrievable.

5.3   Finance records shall be retained for no less than the period of time required by applicable statutes, regulations, and/or contractual requirements. Unless otherwise indicated, those records should be disposed after their minimum retention time is attained (see FA1040-2 FINANCE RECORDS LIST).

5.4   Finance Managers should annually, at a minimum, oversee a review or perform an audit of their respective department' records in accordance with the Company-approved audit procedure, to ensure that records are accurate, up-to-date, and located where they are supposed to be, according to FA1040-2 FINANCE RECORDS LIST.

Effectiveness Criteria:

- Records verify compliance with customer, regulatory, etc., requirements

- Records are accurate and up-to-date

- Clear audit trail

Forms/Records:

- FA1040-1 SAMPLE MASTER FILE GUIDE INDEX

- FA1040-2 FINANCE RECORDS LIST

- FA1040-3 RECORD RETENTION GUIDELINES

References:

A. CFO Manual

- Section 5.1.5 – Record Control

B. Statutory/Regulatory Requirements

The Company should be familiar with and be able to demonstrate compliance with applicable federal, state, and local recordkeeping and record control statutes and regulations; for example:

- **PUBLIC COMPANY ACCOUNTING REFORM AND INVESTOR PROTECTION ACT OF 2002** (aka, "Sarbanes-Oxley," "SOX"). Public companies doing business in the U.S.A. are subject to recordkeeping regulations under the Act. This generally pertains to accounting/financial records and their control, but any record relating to accounting or financial activities, whether or not they contain financial data (e.g., e-mails), may be subject to the requirements of the Act.

- **RIGHT TO FINANCIAL PRIVACY ACT** (12 USC 3401 et seq.). The law is largely procedural and requires government agencies to provide notice and an opportunity to object before a bank or other institution can disclose personal financial information to a government agency, usually for law enforcement purposes. The law was amended in the latter 1980s to allow postponement of notice in investigations dealing with drug trafficking and espionage.

- **SMALL BUSINESS PAPERWORK RELIEF ACT** (44 USC 3504). This Act requires a Task Force (chaired by the Office of Management and Budget and comprised of the Office of Advocacy and other federal agencies) to consider the federal paperwork burdens imposed on small business and to evaluate the feasibility of reducing those burdens.

- **GUIDE TO RECORD RETENTION REQUIREMENTS**

A good source of federal retention requirements is the "Guide to Record Retention Requirements" published by the Office of the Federal Register National Archives and Records Administration. It can be purchased from the U.S. Government Printing Office in Washington DC. Additional sources of information include: IRS regulations, state and local government retention requirements or the AICPA (American Institute of Certified Public Accountants) Filing and Record Retention Procedures Guide.

- **IRS REVENUE PROCEDURE 98-25 - RECORDS RETENTION**

  The Income Tax Regulations require that, except for farmers and wage-earners, any person subject to income tax, or any person required to file an information return with respect to income, must keep such books and records, including inventories, as are sufficient to establish the amount of gross income, deductions, credits, or other matters reported. The books or records required by must be kept available at all times for inspection by authorized internal revenue officers or employees, and must be retained so long as the contents thereof may become material in the administration of any internal revenue law.

  Note: Section 6.01 requires taxpayers to maintain and make available documentation of the business processes that (1) create the retained records, (2) modify and maintain its records, (3) satisfy the requirements of section 5.01(2) of the procedure and verify the correctness of the taxpayer's return, and (4) evidence the authenticity and integrity of the taxpayer's records.

  Section 6.02 sets forth four elements that the documentation required under section 6.01 must establish: (1) the flow of data through the system, (2) internal controls that ensure accurate processing, (3) internal controls that prevent unauthorized record changes, and (4) charts of account.

  Section 6.03 sets forth six specific types of documentation for each retained file: (1) record formats, (2) field definitions, (3) file descriptions, (4) evidence that periodic checks are undertaken to ensure that data remains accessible, (5) evidence that the records reconcile to the taxpayer's books, and (6) evidence that the records reconcile to the taxpayer's return.

  The Internal Revenue Service (IRS), U.S. Department of the Treasury, issues guidelines for maintaining certain types of records. See "Recordkeeping" at http://www.irs.gov/Businesses/Small-Businesses-&-Self-Employed/Recordkeeping

Additional Resources:

A. Accounting Policies and Procedures Manual, Bizmanualz, Inc., 2002 (#ABR31M, ISBN 978-1-9315-9102-7).

B. Internal Control - Integrated Framework: Executive Summary, Framework and Appendices, and Illustrative Tools for Assessing Effectiveness of a System of Internal Control, COSO, 1993. This document establishes a common definition of internal control that addresses needs to assess and improve control systems. Under the COSO Framework, objective setting is considered a precondition to internal control. By setting objectives, management can then identify risks to the achievement of those objectives. To address these risks, management may implement specific *internal controls*. The effectiveness of internal controls is measured by *how well* objectives are achieved and *how effectively* risks are

addressed. This document is available through the AICPA at
http://www.cpa2biz.com/AST/Main/CPA2BIZ_Primary/InternalControls/COSO/
PRDOVR~PC-990025/PC-990025.jsp.

C. Internal Control: Comptroller's Handbook, Office of the Comptroller of the
Currency (OCC), US Department of Treasury, Washington, DC, USA (January,
2001) – http://www.occ.gov/publications/publications-by-type/comptrollers-
handbook/index-comptrollers-handbook.html.

D. Internal Controls: A Guide for Directors, OCC (Sept., 2000) –
http://www.occ.gov/publications/publications-by-type/other-publications-
reports/Internal-Controls.pdf.

E. International Financial Reporting Standards (IFRS), published annually by the
International Accounting Standards Board (IASB). See the IFRS web site,
ifrs.org/pages/default.aspx, for information.

F. "Starting a Business and Keeping Records," IRS Publication 583 (March, 2006),
http://www.irs.gov/publications/p583/index.html.

Revision History:

Revision	Date	Description of Changes	Requested By
0.0	mm/dd/yyyy	Initial Release	

FA1040-1 SAMPLE MASTER FILE GUIDE INDEX

AC	**ACCOUNTING**
AC-100	Accounts Administration
AC-200	Financial Planning
AC-300	General Accounting
310	Checking Account Register
320	Accounts Payable
330	Accounts Receivable
340	Payroll
350	Local, State, Federal taxes {FUTA, FICA, etc.}
360	Banking Services
370	Property Inventory/Fixed Assets
380	Corporate Accountant
390	Corporate Tax Information File
AC-400	Employee Benefit Programs
AC-500	Employee Expense Accounts
AC-600	Petty Cash Management
AC-600	Corporate Loan Management
AC-700	Grants Account Management
AC-800	Purchasing
AC-900	Open

AD	**ADMINISTRATION**
AD-100	General
AD-200	Organizational Manual
AD-300	Organizational Charts
AD-400	Corporate Correspondence Manual
AD-500	Policies and Procedures
AD-600	Records Management and Retrieval
AD-700	Chief Executive Officer Administrative Memorandums
AD-800	Interoffice Staff Administrative Memorandums
AD-900	Open

BU	**BUSINESS**
BU-100	Corporate Business Plan
BU-200	Business Project Management
BU-300	Sub-Corp Business Project Management
BU-400	Business Executive Summaries
BU-500	Sub-Corp Business Executive Summaries
BU-600	Domestic Business Development
BU-700	International Business Development - Europe
BU-800	International Business Development - Asia
BU-900	International Business Development - Canada/S. America

CS	COMPUTER INFORMATION SYSTEMS
CS-100	General
CS-200	Equipment
CS-300	Operation and Maintenance
CS-400	Training in Systems Operation
CS-500	Open

EN	ENGINEERING
EN-100	General Administration
EN-200	Research and Development
EN-300	Chemical Engineering
EN-400	Graphics and Technical Drawings
EN-500	Product Information and Technical Analysis
EN-600	Product Raw Materials Data
EN-700	Engineering Safety Data
EN-800	Product Test Programs
EN-900	Industry Information

IN	INSURANCE
IN-100	General Administration of Insurance
IN-200	Plant and Equipment Policies
IN-300	Corporate Officer Policies
IN-400	Product Liability Policies
IN-500	Corporate Vehicles Policies
IN-600	Health Program Policies
IN-700	Life Insurance Programs for Employees
IN-800	Off Site Special Coverage
IN-900	Open

LG	LEGAL
LG-100	General
LG-200	Reports
LG-300	Contracts
LG-400	Litigation
LG-500	Disputes
LG-600	Legal Personnel Issues
LG-700	Agreements/Partnerships
LG-800	Product Liability
LG-900	Open

MA	MARKETING
MA-100	General
MA-200	Reports / Studies
MA-300	Marketing Plans
MA-400	Customer Relations

OF	OFFICE MANAGEMENT
OF-100	General
OF-200	Procedures
OF-300	Equipment/Furnishings/Telecommunications
OF-400	Information Processing/Communications Procedure
OF-500	Property Lease/Management Agreement
OF-600	Fax/Reproduction/Printing Procedures
OF-700	Protocol to Visitors
OF-800	Maintenance
OF-900	Open

OP	OPERATIONS
OP-100	General
OP-200	Daily Reports
OP-300	Weekly Reports
OP-400	Monthly Reports
OP-500	Quarterly/Annual Reports
OP-600	Performance Analysis
OP-700	Project Management Charts and Plans
OP-800	Manufacturing and Production
OP-900	Open

PE	PERSONNEL
PE-100	General
PE-200	Reports
PE-300	Employee Records
PE-400	Organizational Charts
PE-500	Recruiting
PE-600	Training
PE-700	Benefit Programs
PE-800	Open
PE-900	Open

PP	PATENTS, PERMITS AND PLANS
PP-100	General
PP-200	Reports
PP-300	Licenses/Permits/Plans
PP-400	Open
PP-500	Open

PR	PUBLIC RELATIONS
PR-100	General
PR-200	Reports and Studies
PR-300	Corporate Releases
PR-400	List of Clients/Industry Contacts
PR-500	Open

RG	REGULATORY DATA
RG-100	General
RG-200	Reports
RG-300	Correspondence
RG-400	Acts/Laws/Bills
RG-500	Regulations
RG-600	Agreements
RG-700	Guidelines/ Policies/ Resolutions
RG-800	International Regulations
RG-900	Open

SL	SALES
SL-100	General
SL-200	Domestic Business Development
SL-300	International Business Development
SL-400	Plans and Budgets
SL-500	Corporate Sales Procedures and Project Management

FA1040-2 FINANCE RECORDS LIST

ID	Record Description	Location-Custodian	Minimum Retention[2]	Disposition
	Asset disposal (sale, etc.) records			
	Asset purchase records			
	Bank deposit slips			
	Checkbook register (disbursement journal)			
	Cancelled checks			
	Loan closing statements			
	Credit card transaction records, statements			
	Depreciation deductions			
	Depreciation worksheets			
	Forms 1099-MISC (IRS)			
	General ledger			
	Invoices			
	Journals			
	Paid bills			
	Petty cash records			
	Sales documents			
	Financial statements (statements of cash flows, etc.)			
	Transaction databases			
	Cash account records			
	Equity account records			
	Debt agreements			
	Board of Directors meeting minutes			
	Options agreements			
	Bank statements			

[2] Customers and regulatory agencies may require longer retention periods.

[This page intentionally left blank]

FA1040-3 RECORD RETENTION GUIDELINES

Accident reports and claims (settled cases) ....7 years
Accounts payable ledgers, schedules and trial balances ....7 years
Accounts receivable ledgers, schedules and trial balances ....7 years
Assignments..3 years
Audit reports of accountants .... Permanently
Bank reconciliations ....1 year
Bank statements, cancelled checks, and deposit slips ....7 years
Bills of lading ....3 years
Capital stock and bond records .... Permanently
Cash books .... Permanently
Cash receipts and disbursements ....7 years
Chart of accounts .... Permanently
Checks (cancelled, all other) ....7 years
Checks (cancelled, for important payments, i.e. taxes, property purchases,
special contracts, etc. File checks with the transaction papers).................... Permanently
Construction documents.. Permanently
Contracts and leases (expired) ....7 years
Contracts and leases still in effect..Expiration +7 years
Corporate records and minutes .... Permanently
Correspondence (legal and important matters only) .... Permanently
Correspondence general ....3 years
Credit Applications (Consumer) ....25 Months (after notification)
Credit Applications (Business) .... 1 year (after notification)
Deeds, mortgages, and bills of sale .... Permanently
Depreciation schedules .... Permanently
Duplicate deposit slips...1 year
Electronic fund transfer documents ....7 years
Employee personnel records (after termination)...7 years
Employment applications ....3 years
Expense analyses and Expense distribution schedules ....7 years
Expired contracts and notes receivable ....7 years
Expired purchase contracts ....7 years
Federal, state and local tax returns .... Permanently
Financial statements (end-of-year trial balances) .... Permanently
Fixed asset records and appraisals .... Permanently
Forms W-4 ....7 years
Garnishments ....3 years
General Ledgers (end-of-year trial balances) .... Permanently
I-9s (after termination)..1 year
Insurance records, current accident reports, claims, policies, etc................. Permanently
Interim and year-end financial statements and trial balances....................... Permanently
Inventories of products, materials, and supplies ....7 years
Invoices ....7 years

Journals .... Permanently
Licenses.. Permanently
Loan documents, notes.. Permanently
Minute books of directors and stockholders, including bylaws and charter... Permanently
Monthly trial balances .... Permanently
Notes receivable ledgers and schedules ....7 years
OSHA logs..5 years
Paid bills and vouchers ....7 years
Payroll journals ....7 years
Payroll records and summaries ....7 years
Payroll reports (federal & state) ....7 years
Perpetual inventory records ....7 years
Petty cash vouchers ....7 years
Physical inventory records ....7 years
Physical inventory tags ....7 years
Plant cost ledgers .... Permanently
Polygraph test results and reasons for test ....3 years
Property appraisals by outside appraisers .... Permanently
Property records including costs, depreciation schedules, blueprints, plans .. Permanently
Property titles and mortgages .... Permanently
Purchase journals ....7 years
Purchase orders ....7 years
Receiving sheets..1 year
Requisitions ....7 years
Sales journals ....7 years
Sales records ....7 years
Savings bond registration records of employees ....7 years
Scrap and salvage records (inventories, sales, etc)..7 years
Shipping tickets ....3 years
Stock and bond certificate (cancelled) .... 1 yr
Stockroom withdrawal forms ....7 years
Subsidiary ledgers ....7 years
Tax returns and worksheets, revenue agents' reports and other documents... Permanently
Time books/cards ....7 years
Trade mark registrations .... Permanently
Uncollectible accounts and write offs ....7 years
Voucher for payments to vendors, employees, etc.
(includes all allowances and reimbursement of employees, officers) ....7 years
Voucher register and schedules ....7 years
W-4 forms..4 years
Workman's comp documents ....11 years

Document ID **FA1050**	Title **ANNUAL STOCKHOLDERS' MEETINGS**	Print Date **mm/dd/yyyy**
Revision **0.0**	Prepared By **Preparer's Name / Title**	Date Prepared **mm/dd/yyyy**
Effective Date **mm/dd/yyyy**	Reviewed By **Reviewer's Name / Title**	Date Reviewed **mm/dd/yyyy**
	Approved By **Final Approver's Name / Title**	Date Approved **mm/dd/yyyy**

Policy: The Company shall notify stockholders of annual meetings and record and distribute minutes of the meetings.

Purpose: To keep stockholders informed of business operations, include them in votes on important company actions, and comply with regulatory requirements for "C corporation" shareholder meetings.

Scope: This procedure applies to Top Management and those responsible for planning and executing annual stockholders' meetings.

Responsibilities: The CFO (Chief Financial Officer) is responsible for overseeing that regular shareholder meetings are conducted according the articles of incorporation.

Definitions: Stockholder (or shareholder) – One who owns shares of stock in a corporation (also called stockholder). Ownership includes the right to declared dividends and to vote on certain company matters, including electing the Board of Directors.

Resolution – An official document representing an action or intent of action on the part of the Board of Directors of a corporation.

Articles of Incorporation – A document (also called a charter) filed with a U.S. state by a corporation's founders, describing the purpose, place of business, and other details of a corporation.

C corporation –   A business taxed as a separate entity: a business taxed under Subchapter C of the Internal Revenue Code and legally distinct from its owners.

Bylaws – The rules that govern the internal affairs or actions of a corporation. Bylaws generally include procedures for holding meetings and electing the board of directors and officers. The bylaws also set out the duties and powers of a corporation's officers.

Quorum – The minimum number of people who must be present at a stockholders' meeting, physically or by proxy, in order for a decision made at such a meeting to be binding. The quorum requirements should be stated in the Company's bylaws.

Procedure:

1.0 STRUCTURE OF CORPORATE AUTHORITY

1.1   The stockholders are the collective owners of the Company and they are responsible for the following:

- Electing directors to the Company's board;

- Approving or rejecting major corporate actions (e.g., stock offerings, mergers);

- Amending the corporation's articles; and

- Inspecting the corporate books and records.

1.2   Stockholders elect the Board of Directors to represent them as the Company's governing body, which directs the company through resolutions. The Board's responsibilities include:

- Setting financial and operating policies of the Company;

- Appointing and overseeing Company officers (e.g., President);

- Proper management of the Company; and

- Create and serve on committees (e.g., strategy committee, audit committee).

1.3   Company officers are appointed and empowered by the Board of Directors. Officers can act individually to enter into corporate transactions, subject to the authorization levels given to them by the Board and Board oversight. If an officer exceeds his or her level of authority in a Company transaction, the officer may be held personally responsible for any obligations incurred as a result. Officers' responsibilities include:

- Supervising/directing the day-to-day operations of the Company; and

- Entering into contractual transactions and financial obligations on the Company's behalf.

2.0 STOCKHOLDERS' MEETING NOTIFICATION

2.1   The Company's Articles of Incorporation indicate where and when regular shareholder meetings are to be conducted. Regulations often require that stockholders' meeting be held at least annually and at the same time of year (e.g., the first week of February). Special meetings of stockholders may be called, subject to notification requirements in the Company articles or bylaws.

2.2   The CFO shall establish a record date of ownership for shareholders entitled to vote at the meeting, prior to sending shareholder notices.

2.3   Forty days prior to the meeting, the CFO shall send a notice to each shareholder (see FA1050-1 NOTICE OF SHAREHOLDERS' MEETING) by mail (or by e-mail to shareholders who have granted permission). The notice should include the following:

- A Notice of Internet Availability of Proxy Materials that includes the full website URL where proxy information will be posted;

- The date, time, and place of the meeting;

- A method for ordering proxy materials by mail;

- Financial statements, as required;

- A meeting agenda (a typical agenda includes election of Directors, ratification of Board of Directors' actions of the previous year, amending articles of incorporation, and approving major actions);

- An e-mail correspondence permission form (for those receiving notices by mail); and

- Individual shareholder voting entitlements (see section 2.2, above).

2.4   In order to properly conduct business, a minimum number of shares owned by shareholders must be present at the meeting or represented by proxy (see FA1050-2 AUTHORIZATION OF PROXY TO VOTE SHARES) to form a *quorum*, as prescribed in the Articles of Incorporation. Prior to beginning any meeting, the appointed secretary should determine that a proper quorum exists and inform the chairperson.

2.5   Actions by shareholders can only be taken in unison or by quorum, depending on the Company's bylaws.

3.0   CONDUCTING STOCKHOLDERS' MEETINGS

3.1   Company bylaws shall state who serves as meeting chairperson and secretary.

3.2   The secretary shall be responsible for recording the minutes of the meeting on the FA1050-3 MINUTES OF SHAREHOLDERS' MEETING. Minutes shall include, at a minimum:

- Who presided and acted as secretary;

- Shareholders attending and the number of shares represented in person or by proxy; and

- A summary of actions, in sufficient detail to avoid subsequent disputes over meeting activities and results.

3.3   The first meeting agenda item shall be to read and approve the minutes of the previous meeting (or move to dispense with reading the minutes and to approve as is).

3.4   The meeting shall be conducted through formal proceedings according to parliamentary procedures (e.g., *Robert's Rules of Order*). Items of action shall be properly introduced by a motion and seconded. The item may then be voted upon by either written ballot or by polling the group (e.g., raising of hands), as long as a clear majority of voting shares is demonstrable to the group as either *in favor of* or *opposed to* the item.

3.5   Other items of business listed on the agenda and any other business that comes before the meeting shall be discussed and acted upon.

3.6   The meeting shall conclude with a motion to adjourn that is seconded and carried.

3.7   The meeting minutes shall be maintained in accordance with FA1040 – RECORD CONTROL.

4.0   STOCKHOLDERS' MEETING REVIEW

Within one month after the shareholder meeting, the CFO shall preside over a review meeting to verify the following:

- Meeting notices were sent as scheduled;

- Required information was available to shareholders as scheduled;

- Meeting arrangements were adequate and aided in smooth execution of the meeting;

- Meeting minutes are properly kept and recorded; and

- Compliance with all regulations.

5.0   STOCKHOLDERS' MEETING IMPROVEMENTS

5.1   The CFO shall, as a result of the review (preceding section) or other lessons learned concerning the regular stockholder meetings, recommend improvements to the stockholder meeting procedures, processes, and forms to the Board of Directors.

5.2   The Board shall review the CFO's recommendations and, upon approving them, shall forward them to stockholders of record, asking them to vote on the recommendations in a timely manner.

Effectiveness Criteria:

- Regular shareholder meetings
- Organized meetings that effectively execute shareholder corporate governance
- Notices are sent and information available to shareholders in a timely manner
- Compliance with relevant statutes/regulations

Forms/Records:

- FA1050-1 NOTICE OF SHAREHOLDERS' MEETING
- FA1050-2 AUTHORIZATION OF PROXY TO VOTE SHARES
- FA1050-3 MINUTES OF SHAREHOLDERS' MEETING

References:

A. Finance Policy Manual

- Section 5.1.6 – Annual Stockholders' Meetings

B. Finance Procedures

- FA1040 RECORD CONTROL

C. Robert's Rules of Order (10th edition, revised), Perseus Books Group, 2000. See the Robert's Rules web site, http://www.robertsrules.com/default.html, for more information or to purchase a copy.

Additional Resources:

A. "How to Understand the SEC Compliance Laws for Shareholder Meetings," available at http://www.ehow.com/how_2039474_sec-compliance-shareholder.html.

B. "SEC Division of Corporation Finance Staff Legal Bulletin No. 14 on Shareholder Proposals," available at http://www.sec.gov/pdf/cfslb14.pdf.

Revision History:

Revision	Date	Description of Changes	Requested By
0.0	mm/dd/yyyy	Initial Release	

FA1050-1 NOTICE OF SHAREHOLDERS' MEETING

(COMPANY LETTERHEAD)

NOTICE OF ANNUAL MEETING OF SHAREHOLDERS
TO BE HELD ON _____

Notice is hereby given that the Annual Meeting of Shareholders of Sample Company,
a _____Corporation (the "Company"), will be held in the Company's offices
at _____, _____ __.m., for the purpose of considering and voting on the following matters:

1.   The election of directors for the year beginning _____ and ending _____.

2.   Transacting such other business as may properly come before the meeting or any adjournment
     thereof.

Only those common Shareholders and holders of the Company's Series "A" Convertible Preferred Stock
("Preferred Stock") of record at the close of business on _____(date), shall be entitled to notice of and to
vote in person or by proxy on all matters to be voted upon at the Annual Meeting or any adjournment
thereof.

The Board of Directors of
Sample Company

_____
Secretary

Dated:_____

[This page intentionally left blank]

FA1050-2 AUTHORIZATION OF PROXY TO VOTE SHARES

AUTHORIZATION (PROXY) TO VOTE SHARES

This Proxy is solicited on behalf of management

The undersigned, the owner of _____shares of stock in Sample Company, hereby appoints _____ as Proxy, with the power to appoint a substitute, and hereby authorizes said Proxy to represent and vote these shares for the election of directors and on any other matter as may properly come before the meeting at the Annual Meeting of Shareholders to be held on _____ (date) or any adjournment thereof.

When shares are held by joint tenants, both should sign. When signing as an attorney, executor, administrator, trustee, or guardian, please give full title as such. If a corporation, please sign in the full corporate name, by president or other authorized officer. If a partnership, please sign in the partnership's name by authorized person.

Please Print Name(s):_____

Signature:_____

Signature if held jointly:_____

Dated:_____

Please complete, sign, date, and return this proxy promptly using the
enclosed envelope.

[This page intentionally left blank]

FA1050-3 MINUTES OF SHAREHOLDERS' MEETING

> SAMPLE COMPANY
> MINUTES OF ANNUAL MEETING OF SHAREHOLDERS
> HELD ON _____

The annual meeting of Shareholders of Sample Company, was held in the corporate offices at _____ at _____ o'clock.

The meeting was called to order by _____, President, who chaired the meeting;
_____, Secretary, kept the record of the meeting.

A motion was duly made, seconded and carried to appoint _____ as the Inspector of Elections and certify the results of the meeting and voting.

The Secretary reported that the following Shareholders were present in person:

Shareholder   Number of Voting Shares

and that the following Shareholders were represented by proxy:

Shareholder   Names of Proxies   Number of Voting Shares

Total Number of shares represented:_____

Total Number of shares authorized to vote:_____

The Chairman then announced that there were present in person and represented by proxy the number of shares necessary to constitute a quorum. The proxies were then ordered to be filed with the Secretary of the meeting.

A motion was duly made, seconded and carried to dispense with the reading of the minutes of the last meeting and to be approved as is.

The Chairman then had the Secretary present on a table the stock ledger and transfer books for the corporation, the minutes of the Board of Directors since the last annual meeting and the current annual report which had been mailed to every Shareholder of record. The Chairman then declared the documents to be open for inspection by any Shareholder.

Upon a motion duly made and seconded, it was unanimously Resolved, that all purchases, contracts, contributions, compensations, acts, decisions, proceedings, elections, and appointments by the Board of Directors since the last Annual Meeting of Shareholders held on _____ and all matters referred to in the Annual Report to Shareholders for the fiscal year ended _____, are hereby approved and ratified.

The Chairman stated that the next business to come before the meeting was the election of the Board of Directors to serve for the ensuing year. The following individuals were nominated and seconded as candidates to be directors:

   1.
   2.
   3.

There were no other nominations. Upon motion duly made, seconded and unanimously carried, the nominations were closed.

The ballots of the Shareholders were presented and tallied by the Inspector of Elections. The Inspector of Elections reported that each of the three candidates had received the necessary majority of votes.

The Chairman thereupon declared that the above named persons were duly elected directors of the Corporation to hold office for the ensuing year.

The next item of business to come before the meeting was to vote on an amendment to the Articles of Incorporation to change the name of the Company from _____ to _____. The Chairman declared that an amendment to the articles would require the consent of not less than two thirds of the stock.

A motion was duly made and seconded to Amend the Articles of Incorporation to change the name and title of the Company from _____ to _____ and that the officers of the Company be empowered and directed to file in the office of the Secretary of State the requisite certificate setting forth the change of name.

The ballots of the Shareholders were presented and tallied by the Inspector of Elections which showed:

Votes in Favor of the motion representing _____ shares of stock.

Votes Opposed to the motion representing _____ shares of stock.

Not voting on the motion representing _____ shares of stock.

The Inspector of Elections reported that votes in favor of the resolution constitute more than two thirds of the outstanding shares of stock of the Company.

The Chairman declared that the motion has passed and that the Amendment has been adopted by the shareholders.

There being no further business, upon motion duly made, seconded, and carried, the meeting was adjourned.

_____
Secretary

[This page intentionally left blank]

Document ID **FA1060**	Title **BOARD OF DIRECTORS' MEETINGS**	Print Date **mm/dd/yyyy**
Revision **0.0**	Prepared By **Preparer's Name / Title**	Date Prepared **mm/dd/yyyy**
Effective Date **mm/dd/yyyy**	Reviewed By **Reviewer's Name / Title**	Date Reviewed **mm/dd/yyyy**
	Approved By **Final Approver's Name / Title**	Date Approved **mm/dd/yyyy**

Policy: The Company shall hold regular Board of Director meetings to conduct oversight and management of the Company.

Purpose: To plan, execute, and record Board of Directors meetings.

Scope: This procedure applies to Top Management and the Board of Directors.

Responsibilities: Top Management is responsible for overseeing the Board of Directors Meeting process.

The Board of Directors[1] is responsible for attending Board meetings and making decisions regarding the Company's operations, as required; also referred to in this document as "the Board."

Definitions: Board of Directors – Individuals elected by a corporation's shareholders to oversee the management of the corporation.

Consent Agenda – A practice by which the mundane and non-controversial board action items are organized in a group and passed with one motion.

Procedure:

1.0 PREPARING FOR THE BOARD OF DIRECTORS' MEETING

1.1 Board of Directors' meetings will be scheduled and held in accordance with the Company's bylaws; the Board should meet at least once a year.

1.2 Directors shall receive notice at least ten days prior to Board meetings. Such notice shall include: the date, time, and place of the meeting; meeting agenda; and in the case of a special (i.e., unscheduled) meeting, who is calling the meeting and why.

1.3 The notice should include specific items of business to be discussed and/or resolved at the meeting. At the very first meeting after incorporation, the directors should pass resolutions concerning the following:

- Bylaws for the company;
- Address of the company's principal offices;

---

[1] Private, small to midsize businesses (SMB) sometimes have an informal Advisory Board in place of a Board of Directors; an Advisory Board typically is not given decision making authority. An Advisory Board may consist of legal counsel, a CPA, trusted business associates, and others.

- Designation of the company's official corporate seal;

- Election of Officers;

- Banking arrangements and authorization levels for officers to conduct banking business (e.g., checks, drafts, transfers);

- Form and issuance authorization for stock certificates, where applicable;

- Authorization levels for officers to conduct business transactions and enter into contracts, leases, agreements, etc., on behalf of the Company and/or incur indebtedness to the company; and

- Indemnification for directors and officers.

1.4   Any changes to Section 1.3 above will require the directors to pass new resolutions as needed.

1.5   In order to properly conduct business, a minimum number of directors must be present at the meeting to form a quorum as prescribed per the bylaws.

2.0   BOARD OF DIRECTORS' MEETING PROCEDURE

2.1   The Chairman of the Board will preside over the meeting and the secretary will be responsible for recording the minutes of the meeting; see FA1060-1 MINUTES OF BOARD OF DIRECTORS' MEETING (EXAMPLE) for guidance. At a minimum, the minutes should include:

- Who presided over the meeting;

- Which Directors attended; and

- A summary of resolutions passed at the meeting in sufficient detail to clearly describe what was discussed and agreed upon.

2.2   In addition, the directors may need to address and pass resolutions on an ongoing basis, including, but not necessarily limited to:

- Calling the annual shareholders' meeting (see FA1050 ANNUAL STOCKHOLDERS' MEETINGS) and setting the record date;

- Adopting amendments to the articles of incorporation;

- Approving the annual budget and debt;

- Declaring dividends;

- Changing officers salaries and/or bonus arrangements;

- Adopting employee benefit plan;

- Approving loans to officers; and

- Appointing members to fill any Board vacancy created between annual shareholder meetings.

2.3   The meeting shall be conducted according to parliamentary procedure (see Additional Reference "B"), under which an item of action should be properly introduced by motion and the motion seconded.

2.4   The chair shall use a *consent agenda* to pass non-controversial items.

2.5   At the conclusion of discussions regarding an item, a motion for a resolution should be properly made and shall then be voted upon by polling the group for all those in favor of the resolution, those opposed, and those abstaining.

2.6   When practical, directors with a personal or financial interest in an item to be voted upon by the directors should abstain from voting. Further, the director shall disclose to the other members of the board all material information concerning their interest(s) prior to any voting on the matter.

2.7   The first meeting agenda item shall be to read and approve the minutes of the previous meeting or to make a motion to dispense with reading the minutes and to approve as is. Other items of business listed on the agenda and any other business that comes before the meeting shall be discussed and acted upon. At the conclusion of the meeting, a motion should be made and carried to adjourn the meeting.

2.8   The meeting shall include forming and scheduling key committees such as Audit Committee, Finance Committee, Executive Compensation Committee, Nominating Committee, and Governance Committee.

2.9   The meeting minutes shall be maintained in accordance with FA1040 RECORD CONTROL.

3.0   BOARD OF DIRECTORS' MEETING PROCESS REVIEW

Within one month of the Board of Directors' Meeting, the CFO shall preside over a review meeting to verify that:

- Meeting notices were sent as scheduled;
- Meeting arrangements were adequate and aided in smooth execution of the meeting;
- Meeting minutes are properly kept and recorded; and
- The meeting and all related actions/decisions comply with Company bylaws.

4.0   BOARD OF DIRECTORS' MEETING PROCESS IMPROVEMENTS

The CFO shall, as a result of the review (section 3.0) and/or other lessons learned concerning Board of Directors' Meetings, make improvements to the associated shareholder meeting procedures, processes, and forms.

Effectiveness Criteria:

- Board of Directors' Meeting held according to bylaws and schedule

- Productive Board of Directors' meetings (achieved desired business results)

Forms/Records:

- FA1060-1 MINUTES OF BOARD OF DIRECTORS MEETING (EXAMPLE)

References:

A. CFO Manual

- Section 5.1.7 Board of Directors' Meetings

B. Finance procedures

- FA1040 RECORD CONTROL

- FA1050 ANNUAL STOCKHOLDERS' MEETINGS

Additional Resources:

A. Free Complete Toolkit for Boards (including sample agendas and minutes) available on-line at http://www.managementhelp.org/boards/index.htm.

B. Robert's Rules of Order (10th edition, revised), Perseus Books Group, 2000. (ISBN-10 #0-7382-0307-6 / ISBN-13 #978-0-3068-20205.) See the Robert's Rules web site, http://www.robertsrules.com, for more information or to purchase a copy.

C. Koontz, Harold, Board of Directors and Effective Management (The), Krieger Publishing, 1981.

Revision History:

Revision	Date	Description of Changes	Requested By
0.0	mm/dd/yyyy	Initial Release	

FA1060-1 MINUTES OF BOARD OF DIRECTORS MEETING (EXAMPLE)

SAMPLE COMPANY

MINUTES OF THE BOARD OF DIRECTORS
HELD ON _____

A meeting of the Board of Directors of Sample Company, a _____, Corporation, was held on _____, at _____m., in the Company's offices pursuant to prior notice of the meeting.

Members of the Board of Directors present and in attendance at the meeting were:

Being all the directors of the Corporation. Also in attendance by invitation were _____ and corporate counsel, _____.

_____, President of the Corporation, acted as Chairman of the meeting, and _____, Secretary of the Corporation, acted as Secretary of the meeting. The Chairman announced that a quorum of the directors was present, and that the meeting, having been duly convened, was ready to proceed with its business.

Upon motion duly made, seconded, and unanimously approved, a reading of the minutes of the last meeting of the Board of Directors was waived.

The Chairman then stated that _____ had tendered his written resignation last month as a director of the Corporation in order to devote more time and efforts to the pursuit of his own business interests. Upon motion duly made and seconded, the following resolution was unanimously adopted.

Resolved, that _____ resignation from the Board of Directors of the Company is hereby accepted.

The next item of business involved the election of _____ to the Board of Directors. Her resume was read into the record, to wit:

Following a discussion, and upon motion duly made and seconded, the following resolution was unanimously adopted.

Resolved, that _____ be hereby elected as a Director of the Company and to serve as a member of its Board of Directors until the next annual meeting of the shareholders or until her successor is duly elected and qualified to serve.

The next item of business was the scheduling of the annual shareholders meeting. Following a discussion, and upon motion duly made and seconded, the following resolution was unanimously adopted.

Resolved, that the annual meeting of shareholders of the corporation shall be held on the day of _____, at _____ o'clock. The meeting will be held in the Company's offices. The purposes of the meeting shall be:

1. To elect a new board of directors.
2. To transact any other business that may properly be brought before the meeting or any adjournment thereof.

And that the close of business on _____ is hereby fixed as the time and date for determining the identity of shareholders who shall be entitled to notice of and to the right to vote at the meeting or any adjournment thereof.

The next item of business, the Board was advised that the Company's lease of its present facilities will expire in eight months. Messrs. _____ and _____ noted that the Company may be in a favorable position to negotiate a three year lease with the possibility of being able to obtain an adjoining 5,000 square feet of space for future expansion. Following a discussion, and upon motion duly made and seconded, the following resolution was unanimously adopted.

Resolved, that the Company's officers, _____ and _____, are hereby authorized to commence negotiations with respect to a new lease to the Company's present facilities with the possibility of obtaining an additional 5,000 square feet adjoining the Company's facilities. They are further authorized to evaluate other facilities suitable for the Company's operations and to report to the Board of Directors at the next meeting as to such negotiations and evaluations.

There being no further business to come before the meeting, upon motion duly made, seconded and carried, the meeting was adjourned.

Respectfully submitted,

_____ (Secretary)   Date _____

Finance Policies and Procedures

Section 410

Raising Capital

Section 410
Raising Capital

Document ID **RC1000**	Title **BUSINESS PLAN**	Print Date **mm/dd/yyyy**
Revision **0.0**	Prepared By **Preparer's Name / Title**	Date Prepared **mm/dd/yyyy**
Effective Date **mm/dd/yyyy**	Reviewed By **Reviewer's Name / Title**	Date Reviewed **mm/dd/yyyy**
	Approved By **Final Approver's Name / Title**	Date Approved **mm/dd/yyyy**

Policy: The Company shall develop a Business Plan to guide operations and accomplish defined objectives. Top Management shall review the Company's Business Plan (and update, if necessary) on an annual basis.

Purpose: To direct and manage the Company's growth; to define and prioritize short- and long-range business activities; to develop strategies and objectives that provide foundational guidance to business operations.

Scope: This procedure applies to the Company's Top Management, the Strategy Team, and the Board of Directors.

Responsibilities: Top Management (the CEO and CFO, at a minimum) is responsible for overseeing development and implementation of the RC1000-1 BUSINESS PLAN.

The Strategy Team is responsible for developing the RC1000-1 BUSINESS PLAN.

The Board of Directors[1] is responsible for reviewing and approving the RC1000-1 BUSINESS PLAN.

Definitions: Pro Forma Financial Statements – Statements that have the format of financial statements (balance sheet, income statement, statement of cash flows), but give projections or forecasts instead of actual end of period figures. (See FS1030 FINANCIAL FORECASTING.)

Procedure:

1.0   BUSINESS PLAN – BACKGROUND

1.1   It is important for all individuals involved with developing the Company's Business Plan – the Strategy Team – to remember that the Plan is intended to be a working, action-oriented management tool. A well-written Business Plan is acted on by employees who understand how their daily tasks and responsibilities relate to the overall Company strategy. The Plan should be developed to allow measurement of accomplishment of specific objectives within clearly defined, achievable time frames. The Plan should be a practical, flexible, and timely document for determining and communicating the Company's direction to all

---

[1] Smaller/private companies should have an Advisory Board (a group of trusted business advisors) to help with analysis and decision making. Also see procedure FA1050, "Board of Directors' Meetings."

employees. NOTE: Charts, graphs, photos, etc., should be used frequently in the Business Plan.

1.2   Top Management, under the direction of the Board of Directors, shall have primary responsibility for coordinating development and preparation of the Company's Business Plan.

1.3   Top Management shall form a Strategy Team (see Reference "C") for the purpose of developing a Business Plan, which should address the coming fiscal year and the following two to four years. The Strategy Team should include employees:

- Whose affiliations and interests differ to some degree (i.e., represent various key departments)

- Whose minds are open to change

- Who have a record of (reputation for) innovating

- Who are capable of collaborating

- With a passion for the Company's future

The Strategy Team should include:

> - A sponsor/champion
> - A Team Leader
> - A spokesperson
> - A facilitator and advisors
> - At least one non-stakeholder, to balance stakeholder interests/biases

The Strategy Team Leader should set up Team e-mail and voice mail groups to:

- Schedule meetings;

- Send updates and bulletins

- Encourage collaboration among Team members

1.4   The Strategy Team should base the Business Plan on the following information, at a minimum (see Reference "C"):

> - Stakeholder analysis
> - Vision and mission statement
> - Marketing research and analysis
> - Situational analysis
> - Company goals and objectives
> - Business strategy

The Business Plan itself should contain the following, at a minimum:

> - An Introduction and Summary
> - Company and Management Profiles
> - Products and Services
> - Markets and Marketing
> - Operations
> - Financial Plan and Forecasts
> - Exhibits

1.5   The Strategy Team shall convene annually to review the Company's performance in light of its goals, objectives, and strategies for the current year and update the Business Plan for the coming year. The annual review and update should begin no later than three months prior to the start of the coming fiscal year[2] and be completed prior to the first business day of the new fiscal year.

2.0   DEVELOPING THE BUSINESS PLAN

2.1   **Introduction and Summary**

The *Strategy Team Leader* shall ensure that this section of the Business Plan is developed and adequately serves its purpose. This section should contain, at a minimum:

- A table of contents;

- A "proprietary and confidential" clause; and

- An Executive Summary of the Business Plan.

The purpose of the Executive Summary is to introduce the business opportunity, key themes of the Plan, and subject areas in the body of the Plan. The Summary should be brief – no more than a page in length – and should answer key questions, such as:

> **Why was the Business Plan written?**
>
> **Why should someone invest in the Company?**
>
> **What ROI can the investor expect?**

While it appears *first* in every business plan, the Summary should be prepared *after* the rest of the Business Plan is completed.

---

[2] Strategy, in particular, should be examined and evaluated on an ongoing basis so the budgeting process for the coming year can occur in a timely manner.

2.2   Company and Management Profile

The *Strategy Team Leader* shall assign development of this section to one or more members of the Strategy Team. This section should include the Company mission statement and provide a history of the company's development, identifying its founders and major accomplishments, as well as any setbacks.

The questions this section *should* answer include:

> - What is special about <u>this</u> Management Team?
> - What are their qualifications? Their experience?
> - What are these people capable of? What can they do to make this opportunity work?

It should explain the current and anticipated personnel and management structure, and should include an organization chart with a description of key roles and responsibilities.

Biographies or resumes of key management personnel, consultants, or directors should be presented in brief in this section or in complete in the Exhibits section. Resumes should stress education, training, experiences, and accomplishments of each person in performing functions similar to that person's role in the Company.

Management compensation and ownership should be presented, including any present or anticipated incentive plans.

The Management section should also describe supporting professional services, including legal, accounting, public relations, advertising, banking, management consultants, and other service organizations selected by the Company.

2.3   Products and Services

The *Product and/or Service Manager* shall ensure development of this section of the Business Plan. This section ought to give the answer to such questions as:

> - What is special about your Company's product or service?
> - What is your unique selling proposition (USP)?
> - Why should the market buy <u>*your*</u> product rather than competitors'?

The Company's product and/or service lines are described in this section. The Company's basic and proprietary technology should be explained, with an emphasis on distinctive, *value-adding* features.

Key strengths *and weaknesses* of products/services – competitive advantages *and disadvantages* – should be presented *in detail*. Diagrams, sketches, or pictures should be included (here or in the "Exhibits" section), since illustrations generally improve understanding *and* heighten interest.

Any patent, trade secret, or other proprietary product or feature should be discussed, along with their extension into other potential markets. Regulatory approvals or requirements for specific products/services should also be addressed.

An analysis of the Company's *pricing strategies* should be presented and include comparisons of price differences with competing products based on manufacturing costs, proprietary features, newness, quality, warranty, or service.

A description of the Company's design and development plans for *improving existing* product lines/services or adding new ones should be provided.

The nature and extent of this work, including requirements for personnel, facilities, and equipment, should be fully discussed. Costs and time required to achieve a marketable product or service should be indicated. Timetables with specific development objectives should be determined and listed for each project.

NOTE: Assumptions factored into cost and time estimates, objectives, and timetables should be clearly stated and explained (e.g., "Assume 12 months to develop, based on our recent experience developing similar products").

Brochures, pictures, or sketches of products/services and prototypes should be included in the Exhibits section.

2.4   Markets and Marketing

The *Marketing* and *Sales Managers* shall oversee development of this section, which should answer questions like:

- How will the marketing, distribution, etc., channels you choose help your products – and your *message* – reach your target market?

- How are they better than possible alternatives?

This section should provide a description of the target market(s) for the products/services, marketing strategy, selling and distribution, competitive analysis, and sales forecast. The description of the target market(s) should include:

• The current size of the market	• Market potential
• Buying habits	• Market maturity and trends
• Customer profiles (i.e., who they are, where they're located)	• Seasonality
	• Market share

The Company's marketing strategy for reaching customers should include:

- Targeted market segments;

- Selling and distribution methods (e.g., direct sales, distributors, dealers), including a discussion of anticipated commissions, discount programs, or margins to be given;

- Planned advertising and promotions activities;

- Product or service "imaging" strategies (i.e., product/service features (e.g., quality, price, availability) that will be emphasized to generate sales); and

- Service, customer training, and warranty policies.

Competitors' methods and techniques should be compared and contrasted. The Company's *sales forecast* that forms the basis for the financial forecast should also be presented in this section.

NOTE: Assumptions factored into market size, market potential, the sales forecast, etc., should be clearly stated and explained (e.g., "Assuming market growth of 6% in the coming year based on U.S. Department of Commerce projections and our own trend analysis.").

2.5   **Operations**

The *Operations Manager* shall provide information needed for this section, as well as oversee its development. This section should answer a key question:

> *How does - or how can - the Company achieve a competitive operational advantage?*

This section should describe the Company's capabilities and strategies for *delivering* the forecasted quantities of the Company's products/services.

Service operations should describe the appropriateness of the geographic location, equipment requirements (leased or owned), and the productivity and skill levels of the workforce.

The discussion of production operations should provide the reader with the Company's methods and reasoning with regard to:

- Purchasing policies;

- "Make or buy" decisions (which parts or components will be purchased and which will be produced internally) and the extent of production, assembly and testing to be performed internally;

- Inventory and production control including methods, quality control, critical or sole-source parts;

- Present facilities and equipment with anticipated expansion requirements to satisfy sales projections (should include a discussion of new/used, lease/buy, etc.); and

- Labor force skills, training, and productivity.

A production plan, showing cost-volume information at various sales levels of operation with breakdowns of applicable material, labor, purchased components, and factory overhead, should be presented. Inventory requirements should also be provided for various sales levels or as required for seasonal fluctuations.

2.6   Financial Plan and Forecast

The Company's *CFO* shall supply the necessary information for – and oversee development of – this section of the Business Plan. This section should answer the following questions:

> - *How much capital* is needed?
> - For what *purpose*?
> - For *how long* is it needed? In other words, how long before the lender or investor will recoup their investment?
> - What are the projected earnings or ROI? What is the Company's growth potential?

The purpose of the Financial Plan is to describe the financial potential of the Company as well as capital requirements. The Financial Plan serves as an operating plan for financial management of the Company and incorporates strategies and projections developed elsewhere in the Business Plan.

The Financial Plan should include important conclusions drawn from financial forecasts (see FS1030 FINANCIAL FORECASTING), such as:

- Cash infusions required and whether they should be equity or debt;
- Profits as a percent of sales;
- Growth rates in revenues;
- Break-even level of sales;
- Debt repayment schedules;
- Projected return on investment; and
- Other significant criteria, such as financial ratios (see FS1020 FINANCIAL STATEMENT ANALYSIS).

> **NOTE!** You should *clearly state and explain all assumptions* factored into growth rates, profits, ROI, etc.

The Financial Plan should also cover sources of and potential uses for financing (see RC1030 BANK LOANS, RC1040 STOCK OFFERINGS, and RC1070 LETTERS OF CREDIT for additional information); the Company will use the Business Plan (and, hence, the Financial Plan) to raise capital. The Company needs to be able to answer three basic questions for potential lenders/investors:

2.7   **Exhibits**

The Strategy Team Leader shall ensure completeness of this section, which can contain any items for supporting statements in the Business Plan or provide greater clarification of items that would be too lengthy to include in the narrative sections of the Plan.

Exhibits may include:

• Marketing literature	• Management resumes
• Articles from trade journals	• Engineering studies
• Clinical test results	• Industry financial data, ratios

3.0   REVIEWING AND FINALIZING THE BUSINESS PLAN

3.1   The Strategy Team should review the Business Plan with key Department managers (Marketing, Sales, Production, Customer Service, etc.) at least once prior to submitting the Plan to the Board of Directors, to ensure that all important issues have been covered and to ensure understanding, agreement, and cooperation ("buy-in") of all Departments.

3.2   The Strategy Team should submit the Business Plan to the Board of Directors for consideration before conducting a formal meeting on the topic. The time and place for the formal Business Plan meeting should be agreed upon by all parties.

3.3   After meeting with the Board of Directors on the Business Plan, the Strategy Team may need to adjust/revise the Plan. The Team shall incorporate revisions into the Business Plan, and have Top Management and the Board of Directors review and approve the revised Plan.

3.4   Upon acceptance of the Business Plan, the Strategy Team shall ensure that the Business Plan is communicated appropriately throughout the Company prior to its implementation. See FS1000 FINANCIAL OBJECTIVES for more on this subject.

4.0   MONITORING THE BUSINESS PLAN

4.1   Top Management should continually monitor progress toward the objectives stated in the Business Plan, in accordance with FS1000 FINANCIAL OBJECTIVES, and periodically (quarterly, at a minimum) issue a progress report on the Business Plan to the Board of Directors.

4.2   Top Management should periodically (e.g., quarterly) review the Business Plan, comparing objectives with achievements to date, and determining if/where the Plan needs adjustment. The , and update the Plan as needed.

4.3   Top Management should review the Business Plan whenever significant changes to the Company or the business environment (e.g., natural catastrophe, sudden/ dramatic business downturn, new legislation/regulation) occur.

Effectiveness Criteria:

- Improved income, cash flow, cash position, etc.
- Business activities create new opportunities
- Positive ROI
- Improved ability to respond quickly and appropriately to business downturns

Forms:

- RC1000-1 BUSINESS PLAN

References:

A. Finance Policy Manual

- Section 5.2.1 – Business Plan

B. Finance procedures

- FS1000 FINANCIAL OBJECTIVES
- RC1030 BANK LOANS
- RC1040 STOCK OFFERINGS
- TM1080 ASSET ACQUISITION

C. Regulations/statutes

- None

D. Sales & Marketing Policies and Procedures, Bizmanualz, Inc. Part #ABR44. This product contains explanations and procedures for situational analysis and other topics of importance. See http://www.bizmanualz.com/sales-marketing-procedures-templates for more information.

Additional Resources:[3]

A. SBA Small Business Planner, U.S. Small Business Administration (SBA) – http://www.sba.gov/category/navigation-structure/starting-managing-business; also see section 500 of this product.

B. Business Planning and Financial Statements Template Gallery, Service Corps of Retired Executives (SCORE) – http://www.score.org/resources/business-planning-financial-statements-template-gallery.

C. Business Plans, Entrepreneur.com – http://www.entrepreneur.com/businessplan/index.html.

---

[3] Resources shown are for illustrative purposes only. Their inclusion does not constitute an endorsement of the product or seller, nor is the limited number intended to suggest that viable alternatives do not exist.

Revision History:

Revision	Date	Description of Changes	Requested By
0.0	mm/dd/yyyy	Initial Release	

RC1000-1 BUSINESS PLAN

I.   **Introduction and Summary**

_____

_____

_____

_____

_____

II.   **Company Profile and Management**

_____

_____

_____

_____

_____

_____

III. **Products / Services**

_____

_____

_____

_____

_____

_____

_____

IV. Markets and Marketing

_____

_____

_____

_____

_____

_____

_____

_____

_____

_____

V. Operations

_____

_____

_____

_____

_____

_____

_____

_____

_____

_____

_____

VI.   Financial Plan/Forecasts

_____

_____

_____

_____

_____

_____

_____

_____

_____

VII. Exhibits (attach supporting documentation)

_____

_____

_____

_____

_____

_____

_____

_____

_____

VIII. Approval

_____ Date _____
                        Company President/CEO

_____ Date _____
                        Chief Financial Officer

_____ Date _____
                    Board of Directors Representative

Document ID **RC1010**	Title **CAPITAL PLAN**	Print Date **mm/dd/yyyy**
Revision **0.0**	Prepared By **Preparer's Name / Title**	Date Prepared **mm/dd/yyyy**
Effective Date **mm/dd/yyyy**	Reviewed By **Reviewer's Name / Title**	Date Reviewed **mm/dd/yyyy**
	Approved By **Final Approver's Name / Title**	Date Approved **mm/dd/yyyy**

Policy: The company shall plan to ensure adequate capital at the best available cost to employ long term and medium term business plans and strategies.

Purpose: The Capital Plan should enable the Company to:

- Forecast capital needs and availability;

- Use the best alternatives, considering cost of capital and overall capital structure;

- Create, implement, and monitor results of the Capital Plan and continually improve the Plan.

Scope: This procedure applies to the Finance Department, Top Management, and the Board of Directors.

Responsibilities: The CFO (Chief Financial Officer) is responsible for annually creating a capital plan that aligns with overall business plans and strategies, and for reviewing the capital plan with Top Management and the Board of Directors.

Top Management and the Board of Directors are responsible for reviewing and approving the Capital Plan and any changes to the Plan.

Definitions: Capital – Financial resources available for a business to use; also the assets a business uses to generate income (i.e. cash, property/facilities, equipment).

Capital Asset – Asset that appears on a balance sheet (i.e. manufacturing equipment, inventory).

Leverage – Investing or using financial resources to produce income or positive cash flow. For example, a business borrows $50,000 to buy a piece of equipment (which it will pay back at $11,000 per year including interest over 5 years) that will produce goods it can sell for $20,000 per year for 10 years.

Capital Structure – The means by which a firm is financed. The makeup of the liabilities and stockholders' equity side of the balance sheet, especially the ratio of debt to equity and the mixture of short and long maturities.

Weighted Average Cost of Capital (WACC) – Overall return in

annual percentage that a corporation MUST earn on its existing assets and business operations in order to increase or maintain its current value. WACC is calculated by multiplying the cost of each capital component by its proportional weight and then summing:

$$WACC = \frac{E}{V} * Re + \frac{D}{V} * Rd * (1 - Tc)$$

Where:

Re = cost of equity
Rd = cost of debt
E = market value of the firm's equity
D = market value of the firm's debt
V = E + D
E/V = percentage of financing that is equity
D/V = percentage of financing that is debt
Tc = corporate tax rate

Debt/Equity Ratio – The ratio of long-term debt to shareholder equity that generally describes the company's ability to repay debt. A low debt/equity ratio may indicate that a company is not using debt effectively. A high debt/equity ration may indicate that the company may be over leveraged and have difficulty repaying debts if unanticipated events occur. (D/E = Total Debt/Total Owner& Shareholder Equity)

Earnings Before Interest, Taxes, Depreciation, and Amortization (EBITDA) –The raw operating cash flow of the organization before tax or debt effects.

Working Capital – The total amount of capital needed to operate the business. Typically calculated as Working Capital = (Accounts Receivable + Inventory) – Accounts Payable.

Return on Invested Capital (ROIC) – A ratio which defines how well the capital invested in the organization creates profit. ROIC = (Net Operating Profit -Taxes) / (Total Capital)

Procedure:

1.0   CAPITAL PLAN BACKGROUND

1.1   An important goal of any business is to increase its value for stakeholders, and particularly for the owners/shareholders. The business value stems from owned assets, but even more importantly from the business' ability to reliably generate income (revenue).

1.2   Businesses use capital (financial resources) as leverage to increase business value through increasing capital assets and revenues. The typical sources of capital for a business include:

- Selling shares or interests;
- Debt and credit; and

- Projected profits, retained earnings, and investments.

1.3   Top Management (with Board of Directors approval) should regularly produce business plans and strategies that describe short and long term plans for applying business resources, including financial resources, for improvement and growth. Typical plans that may require capital (financial resources) include:

- New facilities or existing facility renovation/expansion;

- New product research and development;

- Expansion into new markets;

- Acquisitions and mergers;

- Improving or replacing capital equipment or processes; and

- Annual capital budget for improving or replacing equipment, processes, facilities, and other capital assets.

1.4   Business plans and strategies should be reviewed from a financial perspective to assist Top Management and the Board of Directors in determining:

- Financial feasibility and risk;

- Impact on cash flows and working capital (negative or positive); and

- Affect on financial structure and financial statement analysis.

1.5   The CFO creates a capital plan that aligns with the business plan to ensure adequate financial resources are available, and to identify best sources of capital considering the cost of capital (and/or other relevant analysis) and ideal capital structure.

1.6   The completed capital plan should be reviewed by the Top Management and the Board of Directors, and then monitored with actions taken when the plan is not effectively providing financial resources at an efficient cost of capital.

2.0   PREPARING THE CAPITAL PLAN

2.1   The CFO shall create a five-year Capital Plan that identifies the following, at a minimum:

- Working Capital Requirements (overall operating aspects such as working capital, available cash reserves, and credit ratings see TM1000 WORKING CAPITAL.

  a. Working capital policy

  b. Cash and marketable securities management (see RC1050 DEBT & INVESTMENT)

  c. Inventory management (see TM1020 INVENTORY MANAGEMENT)

  d. Credit policy and receivables management

- Dividend Policy

- Financial Forecasts

a. Capital budget (actions that require significant capital)

b. Cash budget

c. Forecast (pro forma) financial statements

d. External financing requirements

e. Financial condition analysis (identifies the best approaches for using financial resources that minimizes the cost of capital and provides favorable financial structure in light of the current business situation, operating environment forecasts, etc.)

- Accounting and Control Plan (actions and milestones required to carry out the capital plan)

2.2   The CFO should review materials that provide information for a capital plan, such as the following:

- Business and/or Strategic Plans

- Strengths, weaknesses, opportunities, and threats (SWOT) analysis

- Market analysis

- Financial, sales, and operational forecasts

- Risk analysis

- Historical performance and financial statements

- Meeting minutes and other available materials concerning creation and review of strategies, plans, analysis, as well as other relevant topics.

2.3   The CFO shall list plans and activities from the short-term business/strategic plan that require capital planning in the short-term Capital Plan section of the RC1010-3 CAPITAL PLAN, and shall list all plans and activities from the long-term business (strategic) plan that require capital planning in the RC1010-3 CAPITAL PLAN.

2.4   The CFO shall conduct financial analysis on the items listed in the RC1010-2 CAPITAL PLAN WORKSHEET in order to determine changes required to the capital structure and complete the worksheet with the appropriate information:

- Enter the values from the last five years to form a baseline;

- Calculate the averages for the last five years along with the associated ratios; and

- Develop various projections based on assumptions for debt, equity, assets, cash, taxes, etc.

2.5   The CFO shall explore alternate capital scenarios using consistent and appropriate financial analysis methods and note such methods on RC1010-2 CAPITAL PLAN WORKSHEET. Analysis methods may include:

- Debt-to-Equity: Effectiveness of shareholders capital.

- Equity Growth: Represents the sustainable growth rate of the organization given the current capital structure. The organization must maintain Equity Growth > Revenue Growth or obtain outside funding at increasing risk.

- EBITDA: Operating cash flow of the organization.

- ROIC: Effectiveness of cash used in the organization.

- ROA: Effectiveness of the assets purchased.

- ROE: Effectiveness of the shareholders ownership.

- Revenue Growth: Effectiveness of the strategy.

- Profit Margin: Effectiveness of the business model.

- WACC: Effectiveness of financing activities.

2.6   The CFO shall use the RC1010-1 CAPITAL ANALYSIS to record and compare analysis results of various capital source scenarios using selected analysis methods (e.g., Debt/Equity and Cost of Capital). While two analysis methods can be used per form, additional forms can be used for employing all the desired alternative analysis methods (See Section 2.4 above.)

2.7   The CFO shall note all results, explanations, and interpretations of financial analysis on the RC1010-1 CAPITAL ANALYSIS, including reasons for selecting particular capital sources and methods. The CFO shall also include any effects or impact of the capital plan on working capital and investments in the notes sections of the RC1010-3 CAPITAL PLAN.

2.8   The CFO shall complete, as a result of analysis conducted in RC1010-1 CAPITAL ANALYSIS, the short-term and long-term sections in the RC1010-3 CAPITAL PLAN with the following information:

- The total amount of capital required to complete the plan or activity

- The number of years the total capital expenditure will occur

- The source of the capital

- Actions required to secure the capital (e.g., to sell stock, secure a loan or bond, liquidate investments)

- Additional notes or references

2.9   The goal of the financial analysis should be to select the most appropriate sources of capital in light of:

- The available capital to execute the desired business plan;

- The cost of capital;

- Strengthening and aligning with the overall financial picture of the company; and

- Feasibility in relation to cash flow and profit forecasts.

2.10   The CFO shall present the RC1010-3 CAPITAL PLAN to Top Management and the Board of Directors for review and approval. On approval of the Plan, the CFO shall oversee its implementation and execution.

3.0   MONITORING THE CAPITAL PLAN

3.1   The CFO shall regularly (e.g., monthly, quarterly) review the results of executing the RC1010-3 CAPITAL PLAN and verify that:

- Financial resources are available in a timely manner to execute the business plan;

- Key analysis goals are being met (i.e. cost of capital, debt/equity, shareholder value, payback period); and

- Overall capital structure and financial position of the Company remain healthy and are improving.

3.2   The CFO shall use the RC1010-3 CAPITAL PLAN to align related financial processes, such as:

- Debt and Investment;

- Working Capital;

- Bank Loans & Bonds;

- Stock Offerings; and

- Asset Acquisition.

See "References" at the end of this procedure.

3.3   The CFO shall note recommended/required corrective actions that will improve the results of the RC1010-3 CAPITAL PLAN and initiate corrective action, where required, in accordance with AC1060 CORRECTIVE ACTION.

4.0   IMPROVING THE CAPITAL PLAN

4.1   The CFO shall present recommendations for improving the Capital Plan, as well as required corrective actions (section 3.3) to Top Management and the Board of Directors.

4.2   Upon approval of changes to the Plan, the CFO shall make changes to the Plan, the process, procedures, and forms, as needed, and take action to implement the desired improvements.

Effectiveness Criteria:

- Financial resources are available to meet the capital needs of the business
- Plan results meet or exceed objectives (strategic, financial, etc.)
- The Capital Plan has a positive impact on the Company's financial health

Forms/Records:

- RC1010-1 CAPITAL ANALYSIS
- RC1010-2 CAPITAL PLAN WORKSHEET
- RC1010-3 CAPITAL PLAN
- RC1000-1 BUSINESS PLAN
- Strategic Plan (may be included in Business Plan)
- Review meeting minutes and reports

References:

A. Finance Policy Manual

- Section 5.2.2 Capital Plan

B. Finance procedures

- AC1060 CORRECTIVE ACTION
- FS1060 FINANCIAL STATEMENT REPORTING
- RC1050 DEBT AND INVESTMENT
- RC1030 BANK LOANS
- RC1040 STOCK OFFERINGS
- RC1060 ASSET ACQUISITION
- TM1000 WORKING CAPITAL

Additional Resources:

A. Siegel, Shim & Dauber, Corporate Controller's Handbook of Financial Management, 2nd Edition, Prentice Hall (1997).

Revision History:

Revision	Date	Description of Changes	Requested By
0.0	mm/dd/yyyy	Initial Release	

RC1010-1 CAPITAL ANALYSIS

Business Plan Item Name/Description _____

Analysis	Scenario 1	Scenario 2	Scenario 3
Capital Sources:			
Analysis Used:			
Results:			
Notes/Explanations: (Impact on cash flow, investments)			
Recommendations:			
Analysis Used:			
Results:			
Notes/Explanations: (Impact on cash flow, investments)			
Recommendations:			

Comments:

Completed by:_____   Date_____

[This page intentionally left blank]

RC1010-2 CAPITAL PLAN WORKSHEET

Five-Year Capital Plan

Metric	FS Data	2003	2004	2005	2006	2007	Average	2008	2009	2010	2011	2012
A. Debt-to-Equity												
	Debt (LT Liabilities)											
	Equity											
B. Equity Growth												
C. EBITDA												
	Net Profit											
	Interest Expense											
	Taxes paid											
	Depreciation											
	Amortization											
D. ROIC												
E. ROA												
F. ROE												
	Other Income											
	Cash & Investments											
	Assets											
G. Revenue Growth												
	Revenue											
H. Profit margin												
I. WACC												
Expectation%	Equity %											
Interest %	LT Debt %											
Interest %	CC % (current)											
	CC											
	Tax Rate %											

[This page intentionally left blank]

RC1010-3 CAPITAL PLAN

Business Activity	Total Capital Required	No. Years	Finance Source	Actions	Notes

Notes:

Completed by: _____   Date _____

Approval: _____   Date _____

[This page intentionally left blank]

Document ID RC1020	Title VALUATION	Print Date mm/dd/yyyy
Revision 0.0	Prepared By Preparer's Name / Title	Date Prepared mm/dd/yyyy
Effective Date mm/dd/yyyy	Reviewed By Reviewer's Name / Title	Date Reviewed mm/dd/yyyy
	Approved By Final Approver's Name / Title	Date Approved mm/dd/yyyy

Policy: The Company shall regularly conduct valuation assessments, and establish valuation targets.

Purpose: To regularly conduct business valuation assessments in order to:

- Monitor valuation and multipliers in relation to valuation and multiplier targets;

- Provide general and industry-specific economic information that affects the business;

- Provide information for business strategic planning; and

- Use worth in equity to raise capital.

Scope: This procedure applies to Top Management and the Finance Department.

Responsibilities: Top Management is responsible for setting valuation schedules, setting valuation targets, for reviewing valuation results in relation to targets, and for monitoring and adjusting business plans and strategies in order to reach valuation targets.

The Chief Financial Officer (CFO) is responsible for executing the valuation process, recording valuation plans, results, improvement plans, and for providing all needed information for the valuation process.

Definitions: Valuation – The process of assessing or estimating the value of a business. There are several valuation approaches, including income (based on expected future cash flow), market (based on value of similar businesses), and asset (based on the net equity of the value of the business assets). The most appropriate method depends on the context or reason for the valuation. Generally, the income method of valuation is most practical for solvent, ongoing businesses.

Multiplier – Generally, the profits/earnings ratio of a business that plays an important role in income method valuation.

Procedure:

1.0 VALUATION PLAN

1.1   Top Management shall create a plan for valuation that includes:

- A schedule for conducting valuations (e.g., every three (3) years);
- The most appropriate valuation method;
- Setting valuation targets; and
- Using valuation to improve the Company's value and performance.

1.2   Top Management shall also identify vital factors and critical points that affect the Company's valuation, which are frequently industry specific. Examples of key factors of valuation include:

- Cash flow;
- Size; and
- Risk.

1.3   The CFO shall assist in completing the valuation plan by:

- Selecting a valuation source (e.g., internal valuation, external appraiser, valuation software);
- Identifying and providing the financial information and other inputs required to conduct the valuation; and
- Collecting industry standards and benchmarks for valuation multipliers.

1.4   The reason for conducting a valuation shall be a major determining factor in selecting the valuation method. Reasons for valuations include:

- Obtaining financing and raising capital (including stock offerings);
- Buying, selling, or succession;
- Litigation; and
- Monitoring and improving the Company's performance.

1.5   Top Management and the CFO shall document the valuation plan in RC1020-1 – VALUATION PLAN and shall review the plan after each valuation process and make improvements as required.

2.0 VALUATION

2.1   Top Management shall set overarching valuation plans (such as frequency of valuation, method of valuation, and valuation targets) and complete Section I of the RC1020-1 VALUATION PLAN with the appropriate information.

2.2   The CFO shall complete the Section II of the RC1020-1 VALUATION PLAN, noting valuation source, valuation inputs, and anticipated valuation start and completion dates.

2.3   The CFO shall conduct the valuation according to the established schedule and methods (if done internally or using valuation software) or and assist in conducting of the valuation if using an external assessor.

2.4   The CFO shall summarize the valuation results in Section II of the RC1020-1 VALUATION PLAN

2.5   The CFO shall enter the appropriate valuation information in the RC1020-3 VALUATION HISTORY.

3.0   VALUATION REVIEW

3.1   The CFO, Top Management, and other affected Managers shall meet at the completion of the valuation process to review the valuation and document the review in Section III of the RC1020-1 VALUATION PLAN. Questions raised during the review should include:

- Does the valuation accurately reflect the business?

- Is the valuation method/technique appropriate for the type of business and the reason for conducting the valuation?

- Does the valuation multiplier seem appropriate?

- Is the schedule for conducting valuations appropriate?

- What light does the valuation shed on the current state of the business, business performance, economic and industry factors, and strengths, weaknesses, opportunities, and threats (SWOT)?

- How does current valuation compare to specified targets?

3.2   The CFO, Top Management, and other affected Managers shall meet at the completion of the valuation to review the RC1020-3 VALUATION HISTORY and determine the Company's success at meeting valuation targets.

3.3   The CFO shall regularly review the valuation plans, history, and results with the Board of Directors.

4.0   REACHING VALUATION TARGETS

4.1   The CFO shall, with input from Top Management and other affected Managers through the valuation review (see Section 3.1) and the valuation history (see Section 3.2), complete the RC1020-3 BUSINESS VALUATION IMPROVEMENT PLAN.

4.2   The RC1020-2 BUSINESS VALUATION IMPROVEMENT PLAN shall focus on meeting valuation targets and multiplier targets.

4.3   Top Management shall approve the RC1020-2 BUSINESS VALUATION IMPROVEMENT PLAN.

4.4   The Company shall implement the RC1020-2 BUSINESS VALUATION IMPROVEMENT PLAN, in order to make improvements necessary to meet valuation targets for the next scheduled valuation.

Effectiveness Criteria:

- Improving business value

- Improving business valuation multiplier

- Effective business plans and strategies using information gained through the valuation process.

- Inventory turns/days inventory

Forms/Records:

- RC1020-1 VALUATION PLAN

- RC1020-2 VALUATION IMPROVEMENT PLAN

- RC1020-3 VALUATION HISTORY

- Review Meeting Minutes

References:

A. Finance Policy Manual

- Section 5.2.3 – Valuation

B. Finance procedures

- FS1000 FINANCIAL OBJECTIVES

- RC1000 BUSINESS PLAN

Additional Resources:

A. S. Gabehart & R. Brinkley, <u>Business Valuation Book (The)</u>, American Management Association (AMACOM) press, 2002.

B. Lawrence W. Tuller, <u>Small Business Valuation Book (The)</u>, Adams Media, Second Edition, 1998.

Revision History:

Revision	Date	Description of Changes	Requested By
0.0	mm/dd/yyyy	Initial Release	

RC1020-1 VALUATION PLAN

I) Valuation Plan

Date _____   Completed By _____

Valuation Schedule

_____

_____

Valuation Reasons/Goals

_____

_____

Valuation Methods

_____

_____

Valuation Responsibilities

_____

_____

Valuation Vital Factors/Benchmarks

_____

_____

_____

Valuation Targets

_____

_____

_____

_____

II) Valuation Process & Results

Date _____   Completed By _____

Valuation Source (and reasons for selection)

_____

_____

_____

Valuation Begin & Complete Dates

_____

_____

_____

Valuation Required Input Information

_____

_____

_____

_____

Valuation Result Summary

_____

_____

_____

_____

_____

_____

III) Valuation Review

Valuation Accuracy Comments

_____

_____

_____

Valuation Multiplier Accuracy Comments

_____

_____

_____

Valuation Techniques Comments

_____

_____

_____

Valuation Schedule Comments

_____

_____

_____

Overall Valuation Effectiveness Comments

_____

_____

_____

_____

_____

[This page intentionally left blank]

RC1020-2 VALUATION IMPROVEMENT PLAN

Date _____   Completed By _____

Meeting Valuation Targets

_____

_____

_____

Meeting Multiplier Targets

_____

_____

_____

Valuation Strengths - Weaknesses- Opportunities - Threats

_____

_____

_____

Meeting Income and Asset Productivity Targets

_____

_____

_____

Other

_____

_____

_____

Approved By _____   Date _____

[This page intentionally left blank]

RC1020-3 VALUATION HISTORY

Valuation Method	Date	Target Valuation	Actual Valuation	Notes

Comments:

_____

_____

_____

[This page intentionally left blank]

Document ID **RC1030**	Title **BANK LOANS**	Print Date **mm/dd/yyyy**
Revision **0.0**	Prepared By **Preparer's Name / Title**	Date Prepared **mm/dd/yyyy**
Effective Date **mm/dd/yyyy**	Reviewed By **Reviewer's Name / Title**	Date Reviewed **mm/dd/yyyy**
	Approved By **Final Approver's Name / Title**	Date Approved **mm/dd/yyyy**

Policy: The Company shall develop a plan for financing its capital needs.

Purpose: To provide guidelines for determination of suitable lending requirements and format and preparation of loan proposals.

Scope: This procedure applies to bank loan applications but can be used for alternate forms of financing. Proposals can be used for loan applications for one or more banks or lending institutions.

Responsibilities: The Chief Financial Officer (CFO) is responsible for directing the Finance Department in developing borrowing and financial plans to meet the needs of the Company's operations.

The Board of Directors is responsible for authorizing the raising of capital through bank loans.

Definitions: Collateralization – Securing a debt in part or in full by a pledge of collateral (an asset pledged as security to ensure payment or performance of an obligation).

Covenant – Condition that a borrower must comply with according to the terms of the loan agreement; if the borrower does not act in accordance with a covenant, the loan can be considered in default, in which case the lender has the right to demand payment, usually in full.

Credit scoring – Measuring and evaluating creditworthiness of a loan applicant; profitability, solvency, management ability, liquidity, and other information may be factored into an applicant's credit score.

Securitization – Pooling of non-traded assets for the purpose of issuing standardized securities backed by those assets, which can then be traded like any other security; bundling and resale of debt instruments to investors, permitted only for parties licensed and regulated by the SEC; process of selling non-conventional loan packages to investors (public or private) who represent an interest in the cash flow generated by asset-backed loans.

Takedown – Transfer of money from a lender to a borrower under a loan agreement, loan commitment, or line of credit.

Procedure:

1.0   ASSESSING CAPITAL REQUIREMENTS

1.1   The Budget Committee shall develop borrowing and financial plans to meet the needs of the Company's operations (see RC1010 CAPITAL PLANNING). These plans shall take into account current and projected business conditions and cycles and may include the following criteria:

- Capital requirements to satisfy company growth in relation to risk;
- Ability of the Company to meet present obligations as well as assume new debt under worst-case conditions;
- Appropriateness of capital or debt structure;
- Level or type of debt that does not preclude future borrowing or funding capacity; and
- The cost of capital in relation to internal return on investment from use of funds obtained.

1.2   The CFO shall designate institutions to be contacted for borrowing purposes.

1.3   The CFO shall oversee preparation of the Company's loan application(s), which shall include all required supporting analyses and documentation.

2.0   PREPARING THE LOAN APPLICATION

2.1   The CFO should draft the loan proposal to include the following information, where applicable:

DATE	The proposal for each bank (lender) should show the date the proposal will be presented to the bank.
BORROWER	The specific legal name of the intended borrowing entity (e.g., parent Company, subsidiary, holding company) should be listed, to avoid confusion with other borrowers.
TYPE OF LOAN	The specific type of loan requested (e.g., equipment loan, line of credit) should be listed, to eliminate any guessing or assumptions by the loan officer.
AMOUNT	The amount of the loan requested should be determined and listed. It is very important to establish credibility with the loan officer and committees - asking for too much or too little money can convey uncertainty or doubt about the company's ability to implement successfully the plans for the loan proceeds. All numbers - actual and forecast - should be supported with appropriate documentation.
USE OF PROCEEDS	As above, the use of proceeds should be listed and well supported by documentation in the company's business plan and forecasts.
TERM	The desired term of the loan should be listed. If deemed possible, longer terms should be requested to avoid the process of having to renew the loan frequently.

CLOSING DATE	Set a closing date. For renewals, approximately 30 days after application; for new banks or loan applications, approximately 60 days after application. This communicates a bit of negotiating edge for the Company by conveying the message that the matter is to be resolved or the Company will use other banks willing to work within this schedule.
TAKEDOWN AT CLOSING	The amount of funds to drawn immediately at closing of the loan should be listed. As with the loan amount, this should reflect the business plan and convey that the Company understands its business and financial requirements.
COLLATERAL	Any assets to be used as collateral for the loan (e.g., equipment, inventory, accounts receivable) should be listed and should appropriately reflect the type of loan.
GUARANTEES	This should normally be completed with "none" - the Company should always propose loans based upon its creditworthiness. However, in certain situations, personal guarantees by the officers may be necessary.
COVENANTS	Lenders usually add covenants to maintain loan quality, ensure adequate cash flow, preserve equity In a borrower with a known weakness in its capital structure as a measure to improve this weakness, and have an updated picture of the borrower's financial performance and condition. Examples of covenants include maintaining hazard insurance, paying taxes, providing financial information periodically, and maintaining at least minimum financial ratios.
RATE	For negotiating purposes, rather than have the bank "suggest" the interest rate, it is better to state a reasonable but fair rate for the Company. The rate should reflect the type of loan, the prevailing rate for that loan type, and the level of risk Company officers feel the Company represents to the bank.
REPAYMENT SCHEDULE	A realistic repayment schedule should be determined, which should correspond to the Company's business plan (strategy) and its financial forecasts.
SOURCE OF FUNDS FOR REPAYMENT	The specific source of cash to be used for repayment should be identified.
ALTERNATE SOURCE OF FUNDS FOR REPAYMENT	To satisfy the bank's concerns that in the event the Company does not meet its financial projections, a contingency plan for meeting the repayment schedule should be listed. For example, liquidating assets or equity from a private placement could be used to repay the loan.

2.2 The CFO should gather information the bank will need to evaluate and process the loan application, using RC1030-1 LOAN APPLICATION CHECKLIST for guidance, then submit the application to the Company's Board of Directors (or Advisory Board) for review and approval.

2.3 The Board of Directors (or Advisory Board), once it has decided to approve the application, shall draw up a formal resolution authorizing the borrowing of funds.

3.0 APPLYING FOR THE LOAN

3.1 The CFO shall submit the complete loan application package to the approved lending institution(s).

3.2   On approving the loan application, the lending institution will generally issue a formal Loan Commitment, which may be a simple one-page form letter or could be a multiple-page loan acceptance form.

4.0   CLOSING THE LOAN

4.1   The CFO shall review the Loan Commitment, paying special attention to terms (interest rate, payback period, insurance requirements, etc.) set forth by the lender. The CFO should have qualified legal counsel review the Commitment, to ensure that it conforms to legal requirements and to ensure that the Company's best interests are protected.

4.2   The CFO should negotiate with the lender in order to gain terms more favorable to the Company. All terms and conditions are negotiable; particular examples include rate and repayment terms, collateralization, and securitization.[1] See Additional Reference "D."

4.3   Once the Company and lender agree to terms, they will schedule the loan closing. At the closing, the CFO, President, or other authorized representative of the Company[2] typically reviews and recaps the loan agreement with the lender's loan officer, after which both parties sign and date the agreement. Following that, the lending institution disburses funds to the Company.

5.0   LOAN SERVICING AND REPORTING

5.1   The CFO shall disburse loan proceeds within the Company in accordance with the Capital Plan (see RC1010 CAPITAL PLANNING).

5.2   The CFO shall periodically monitor capital project activity in accordance with the Capital Plan.

5.3   The CFO shall monitor items listed in the "Terms and Conditions" section of the loan agreement (e.g., financials, insurance, covenants, restrictions, other loan requirements) and submit periodic reports to the lender, in accordance with the terms of the loan agreement.

5.4   At the end of the loan (after the loan balance has been paid down to zero), the CFO shall obtain a lien release of the collateralized assets.

6.0   LOAN ANALYSIS

6.1   Each Project Lead should report periodically (e.g., weekly) on the progress of his/her capital project, in accordance with RC1010, "Capital Planning."

6.2   The CFO shall periodically (at least monthly) review utilization of loan funds for capital projects, comparing actual with budgeted amounts, verifying that deadlines are being met, and analyzing trends. Where trends appear to be out of line with estimates, the CFO may request corrective actions in accordance with AC1060, "Corrective Action."

---

[1] Lenders generally try to protect their interests by collateralizing/securing as many assets as possible.
[2] One who is authorized to legally bind the Company to agreements it makes.

6.3   At the end of the loan (after all funds have been repaid), the Budget Committee shall review the Company's performance on the loan and keep a record of the review for use in subsequent occasions where capital must be raised.

Effectiveness Criteria:

- Company receives most favorable terms when borrowing.

- Company is discharging obligations effectively and in a timely manner.

- Bank loans are helping to optimize the Company's capital structure.

Forms/Records:

- RC1030-1 LOAN APPLICATION CHECKLIST

- Loan application package

- Records of Budget Committee reviews

- Project progress reports

References:

A. Finance Policy Manual

- Section 5.2.4 – Bank Loans

B. Finance Procedures

- AC1060 CORRECTIVE ACTION

- RC1000 BUSINESS PLAN

- RC1010 CAPITAL PLANNING

- RC1040 STOCK OFFERINGS

- RC1070 LETTERS OF CREDIT

Additional Resources:

A. Finance Your Business, SBA Small Business Planner – http://www.sba.gov/category/navigation-structure/starting-managing-business/starting-business/prepare-your-business-f-0.

B. Explore Loans, Grants, & Funding, SBA Small Business Planner. http://www.sba.gov/category/navigation-structure/starting-managing-business/starting-business/loans-grants-funding.

Revision History:

Revision	Date	Description of Changes	Requested By
0.0	mm/dd/yyyy	Initial Release	

RC1030-1 LOAN APPLICATION CHECKLIST

☐	Personal Federal tax returns, including schedules, for past three (3) years.
☐	USA – IRS Form 4506, to authorize verification of your tax return.
☐	Personal state tax returns, including schedules, for past three (3) years.
☐	Federal business tax returns, including schedules, for past three (3) years, if available.
☐	State business tax returns, including schedules, for past three (3) years, if available.
☐	Business financial statements for last three years, if available.
☐	Personal financial statements (optional).
☐	Interim Financial Statement, to include balance sheet and income statement dated within forty-five (45) days of the application.
☐	Accounts receivable and accounts payable aging (same date as Interim Financial Statement.)
☐	Complete business plan, including three-to-five-year projections (pro forma statements), with assumptions stated.
☐	Articles of incorporation and other documentation of legal identity.
☐	Site description/location demographics, from commercial property manager or real estate agent.
☐	Copy of current lease, if applicable.
☐	Copy of proposed lease or letter from landlord outlining proposed terms, if applicable.
☐	Uniform Franchise Offering Circular (UFOC) and franchise agreement or letter of intent from franchiser.

[This page intentionally left blank]

Document ID	Title	Print Date
RC1040	**STOCK OFFERINGS**	**mm/dd/yyyy**
Revision	Prepared By	Date Prepared
0.0	**Preparer's Name / Title**	**mm/dd/yyyy**
Effective Date	Reviewed By	Date Reviewed
mm/dd/yyyy	**Reviewer's Name / Title**	**mm/dd/yyyy**
	Approved By	Date Approved
	Final Approver's Name / Title	**mm/dd/yyyy**

Policy: The Company shall plan and prepare stock offerings to ensure capital/finance goals are reached in a timely and efficient manner.

Purpose: To generate the desired funds through offering Company stock publicly; employing best practices in conducting stock offerings effectively and efficiently.

Scope: This procedure applies to the Top Management, Finance, and Accounting departments.

Responsibilities: Top Management is responsible for creating the stock offering plan, and overseeing/reviewing the stock offering process.

The CFO (Chief Financial Officer) is responsible for advising Top Management in the stock offering process, and for executing the stock offering process.

Department Managers shall assist in the stock offering process as necessary.

The Board of Directors approves all stock offerings.

Definitions: Due Diligence – Investigation into the company by the SEC Regulators and potential investors to ensure the representations made in the company's prospectus about its financial condition, operations, and other facets of the company are correct and verifiable.

Investment/Underwriting Bank – A bank selected by the company to advise and assist in executing an initial or secondary public offering.

Prospectus – A formal legal document providing details about a corporation; generally used during a stock offering.

SEC General Rules and Regulations of the Securities Act of 1933 (17 CFR 230, USA) – Securities law containing rules for public stock offerings.

United States Securities and Exchange Commission (SEC) – Government commission created by the Securities Exchange Act of 1934 to regulate securities markets and protect investors.

Procedure:

1.0   STOCK OFFERING PLAN

1.1   When the Company elects to sell shares of stock in the company to the public, The CFO, with Top Management's help, shall create a detailed plan (in the form of a checklist or action plan) for executing the stock offering. The Plan should address elements such as:

- Determining the number of shares to offer, types of shares to offer, the estimated price, and the amount of capital to raise;

- Review of Articles of Incorporation for limits or other criteria for selling shares, and the strategy for gaining approval of the Board of Directors;

- Approval of the Board of Directors;

- A schedule for executing the stock offering;

- Reviewing and updating the Business Plan to ensure it describes the planned use of capital;

- Criteria for selecting the Underwriting Bank;

- Creating SEC or other registration materials, and complying with all SEC Regulations and other legal requirements;

- Meeting rules and regulations in all states where the stock will be sold;

- Meeting due diligence requirements;

- Providing for legal review;

- Generating an initial and final prospectus;

- Marketing the shares;

- Setting final shares price;

- Printing and delivering shares; and

- Closing the offering process.

1.2   The CFO shall review the plan with Top Management and other involved Managers, to ensure that all aspects of the stock offering are addressed.

1.3   The CFO shall be responsible for overseeing the execution of the stock offering plan.

1.4   The CFO shall record actions, results, and notes from executing the stock offering process in the RC1040-1 STOCK OFFERING PLAN.

1.5   The CFO, Top Management, and other involved Managers shall meet to review the stock offering process after its completion to ensure all activities are closed and to document lessons learned and other useful information.

2.0   EXECUTING THE STOCK OFFERING

2.1   Top Management, the CFO, and other involved Department Managers shall meet to create the plan for executing the stock offering process.

2.2   The CFO shall be responsible for documenting the stock offering plan and schedule in Section I of the RC1040-1 STOCK OFFERING PLAN and note the responsible person, department, or entity for carrying out particular actions, as well as the date actions are completed.

2.3   The CFO, with input from Top Management and approval of the Board of Directors, complete Section II of RC1040-1 with the goals of the stock offering and note the actual results when the stock offering is complete.

2.4   Top Management, the CFO, and other involved managers and departments, shall note detailed plans and strategies for meeting and completing stock offering process activities in Sections III through XIV of RC1040-1.

2.5   The CFO and other managers with assigned responsibilities shall execute the stock offering process according to RC1040-1.

2.6   Top Management, the CFO, and other involved managers and departments, shall record notes, comments, and results (including delays, unforeseen problems, and other lessons learned) of executing stock offering process activities in Section XV of RC1040-1.

3.0   REVIEWING THE STOCK OFFERING PROCESS

3.1   At the completion of the stock offering process, the CFO, Top Management, and other involved Managers shall meet to review the stock offering process and the information recorded in RC1040-1.

3.2   At the review meeting, attendees will analyze, review, and discuss the key results of the stock offering process, answering such questions as:

- Were stock offering actions completed according to schedule?

- Was the desired amount of investment funds raised?

- Were there issues, problems, or delays in meeting regulatory or legal requirements/filings?

- Were there other issues or problems with executing the stock offering process that caused delays, rework, or other unexpected efforts?

- Did the Stock Offering Plan address all key elements of a stock offering?

- What improvements to the plan would improve the execution and results of future stock offerings?

3.3   The CFO shall complete a closing report, clearly documenting the results of the stock offering process review meeting, including all issues discovered and addressed, lessons learned, results, reasons for results, and other important items related to the stock offering just completed.

4.0   IMPROVING THE STOCK OFFERING PROCESS

4.1   The CFO shall, as a result of executing the stock offering plan, the process review meeting, and the closing report, make improvements to this procedure and to the RC1040-1 – STOCK OFFERING PLAN form, as needed.

Effectiveness Criteria:

- Meeting investment generation goals (the desired number of stock sold at the desired price).

- No delays, additional efforts required, etc., in the execution of RC1040-1 STOCK OFFERING PLAN; stock offering completed on schedule.

- No regulatory issues (e.g., delays, rework, refiling) in creating and filing required SEC and state required documents.

Forms/Records:

- RC1040-1 STOCK OFFERING PLAN

- Review Meeting Minutes

- Stock Offering Process Final Report

References:

A. Finance Policy Manual

   - Section 5.2.5 – Stock Offerings

B. Finance procedures

   - None

C. **SECURITIES & EXCHANGE ACT OF 1934** (USA). Provides for the regulation of securities exchanges and of over-the-counter markets operating in interstate and foreign commerce and through the mails, to prevent inequitable and unfair practices on such exchanges and markets, and for other purposes (short title – Securities & Exchange Act of 1934; SEC General Rules and Regulations, The Securities and Exchange Act of 1934 (12B CFR 240)

D. **SECURITIES ACT OF 1933** (USA). SEC General Rules and Regulations, 17 CFR 230.

E. **SARBANES-OXLEY ACT OF 2002** (USA). The purpose of the Act is to protect investors in public companies by improving the accuracy and reliability of corporate disclosures made pursuant to the securities laws and for other purposes.

Additional Resources:

A. General Rules and Regulations – Securities Act of 1933 (17 CFR 230; contains Regulation D) available on-line at http://www.sec.gov/divisions/corpfin/ecfrlinks.shtml

B. Securities Exchange Act of 1934 available at http://www.sec.gov/about/laws/sea34.pdf and at http://www.sec.gov/divisions/corpfin/34act/index1934.shtml

C. Q & A: Small Business and the SEC (A guide to help understand how to raise capital and comply with the federal securities laws). Available at http://www.sec.gov/info/smallbus/qasbsec.htm

D. SEC Form S-1 Registration Statement Under the Securities Act of 1933 available on-line in PDF format at http://www.sec.gov/about/forms/forms-1.pdf

E. Changeover to the SEC's New Smaller Reporting Company System by Small Business Issuers and Non-Accelerated Filer Companies, A Small Entity Compliance Guide. Available at www.sec.gov/info/smallbus/secg/smrepcosysguid.pdf

F. SEC Rule 504 of Regulation D – Exemption from the registration requirements of the federal securities laws for some companies when they offer and sell up to $1,000,000 of their securities in any 12-month period. See http://www.sec.gov/answers/rule504.htm.

G. SEC Rule 506 of Regulation D – "Safe harbor" for the private offering exemption of Section 4(2) of the Securities Act. Companies using the Rule 506 exemption can raise an unlimited amount of money. See http://www.sec.gov/answers/rule506.htm

H. Description of SEC Regulation D available at http://www.sec.gov/answers/regd.htm

I. IPOs, Inc.com – http://www.inc.com/guides/finance/20713.html

J. Geddes, Ross, IPOs and Equity Offerings, Butterworth-Heinemann, 2003.

K. Wasserman, Elizabeth, "How to Prepare a Company for an Initial Public Offering," Inc.com – http://www.inc.com/guides/preparing-for-initial-public-offering.html

L. Westenberg, David A., Initial Public Offerings: A Practical Guide to Going Public, 2nd Edition, Oct. 2013 (ISBN #978-1402418952) – http://www.ipoguidebook.com/index.html

Revision History:

Revision	Date	Description of Changes	Requested By
0.0	mm/dd/yyyy	Initial Release	

RC1040-1 STOCK OFFERING PLAN

Date _____   Completed by _____

I) Stock Offering Checklist and Schedule

Stock Offering Action	Planned Completion	Actual Completion	Notes
Set Stock Offering Goals			
- Determine Types of Shares			
- Determine Number of Shares			
- Determine Desired Price			
- Determine Capital Goals			
- Set Stock Offering Schedule			
Review of Articles of Incorporation			
Gain Approval of Board of Directors			
Set Underwriting Bank Criteria			
Select Underwriting Bank			
Legal Review			
Determine SEC Compliance Requirements			
Complete SEC Filings/Registration			
Determine State Legal/Filing Requirements			
Complete State Legal/Filing Requirements			
Complete Initial Prospectus			
Complete Final Prospectus			
Strategy for Marketing Stock			
Set Final Price			
Stock Offering			
Share Delivery			
Closing Actions			

II) Stock Offering Goals and Results

Stock Offering Performance	Goal	Actual	Notes
Shares Offered			
Shares Sold			
Share Price			
Total Investment Generated			

III) Setting Stock Offering Goals

(Actions)
_____

_____

_____

(Results)
_____

_____

_____

IV) Review of Articles of Incorporation and Board of Directors Approval

(Actions)
_____

_____

_____

(Results)
_____

_____

_____

V) Selecting Advising Bank (Criteria and Process)

(Actions)
_____

_____

_____

(Results)
_____

_____

_____

VI) SEC Registration and Compliance (Responsibilities, Information)

(Actions)
_____

_____

_____

(Results)
_____

_____

_____

VII) Legal Review

(Actions)
_____

_____

(Results)
_____

_____

_____

VIII) Determining and Meeting State Registration/Legal Requirements

(Actions)

_____

_____

_____

(Results)

_____

_____

_____

IX) Completing Initial and Final Prospectus

(Actions)

_____

_____

_____

(Results)

_____

_____

_____

X) Marketing Stock

(Actions)

_____

_____

_____

(Results)

_____

_____

_____

XI) Setting Final Stock Price – Other Final Activities

(Actions)

_____

_____

_____

(Results)

_____

_____

_____

XII) Executing the Offering

(Actions)

_____

_____

_____

(Results)

_____

_____

_____

XIII) Delivering Shares

(Actions)

_____

_____

_____

(Results)

_____

_____

_____

XIV) Closing the Stock Offering Process

(Actions)

_____

_____

_____

(Results)

_____

_____

_____

XV) Process Notes and Comments

_____

_____

_____

_____

_____

_____

_____

_____

_____

Completed by _____   Date _____

Approved by _____   Date _____

Document ID **RC1050**	Title **DEBT AND INVESTMENT**	Print Date **mm/dd/yyyy**
Revision **0.0**	Prepared By **Preparer's Name / Title**	Date Prepared **mm/dd/yyyy**
Effective Date **mm/dd/yyyy**	Reviewed By **Reviewer's Name / Title**	Date Reviewed **mm/dd/yyyy**
	Approved By **Final Approver's Name / Title**	Date Approved **mm/dd/yyyy**

Policy: The Company shall plan for and establish guidelines for managing surplus funds (i.e. invest, distribute to owners, or pay off debt), and create acceptable criteria for investment vehicles.

Purpose: To receive the most return and benefit from surplus funds while minimizing risk and costs, and reduce overall cost of capital in pursuing business plans and strategies.

Scope: This procedure applies to the Finance Department and to Top Management.

Responsibilities: The CFO (Chief Financial Officer) is responsible for overseeing surplus funds investing and debt pay down.

Top Management and the Board of Directors are responsible for reviewing and approving

Definitions: Surplus Funds – Profits and/or cash flow not needed for working capital, or part of cash management accounts (also called excess cash); should be invested for future use, used to pay debt, or distributed to shareholders.

Net Present Value – Used to analyze the profitability of an investment or project. The present value of an investment's future net cash flow minus the initial investment. Formula:

$$NPV = \sum_{t=1}^{T} \frac{C_t}{(1+r)^t} - C_0$$

Where:

t = the total number of payments

C_t = future cash flows

C_0 = initial cash flows

r = return on comparable investment

Weighted Average Cost of Capital (WACC) – Overall return that a corporation must earn on existing assets and business operations in order to increase or maintain its current value; calculated by multiplying the cost of each capital component by its proportional weight and then summing:

$$WACC = \frac{E}{V} * Re + \frac{D}{V} * Rd * (1 - Tc)$$

Where:

Re = cost of equity
Rd = cost of debt
E = market value of the firm's equity
D = market value of the firm's debt
V = E + D
E/V = percentage of financing that is equity
D/V = percentage of financing that is debt
Tc = corporate tax rate

Procedure:

1.0   DEBT AND INVESTMENT PLAN

1.1   The CFO shall annually set or review policies, objectives, plans, and activities for dealing with surplus funds or excess cash. General categories for using surplus funds include:

- Paying down debt;

- Distributing cash to owners and/or stockholders;

- Holding and investing surplus funds/cash reserves (as emergency funds or for future capital needs) so as to balance risk and return; and

- Find ways to invest in the business.

1.2   The CFO, Board of Directors, and Top Management shall annually set and/or review general policies as needed for acceptable investments that balance the Company's desire for return and acceptable risk, including investment attributes, such as:

- Ratings, insurance, and other risk factors of accounts and investments;

- Diversification requirements of investments including maximum and minimum dollar amounts in investment types and investment mixes;

- Types and categories of acceptable or unacceptable investments;

- Liquidity requirements; and

- Tax considerations.

1.3   All investments shall be in accordance with the investment policy established by the Board of Directors.

1.4   Using key forecasts and pro forma financial statements, the CFO shall analyze options available for using surplus funds (see Section 1.1 above) and create a debt-investment plan for the best use of surplus funds, including specific actions and objectives.

1.5   The debt-investment plan directly aligns with RC1010-1 CAPITAL PLAN to ensure that required financial resources are available, particularly for capital intensive business plans.

1.6   Top Management and the Board of Directors shall approve the Debt & Investment plan.

1.7   The CFO shall monitor Debt and Investment activities and make adjustments and corrections as needed to achieve plan goals.

2.0   DEBT AND INVESTMENT ACTIVITIES

2.1   The CFO shall review the policies and goals for using surplus funds with Top Management and the Board of Directors (See Section 1.2 above) and describe the established policies and goals in part I of RC1050-1 DEBT AND INVESTMENT PLAN.

2.2   The CFO shall perform an analysis of various options for using surplus funds to determine:

- Which use of surplus funds (See Section 1.1 above) option provides the best overall financial result (using methods such as Net Present Value and Cost of Capital);

- Which options create a positive overarching financial position for company according to standard financial statement analysis; and

- Which options meet established investment criteria (see Sections 1.2, 1.3, and 2.1 above).

2.3   The CFO shall note the methods and results of the analysis, along with recommendations for using surplus funds, in part II of RC1050-1.

2.4   The CFO shall use results and recommendations (from analysis in Section 2.2, above) for surplus funds to create a list of actions required to accomplish surplus fund goals and meet all established investment and surplus funds criteria. These activities shall be listed on the RC1050-2 DEBT AND INVESTMENT ACTION LOG. Activities can include specific actions such as:

- Pay certain amounts toward certain debts over specified period of time;

- Invest certain amounts in specifically listed investment accounts and funds over a specific period of time; and

- Distribute specific funds to shareholders or owners during a specific period of time.

2.5   The CFO shall record the completion and results of debt and investment activities on RC1050-2.

3.0   DEBT AND INVESTMENT REVIEW

3.1   The CFO shall regularly (weekly, monthly) monitor the RC1050-2 DEBT AND INVESTMENT ACTION LOG to ensure activities are carried out as scheduled and that results are consistent with the RC1050-1 DEBT AND INVESTMENT PLAN.

3.2   The CFO shall annually review the RC1050-1 DEBT AND INVESTMENT PLAN with Top Management and the Board of Directors shall verify that:

- The policies, plans, and goals for the general use of surplus funds still suit the overall needs of the Company;

- The policies and requirements for types of investments continue to meet objectives for risk, return, and liquidity and for the overall cost of capital; and

- The results of activities in terms of return on investments, overall financial health in terms of cash flow, financial statement analysis, achieving investment goals.

4.0   DEBT AND INVESTMENT PLAN IMPROVEMENT

4.1   As a result of the information exchanged and lessons learned in the course of the debt and investment review (see Section 3.0), the CFO shall make recommendations for modifying policies and the process of surplus funds management.

4.2   The CFO shall submit recommendations to the Board of Directors, which must approve recommended revisions before they are implemented.

4.3   Upon receiving the Board of Directors' approval, the CFO shall ensure the necessary changes are made to the Debt and Investment Plan and the Plan is implemented and monitored as revised.

Effectiveness Criteria:

- Planned use of surplus funds the best meet the Company needs

- Effective returns on investments of surplus funds and minimized cost of capital

- Investments that meet risk, return, and liquidity objectives

Forms/Records:

- RC1050-1 DEBT AND INVESTMENT PLAN

- RC1050-2 DEBT AND INVESTMENT ACTION LOG

- Review Meeting minutes

References:

    A. Finance Policy Manual

- Section 5.2.6 – Debt and Investment

    B. Financial procedures

- None

Additional Resources:

    A. "What to Do with Your Excess Cash," Edward Lowe Foundation. Available at edwardlowe.org/digital-library/what-to-do-with-your-excess-cash.

B. <u>Corporate Cash Management, Excess Cash, and Acquisitions</u>, Taylor & Francis, 2000, ISBN #978-0815335528.

C. <u>Excess Cash Flow: A Signal for Institutional and Corporate Governance</u>, Rahul Dhumale, Palgrave Macmillan, Jan. 2003, ISBN #978-1403900395.

Revision History:

Revision	Date	Description of Changes	Requested By
0.0	mm/dd/yyyy	Initial Release	

[This page intentionally left blank]

RC1050-1 DEBT AND INVESTMENT PLAN

I)   Policies, Plans, Goals

Risk Requirements: (i.e. ratings, insurance, and guarantees)

_____

_____

_____

_____

Diversification Requirements:

_____

_____

_____

_____

Liquidity Requirements:

_____

_____

_____

_____

Investment Return Goals:

_____

_____

_____

_____

_____

_____

II)   Surplus Funds Analysis

Pay Debt Analysis:

Methods Used: _____

Results: _____

_____

_____

Dividend Analysis:

Methods Used: _____

Results: _____

_____

_____

Investment Analysis:

Methods Used: _____

Results: _____

_____

_____

List/Explain Debt & Investment General Plans and Strategies:

_____

_____

_____

_____

_____

_____

_____

_____

RC1050-2 DEBT AND INVESTMENT ACTION LOG

Action	Projected Complete	Actual Complete	Projected Result	Actual Result

Comments:

[This page intentionally left blank]

Document ID **RC1060**	Title **ASSET ACQUISITION**	Print Date **mm/dd/yyyy**
Revision **0.0**	Prepared By **Preparer's Name / Title**	Date Prepared **mm/dd/yyyy**
Effective Date **mm/dd/yyyy**	Reviewed By **Reviewer's Name / Title**	Date Reviewed **mm/dd/yyyy**
	Approved By **Final Approver's Name / Title**	Date Approved **mm/dd/yyyy**

Policy: The Company shall establish methods and guidelines in order to evaluate appropriate use of capital for asset acquisition through using financial analysis tools.

Purpose: To ensure capital used for purchasing fixed assets meet established financial guidelines.

Scope: This procedure applies to the Finance Department and other affected departments.

Responsibilities: The CFO (Chief Financial Officer) is responsible for overseeing the asset acquisition process and reviewing the ROI Worksheet with the Capital Budget Committee.

Department Managers are responsible for completing and submitting asset acquisitions for approval.

The Capital Budget Committee shall review and approve or disapprove each RC1060-2 ASSET ACQUISITION REQUEST/WORKSHEET based on:

- Return on investment (or other financial analysis criteria);

- Allocation and availability in the capital budget;

- Alignment with business plans;

- Associated risk; and

- Potential positive or negative impact on the business.

Definitions: Return on Investment (ROI) – The return ratio that compares the net benefits of a project verses its total costs. Formula: Annual ROI = [(net profit / total investment × 100) / year] .

Net Present Value (NPV) – Used to analyze the profitability of an investment or project. The present value of an investment's future net cash flows minus the initial investment. Formula:

$$NPV = \sum_{t=1}^{T} \frac{C_t}{(1+r)^t} - C_o$$

Where:

> T = the total number of payments (per period)
> Ct = future cash flows
> C0 = initial cash flows
> r = return on comparable investment

Payback Period (PP) – The amount of time taken to break even on an investment. Since this method ignores the time value of money and cash flows after the payback period, it can provide only a partial picture of whether the investment is worthwhile. Formula: PP = Total investment/Annual cash flows.

Weighted Average Cost of Capital (WACC) – Overall return that a corporation must earn on its existing assets and business operations in order to increase or maintain its current value. WACC is calculated by multiplying the cost of each capital component by its proportional weight and then summing. Formula:

$$WACC = \frac{E}{V} * Re + \frac{D}{V} * Rd * (1 - Tc)$$

Where:

> Re = cost of equity
> Rd = cost of debt
> E = market value of the firm's equity
> D = market value of the firm's debt
> V = E + D (per period)
> E/V = percentage of financing that is equity
> D/V = percentage of financing that is debt
> Tc = corporate tax rate

Capital Budget – Long-term and yearly expenditure plan for acquisition of capital assets, construction, or improvement of fixed assets such as land and buildings.

Capital Asset – Tangible, long-term such as buildings, machinery, fixtures, furniture and equipment (typically more than $2000 depreciated over 2 or more years). It does not include items normally consumed in the course of business operation or production.

Procedure:

1.0   ASSET ACQUISITION PLANNING

1.1   A Capital Budget Committee shall be formed and headed by the CFO. The Committee shall consist of selected members of Top Management, the Accounting, Finance, and Operation departments, and other departments, as required. Required approvals (CFO, CEO, or Board of Directors) for levels of expenditures shall also be created and reviewed periodically.

1.2   The CFO and the Capital Budget Committee shall establish basic criteria for reviewing the use of the capital budget for the acquisition of assets. While these criteria should be fairly standard, they should also be modified and improved according to the situation and lessons learned. Standard methods of analysis should include methods such as internal return on investment, payback period, and net present value (NPV). These criteria can vary according to:

- The financial analysis used (see Section 1.3 below);

- Certainty versus risk: Assets that have a high degree of certainty may be considered if they return the cost of capital and profit goals (i.e. 10% + 20% = 30% ROI): High risks might require 100 to 200% ROI;

- Availability of Capital: The funds available in the capital budget (ability to fund a few or a large number of asset acquisition requests) plays a large role is establishing criteria;

- Performance History: Past performance of similar assets, particularly in reference to predicted ROI;

- Tax and Regulatory Consequences: Whether the asset provides tax savings (or, conversely, regulatory costs); and

- Competition and Business Strategy: Providing a strong competitive advantage or it aligning with over-arching business strategy might increase a willingness to accept risk or lower acceptable ROI.

1.3   The CFO and the Capital Budget Committee shall establish types of financial analysis used according to best practices, situations, and factors. Examples include:

- Internal Rate of Return for screening decisions (i.e., making a yes or no decision on an individual asset);

- Net Present Value for preference decisions (selecting between competing asset choices); and

- Payback Period when risk and liquidity are concerns (high-tech assets).

1.4   A Department Manager requesting use of the capital budget to purchase a capital asset shall complete an RC1060-2 ASSET ACQUISITION REQUEST/WORKSHEET.

1.5   CFO shall review each submitted RC1060-2 ASSET ACQUISITION REQUEST/WORKSHEET to ensure the following:

- The ROI worksheet is completed fully and properly;

- The information appears thorough and correct; and

- The described project or purchase aligns with overall business goals and strategies.

1.6   The CFO shall meet with the Capital Budget Committee to review, and then approve or disapprove, capital assets requests based upon established criteria (see sections 1.2 and 1.3 above).

1.7   Asset acquisitions and the asset acquisition process shall be regularly reviewed by the CFO, Top Management, Capital Budget Committee, and the Board of Directors (if required) to evaluate and improve, as needed, and ensure:

- Proper selection criteria are being established and used;

- Capital budgets are being properly used and not exceeded; and

- Assets are yielding projected returns.

2.0   ASSET ACQUISITION

2.1   The CFO and the Capital Budget Committee shall complete the RC1060-1 ASSET ACQUISITION CRITERIA by listing the following:

- Noting in Section I the types of analysis used according to asset type, category, or department (typically more than one method of financial analysis is used to consider asset acquisition);

- Standards for approval, such as minimum return on investment or payback period, that can also vary according to the asset type or category; and

- Other important factors that should be considered (e.g., fulfills the objectives in the Business Plan).

2.2   To request the purchase of a capital asset, the appropriate Department Manager shall complete a RC1060-2 ASSET ACQUISITION REQUEST/WORKSHEET (with the assistance of the CFO or other Finance Dept. representative) in order to request the purchase of a capital asset, including information about:

- Projected costs associated with the asset, including acquisition costs and maintenance/operation over the life of the asset;

- Projected cash flows and/or cost savings over the life of the asset benefits;

- Other material benefits and information about the asset ("fulfills core mission," "provides competitive advantage," etc.);

- Projected affects on Working Capital needs resulting from asset purchase; and

- Appropriate ROI, NPV, or PBP analysis results (according to analysis as specified in the RC1060-1 ASSET ACQUISITION CRITERIA).

2.3   Completed RC1060-2 ASSET ACQUISITION REQUEST/WORKSHEET forms shall be submitted to the CFO, who shall review them to ensure they are thorough and correct, and seek additional information from the submitting Department Manager as required.

2.4   The CFO shall periodically (e.g., weekly) convent the Capital Budget Committee to review the submitted RC1060-2 ASSET ACQUISITION REQUEST/ WORKSHEET forms and approve, disapprove, or table requests (to gather more information, etc.). Tabled requests must be reviewed for approval or disapproval within one month.

2.5   The CFO shall note and take appropriate action for each reviewed RC1060-2 ASSET ACQUISITION REQUEST/WORKSHEET, such as:

- For approved acquisitions, notify requester of approval, assign budget and account number (or notify accounting department to do so), designate capital asset number, etc.;

- For acquisition requests that are not approved, the CFO shall notify requester that asset acquisition is not approved along with clear, meaningful, and constructive explanation (that does not discourage future requests);

- For tabled requests, assign action items to collect information in order to complete review within 30 days; and

- Approved requests receive appropriate authorization (e.g., less than $50,000 – CFO and Committee approval/more than $50,000 but less than $100,000 – CEO approval/over $100,000 – Board of Directors approval).

2.6   The CFO shall maintain the RC1010-3 CAPITAL BUDGET LOG after each Capital Budget Committee meeting to track capital budget status, to ensure that:

- The capital budget will be utilized, but not exceeded;

- The capital budget is used in a timely manner (i.e., spending is fairly equal by quarter, rather than used all in the last month); and

- The current state of the capital budget is known.

3.0   ASSET ACQUISITION REVIEW

3.1   The CFO shall be responsible for annually reviewing or auditing several (five to ten, for example) approved RC1060-2 ASSET ACQUISITION REQUEST/WORKSHEET forms from the previous two to five (2-5) years to verify:

- Actual cash flows and/or demonstrated savings (i.e., actual ROI, NPV compared with projections);

- How actual costs and expenses compared to projections;

- The projected return of the asset is being fulfilled;

- Other material benefits projected or realized; and

- Other relevant information.

3.2   The CFO shall report findings of the review described in Section 3.1, above, to the Capital Budget Committee, Top Management, and the Board of Directors.

3.3   The CFO shall regularly (e.g., weekly, monthly) review the status of the capital
        budget (RC1010-3 CAPITAL BUDGET LOG) and notify Top Management
        immediately of any concern.

4.0   IMPROVING THE ASSET ACQUISITION PROCESS

The CFO shall hold an annual review meeting with the Capital Budget Committee
and Top Management to present findings of the conducted audits and reviews (see
Section 3.0, preceding). Any issues should be addressed by improving the:

- Asset acquisition process or forms;
- Analysis or criteria established for evaluating asset acquisition; and
- Increasing or decreasing the capital budget.

Effectiveness Criteria:

- Investing in assets that provide adequate return on investment.
- Proper use of the capital budget; capital budget not exceeding.
- Asset investments that align with business plans and liquidity objectives.

Forms/Records:

- RC1060-1 ASSET ACQUISITION CRITERIA
- RC1060-2 ASSET ACQUISITION REQUEST/WORKSHEET
- RC1010-3 CAPITAL BUDGET LOG
- Review Meeting minutes

References:

A. Finance Policy Manual

- Section 5.2.7 – Asset Acquisition

B. Finance procedures

- RC1010 CAPITAL PLAN

Additional Resources:

A. Siegel, Shim & Dauber, Corporate Controller's Handbook of Financial
    Management 2008-09 Ed., CCH, Inc. (2008). ISBN #978-0808091721.

Revision History:

Revision	Date	Description of Changes	Requested By
0.0	mm/dd/yyyy	Initial Release	

[This page intentionally left blank]

RC1060-1 ASSET ACQUISTION CRITERIA

Completed by _____   **For Fiscal Year** _____

I) Type of Analysis

Analysis Methods	Dept./Type of Asset				
	Operations	Research & Development	Sales & Marketing	Information Technology	
ROI					
NPV					
PBP					

Comments:

II) Minimum Criteria

Asset Category	Minimum Required Return				
	Operations	Research & Development	Sales & Marketing	Information Technology	
Very High Risk					
High Risk					
Moderate Risk					
Low Risk					
Very Low Risk					
Other Factors					

Comments:

[This page intentionally left blank]

RC1060-2 ASSET ACQUISTION REQUEST/WORKSHEET

Completed by _____   Date _____

I) Basic Information

Asset Name: _____ Dept.: _____

Contact: _____

Description: _____

_____

_____

Costs	# Years	Avg $/Year		Total
Acquisition				
Operation/Maintenance				
Other Costs				
Total Costs				
Projected Earnings	# Years	Avg $/Year		Total
Sales				
Savings				
Other Income				
Totals				
Other Material Benefits:				

II) Financial Analysis

Internal Return on Investment Results: _____

Net Present Value Results: _____

Pay Back Period Results: _____

Regulatory Implications: _____

_____

_____

III) Approvals

Capital Budget Committee Recommendation: (Check and Chairperson Initial)

Approve		Disapprove		Tabled Until:		Date

Reasons for
Approval or
Disapproval

_____
_____
_____
_____
_____
_____
_____
_____
_____
_____

Approved By   **Date:**

CFO: _____   _____
CEO: _____   _____
Board Chair: _____   _____
              _____   _____

Account No.:		Created By:		Date:	

Comments:

_____

_____

_____

_____

_____

Document ID **RC1070**	Title **LEASING**	Print Date **mm/dd/yyyy**
Revision **0.0**	Prepared By **Preparer's Name / Title**	Date Prepared **mm/dd/yyyy**
Effective Date **mm/dd/yyyy**	Reviewed By **Reviewer's Name / Title**	Date Reviewed **mm/dd/yyyy**
	Approved By **Final Approver's Name / Title**	Date Approved **mm/dd/yyyy**

Policy: The Company shall explore and consider lease and buy options when purchasing capital equipment and other major expenditures, and make decisions based on the overall good of the company, and alignment with overall financial strategies and objectives.

Purpose: To ensure lease and buy decisions are made after considering and comparing the lease options to ownership, especially in calculating total equipment costs which can include operation and maintenance, tax benefits, and economic life.

Scope: This procedure applies to the Finance department and any department requesting capital equipment.

Responsibilities: The CFO (Chief Financial Officer) is responsible for reviewing lease/buy considerations for capital equipment.

Department Managers are responsible evaluating lease/buy decisions that affect their department.

Definitions: Present Value Interest Factor (PVIF) – Serves to discount future values to account for the opportunity cost of time.

Operating Lease – Lease that, for operational purposes, is treated as a monthly expense.

Capital Lease – A lease that for operational purposes is treated like an asset purchase.

Lease-Buy Evaluation – Considering all factors in comparing the total cost of leasing and the total cost of ownership in order to make a lease or buy decision.

Total Cost – The cost of leasing or buying equipment, including monthly payments, interest/fees, taxes, operations/ maintenance, royalties, down payments, etc.

Procedure:

1.0   LEASING PLAN

1.1   The CFO shall oversee the process for analyzing whether it is best to lease or buy equipment, based on situational and financial considerations that factor into the total cost over the life of the equipment use, in accordance with procedure RC1010 CAPITAL PLAN. Typical considerations can include:

- Economic life of the equipment and time to obsolescence;

- Tax advantages/disadvantages;

- Cost of operation and maintenance;

- Short term or seasonal use;

- Best use of capital;

- Alignment with financial strategies and objectives; and

- Average invested capital.

1.2   The CFO shall set and regularly review the buy/lease policy with Department managers (e.g., Information Technology, Facilities Management) for equipment types or functions that, individually, do not equal a large capital expense but collectively are a significant cost. Examples include:

- Computers and related equipment (e.g., scanners, printers, routers);

- Office electronics (copiers, phones, calculators, fax machines);

- Office furniture (desks, chairs, bookcases, file cabinets); and

- Small equipment (e.g., dollies, scales).

1.3   The CFO shall assist and oversee department managers in following the review and assessment procedure for equipment lease/buy decisions.

1.4   The general guide for making lease/buy decisions shall be the total cost and return on investment over the life of the equipment. Occasionally, however, situational factors and concerns may override the total cost result. In these cases, the overriding factors should be clearly documented and explained on the RC1070-1 LEASE/BUY FINANCIAL ANALYSIS.

1.5   Particular factors of the lease agreement determine if the lease is considered an "operating lease" and a monthly expense or a "capital lease" and treated as a purchase (i.e., the cost is amortized over an appropriate period). If any of the following applies, the lease is considered a capital lease:

- Transfer of ownership at the end of the lease;

- Bargain purchase options at the end of the lease;

- Lease term exceeds 75% of economic life of the equipment; and/or

- Lease payments exceed 90% of equipment fair market value.

1.6   Careful consideration shall be made to determine proper tax definition (purchase or lease) using factors such as:

- The right of the lessee to purchase the equipment at the expiration of the lease for a nominal price in relation to the fair market value. Purchase options for one or ten dollars are common examples;

- The payment of substantial rentals for a short original lease term in relation to the expected useful life of the property, followed by relatively nominal rental for an additional term approximately equal to the remaining useful life;

- The fact that the equipment will be virtually worthless at lease end;

- Requiring the lessee to repair and maintain the equipment and to assume all risk of loss and damage;

- The intent of the parties that the lessee will keep the equipment when the lease expires; and

- The designation of some portion of the lease payments as interest.

2.0   LEASING EVALUATIONS

2.1   The CFO shall request the information from the appropriate department manager to complete the RC1070-1 LEASE/BUY FINANCIAL ANALYSIS when a lease or buy decision is required.

2.2   The CFO shall complete RC1070-1 and review the information with the appropriate Department managers and together reach a lease-buy decision. (Alternate methods such as Net Present Value after tax may also be used.)

2.3   The CFO and the appropriate department manager shall make the lease-buy decision based on Total Cost of leasing or buying the equipment, unless other factors and concerns outweigh the cost.

2.4   When other factors override total cost in making lease-buy decisions, the CFO shall clearly document these reasons in the Comments sections of RC1070-1 (i.e., estimated life far exceeds length of the loan, significantly decreasing the lifetime annual cost of the equipment).

3.0   REVIEWING LEASE EVALUATIONS

3.1   The CFO shall annually review lease-buy decisions made in the preceding one-to-three (1-3) years to determine if the lease evaluation process accurately estimates the total costs of leasing or buying particular equipment or equipment types and if all relevant factors have been considered in making lease-buy decisions.

3.2   As part of the review process, the CFO shall meet with Department managers (e.g., operations, facilities, and accounting), tax accountants or other tax advisors, the controller, and other advisory and/or accounting committees to review lease/ buy decisions.

4.0   IMPROVING THE LEASE EVALUATION PROCESS

4.1   The CFO shall, as a result of any findings during the review process (see Section 3.1 and 3.2) revise and improve the Lease Evaluation procedure and/or the RC1070-1 LEASE/BUY FINANCIAL ANALYSIS, as needed, to ensure accurate and relevant information is collected, recorded, and considered during the lease-buy decision process.

Effectiveness Criteria:

- Total cost analysis (made during the lease/buy decision process) accurately reflects the true *total cost* of equipment.

- Lease-buy decisions are made using proper and adequate information and considerations.

Forms/Records:

- RC1070-1 LEASE/BUY FINANCIAL ANALYSIS
- Review meetings

References:

A. Finance Policy Manual

- Section 5.2.8 – Leasing

B. Finance procedures

- RC1010 CAPITAL PLAN

Additional Resources:

A. GAAP Handbook of Policies and Procedures, CCH, Inc.

B. FASB Statement of Financial Standards #13, "Accounting for Leases," Financial Standards Accounting Board, PO Box 5116, Norwalk, CT 06856.

This Statement establishes standards of financial accounting and reporting for leases by lessees and lessors. For lessees, a lease is a financing transaction called a capital lease if it meets any one of four specified criteria; if not, it is an operating lease. Capital leases are treated as the acquisition of assets and the incurrence of obligations by the lessee. Operating leases are treated as current operating expenses. For lessors, a financing transaction lease is classified as a sales-type, direct financing, or leveraged lease. To be a sales-type, direct financing, or leveraged lease, the lease must meet one of the same criteria used for lessees to classify a lease as a capital lease, in addition to two criteria dealing with future uncertainties. Leveraged leases also have to meet further criteria. These types of leases are recorded as investments under different specifications for each type of lease. Leases not meeting the criteria are considered operating leases and are accounted for like rental property.

See http://www.fasb.org/pdf/fas13.pdf for the full text.

Revision History:

Revision	Date	Description of Changes	Requested By
0.0	mm/dd/yyyy	Initial Release	

[This page intentionally left blank]

RC1070-1 LEASE/BUY FINANCIAL ANALYSIS

Equipment Description: _____

Department/Manager: _____ Date Needed: _____

Completed by: _____ Date: _____

Lease Calculation:

A: Lease Length (Yrs.)	B: Annual Lease Payments	C: Annual Lease Tax Benefits	D: Other Annual Lease Expenses	E: Net Annual Lease Cost (B-C+D)	F: Adjusted Annual Lease Cost (E•PVIF[1])	G: Total Cost (A•F)

Buy Calculation:

A: Estimated Life (Years)	B: Length of Loan (Years)	C: Annual Loan Payments	D: Annual Interest Portion of Payments	E: Annual Depreciation	F: Total Tax Benefits (D+E)	G: Other Annual Ownership Costs	H: Net Annual Purchase Cost (C+G-F)	I: Adjusted Annual Purchase Cost (G•PVIF)	J: Total Cost (B•H)

Decision: Lease _____ Buy _____ Difference _____

Comments: _____

_____

_____

[1] PVIF: Present Value Interest Factor

[This page intentionally left blank]

Finance Policies and Procedures

Section 420

Treasury Management

Section 420

Treasury Management

Document ID **TM1000**	Title **WORKING CAPITAL**	Print Date **mm/dd/yyyy**
Revision **0.0**	Prepared By **Preparer's Name / Title**	Date Prepared **mm/dd/yyyy**
Effective Date **mm/dd/yyyy**	Reviewed By **Reviewer's Name / Title**	Date Reviewed **mm/dd/yyyy**
	Approved By **Final Approver's Name / Title**	Date Approved **mm/dd/yyyy**

Policy:
The Company shall properly manage the working capital invested to operate the business in areas such as Accounts Receivable, Accounts Payable, and Inventory, in order to minimize working capital while still meeting all operational needs.

Purpose:
(a) Minimize and make best use of working capital; (b) set working capital goals; (c) Monitor, review, and improve working capital performance in such areas as:

- Accounts Payable (i.e. Days Payable Outstanding);
- Account Receivable (i.e. Days Sales Outstanding);
- Inventories (i.e. Days Inventories Outstanding); and
- Total Working Capital.

Scope:
This procedure applies to the Finance, Accounting, Sales, and Operations departments.

Responsibilities:
The Chief Financial Officer (CFO) is responsible for overseeing working capital and for completing the TM1000-1 WORKING CAPITAL PLAN.

Top Management is responsible of approving the TM1000-1 WORKING CAPITAL PLAN.

Definitions:
Total Working Capital – The total amount of capital needed to operate the business. Typically calculated as:

(Accounts Receivable + Inventory) – Accounts Payable.

Accounts Receivable – Money owed to the Company (credits) for goods and services delivered, and it frequently refers to the department and/or processes in place to collect these payments including invoicing, processing payments, and collections and deposits.

Days Sales Outstanding (DSO) – The average number of days it takes to collect payment after the sale is made, typically calculated as:

Accounts Receivable ÷ Sales x Days

Days are the number of days in the period you are using to

calculate DSO (e.g., month=30; quarter=90; year=365).

Accounts Payable – Payments owed (liabilities) by the Company to suppliers, service providers, and other creditors for goods and services provided, and it frequently refers to the department and/or processes in place to make such payments.

Days Payable Outstanding (DPO) – The average number of days it takes the Company to pay invoices and other payables; typically calculated as:

Accounts Payable ÷ Net Sales x Days

Inventory – Quantity of goods and materials on hand in the form of raw and purchased materials, work-in-process, and finished goods (and for retailers, resale goods); typically appears as an asset on the Company's Balance Sheet.

Days Inventory Outstanding (DIO) – The average number of days of inventory the Company has in stock or in process, typically calculated as:

Average Inventory ÷ Net Sales x Days

Collections – Process of collecting a delinquent Accounts Payable amount.

Procedure:

1.0   WORKING CAPITAL PLAN

1.1   The CFO shall regularly set and review working capital plans and performance to ensure the working capital (in Accounts Receivable, Accounts Payable, and Inventory) needed to operate the business is:

- Minimized to a practical degree, particularly in relation to benchmarks established by top performers in similar industries;

- Managed and used in ways that align with overarching operational and financial goals established in Business Plans, Financial Objectives, and the Capital Plan; and

- Adequately available to ensure operation of the business.

1.2   The CFO shall ensure that clear goals and processes are in place to collect Accounts Receivables and Collections, including:

- Prompt invoicing;

- Swift processing and deposits of payments;

- Effective collection activities of late accounts; and

- Produce regular reports and conduct reviews of accounts payable effectiveness (i.e., Days Sales Outstanding Reports).

1.3   The CFO shall ensure that clear goals and processes are in place to disburse accounts payable that include the following:

- Invoices are paid in a timely and optimum manner (i.e., mailed 5 days prior to due date);

- A clear policy for making early payments, for example, at least a 2% discount if paid within 10 days (2-10 net 30); and

- Regular reports and review of accounts payable effectiveness (i.e., Days Payable Outstanding Reports).

1.4   The CFO shall monitor and review cash accounts inventory in accordance with TM1010 CASH MANAGEMENT.

1.5   The CFO shall monitor and review inventory in accordance with TM1020 INVENTORY MANAGEMENT.

1.6   The CFO shall conduct regular review meetings with Top Management to review working capital plans and performance, including:

- Aligning working capital goals with overall Company strategic, operational, and financial goals;

- Creating or modifying specific working capital goals, strategies, and practices; and

- Reviewing past and current performance of working capital according to established criteria and industry benchmarks.

1.7   The CFO shall document the working capital goals (see Sections 1.1 through 1.5 above) and list the activities and resources required to meet them in TM1000-1 WORKING CAPITAL PLAN.

2.0   WORKING CAPITAL PERFORMANCE

2.1   The CFO shall meet regularly with the owners /managers of the working capital processes (Accounts Receivable, Accounts Payable, Inventories) to establish and/or review goals/objectives, set measurement and reports (monthly and/or quarterly), and to review performance results. Goals and objectives shall be established in light of:

- Overarching business plans and objectives;

- Industry leaders (benchmarks); and

- Current performance and realistic steps/progress toward industry leader performance

2.2   The CFO shall note all established goals and objectives of working capital processes on the TM1000-1 WORKING CAPITAL PLAN.

2.3   The CFO shall be responsible for collecting established regular reports (see section 2.1 above) regarding working capital processes and record relevant results on the TM1000-1 WORKING CAPITAL PLAN.

3.0   REVIEWING THE WORKING CAPITAL PLAN

3.1   The CFO shall regularly review performance results contained in regular reports and entered in the TM1000-1 WORKING CAPITAL PLAN. The CFO shall pay particular attention to key measurements for individual components of working capital (i.e. Accounts Receivable, Accounts Payable, Inventories) and monitor the total capital required to operate the business.

3.2   The CFO shall hold regular review meetings (weekly/monthly/quarterly) with the working capital process owners to review working capital performance and compare performance with established working capital goals listed in the TM1000-1 WORKING CAPITAL PLAN.

3.3   The CFO shall annually review working capital goals and performance with Top Management to ensure the TM1000-1 WORKING CAPITAL PLAN aligns with overall business strategies and plans.

4.0   IMPROVING THE WORKING CAPITAL PLAN

The CFO shall, as a result of working capital review (See Section 3.0), modify the TM1000-1 WORKING CAPITAL PLAN as required to meet working capital goals and needs. Key improvement areas can include:

- Improving processes and procedures used to implement areas of working capital in order to reach goals;

- Improving reporting and measurement capabilities to more effectively execute and monitor working capital processes (particularly through the use of automation and technology); and

- Revisiting goals and objectives to ensure they are realistic and reachable.

Effectiveness Criteria:

- Total working capital invested in operations
- Days Sales Outstanding
- Days Payable Outstanding
- Days Inventory Outstanding
- Total Inventory Investment

Forms/Records:

- TM1000-1 WORKING CAPITAL PLAN
- Meeting notes (minutes)

References:

A. Finance Policy Manual

- Section 5.3.1 – Working Capital

B. Finance procedures

- FS1000 FINANCIAL OBJECTIVES

- RC1000 BUSINESS PLAN
- RC1010 CAPITAL PLAN
- TM1010 CASH MANAGEMENT
- TM1020 INVENTORY MANAGEMENT

Additional Resources:

A. "How To Calculate Working Capital Needs Based on Business Cycles," available at http://www.googobits.com/articles/p0-3029-how-to-calculate-working-capital-needs-based-on-business-cycles.html.

Revision History:

Revision	Date	Description of Changes	Requested By
0.0	mm/dd/yyyy	Initial Release	

[This page intentionally left blank]

TM1000-1 WORKING CAPITAL PLAN

Date _____

Completed by _____

Working Capital Activity	Goal	Benchmarks	Q1 Results	Q2 Results	Q3 Results	Q4 Results
Accounts Receivable						
Policies-Procedures-Training						
Measurements-Reporting						
Reviews						
Days Sales Outstanding						
Deposits						
Resources						
Accounts Payable						
Policies-Procedures-Training						
Measurements-Reporting						
Reviews						
Days Payable Outstanding						
Early Payments						
Resources						

TM1000-1 WORKING CAPITAL PLAN

Working Capital Activity	Goal	Benchmarks	Q1 Results	Q2 Results	Q3 Results	Q4 Results
Inventory						
Raw Materials						
Purchased Parts						
Work-in-Process						
Finished Goods						
Resale Goods						
Reports						
Reviews						
Resources						
Total Working Capital						
Working Capital Reduction						
Working Capital Management						
Reports						
Reviews						
Resources						

Comments/Notes:

Document ID **TM1010**	Title **CASH MANAGEMENT**	Print Date **mm/dd/yyyy**
Revision **0.0**	Prepared By **Preparer's Name / Title**	Date Prepared **mm/dd/yyyy**
Effective Date **mm/dd/yyyy**	Reviewed By **Reviewer's Name / Title**	Date Reviewed **mm/dd/yyyy**
	Approved By **Final Approver's Name / Title**	Date Approved **mm/dd/yyyy**

Policy: The Company shall ensure cash availability through managing cash on hand, cash deposits in daily, medium, and long term accounts, and cash disbursements to best meet the Company cash and liquidity needs while managing risk.

Purpose: To plan, track, and manage cash accounts to ensure proper cash utilization and availability, including:

- Planned and proper use of cash resources;
- Preventing cash shortfalls; and
- Balancing risk, liquidity, return, and cost of cash accounts.

Scope: This procedure applies to the Finance and Accounting departments.

Responsibilities: The CFO (Chief Financial Officer) is responsible for overseeing cash management processes to ensure proper cash availability and best practices in cash management, and for completing the TM1010-1 CASH MANAGEMENT PLAN

Top Management is responsible for approving the TM1010-1 CASH MANAGEMENT PLAN.

Definitions: Liquidity – Ability to convert an asset into cash quickly and without a price discount.

Sweep Account – An account that automatically transfers excess balances out of a cash account and into interest bearing accounts, or vice versa (e.g., from a money market account into a checking account to prevent a shortfall/overdraft).

Liquidity Tree – Dispersing cash among different types of accounts (daily, medium, and long term) to improve return, balance risks, and maintain needed access to funds.

Daily Account – An account that provides immediate access to funds but typically provides no rate of return, such as a checking account.

Medium Term Account – An account that has limited fund availability (e.g., only two withdrawals allowed per month) but provides a better rate of return than a checking account; an example is a money market account.

> Long Term Account – An account that has more restrictive limits on availability (e.g., available every 90 days) but offers a higher rate of return; an example of an LTA is a U.S. Treasury Bill.

Procedure:

1.0   CASH MANAGEMENT PLAN

1.1   The CFO shall conduct monthly meetings with Top Management to set, review, and improve cash management including the following:

- Setting cash management goals and policies, and aligning them with overall Business Plans, including Company strategic, operational, and financial goals.

- Reviewing cash management performance according to established policies, goals, and objectives.

1.2   The CFO shall note the cash requirements determined (usually in terms of months or in dollar amounts) at all levels of the liquidity tree in Part I of the TM1010-1 CASH MANAGEMENT PLAN. For example; one month of cash in daily accounts, two months in medium term accounts, and one month in long term accounts.   Considerations to determine cash requirements include the following:

- The amount needed for cash balances will vary dependent on the business or organization. Organizations with large inventories and long payables period will need larger cash balances than low inventory, cash businesses.

- A standard, straightforward formula for dispersion may be adequate (i.e. 1/3 of cash in each account) or some businesses require a less straightforward approach (i.e. a formula that varies according to season or cash balances)

1.3   The CFO shall determine the activities, and measurements required to meet the goals for cash account balances and dispersion, and record them in Part I of the TM1010-1 CASH MANAGEMENT PLAN. Activities may include:

- Tracking and planning of cash account balances and cash flow (in relation to budgets and forecasts) to ensure availability of operational funds, including setting average targets;

- Managing accounts to maximize return on cash balances (i.e. use of sweep accounts) while minimizing fees (See RC1070 MANAGING BANK RELATIONSHIPS); and

- Establishing and managing the number of banks/accounts required to meet cash management needs, important criteria for selecting banks/accounts, and the personnel authorized to open and have access to accounts.

1.4   The CFO shall note policies and goals for liquidity requirements and acceptable risks[1] associated with various cash account options in Part II of the TM1010-1 CASH MANAGEMENT PLAN. Risk considerations can include:

- Whether deposits are insured, and insurance levels;

---

[1] See procedure AC1020, "Risk Assessment."

- Rating of bonds, funds, securities, banks, etc.;
- Diversity of investments, staggered maturation times
- Negative impact of various levels of investment loss

1.5   The CFO shall determine the strategies, activities, and measurements required to meet the policies and goals for liquidity requirements and acceptable risks associated with various cash account options and list them in Part II of the TM1010-1 CASH MANAGEMENT. Strategies may include managing daily, medium, and long term cash accounts to balance liquidity and risk according to established guidelines and policy.

1.6   The CFO shall note policies and goals for meeting cash shortfalls in the cash accounts in Part III of the TM1010-1 CASH MANAGEMENT PLAN. Cash shortfall contingency plans may include:

- Overdraft protection;
- Lines of credit or pre-approved loans; and
- Average-balance accounts.

1.7   The CFO shall determine the strategies, activities, and measurements required to meet the policies and goals for meeting cash shortfalls in the cash accounts in Part III of the TM1010-1 CASH MANAGEMENT PLAN.

- Manage daily, short term, and long term cash accounts to balance liquidity and risk according to established guidelines and policy (see Section 1.1);
- Create contingency plans for cash shortfalls (i.e. establish line of credit);
- Establish and manage the number of banks/accounts required to meet cash management needs, important criteria for selecting banks/accounts, and the personnel authorized to open and have access to accounts (See RC1070 MANAGING BANK RELATIONSHIPS); and
- Ensure all cash disbursements are timely and accurate.

1.8   The CFO shall enter cash account goals and results in Part IV of the TM1010-1 CASH MANAGEMENT PLAN, including daily accounts (i.e. checking), Short term accounts (i.e. money market) and long term accounts (Certificate of Deposit, Treasury Bills, Bonds). (See TM1000 WORKING CAPITAL).

2.0   CASH MANAGEMENT

2.1   The CFO shall monthly review account statements from the cash management accounts and record the required information in Part IV of the TM1010-1 CASH MANAGEMENT PLAN, including information such as the following

- Account minimum, maximum, and average balances;
- Interest rates; and
- Fees.

2.2   The CFO shall note any trends or other useful information found while recording account information and prepare analysis and reports for Top Management.

2.3   The CFO shall take action according to contingency plans if cash account trends indicate an impending shortfall.

3.0   REVIEWING THE CASH MANAGEMENT PLAN

3.1   The CFO shall review the following on a monthly basis:

- Cash management results and performance relative to established goals and objectives (especially interest rates, balances);

- Cash account dispersion and liquidity;

- Account sweep activities;

- Cash income and outlays, particularly daily cash accounts, in relation to cash forecasts and budgets; and

- Actions taken to prevent cash shortfalls.

3.2   The CFO shall present cash management activity results to Top Management at regular cash management reviews (see Section 1.1).

4.0   IMPROVING THE CASH MANAGEMENT PLAN

4.1   The CFO shall, as a result of cash management review (See Section 3.0), modify the TM1010-1 CASH MANAGEMENT PLAN as required to meet cash goals of the Company and improve cash management performance. (See RC1070 MANAGING BANK RELATIONSHIPS.)

Effectiveness Criteria:

- Effective use of cash to meet Company needs (goals and strategies).
- Total return on cash accounts.
- No cash shortfalls.
- Cash account dispersion meets Company policies and goals.

Forms/Records:

- TM1010-1 CASH MANAGEMENT PLAN
- Review Meeting Notes

References:

A. Finance Policy Manual

- Section 5.3.2 – Cash Management

B. Finance procedures

- AC1020 RISK ASSESSMENT
- FA1000 FINANCIAL OBJECTIVES
- RC1030 BANK LOANS
- RC1070 MANAGING BANK RELATIONSHIPS
- TM1000 WORKING CAPITAL

Additional Resources:

A. *Liabilities, Liquidity, and Cash Management: Balancing Financial Risks* by Dimitris N. Chorafas. John Wiley & Sons (2001). ISBN #978-0471106302.

B. *Corporate Treasury and Cash Management (Finance and Capital Markets)* by Robert Cooper. Palgrave Macmillan (2001). ISBN #978-1403916235.

Revision History:

Revision	Date	Description of Changes	Requested By
0.0	mm/dd/yyyy	Initial Release	

[This page intentionally left blank]

TM1010-1 CASH MANAGEMENT PLAN

I) Balance and Dispersion of Cash Accounts:

Policies and Goals:

_____

_____

Strategies, Activities, and Measurements:

_____

_____

II) Liquidity and Risk of Cash Accounts:

Policies and Goals:

_____

_____

Strategies, Activities, and Measurements:

_____

_____

III) Contingency Plans for Cash Shortfalls:

Policies and Goals:

_____

_____

_____

Strategies, Activities, and Measurements:

_____

_____

_____

Comments:

Completed By:

_____   Date _____

Approval:

_____   Date _____

IV) Cash Account Performance

Year _____   Completed by _____

Month	Average Balance		Minimum Balance		Maximum Balance		Int. Rate		Total Return		Fees	
Daily Accounts	Goal	Actual	Goal	Actual	Goal	Actual	Goal	Actual	Goal	Actual	Goal	Actual
January												
February												
March												
April												
May												
June												
July												
August												
September												
October												
November												
December												
Totals & Averages												

Comments/Notes:

_____

_____

Medium & Long Term Accounts

Month	Average Balance		Minimum Balance		Maximum Balance		Int. Rate		Total Return		Fees	
	Goal	Actual	Goal	Actual	Goal	Actual	Goal	Actual	Goal	Actual	Goal	Actual
Medium												
1st Quarter												
2nd Quarter												
3rd Quarter												
4th Quarter												
Totals & Averages												
Long												
1st Quarter												
2nd Quarter												
3rd Quarter												
4th Quarter												
Totals & Averages												

Comments/Notes:

Document ID **TM1020**	Title **INVENTORY MANAGEMENT**	Print Date **mm/dd/yyyy**
Revision **0.0**	Prepared By **Preparer's Name / Title**	Date Prepared **mm/dd/yyyy**
Effective Date **mm/dd/yyyy**	Reviewed By **Reviewer's Name / Title**	Date Reviewed **mm/dd/yyyy**
	Approved By **Final Approver's Name / Title**	Date Approved **mm/dd/yyyy**

Policy: The Company shall minimize inventory and minimize cost of inventory ownership, while ensuring inventory practices align with overall company financial objectives and meet operational needs.

Purpose: The purpose of inventory management is:

- To minimize and monitor inventory performance through metrics such as Days Inventory and Inventory Turns;

- To minimize and monitor Cost of Ownership;

- To ensure that inventory practices do not adversely affect the Company's financial performance; and

- To ensure that best inventory practices are employed and that they meet the Company's needs.

Scope: This procedure applies to the Finance, Accounting, Purchasing, Sales, and Operation departments, as well as other departments involved in managing inventories.

Responsibilities: The CFO (Chief Financial Officer) is responsible for overseeing the Company's financial investment in inventories and for assisting in developing and reviewing the TM1020-1 INVENTORY MANAGEMENT PLAN.

Top Management is responsible for developing inventory policies and overarching inventory goals documented in the TM1020-1 INVENTORY MANAGEMENT PLAN.

Involved Department Managers are responsible for helping to complete the review of and implementing the TM1020-1 INVENTORY MANAGEMENT PLAN.

Definitions: Inventory – Quantity of goods and materials on hand in the form of raw and purchased materials, work-in-process, and finished goods (and for retailers, resale goods); typically appears as an asset on the Company's Balance Sheet.

Work-In-Process (WIP) – All incomplete products and components in various stages of the manufacturing/assembly process.

Finished Goods – Complete products ready for sale and shipment.

Inventory Turns – The number of times that a company's inventory cycles or turns over per year. Calculation methods vary slightly depending on the type of inventory being calculated (i.e. for raw/purchased inventory: cost of materials used/average cost of materials in inventory; for finished goods inventory: cost of goods sold/average cost of goods in inventory).

Days Inventory – The average number of days of inventory on hand per accounting period (i.e. Turns per year = 365 days/Inventory turns).

Average Inventory – Usually calculated as the starting inventory number at the start of a period (week, month, quarter) minus the ending period inventory number divided by two.

Cost of Ownership – The total cost of maintaining inventory; includes the purchase price. Can include warehouse space (including utilities and maintenance), finance costs, personnel, equipment, shrinkage, obsolescence, and insurance.

Inventory Obsolescence – Inventory no longer in demand (e.g., not selling or selling at a very slow rate) or no longer used to produce product. A clear policy should be developed to dispose of obsolescent inventory items in a timely way, to remove non-performing assets from the books and eliminate the cost of ownership of unneeded items.

Procedure:

1.0   INVENTORY MANAGEMENT OVERVIEW

1.1   Inventory levels are an important facet of financial management. Carrying large inventories mean significant costs of ownership. While organizations may need to make significant investments in the materials used to make products, in products in various stage of assembly, and in complete products ready for sale, these investments should align with overall financial objectives.

1.2   The overarching goal of any organization should be to minimize inventory levels of all types through the use of best inventory management practices that meet the organizational needs and service level goals (i.e. on-time shipping), and the use of technology to provide accurate and immediate inventory information.

1.3   The CFO shall have a role in overseeing the use of the Company's financial resources into various types of inventory, including understanding how inventory practices/levels mask performance issues. For example:

HIGH LEVELS OF	INDICATE INEFFICIENCIES IN
Raw/purchased materials	Purchasing and/or supplier practices
Work in process	Manufacturing processes
Finished goods	Sales & marketing and/or customer practices

1.4   The CFO shall seek to increase inventory turns to be in inline with industry segment leaders. The higher the number of turns of any inventory type, then the more accurate measures of business performance become (no longer being masked by higher than needed inventories). Increasing inventory turns also reduces the opportunity of errors and other problems in inventory accounting techniques.

1.5   The CFO shall ensure alignment of the inventory management plan with TM1000-1 – WORKING CAPITAL PLAN (see Reference "B").

2.0   INVENTORY MANAGEMENT PLANNING

2.1   The CFO and other involved Department Managers shall meet annually with Top Management to discuss and set overarching inventory policies and practices that are best suited to meet organizational needs and goals. Inventory Management includes all types of inventory, including:

- Raw and Purchased Materials;

- Work-in-Process;

- Finished Goods; and

- Resale Goods.

2.2   The CFO shall review industry standards and benchmarks, as well as overall working capital requirements, to fulfill operational needs in order to properly establish Company inventory objectives.

2.3   The CFO shall meet with and assist Department Managers in setting inventory plans, goals, strategies, and practices (i.e. economic order quantities, safety stock) to ensure that the Company's investment in inventory aligns with its organizational and financial goals.

2.4   As a result of the meeting described in section 2.2 above, the CFO shall note specific objectives for reaching and maintaining minimal levels of inventory while meeting organizational needs and service levels (e.g., on-time shipping), including performance metrics such as:

- Days Inventory;

- Cost of Ownership;

- Obsolete and slow-moving inventory; and

- Total financial investment in inventory categories.

2.5   The CFO shall regularly meet with inventory process owners to compare actual performance or inventory processes with established inventory goals and objectives.

2.6   The CFO shall, as a result of regular meeting with (see section 2.5 above), improve inventory management, including inventory processes, measurement tools, established objectives, as required.

3.0   INVENTORY MANAGEMENT

3.1   The CFO shall note specific inventory management objectives (set through meeting with inventory managers and process owners – see section 2.3 and 2.4 above) on the TM1020-1 INVENTORY MANAGEMENT PLAN.

3.2   The CFO shall regularly (i.e. weekly, monthly) review inventory performance (from regular inventory reports) and record inventory performance information on the TM1020-2 INVENTORY MANAGEMENT RESULTS.

3.3   The CFO shall meet with related Department Managers regularly (i.e. weekly or monthly) to review inventory performance relative to established goals and objectives. The appropriate portion of Section II of the TM1020-2 INVENTORY MANAGEMENT RESULTS shall be completed during each meeting. Inventory information can be collected and reviewed according to appropriate categories, for example:

- Individual part numbers;
- Product lines or types;
- Business segments or divisions; and
- Product value streams.

4.0   REVIEWING THE INVENTORY MANAGEMENT PLAN

4.1   During the regular weekly/monthly meetings (see Section 3.3), the CFO shall review inventory's performance against stated inventory objectives in the most recent period (see TM1020-2 – INVENTORY MANAGEMENT RESULTS) with involved Department Managers.

4.2   The CFO shall discuss the following with appropriate department managers:

- Process and/or performance issues or obstacles that result in goals not regularly being reached; and
- If established goals and objectives are appropriate (unrealistic or not challenging).

4.3   The CFO shall periodically meet with members of Top Management to discuss inventory management goals and progress toward improving inventory management in light of overarching business plans and financial objectives.

5.0   IMPROVING INVENTORY MANAGEMENT

5.1   The CFO and other involved Department Managers shall, as part of the regular review meetings (see Section 4.1), discuss ways to improve inventory management methods and performance through improved practices, or discuss re-aligning objectives, particularly if performance metrics are not regularly being met. Review areas could include:

- Lean manufacturing;
- Activity analysis;
- Customer & product profitability;

- Just-in-time (JIT) inventory;
- Common parts analysis; and
- Supplier agreements

5.2   The CFO shall note any changes to inventory practices or objectives in the TM1020-1 INVENTORY MANAGEMENT PLAN and/or TM1020-2 INVENTORY MANAGEMENT RESULTS.

Effectiveness Criteria:

- Minimal raw/purchased material inventory
- Minimal work-in-process inventory
- Minimal finished goods inventory
- Low cost of ownership
- Inventory turns/days inventory

Forms/Records:

- TM1020-1 INVENTORY MANAGEMENT PLAN
- TM1020-2 INVENTORY MANAGEMENT RESULTS
- Review Meeting Notes

References:

A. Finance Policy Manual

- Section 5.3.3 – Inventory Management

B. Finance procedures

- TM1000 WORKING CAPITAL

Additional Resources:

A. Wild, Tony, Best Practice in Inventory Management, Elsevier Science (2002). ISBN 978-0750654586.

B. Muller, Max, Essentials in Inventory Management, AMACOM Press, 2nd Ed. (2011). ISBN #978-0814416556.

Revision History:

Revision	Date	Description of Changes	Requested By
0.0	mm/dd/yyyy	Initial Release	

TM1020-1 INVENTORY MANAGEMENT PLAN

Completed by _____

1) Top Management Inventory Review
Date _____

1) General Inventory Policy

_____

_____

2) General Inventory Goals

_____

_____

3) Inventory Notes/Comments

_____

_____

_____

TM1020 Inventory Management

[This page intentionally left blank]

TM1020-2 INVENTORY MANAGEMENT RESULTS

II) Monthly Inventory: Objectives - Performance - Action

Date _____   Completed by _____

Inventory Management	Objectives	Results	Actions
Raw/Purchased Materials			
Work In Process			
Finished Goods			

Comments/Notes:

_____

_____

Document ID **TM1030**	Title **RELATED PARTY TRANSACTIONS**	Print Date **mm/dd/yyyy**
Revision **0.0**	Prepared By **Preparer's Name / Title**	Date Prepared **mm/dd/yyyy**
Effective Date **mm/dd/yyyy**	Reviewed By **Reviewer's Name / Title**	Date Reviewed **mm/dd/yyyy**
	Approved By **Final Approver's Name / Title**	Date Approved **mm/dd/yyyy**
Applicable Standards/Regulations: **Security & Exchange Commission Regulation S-K Item 404(b); FASB Statement Number 57.**		

Policy: The company shall establish and follow policies for reviewing and approving related party transactions to ensure that such transactions are in the best interest of the Company and that all related party transactions meet disclosure compliance requirements.

Purpose: The purpose of this procedure is to monitor related party transactions by:

- Setting clear policies and guidelines so that all potential conflicts of interest through related party transactions are reviewed, approved, and disclosed;

- Communicating policies to affected members of the organization; and

- Complying with disclosure regulations.

Scope: This procedure applies to the Finance Department, the Board of Directors, and to all related party transactions.

Responsibilities: The Chief Financial Officer (CFO) is responsible for annually reviewing and updating related party transaction policies and procedures with Top Management and the Board of Directors; and reviewing, approving, and disclosing related party transactions. The CFO is also responsible for annually distributing the Related Party Transaction Conflict of Interest Questionnaire.

The Board of Directors shall review approved related party transactions and set auditing or monitoring practices according to the requirements of each individual case.

Definitions: Related Party Transactions – A business deal or arrangement between two parties who have an existing, prior relationship (i.e. a purchasing agent buying materials from a company owned by a spouse). Transactions that exceed $120,000 per year concerning executives, directors, and stockholders with 5% or more of Company stock (or an immediate family member) legally require disclosure to the SEC for publicly traded companies per Security & Exchange Commission Regulation S-K Item 404(b).

Securities and Exchange Commission (SEC - USA) – Government

commission created by the Securities Exchange Act of 1934 to regulate securities markets and protect investors.

Procedure:

1.0   RELATED PARTY TRANSACTIONS PLAN

1.1   The CFO shall meet with Top Management and the Board of Directors to create/review the Company policy for reviewing, approving, and reporting related party transactions. The policy shall appear in Section I of the TM1030-1 RELATED PARTY TRANSACTION POLICY & CONFLICT OF INTEREST QUESTIONNAIRE. The policy shall address relevant matters such as:

- Fairness of terms for the Company;

- Materiality of the transaction (i.e. in annual or total dollar amounts);

- Role of related party in the transaction;

- Structure of the transaction; and

- Interests of all parties to the transaction.

1.2   The CFO shall be responsible for annually creating a list of employees where potential for related party transactions may exist due to position, authorities, etc. Typically, employees who may potentially have related party transaction conflicts of interest include:

- Sales staff;

- Purchasing staff;

- Design/project engineers;

- Project Managers;

- Facility Managers;

- Director level staff and above;

- Shareholders with 5% or more of Company stock; and

- Members of the Board of Directors.

1.3   The CFO shall annually create a memo and questionnaire concerning related party transactions and send to those listed employees (see Section 1.2, above) to be completed and returned.

1.4   The CFO shall review the returned questionnaires, evaluate and tentatively approve all related party transactions, and submit them to the Board of Directors Audit Committee for review and final approval.

1.5   The CFO shall list and properly disclose all approved related party transactions as required by law.

2.0   RELATED PARTY TRANSACTIONS

2.1   The CFO shall create a TM1030-1 RELATED PARTY TRANSACTION POLICY & CONFLICT OF INTEREST QUESTIONNAIRE (with the assistance of legal council as required).

2.2   The CFO shall complete the TM1030-2 RELATED PARTY TRANSACTION QUESTIONNAIRE LOG by listing employees or others who should complete a TM1030-1 RELATED PARTY TRANSACTION POLICY & CONFLICT OF INTEREST QUESTIONNAIRE.

2.3   The CFO shall send the TM1030-1 RELATED PARTY TRANSACTION POLICY & CONFLICT OF INTEREST QUESTIONNAIRE to those listed on TM1030-2 RELATED PARTY TRANSACTION QUESTIONNAIRE LOG.

2.4   The CFO shall note the date the questionnaire is sent, the date it is returned, and verify that the questionnaire is properly signed. The CFO shall follow up every thirty days with employees who have not returned a completed and signed questionnaire.

2.5   The CFO shall collect appropriate information about related party transactions from returned questionnaires, consider and approve or disapprove individual disclosed reporting related party transactions, and complete Section III of the TM1030-1 RELATED PARTY TRANSACTION POLICY & CONFLICT OF INTEREST QUESTIONNAIRE with the following:

- A sequential number for each related party transaction for the calendar or fiscal year (i.e. 2008-001);

- Name, title or affiliation, and contact information of related party;

- The related person's interest in the transaction, including their relationship with any other entity that has an interest in the transaction;

- The approximate dollar value or annual dollar value of the transaction;

- In case of loans/debts, the outstanding principal and interest paid (or to be paid);

- Other material information deemed relevant or required;

- CFO approval and date; and

- The Board of Directors Audit Committee review and date.

2.6   The CFO shall properly disclose all related party transactions in SEC filings in accordance with applicable regulations, particularly those stipulated in SEC Regulation S-K Item 404(b), the Security Act of 1933, and the Security Exchange Act of 1934.

2.7   The CFO shall report related party transactions to the Board of Directors Audit Committee, along with the tentative approval or disapproval and supporting evidence or reasoning.

2.8   The CFO shall also disclose the Company policy and procedure for review and approval of related party transactions when filing form 10-K with the SEC.

3.0   RELATED PARTY TRANSACTIONS REVIEW

3.1   The Board of Directors Audit Committee shall review CFO-approved related party transactions to ensure that they:

- Conform to established policies and guidelines;

- Are fair and beneficial to the company;

- Comply with legal and ethical standards; and

- Verify ongoing monitoring, audit, or review requirements required for each individual related party transaction.

3.2   In accordance with procedure AC1040 EXTERNAL AUDITING and/or AC1050 INTERNAL AUDITING, the CFO shall review and investigate:

- Any audit opinion pertaining to related party transactions and purchasing processes (e.g., vendor verification and validation) that is *not "unqualified"*; and/or

- Any discovered related party transaction found after the fact not to be properly disclosed (disclosed internally or legally required disclosure).

4.0   IMPROVING RELATED PARTY TRANSACTIONS

4.1   The CFO shall be responsible for improving related party transactions process, including review, approval, and disclosures, particularly as a result of any review, monitoring, and investigations carried out as described in Section 3.0 above.

4.2   The CFO shall annually review results of related party transaction activities with the Board of Directors Audit Committee to determine improvements in related party transactions processes.

Effectiveness Criteria:

- A clear and well communicated related party transactions policy.

- All related party transactions properly reviewed and disclosed and legal requirements fulfilled.

- All affected personnel annually submit a signed related party transactions questionnaire.

Forms/Records:

- TM1030-1 RELATED PARTY TRANSACTION POLICY & CONFLICT OF INTEREST QUESTIONNAIRE

- TM1030-2 RELATED PARTY TRANSACTION QUESTIONNAIRE LOG

- Review meeting minutes and reports

References:

A. Finance Policy Manual

- Section 5.3.4 – Related Party Transactions

B. Finance procedures

- AC1040 EXTERNAL AUDITING

- AC1050 INTERNAL AUDITING

- FS1010 FINANCIAL STATEMENT REPORTING

C. **SECURITIES EXCHANGE ACT OF 1934** (USA). The Act provides for regulation of securities exchanges and over-the counter (OTC) markets operating in interstate and foreign commerce and through the mails in order to prevent "inequitable and unfair" practices on such exchanges and markets.

D. **SEC GENERAL REGULATION S-K** (17 CFR 229, USA)

E. FASB Statement of Financial Accounting Standards No. 57, "Related Party Disclosures."

Additional Resources:

A. Securities Exchange Act of 1934 available at http://www.sec.gov/about/laws/sea34.pdf.

B. Title 17, Part 240, SEC General Rules and Regulations, The Securities Exchange Act of 1934, available at: http://ecfr.gpoaccess.gov/cgi/t/text/text-idx?c=ecfr&sid=47b43cbb88844faad586861c05c81595&rgn=div5&view=text&node=17:3.0.1.1.1&idno=17.

C. Title 17, Part 229, SEC General Regulation S-K (17 CFR 229) available at http://www.sec.gov/about/forms/regs-k.pdf and http://ecfr.gpoaccess.gov/cgi/t/text/text-idx?c=ecfr&sid=20c66c74f60c4bb8392bcf9ad6fccea3&rgn=div5&view=text&node=17:2.0.1.1.11&idno=17.

D. Statement of Financial Accounting Standards No. 57 – Related Party Disclosures (Mar. 1982), available at http://www.fasb.org/pdf/fas57.pdf.

Revision History:

Revision	Date	Description of Changes	Requested By
0.0	mm/dd/yyyy	Initial Release	

TM1030-1 RELATED PARTY TRANSACTION POLICY & CONFLICT OF INTEREST QUESTIONNAIRE

I) Related Party Transactions Policy

All potential conflicts of interest through related party transactions must be reviewed and disclosed periodically to ensure that Company interests are protected. Conflict of interest may relate to you, your spouse and immediate family members, and/or associates. Conflicts of interest may arise when one party has the ability to significantly influence the management, operating policies, purchasing, or other fiscal matters, of the other; to the extent that one of the transacting parties might be prevented from fully pursuing the interests of the Company rather than his/her own separate or related-party interests.

II) Related Party Transactions Questionnaire

Considering the period from _____ to date:

	Yes[1]	No
1. I (or a party related to me) hold, directly or indirectly, a position of financial interest in an outside concern from which the organization secures goods or services.	____	____
2. I (or a related party of mine) render directive, managerial, or consultative services to, or am an employee of, any outside concern that does business with the Company.	____	____
3. I have accepted gifts or other benefits valued at $100 or more from any outside concern that does, or is seeking to do, business with the Company.	____	____
4. I have participated in management decisions concerning transactions that affect or benefit me, my family, or my personal financial interests (other than ordinary management decisions on employment matters such as compensation).	____	____
5. I (or a related party of mine) have been indebted to the Company at some time during the above stated period. If so, please note the nature, date, terms, and amount.	____	____
6. The Company has been indebted to me (or a related party of mine) at some time during the above stated period. If so, please note the nature, date, terms, and amount.	____	____

---

[1] If you answer "Yes" to any statement, please provide further explanation and information on any related-party transaction on the other side of this form.

If you answered "Yes" to any of the preceding questions, please explain and provide
   any material information on related-party transactions.

_____

_____

_____

_____

_____

_____

I have completed this questionnaire to the best extent of my knowledge. I have also read and understand the Company
policy regarding related party transactions.

_____   _____   _____
(Print Name)   (Signature)   (Date)

III) Related Party Transactions Information/Review (CFO use only)

RPT #:	Type of Transaction:	Amount of Transaction: Annually Total
Name:	Interest/Relationship with Transaction Party:	P.O./Invoice/Contract #:
Title/Affiliation: Dept/Ext:	Notes (Explain reason or advantages):	
CFO Review Date:	CFO Approval:	Audit Comm. Review Date:	Audit Comm. Approval
Review Notes & Auditing Activities			

TM1030-2 RELATED PARTY TRANSACTION QUESTIONNAIRE LOG

Year _____

Name	Title	Mail Stop/Email	Date Sent	Date Returned	Signed (√)

Comments:

Completed by:

_____ Date _____

[This page intentionally left blank]

Document ID	Title	Print Date
TM1040	**FOREIGN EXCHANGE MANAGEMENT**	**mm/dd/yyyy**
Revision	Prepared By	Date Prepared
0.0	**Preparer's Name / Title**	**mm/dd/yyyy**
Effective Date	Reviewed By	Date Reviewed
mm/dd/yyyy	**Reviewer's Name / Title**	**mm/dd/yyyy**
	Approved By	Date Approved
	Final Approver's Name / Title	**mm/dd/yyyy**

Policy: The Company shall analyze potential risks of receiving and disbursing in foreign currency and set a foreign exchange management policy that guides sound practices in dealing with foreign currency.

Purpose: To make thoughtful and intelligent decisions about foreign currency exchange that minimize the associated risk of less than expected returns or higher than expected costs due to fluctuations in exchange rates.

Scope: This procedure applies to the Finance and Accounting departments.

Responsibilities: The <u>CFO</u> (Chief Financial Officer) is responsible for assessing risks and exposure due to business conducted in foreign currency. The CFO shall prepare a report and recommendations for dealing with foreign currencies. The CFO shall follow and execute the established foreign exchange management policy.

<u>Top Management</u> and the <u>Board of Directors</u> shall review and access foreign exchange risks and policy options, and then set the Company foreign exchange management policy.

Definitions: <u>Foreign exchange risk</u> – Risk that currency movements alone may affect the value of an investment; also called "currency risk."

<u>FX</u> – Common abbreviation for "foreign currency exchange."

<u>Hedge</u> – Insure against lost revenue due to foreign currency fluctuations.

<u>Translation</u> – Actual act or method of converting one form of currency to another.

Procedure:

1.0 FOREIGN EXCHANGE MANAGEMENT PLAN

1.1 The CFO shall analyze risk or exposure from accepting or disbursing foreign currency annually or as needed, due to conditions and opportunities. Converting or translating currency (to/from US dollars, euros, yen, etc.) can diminish sales income or lead to higher-than-expected costs because of rate fluctuation – this is referred to as *currency risk* or *foreign exchange risk*. Important factors to consider in foreign exchange management include:

- Annual sales (receivables) and purchases (payables) made in foreign currencies;

- Historical volatility of any foreign currency (in relation to U.S. Dollars) in which the Company has receivables and payables; and

- Current conditions or potential future conditions that could cause volatility of particular foreign currencies or exchange rates in general.

1.2   The CFO shall annually prepare and present a report to Top Management and Board of Directors clearly describing any material risk for the Company regarding foreign currency. The report shall cover, at a minimum:

- The Company exposure in foreign currency exchange based on research and findings (particularly worst case scenarios) regarding issues listed in Section 1.1;

- Recommended strategies for making risks and exposure acceptable (according to Top Management's and Board of Director's willingness to accept risk); and

- Recommended or best methods for hedging foreign currency exchange and the best methods for translating foreign currency.

1.3   The Board of Directors, along with Top Management, shall consider the report presented by the CFO, as well as its own research and experience, and set clear policies regarding foreign currency exchange based on the Company's willingness to accept associated risk (*risk tolerance*). The policy should clearly state how each currency should be handled. Examples of hedging policies include:

- Hedge all foreign currency;

- Hedge all foreign currencies payable or receivable more than one month out;

- Never hedge particular currencies and always hedge particular currencies (accompanied by a specific list);

- Never hedge foreign currency; and

- Never accept foreign currency.

1.4   If the policy includes always hedging or sometimes hedging foreign currency, then specific recommended hedge vehicles should be included (see Additional Resource "B").

1.5   The Board of Directors and Top Management shall also set clear policies on how foreign currency shall be translated. Options include:

- Using established banks and accounts in accordance with TM1050 MANAGING BANK RELATIONSHIPS;

- Opening foreign bank accounts;

- Using currency markets or other alternate methods; and

- Using credit card accounts.

1.6   The CFO shall clearly document the foreign exchange policy prescribed by the Board of Directors and Top Management in the TM1040-1 FOREIGN EXCHANGE MANAGEMENT PLAN.

1.7   The CFO shall document the results of foreign exchange management, including analysis of alternative exchange policies, in the TM1040-2 FOREIGN EXCHANGE RESULTS. (For example, the CFO might compare the actual results of the Company's "always hedge" policy with likely results if a "never hedge" policy had been implemented.)

2.0   FOREIGN EXCHANGE MANAGEMENT

2.1   The CFO shall execute foreign exchange management in accordance with TM1040-1.

2.2   The CFO shall ensure the recording of outcomes of executing TM1040-1 on TM1040-2. Results including methods, outcomes, fees, ratings, etc., shall be recorded in a manner appropriate to the business model and business operation. For example:

- For a business recording a few large payments or receipts (e.g., a building company or a heavy equipment company), each transaction (receivable and payment) should be recorded separately.

- For a business recording a large number of payments or receipts (e.g., a clothing retailer), then transactions over a financial period (per month or per quarter) can be grouped together according to foreign currency denomination.

2.3   The CFO shall research and record the results of employing alternate foreign exchange policies and methods on the TM1040-2 FOREIGN EXCHANGE RESULTS (e.g., if the FX policy calls for always hedging, what would the result have been if "never hedge" had been the policy?)

3.0   REVIEWING FOREIGN EXCHANGE MANAGEMENT

The CFO shall conduct a review meeting annually, at a minimum, or as needed with Top Management and the Board of Directors to discuss the results of the TM1040-1 FOREIGN EXCHANGE MANAGEMENT PLAN, comparing TM1040-2 FOREIGN EXCHANGE RESULTS with plans and objectives.

4.0   IMPROVING FOREIGN EXCHANGE MANAGEMENT

4.1   Based on the results of the FX review meeting, the CFO shall make the necessary revisions to the TM1040 FOREIGN EXCHANGE MANAGEMENT PLAN, as directed by Top Management and the Board of Directors, and submit the revised plan to the Board.

4.2   On the approval of the Board, the CFO shall implement the revised Plan, continually monitoring and periodically reporting on its performance as described in section 2.0.

Effectiveness Criteria:

- Understanding and managing risk associated with business conducted in foreign currency.

- Reducing unexpected revenue loss due to currency exchange fluctuation.

Forms/Records:

- TM1040-1 FOREIGN EXCHANGE MANAGEMENT PLAN

- TM1040-2 FOREIGN EXCHANGE RESULTS

- FX Review Meeting minutes and reports

References:

A. Finance Policy Manual

- Section 5.3.5 – Foreign Exchange Management

B. Finance procedures

- TM1050 MANAGING BANK RELATIONSHIPS

Additional Resources:

A. IRS Form TD F 90-22.1, "Report of Foreign Bank Accounts," Internal Revenue Service (IRS) – http://www.irs.gov/Businesses/Small-Businesses-&-Self-Employed/Report-of-Foreign-Band-and-Financial-Accounts-FBAR.

B. Nobile, John, "Types of Currency Hedging Vehicles," (eZine article) – http://ezinearticles.com/?Types-of-Foreign-Currency-Hedging-Vehicles&id=33053.

C. Gillani, Dilshad F., "Managing Your Foreign Currency Exposure," *CMA-The Management Accounting Magazine*, Vol. 70, No. 5 (June 1996).

Revision History:

Revision	Date	Description of Changes	Requested By
0.0	mm/dd/yyyy	Initial Release	

[This page intentionally left blank]

TM1040-1 FOREIGN EXCHANGE MANAGEMENT PLAN

Date: _____ Prepared By _____

I) Foreign Currency Exposures and Risk Assessments:

Foreign Currency	Annual Sales or Purchases (U.S. $)	Historical Volatility (High-Medium-Low)	Currency Exchange Risks (High-Medium-Low)	Exchange Policy Notes

Comments:

_____

_____

_____

II) General Description of Foreign Exchange Risk : _____

_____

_____

_____

_____

III) General Statement of Foreign Exchange
Policy: _____

_____

_____

_____

_____

IV) General Description of Translation Method Policy : _____

_____

_____

_____

_____

Comments:

_____

_____

_____

Approval: _____ **Date:** _____

_____ **Date** _____

TM1040-2 FOREIGN EXCHANGE RESULTS

Fiscal Year _____   Prepared By _____

Transaction	Method	Amount	FX From	FX To	Net Result
	Actual				
	Alternative 1				
	Alternative 2				
	Actual				
	Alternative 1				
	Alternative 2				
	Actual				
	Alternative 1				
	Alternative 2				
	Actual				
	Alternative 1				
	Alternative 2				
	Actual				
	Alternative 1				
	Alternative 2				
	Actual				
	Alternative 1				
	Alternative 2				
	Actual				
	Alternative 1				
	Alternative 2				
	Actual				
	Alternative 1				
	Alternative 2				
	Actual				
	Alternative 1				
	Alternative 2				
	Actual				
	Alternative 1				
	Alternative 2				

Comments:

_____

_____

_____

[This page intentionally left blank]

Document ID **TM1050**	Title **MANAGING BANK RELATIONSHIPS**	Print Date **mm/dd/yyyy**
Revision **0.0**	Prepared By **Preparer's Name / Title**	Date Prepared **mm/dd/yyyy**
Effective Date **mm/dd/yyyy**	Reviewed By **Reviewer's Name / Title**	Date Reviewed **mm/dd/yyyy**
	Approved By **Final Approver's Name / Title**	Date Approved **mm/dd/yyyy**

Policy: The Company shall meet regularly with bank managers to determine optimal banks and banking services to meet business needs.

Purpose: To ensure the Company is maximizing the benefits of its bank-business relationship by:

- Taking advantage of useful banking services and accounts; and
- Maximizing return on bank-held assets while minimizing the cost of banking.

Scope: This procedure applies to the Finance department.

Responsibilities: The Chief Financial Officer (CFO) is responsible for managing banking relationships.

Top Management is responsible for overseeing banking relations and approving bank management authorities (e.g., ability to open, close accounts).

Definitions: Sweep Account – Bank account that, at the close of each business day, automatically transfers funds that exceed or fall short of a specified amount into or from a higher-interest earning account.

Procedure:

1.0   BANK RELATIONSHIP PLAN

1.1   The CFO shall regularly review the Company's banking needs, determining requirements and ascertaining banks and banking services available in the marketplace. Such a review should include:

- Account statements;
- Usage reports;
- Company needs (e.g. business plan, working capital plan, cash management plan);
- Bank web pages and promotional materials;
- Business banking literature, seminars, and presentations; and
- Information from peers and through networking.

1.2   The CFO shall create a schedule to review banking service needs (e.g., semiannually), meeting with managers from banks where the Company has accounts, as well as banks where the Company does not currently have an account. For example, the CFO may set a goal of meeting with the current bank and at least one *potential* banking partner during each review cycle.

1.3   The CFO shall meet with bank managers to discuss and review banking issues important to the company, such as:

- Pending or future needs for financing or lines of credit;

- The range of services, locations, convenience, benefits, etc.;

- Fees and costs for accounts and services;

- Match of accounts and account types to Company needs (e.g., sweep accounts, interest rates, fees);

- Managing merchant accounts, foreign exchange, or other business needs; and

- Other items of note discovered during the review of statements, reports, bank promotional materials and websites, literature review, and other sources of information.

1.4   The CFO shall invite the CEO, Controller, or other managers involved with bank relationships to attend meetings with bank managers as deemed appropriate and necessary.

1.5   The CFO shall note the results of meetings with bank managers for use as a reference in meeting the Company's banking needs.

1.6   The CFO shall manage the banking relationships based the overarching benefit it brings to the Company when all factors (those listed in Section 1.3, as well as aspects such as relationship history, service level, and industry standing) are considered.

2.0   MANAGING BANK RELATIONSHIPS

2.1   The CFO shall record the desired meeting schedule (i.e. quarterly or annually) in the TM1050-1 BANKING RELATIONSHIP CONTACT MANAGEMENT LOG.

2.2   According to the schedule, the CFO shall list all banks with which the Company has existing accounts in the TM1050-1 BANKING RELATIONSHIP CONTACT MANAGEMENT LOG, and banks with which the Company may consider creating a relationship (see Section 1.3).

2.3   The CFO shall set appointments with bank managers with banks listed in the TM1050-1 BANKING RELATIONSHIP CONTACT MANAGEMENT LOG, and note each scheduled appointment.

2.4   Prior to a meeting with a bank manager, the CFO shall create a meeting agenda on the TM1050-2 BANKING RELATIONSHIP MEETING AGENDA/MINUTES, and forward the agenda to the appropriate bank manager at least one business day prior to the meeting. Typical agenda items should reflect the following:

- Items such as those listed in Section 1.3, above;

- Comparisons of these items with competitors and alternatives;

- Specific and general Company needs; and

- Company goals and expectations in banking relationships.

2.5   The CFO shall meet with bank managers according the schedule set in the TM1050-1 BANKING RELATIONSHIP CONTACT MANAGEMENT LOG, and record noteworthy items, actions, and results from each meeting in the Minutes portion of the TM1050-2 BANKING RELATIONSHIP MEETING AGENDA/MINUTES.

2.6   After each bank manager meeting, the CFO shall update the TM1050-1 BANKING RELATIONSHIP CONTACT MANAGEMENT LOG with the date of the meeting.

3.0   REVIEWING BANK RELATIONSHIPS

3.1   After meeting with the bank managers, the CFO shall review the Company needs in relation to the services offered by each bank (see Sections 1.2, 1.4, and 2.4). The CFO shall evaluate the information to ensure the Company's needs are being met, and/or what changes in bank supplied services seem warranted after considering all factors.

3.2   The CFO shall annually review the TM1050-1 BANKING RELATIONSHIP CONTACT MANAGEMENT LOG and the TM1050-2 BANKING RELATIONSHIP MEETING AGENDA/MINUTES to verify the following:

- Are bank relationship meetings taking place according to schedule?

- Are agendas being forwarded to bank managers prior to the meeting?

- Is the meeting schedule appropriate (i.e., should meeting frequency be increased or decreased)?

- Are there tangible, useful, and positive results of regular meetings (e.g., greater awareness of: better suited accounts or services; cost/fee savings; quick, problem-free loans; line-of-credit approvals)?

4.0   IMPROVING THE MANAGEMENT OF BANK RELATIONSHIPS

4.1   As a result of reviewing bank relationships (see Section 3.1), the CFO may improve banking services by shifting accounts within or between banks, based on authorization and management approval requirements.

4.2   As a result of reviewing the bank relationship management process (see Section 3.2), the CFO shall make any necessary improvement to this procedure, the TM1050-1 BANKING RELATIONSHIP CONTACT MANAGEMENT LOG, or the TM1050-2 BANKING RELATIONSHIP MEETING AGENDA/MINUTES forms. Revisions shall be implemented only after review by and approval of Top Management.

Effectiveness Criteria:

- Regular meetings with bank managers.

- A clear understanding of the relationship and coordination of bank services and Company banking needs.

- Proactive planning and management of bank services to receive the most benefit and return while minimizing costs.

- Using bank relationships to enhance cash management and working capital.

Forms/Records:

- TM1050-1 BANKING RELATIONSHIP CONTACT MANAGEMENT LOG

- TM1050-2 BANKING RELATIONSHIP MEETING AGENDA/MINUTES

References:

A. Finance Policy Manual

- Section 5.3.6 – Managing Banking Relationships

B. Finance procedures

- RC1030 BANK LOANS
- TM1000 WORKING CAPITAL
- TM1010 CASH MANAGEMENT

Additional Resources:

A. Platz, Theodore A., and Fitch, Thomas, <u>Business Banking</u>, Barron's Educational Series (2nd Edition, 2001). ISBN-13 # 978-0-7641-1398-7

Revision History:

Revision	Date	Description of Changes	Requested By
0.0	mm/dd/yyyy	Initial Release	

TM1050-1 BANKING RELATIONSHIP CONTACT MANAGEMENT LOG

Date _____   Completed by _____

I) Bank Meeting Schedule

Bank	Meeting Frequency	Manager Name	Contact Information

II) Bank Meeting Plan/Log

Manager Name/Bank	Scheduled Meeting Date	Actual Meeting Date	Notes

[This page intentionally left blank]

TM1050-2 BANKING RELATIONSHIP MEETING AGENDA/MINUTES

I) Meeting Agenda

Date _____   Time _____   Location _____

Invited Attendees/Participants:

_____

_____

_____

Topics:

_____

_____

_____

_____

_____

_____

_____

_____

_____

_____

_____

_____

II) Meeting Minutes

Actual Attendees/Participants:

_____

_____

_____

Minutes/Notes:

_____

_____

_____

_____

_____

_____

_____

_____

_____

_____

_____

_____

Completed by _____   Date _____

Document ID **TM1060**	Title **MERCHANT ACCOUNTS**	Print Date **mm/dd/yyyy**
Revision **0.0**	Prepared By **Preparer's Name / Title**	Date Prepared **mm/dd/yyyy**
Effective Date **mm/dd/yyyy**	Reviewed By **Reviewer's Name / Title**	Date Reviewed **mm/dd/yyyy**
	Approved By **Final Approver's Name / Title**	Date Approved **mm/dd/yyyy**

Policy: The Company shall plan for, monitor, and review its merchant accounts in order to ensure the greatest value for the service.

Purpose: To ensure the selection of a merchant account that meets the Company's need to balance best service and lowest cost.

Scope: This procedure applies to the Finance Department.

Responsibilities: The Chief Financial Officer (CFO) is responsible for overseeing the selection of merchant accounts and for conducting periodic reviews of merchant accounts.

Definitions: Merchant Account – Service provider that processes credit card payments for a merchant (business), such as our Company.

        Chargeback – Reversal of a credit card transaction; can be accompanied by penalties and fees to the merchant.

        Discount Rate – Fee paid by the merchant as a percentage of the transaction amount (e.g., 3%).

        Fixed Transaction Fee – Flat fee paid by a merchant on every transaction.

        Holdback – Percentage of transactions paid by the merchant and held by the merchant account provider to cover any transaction related dispute. Funds in the "holdback account" are released to the merchant at a predetermined time (e.g., after six (6) months).

Procedure:

1.0 MERCHANT ACCOUNT PLAN

1.1 The CFO shall periodically (e.g., annually) review the Company's use of merchant accounts, to ensure that the Company is receiving the required service level and that fees are competitive. A small reduction in fees can result in significant overall savings, especially for high volume and high dollar amount transactions; however, cost must be balanced with the level of service. Credit card transactions must be conducted swiftly and smoothly, and without interruption of service.

1.2 The CFO shall periodically review existing and potential merchant account providers, considering and comparing attributes such as:

  • Monthly fixed fees;

- Discount rates;
- Fixed transaction fees;
- Chargebacks;
- Termination fees and contract requirements;
- Accuracy and timeliness of the existing merchant account's processing and reporting; and
- Return fees and policies.

1.3   The CFO shall create a total cost estimate for each month or quarter based on fee information gathered (Section 1.2), using historical merchant account use and projecting future use.

1.4   The CFO shall create a method for evaluating merchant account service levels (for example, listing key service areas required by the Company and rating availability of the service by existing and potential merchant accounts). Examples of important service features include:

- Chargebacks;
- Customer service availability (responsiveness, speed of resolution);
- Ease of use;
- Reliability; and
- Holdback policies.

1.5   Based on the review of overall fees and service levels (see Sections 1.1, 1.2), the CFO shall:

- Continue the existing merchant account under the current terms;
- Attempt to renegotiate terms with the existing merchant account; or
- Find and negotiate with an alternate merchant account provider.

2.0   MERCHANT ACCOUNT COMPARISONS

2.1   The CFO shall annually complete the TM1060-1 MERCHANT ACCOUNT REVIEW with existing and potential merchant account provider's fee information.

2.2   The CFO shall calculate the estimated total fees per period (e.g., month, quarter) for existing and potential merchant account providers and record the estimated total fees on TM1060-1. The CFO shall consider the following when calculating estimates:

- Information about the various merchant account fees;
- Historical merchant account use;
- Projected future merchant account use;

2.3   The CFO shall list and rate important service features of existing and potential merchant account provider's on the TM1060-1 MERCHANT ACCOUNT REVIEW form (see Section 1.4).

3.0   MERCHANT ACCOUNT COMPARISON REVIEW

3.1   The CFO shall use the information on the TM1060-1 form to determine if any action is required in the Company's merchant account provider (see Section 1.5).

3.2   The CFO shall list reasons and justifications for the decision to continue, renegotiate, or change merchant accounts on TM1060-1.

4.0   MERCHANT ACCOUNT IMPROVEMENTS

4.1   The CFO shall make changes and adjustments to its merchant accounts, in accordance with the decision described on TM1060-1.

4.2   As part of the annual merchant provider review, the CFO shall (re)evaluate the merchant provider evaluation process, to ensure its continuing suitability and usefulness. The CFO shall be responsible for making any recognized improvement to this procedure and the associated form TM1060-1 to enhance the merchant account review/selection process.

Effectiveness Criteria:

- Lowest merchant account total fees
- Effective merchant account service
- Merchant account ease of use

Forms/Records:

- TM1060-1 MERCHANT ACCOUNT REVIEW

- Meeting minutes and reports

References:

A. Finance Policy Manual

- Section 5.3.7 – Merchant Accounts

Additional Resources:

A. Carroll, Jim, and Broadhead, Rick, Selling Online: How to Become a Successful E-Commerce Merchant, Dearborn Trade, a Kaplan Professional Company, 2001. ISBN #978-0793145171.

B. Ogden, Anthony L., What Every Business Should Know About Accepting Credit Cards, BankCardLaw Media Corp., June, 2004. ISBN # 978-0975960509.

C. "Choosing an Internet Merchant Account", available at http://www.findmyhosting.com/web-resources/Articles/internet-merchant.htm.

D. "How to Choose a Merchant Account Provider," NFIB.com (July 17, 2013) – http://www.nfib.com/article/how-to-choose-a-merchant-account-provider-63319/

E. Hayes, Mark, "How to Ensure Your Merchant Account Application Is Approved," Shopify Ecommerce blog (Sept. 25, 2012) – http://www.shopify.com/blog/6614567-how-to-ensure-your-merchant-account-application-is-approved#axzz2vai8Nrjl

Revision History:

Revision	Date	Description of changes	Requested By
0.0	mm/dd/yyyy	Initial Release	

TM1060-1 MERCHANT ACCOUNT REVIEW

1. Merchant Account Fees

Merchant Account Provider	Fixed Fees	Discount Rate	Transaction Fees	Termination Fees	Misc. Fees	Estimated Total Fees (per period)

Comments:

2. Merchant Account Services

Merchant Account Provider List Specific Service Feature —>	Service Feature 1	Service Feature 2	Service Feature 3	Service Feature 4

Comments:

Decisions, Justifications, and Actions for Merchant Accounts

_____

_____

_____

Approval:

_____   Date _____

[This page intentionally left blank]

Document ID TM1070	Title LETTERS OF CREDIT	Print Date mm/dd/yyyy
Revision 0.0	Prepared By Preparer's Name / Title	Date Prepared mm/dd/yyyy
Effective Date mm/dd/yyyy	Reviewed By Reviewer's Name / Title	Date Reviewed mm/dd/yyyy
	Approved By Final Approver's Name / Title	Date Approved mm/dd/yyyy

Policy:
The Company shall ensure Letters of Credit are consistently processed in an efficient and timely manner, avoiding unnecessary delays in payments or shipments.

Purpose:
To develop and build best practices in processing a Letter of Credit quickly and efficiently in order to process foreign transactions where a known or unclear level of risk prohibits normal purchasing and sales processes.

Scope:
This procedure applies to the Finance, Accounting, Purchasing, and Sales departments, or other departments involved in using a Letter of Credit to process transactions.

Responsibilities:
The Chief Financial Officer (CFO) is responsible for setting and overseeing the process of providing and/or receiving a Letter of Credit, and is responsible for all related bank communication and transactions.

Department Managers are responsible for following the proper procedure for issuing or receiving a Letter of Credit.

Definitions:
Letter of Credit – Bank monitored/controlled exchange of funds for a product or service, typically used in international trade where performance is considered a risk.

Bill of Lading – Legal document prepared by a carrier, as a contract, accepting goods for transport from the shipping party. It details the type, quantity and destination of the good being carried and serves as a receipt of shipment when the good is delivered. It accompanies the shipped goods, no matter the form of transportation, and must be signed by an authorized representative from the carrier, the shipper and the receiver.

Warranty Title – Legal statement from the seller that the title being conveyed is good and the transfer is legal and rightful.

Letter of Indemnity – Letter typically issued by the issuing bank protecting the buyer in the case the seller fails to deliver the goods/services as promised (fails to perform).

Issuing Bank – Bank selected and used by the buyer to reserve, and then issue funds, after evidence of successful performance by the seller (typically, delivery of required documents including a Bill of Lading from a contracted carrier).

Advising Bank – Selected by the seller to accept and review documents provided by the seller that provide evidence of performance. It then forwards the documents to the issuing bank to prompt the transfer of funds from the issuing bank (set up by the buyer) to the advising bank for eventual payment to the seller.

Carrier – A company in the business of transporting freight.

Procedure:

1.0   LETTER OF CREDIT PLAN

1.1   A Letter of Credit, due to the time and expense involved, shall be used as a last resort for conducting transactions. The CFO, Purchasing, Sales, or other department manager shall use this highly secure method of delivering or receiving payment only when they believe there is a less-than-acceptable risk (typically with an off-shore provider/receiver) in the performance of the other party.

1.2   The CFO shall be responsible for creating and maintaining the TM1070-1 LETTER OF CREDIT CHECKLIST, which lists the requirements for accepting a Letter of Credit for deliverables, or for creating a Letter of Credit for purchases.

1.3   The CFO or other Department Manager (i.e. Sales, Operations) shall use the TM1070-1 LETTER OF CREDIT CHECKLIST to ensure that the terms of the sale are clearly listed and agreed upon between the buyer and seller, including:

- Quantity;
- Price;
- Part numbers;
- Descriptions and nomenclature;
- Payment terms;
- Ship date, mode of transport, and delivery date; and
- Expiration date of the Letter of Credit.

1.4   The CFO or Department Manager shall use TM1070-1 to ensure that the required documents needed to complete the Letter of Credit are clearly listed and agreed upon between the buyer and seller, including:

- Invoice;
- Bill of Lading;
- Warranty Title; and
- A Letter of Indemnity.

1.5   The CFO or other Department Manager shall use TM1070-1 LETTER OF
        CREDIT CHECKLIST for issuing as Buyer or accepting as Seller a Letter of
        Credit. Both shall reflect the basic Letter of Credit process:

- Buyer and Seller negotiate clear terms, documentation requirements, and
  schedule for the Letter of Credit, and this information is listed on TM1070-1;
- Buyer creates a Letter of Credit draft for the agreed amount of purchase in
  cooperation with an issuing bank using established credit, deposit, or a
  holding or reserve account;
- After the Buyer and Seller both agree to the terms and the required
  documentation (listed on TM1070-1) and review a Letter of Credit draft (if
  required); the buyer then proceeds with having the issuing bank create a Letter
  of Credit and transmitting it to the advising bank, which authenticates it;
- After the Letter of Credit is established, authenticated, and received by the
  advising bank and the seller, the seller ships the ordered goods with a carrier
  (receiving a bill of lading), then sends the required document set required by
  the Letter of Credit and listed on TM1070-1 to the advising bank;
- Advising bank verifies the documentation in accordance with the terms of the
  Letter of Credit, then releases the funds set forth in the Letter of Credit to the
  seller;
- Advising bank forwards documentation to issuing bank, which, upon
  verification, transfers or releases the appropriate funds to the advising bank;
  and
- Issuing bank delivers the documents to the buyer (and closes out any required
  payments or other transactions), which then allows the buyer to claim or
  arrange delivery of the purchased goods from the carrier.

2.0   EXECUTING A LETTER OF CREDIT AS A BUYER

2.1   The CFO shall approve the use of the Letter of Credit and ensure that TM1070-1
        is employed each time the Company uses a Letter of Credit as a buyer.

2.2   If the Company is the buyer, the CFO, purchasing manager, or appropriate
        department manager (acting as the buyer) shall collect the necessary information
        from the seller to complete the TM1070-1.

2.3   The CFO or manager acting as the buyer shall send the TM1070-1 to the seller to
        ensure all the required information is present and correct for the Company to
        generate a Letter of Credit. The seller shall confirm the information is correct by
        completing the Seller section at the bottom of the TM1070-1 and returning it to
        the CFO or manager acting as the buyer.

2.4   The CFO or manager acting as the buyer shall review a draft of the Letter of
        Credit (if needed) before final approval, particularly if the Company rarely uses or
        receives a Letter of Credit.

2.5   When TM1070-1 is complete and all terms/documentation is agreed upon
        between the Company and the seller (and the Letter of Credit draft is reviewed
        and approved as required), the CFO or other authorized Finance/Accounting
        Department manager shall create the Letter of Credit with the selected issuing

bank, and note on TM1070-1 LETTER OF CREDIT CHECKLIST the date of issuance and anticipated date of completion (delivery of funds to the seller) and expected delivery date.

2.6   The CFO or authorized Finance/Accounting Department manager shall note on TM1070-1 the date the Letter of Credit is complete, and should record in Comments/Notes section any problems, delays, or other issues with the execution of the Letter of Credit, and what corrective actions were required to expedite the Letter of Credit.

3.0   EXECUTING A LETTER OF CREDIT AS A SELLER

3.1   The CFO shall approve the use of the Letter of Credit and ensure that TM1070-1 is employed each time the Company uses a Letter of Credit as a seller.

3.2   If the Company is the seller, the CFO, sales manager, or appropriate department manager (acting as the seller) shall complete TM1070-1.

3.3   The CFO or manager acting as the seller shall send TM1070-1 to the buyer in order to verify that all the required information appears and is correct, and will allow the buyer to generate a Letter of Credit. The buyer shall complete the Buyer section at the bottom of TM1070-1, verifying the information is correct, and return it to the CFO or manager acting as the seller.

3.4   When TM1070-1 is complete and all terms/documentation are agreed upon between the Company and the buyer, then the CFO or other authorized Finance/Accounting Department manager shall coordinate acceptance of the Letter of Credit with the selected advising bank, and note on TM1070-1 the anticipated date of issuance and date of completion (delivery of funds to the seller).

3.5   The CFO or other manager acting as the seller shall note on TM1070-1 the date that the Letter of Credit is complete, and should record in Comments/Notes section any problems, delays, or other issues with the execution of the Letter of Credit, and what actions were required to correct them or to expedite the Letter of Credit.

4.0   REVIEWING THE LETTER OF CREDIT PROCESS

The CFO shall review the Letter of Credit process with the managers and personnel involved with executing the Letter of Credit process to determine if there were delays or additional efforts required to complete the Letter of Credit transaction. For example:

- Was all the required information clearly negotiated and recorded between the buyer and seller through using TM1070-1?

- Was all the required documentation recognized and agreed upon between the buyer and seller, through the use of the checklist, while initializing or setting up the Letter of Credit?

- Were any amendments required to complete the Letter of Credit?

- Were there any problems or oversights in generating or receiving a Letter of Credit that resulted in delays, or extra time and effort, in completing the Letter of Credit?

- Are there any ways to reduce or combine required steps to streamline the process?

5.0 IMPROVING THE LETTER OF CREDIT PROCESS

The CFO shall, as a result of the review of the Letter of Credit process and of TM1070-1 LETTER OF CREDIT CHECKLIST, including investigating root causes for delays or other problems, modify the policy, procedure, and/or TM1070-1, as needed, to improve timely and efficient execution of a Letter of Credit.

Effectiveness Criteria:

- Efficient and effective use of Letters of Credit when required.
- Letters of Credit completed according to plan/schedule, with no problems or delays requiring additional time and effort to resolve.

Forms/Records:

- TM1070-1 LETTER OF CREDIT CHECKLIST
- The bank's Letter of Credit

References:

A. Finance Policy Manual

  - Section 5.3.8 – Letters of Credit

B. Finance Procedures

  - TM1050 MANAGING BANK RELATIONSHIPS

Revision History:

Revision	Date	Description of Changes	Requested By
0.0	mm/dd/yyyy	Initial Release	

TM1070-1 LETTER OF CREDIT CHECKLIST[1]

Date _____   Completed by _____
Seller _____   For Department _____

Letter of Credit (LOC) Requirements	Name/Number/...	√	Notes
Information			
Part Number			
Nomenclature/Description			
Quantity			
Unit Price			
Total Price			
Shipping/Handling/Other Fees			
Terms/ LOC Expiration			
Shipment Date			
Delivery Date			
Transport Mode(s)			
Documentation			
Invoice			
Bill of Lading			
Warranty Title			
Letter of Indemnity			
Purchase Order			
Other			
Issuing Bank			
Advising Bank			
Projected Completion Date			
Actual Completion Date			

Comments/Notes (particularly delays, additional efforts):

Seller: The information above is sufficient and correct for accepting a Letter of Credit.
Name (printed)_____   Title_____
Signature_____   Date_____
Company_____   Location_____

_____
[1] Buyer's copy

TM1070-1 LETTER OF CREDIT CHECKLIST[2]

Date _____   Completed by _____

Buyer _____   For Department _____

Letter of Credit (LOC) Requirements	Name/Number/...	√	Notes
Information			
Part Number			
Nomenclature/Description			
Quantity			
Unit Price			
Total Price			
Shipping/Handling/Other Fees			
Terms/ LOC Expiration			
Shipment Date			
Delivery Date			
Transport Mode(s)			
Documentation			
Invoice			
Bill of Lading			
Warranty Title			
Letter of Indemnity			
Purchase Order			
Other			
Issuing Bank			
Advising Bank			
Projected Completion Date			
Actual Completion Date			

Comments/Notes (particularly delays, additional efforts):

Buyer: The information above is sufficient and correct for generating a Letter of Credit.

Name (printed)_____   Title_____

Signature_____   Date_____

Company_____   Location_____

---

[2] Seller's copy

Finance Policies and Procedures

Section 430

Financial Statements

Section 430
Financial Statements

Document ID **FS1000**	Title **FINANCIAL FORECASTING**	Print Date **mm/dd/yyyy**
Revision **0.0**	Prepared By **Preparer's Name / Title**	Date Prepared **mm/dd/yyyy**
Effective Date **mm/dd/yyyy**	Reviewed By **Reviewer's Name / Title**	Date Reviewed **mm/dd/yyyy**
	Approved By **Final Approver's Name / Title**	Date Approved **mm/dd/yyyy**

Policy: The Company shall conduct financial forecasting and create projected or forecasted financial statements (forecasted statements) to assist with proper financial planning and management.

Purpose: To make thoughtful and intelligent predictions regarding revenue and expenses that allow for capital planning, creating budgets, and financial management that aligns with overall Company objectives and strategies, and that help ensure the financial resources for operating the business are in place.

Scope: This procedure applies to the Finance and Accounting departments.

Responsibilities: The Chief Financial Officer (CFO) is responsible for preparing forecasted financial statements, and for preparing reports and recommendations to Top Management and the Board of Directors concerning forecasted financial statements.

Top Management from key departments such as Sales and Operations is responsible for providing the CFO with projections regarding sales and operations that are necessary for financial forecasting.

The Chief Executive Officer (CEO), Top Management, and the Board of Directors are responsible for reviewing financial forecasts and forecasted financial statements.

Definitions: Balanced Scorecard – Analysis technique designed to translate the Company's mission statement and overall business strategy into specific, quantifiable goals and monitor the Company's performance in terms of achieving those goals.

Forecasted Financial Statements – Statements that have the format of financial statements (balance sheet, income statement, statement of cash flows), but give projections or forecasts instead of actual end-of-period figures.

United States Securities and Exchange Commission (SEC) – A government commission created by the Securities Exchange Act of 1934 to regulate securities markets (stocks, bonds, derivatives, etc.) and protect investors.

Public Company – Company that has issued securities (transferable

interest representing financial value) through an initial public
offering (IPO), which are traded on at least one stock exchange or
over-the-counter market; also referred to as a "publicly traded
company."

Procedure:

1.0   FINANCIAL FORECASTING PLAN

1.1   The CFO shall create financial forecasts (forecasted financial statements at a
minimum) at least once per year. The CFO shall re-forecast and rework
forecasted financial statements if there is a major change that will affect
forecasting or budget accuracy, such as:

- An acquisition or merger;

- Purchase or sale of major properties or assets;

- Loss or gain of major customers; or

- A substantial change in the general financial picture (e.g., interest rates,
exchange rates, significant market fluctuations).

1.2   The CFO shall list all required forecasts and forecasted financial statements on a
Financial Forecast Checklist that, at minimum, should include:

- Sales forecasts, production plans, and cost estimates;

- Forecasted Income Statement;

- Forecasted Statement of Cash Flows (annual);

- Period budgets (monthly and quarterly);

- Forecasted Balance Sheet; and

- Assumptions on which forecasts are based.

1.3   The CFO shall receive sales projections from Sales management and production
plans and cost projections from Operations management.

1.4   The CFO shall review the financial forecasts with Top Management and the
Board of Directors and modify financial forecasts, as required.

1.5   For public companies (US), the CFO shall submit financial forecasts to the SEC
as required by law. For public *and* private companies, the CFO shall submit
financial forecasts to federal, state, and local governments, as required.

The CFO shall submit financial forecasts to business partners (e.g., banks,
investors, creditors) in accordance with contractual and/or regulatory
requirements.

1.6   The CFO shall use the information from financial forecasts to ensure the financial
needs of the Company are met through the coming business year.

2.0   COLLECTING INFORMATION FOR FINANCIAL FORECASTS

2.1   The CFO shall list on the FS1000-1 FINANCIAL FORECAST CHECKLIST all the required items and information needed to complete the financial forecast process, and note the date and other relative information when these items are received.

2.2   The CFO shall receive sales projections for the coming fiscal year from Sales Management at least ninety days prior to the end of the current fiscal year,[1] including:

- Sales projections per quarter; and

- Sales projections by product, product line, or type.

In addition, Sales Management shall provide clear notes and descriptions about any *assumptions* on which those projections are based and the associated *risks*.

2.3   The CFO shall review sales projections with Top Management to ensure that:

- Sales projections align with overall company strategies, objectives, and business plans; and

- They account for potential constraints on growth (e.g., ability to raise capital, physical and human resource capacity, absorption).

2.4   The CFO shall receive operation or production plans and operational cost projections from the operations or production manager within 30 days after the review and finalization of the sales projections, and shall include:

- Number of facilities;

- Number of production lines;

- Number of employees;

- Notes on what assumptions are being made that affect production plans;

- Fixed overhead and administrative expenses;

- Flexible expenses bases on sales, materials, and production; and

- Assumptions that may affect expenses.

2.5   The CFO shall review operations and cost projections with Top Management to ensure that they align with overarching company strategies, goals, objectives, and capabilities.

2.6   Once sales and operation/cost projections are complete and have been reviewed and accepted by Top Management, the CFO shall create financial forecasts and forecasted statements.

---

[1] A number of variables (size/complexity of forecasts, etc.) may affect the lead time for projections.

3.0   CREATING FINANCIAL FORECASTS

3.1   The CFO shall list all the required financial forecasts, as well as the information needed to complete the financial forecast process, on the FS1000-1 FINANCIAL FORECAST CHECKLIST.

3.2   CFO shall use the projected sales and costs to create pro-forma financial statements and budgets:

- Sales and costs projections used to create forecasted income statement;

- Forecasted income statement used to complete a forecasted statement of cash flows;

- Forecasted statement of cash flows to create cash budgets for each designated financial period (months, quarters); and

- Forecasted income statement and forecasted statement of cash flows used to create a forecasted balance sheet.

3.3   As forecast items are completed, the CFO shall note information on each document, forecast, and forecasted statement listed on FS1000-1 FINANCIAL FORECAST CHECKLIST, including:

- The date on which the item was completed;

- The required submission date for that item;

- The organization/person/agency requiring (requesting) the item;

- The actual submission date; and

- Any relevant notes regarding the item.

4.0   REVIEWING AND COMPLETING FINANCIAL FORECASTS

4.1   The CFO shall hold a review meeting with the CEO and Top Management prior to the end of the fiscal year to present and review the financial forecasts for the coming fiscal year, particularly in light of Company strategies, goals objectives, and the balanced scorecard.

4.2   The CFO shall revise the financial forecasts as agreed necessary and prudent by the CEO, CFO, and Top Management.

4.3   The CFO shall complete and release the final versions of the forecasted financial statements listed on FS1000-1 FINANCIAL FORECAST CHECKLIST, as required and in the required formats; for example:

- For internal purposes (such as for the CEO, Top Management, the Board of Directors, partners, etc.);

- For public companies (USA), submission to the SEC in accordance with Regulation S-X, Article 11;

- Submission to other federal, state, and local governments and regulatory bodies, as required; and/or

- For reporting to creditors, investors, banks, or other interested parties.

5.0   FINANCIAL RE-FORECASTING

5.1   The CFO should review – and update, if necessary – the Company's pro forma financial statements periodically (e.g., quarterly) or whenever a significant event that may have an effect on the accuracy of the current forecast occurs. The CFO should consider events/issues such as:

- Acquisitions or mergers;

- Possible purchase/sale of major properties or assets;

- Losing or gaining major customers; and

- Substantial changes in the business/financial environment (e.g., interest rate fluctuations, market trends).

5.2   If forecasting revisions are necessary, the CFO shall request revised/updated sales projections from Sales management and revised/updated cost projections from Production (Operations) management. After receiving the requested revisions/ updates, the CFO shall revise pro forma statements and related forecast documents listed on FS1000-1 FINANCIAL FORECAST CHECKLIST.

5.3   On FS1000-1, the CFO shall clearly indicate revision dates for pro forma financial statements and related documents, revision ID's (where applicable), as well as which forecasted financial statements are superseded and their original dates of publication.

5.4   The CFO shall send the revised pro forma statements and related documentation to all parties identified on FS1000-1 FINANCIAL FORECAST CHECKLIST as having received original pro forma financial statements and related material.

6.0   IMPROVING THE FINANCIAL FORECASTING PROCESS

6.1   The CFO shall periodically review the process of creating financial forecasts and forecasted financial statements, considering issues such as:

- How correct and accurate previous financial forecasts have been at successfully projecting financial information for financial management and budgeting, and how can it be improved for future financial forecasts;

- Whether the information available to the CFO was accurate and timely; and

- How the accuracy and availability of information related to creating financial forecasts might be improved.

6.2   After reviewing the success or accuracy of previous financial forecasts, as well as reviewing the process, the CFO should develop improvements to the financial forecasting procedure, as needed, and submit the revised procedure to Top Management and/or the Board of Directors for review and approval. On approval of the revised process, the CFO shall ensure its timely implementation.

6.3 The CFO shall review FS1030-1 FINANCIAL FORECAST CHECKLIST near the end of each fiscal year,[2] verifying that all required forecast documents are listed and that all listed documents are created and submitted, as required.

Effectiveness Criteria:

- Financial forecasts and forecasted financial statements created according to established plan.
- Improving financial forecasting accuracy through reviewing and reflecting on the forecasting process.
- Information required to create forecasts available in a timely manner.

Forms/Records:

- FS1000-1 FINANCIAL FORECAST CHECKLIST
- Review Meeting Minutes and Reports
- Forecasted Financial Statements

References:

A. Finance Policy Manual

   - Section 5.4.1 – Financial Forecasting

B. Financial Procedures

   - RC1010 CAPITAL PLAN

C. **SEC REGULATION S-X, ARTICLE 11** (17 CFR 210, USA)

   This article specifies requirements for the preparation and presentation of pro forma financial information and forecasts. Details of Article 11 may be found at http://ecfr.gpoaccess.gov/cgi/t/text/text-idx?c=ecfr&sid=20c66c74f60c4bb8392bcf9ad6fccea3&rgn=div5&view=text&node=17:2.0.1.1.8&idno=17#17:2.0.1.1.8.0.29.

Additional Resources:

A. none

---

[2] Lead time depends on the size and complexity of forecasts, the number of parties requiring them, etc.

Revision History:

Revision	Date	Description of Changes	Requested By
0.0	mm/dd/yyyy	Initial Release	

[This page intentionally left blank]

FS1000-1 FINANCIAL FORECASTING CHECKLIST

For Fiscal Year _____

Financial Forecast Document	Required Date	Submitted To	Submission Date	Notes
Sales Projections				
Cost/Operation Projections				
List of Significant Assumptions				
Forecasted Income Statement				
Forecasted Statement of Cash Flows				
Forecasted Balance Sheet				
Financial Period Budgets				
List of Assumptions:				

Comments:

_____

_____

_____

Completed by _____ Date _____

[This page intentionally left blank]

Document ID **FS1010**	Title **FINANCIAL REPORTING**	Print Date **mm/dd/yyyy**
Revision **0.0**	Prepared By **Preparer's Name / Title**	Date Prepared **mm/dd/yyyy**
Effective Date **mm/dd/yyyy**	Reviewed By **Reviewer's Name / Title**	Date Reviewed **mm/dd/yyyy**
	Approved By **Final Approver's Name / Title**	Date Approved **mm/dd/yyyy**

Policy: The Company shall prepare and submit all financial reports as legally and ethically required, and for additional business purposes as needed.

Purpose: To ensure that all financial reporting is:

- Completed in accordance with legal and ethical requirements and accepted accounting practices;

- Completed within the required time frame(s) and forwarded to required agencies;

- Reviewed and signed by Company officers who, by signing reports, attest to the reasonable accuracy of the information and effectiveness of internal controls, as required; and

- Available for the Company's needs.

Scope: This procedure applies to the Finance and Accounting departments.

Responsibilities: The Chief Financial Officer (CFO) is responsible for preparing and submitting all financial statements as required by law and by company policy.

The CFO and the Chief Executive Officer (CEO) are responsible for signing all reported financial statements.

Top Management and the Board of Directors are responsible for reviewing and approving all submitted financial reports.

The Controller is responsible for providing audited financial reports to the CFO annually, and unaudited financial reports quarterly.

Definitions: Financial Statements – Statements that give an overall picture of the Company's business operations and financial condition.

United States Securities and Exchange Commission (SEC) – Government commission, created by the Securities Exchange Act of 1934 to regulate securities markets (stocks, bonds, derivatives, etc.) and protect investors.

Form 10-Q – The form and instructions needed for submitting quarterly financial reports to the SEC.

Form 10-K – The form and instructions needed for submitting

annual financial reports to the SEC.

Annual Stockholders Report (ASR) – Information about the financial status of the Company, sent to stockholders prior to or with proxy statements and the notice of the scheduled annual stockholders' meeting in accordance with reporting requirements.

Generally Accepted Accounting Principles (GAAP) – Standards, conventions, and rules (including creation of financial statements) followed by accountants practicing in the US; established by the Financial Accounting Standards Board (FASB).

Procedure:

1.0   FINANCIAL STATEMENT REPORTING PLAN

1.1   The CFO shall create a FS1010-1 FINANCIAL REPORT CHECKLIST that lists all required financial statement reports that must be prepared and submitted during a fiscal year.   Financial statements for reporting are typically distributed:

Quarterly, to
- The SEC (USA)
- Federal, state, and local governments
- Associated stock exchanges
- Internally (for a variety of purposes)

Annually, to
- SEC (USA)
- Federal, state, and local governments
- Associated stock exchanges
- Stockholders of record as of a specific date
- Internally

1.2   The CFO shall produce (or ensure production of) financial statement reports and ancillary materials for submission. Such materials shall be submitted to Top Management and the Board of Directors for review and approval. Upon their approval, the CEO, the CFO, and other Company officials shall sign the reports, as required.

1.3   The CFO shall ensure that all financial statements are submitted in accordance with time requirements (deadlines) and note all financial statements sent to any person or organization on the FS1010-1 FINANCIAL REPORT CHECKLIST.

1.4   The CFO should be familiar with all relevant laws and regulations relating to the preparation and submission of financial statement reports (see "References" at the end of this procedure). The CFO should seek the advice of qualified, licensed legal counsel while preparing financial reports and should have counsel review such reports to help ensure compliance.

2.0   FINANCIAL STATEMENT CERTIFICATION

2.1   If certification is required both the CEO and the CFO shall review the financial controls used to produce the financial statements and the financial statements themselves to ensure that no untrue statements or omissions of a material fact as of the end of the period covered by the report exist.

2.2   Both the CEO and the CFO shall use two separate forms, FS1010-2 CEO/CFO CERTIFICATION STATEMENT, to attest to the fact that no untrue statements or omissions of a material fact as of the end of the period covered by the report exist.

2.3   Each of the certification statements shall be notarized and filed accordingly with the financial statements in accordance with FA1040 RECORD CONTROL

3.0   ANNUAL REPORT TO STOCKHOLDERS

3.1   The CFO shall prepare and publish an annual report to stockholders that contains financial statement information, financial performance, and other business information in accordance with relevant regulations (see "References").

3.2   The CFO shall submit the Annual Report to Stockholders ("Annual Report") to Top Management and the Board of Directors for review and approval.

3.3   Upon approval of the Annual Report, the CFO shall send the Report or notice of its availability to stockholders at least sixty days prior to the annual shareholders' meeting, in accordance with FA1050 ANNUAL STOCKHOLDERS' MEETINGS.

3.4   The CFO shall note on the FS1010-1 FINANCIAL REPORT CHECKLIST when the Annual Report to Stockholders has been released or mailed.

4.0   FINANCIAL STATEMENTS FOR BUSINESS OPERATIONS

4.1   The CFO shall prepare financial statements for issuing to business partners who request – and have legitimate needs for – them, such as:

- Banks and lending institutions;
- Suppliers giving credit or terms; and/or
- Suppliers or customers entering into long-term or large capital projects with the Company.

4.2   The CFO shall release prepared financial statements in accordance with FS1050 FINANCIAL STATEMENT RELEASE.

4.3   The CFO shall approve all financial report releases, noting approval as well as recipients and dates of release on the FS1010-1 FINANCIAL REPORT CHECKLIST.

5.0   ADDITIONAL FINANCIAL STATEMENT REPORTING

5.1   The CFO shall determine which financial statement reports are required for federal, state, and/or local governments and for affiliated stock exchanges and list all required financial statement reports on FS1010-1.

5.2   The CFO shall complete and submit all required financial statement reports in accordance with government and exchange authority requirements. The CFO shall note dates of release and recipients of all financial statement reports on FS1010-1 FINANCIAL REPORT CHECKLIST.

6.0   PUBLIC COMPANY QUARTERLY REPORTING

6.1   The CFO shall receive unaudited quarterly financial statements from the Controller within fifteen (15) days of the end of the quarter for each of the first three quarters of the fiscal year (no quarterly report is required for the end of the fiscal year). Financial statements should, at a minimum, include:

- The Balance Sheet;

- Income Statement; and

- Statement of Cash Flows.

6.2   The CFO shall ensure that quarterly financial statement reports and ancillary materials are prepared and submitted in accordance with applicable regulations and guidelines and in accordance with AC1000 SARBANES-OXLEY COMPLIANCE (see "References").

6.3   The CFO shall follow applicable regulatory guidelines for filing electronically (see Reference "G").

6.4   The CFO shall ensure that quarterly reports are filed in the required time frame in accordance with applicable guidelines and statutes (see Reference "J").

6.5   The CFO shall note the submission of all quarterly reports on FS1010-1.

7.0   PUBLIC COMPANY ANNUAL REPORTING

7.1   The CFO shall receive audited annual financial statements from the Controller within twenty days of the end of the fiscal year which should, at a minimum, include:

- The Balance Sheet;

- Income Statement; and

- Statement of Cash Flows

7.2   The CFO shall ensure that annual financial reports and ancillary materials are prepared and submitted to the SEC in accordance with the instructions on SEC Form 10-K, in accordance with GAAP for creating financial statements, and with proper approval and signatures.

7.3   The CFO shall follow the guidelines specified by SEC Regulation S-T if financial reports are filed electronically.

7.4   The CFO shall ensure annual reports to SEC are filed in the required time frame in accordance with 10-K (currently within 60 days of the end of the fiscal year for large accelerated filers, 75 days for accelerated filers, and 90 days for all others).

7.5   The CFO shall note all annual reports submitted to the SEC on FS1010-1
        FINANCIAL REPORT CHECKLIST.

8.0   IMPROVING THE FINANCIAL STATEMENT REPORTING PROCESS

8.1   The CFO shall hold a meeting during the fourth quarter of the fiscal year with
        Top Management and key managers from Accounting, Finance, and other
        departments that may be associated with financial reporting in order to review the
        process of creating and submitting the Company's financial statement reports.

8.2   The CFO shall list and assign actions items needed to improve the process of
        creating and submitting financial statement reports as a result of the review
        meeting.

8.3   The CFO shall ensure the procedure and process is modified as required to
        improve the process of creating and submitting financial statement reports, and
        monitor the completion of assigned action items noted.

Effectiveness Criteria:

- Financial statements for reporting prepared and submitted in a timely manner
- Meeting legal and ethical requirements for reporting financial statements.
- Prepared financial statements to use for business operation needs.

Forms/Records:

- FS1010-1 FINANCIAL REPORT CHECKLIST
- FS1010-2 CEO/CFO CERTIFICATION STATEMENT
- Required financial statement reports
- Meeting minutes and reports

References:

A. Finance Policy Manual

   - Section 5.4.2 Financial Reporting

B. Finance procedures

   - AC1000 SARBANES-OXLEY COMPLIANCE
   - FA1050 ANNUAL STOCKHOLDERS' MEETINGS

C. Bizmanualz© Accounting Policies and Procedures.

   - G&A104 MANAGEMENT REPORTS
   - G&A105 PERIOD END REVIEW & CLOSING
   - G&A109 CONFIDENTIAL INFORMATION RELEASE

D. **SECURITIES AND EXCHANGE ACT OF 1934** (USA); **SEC GENERAL
   RULES AND REGULATIONS**, the Securities and Exchange Act of 1934 (12B
   CFR 240). The Act was designed to provide for regulation of securities

exchanges and over-the counter markets operating in interstate and foreign commerce and through the mails, to prevent inequitable and unfair practices on such exchanges and markets.

E. **SEC ACCOUNTING REGULATION S-X** (17 CFR 210, USA)

F. **SEC GENERAL REGULATION S-K** (17 CFR 229, USA)

G. **SEC GENERAL RULES FOR ELECTRONIC FILING REGULATION S-T** (17 CFR 232, USA)

H. **SARBANES-OXLEY ACT OF 2002** (USA). The Act was designed to protect investors by improving the accuracy and reliability of public companies' disclosures.

I. **SEC REGULATION 14A SOLICITATION OF PROXIES** (14A CFR 240)

Additional Resources:

A. GAAP Handbook of Policies and Procedures, CCH, Inc.

B. Securities Exchange Act of 1934 available at
http://www.sec.gov/about/laws/sea34.pdf

C. SEC General Rules and Regulations, The Securities and Exchange Act of 1934 (12B CFR 240) available at http://ecfr.gpoaccess.gov/cgi/t/text/text-idx?c=ecfr&sid=47b43cbb88844faad586861c05c81595&rgn=div5&view=text&node=17:3.0.1.1.1&idno=17

D. SEC Accounting Regulation S-X (17 CFR 210) available at
http://www.sec.gov/divisions/corpfin/ecfrlinks.shtml

E. SEC General Regulation S-K (17 CFR 229) available at
http://www.sec.gov/divisions/corpfin/ecfrlinks.shtml

F. SEC General Rules for Electronic Filing Regulation S-T (17 CFR 232) available at http://www.sec.gov/divisions/corpfin/ecfrlinks.shtml

G. Accounting & Financial Reporting Guidance/Contacting Staff for Advice – http://www.sec.gov/divisions/corpfin/cfreportingguidance.shtml

H. SEC Form 10-Q may be found at http://www.sec.gov/about/forms/form10-q.pdf.

I. SEC Form 10-K may be found at http://www.sec.gov/about/forms/form10-k.pdf.

Revision History:

Revision	Date	Description of Changes	Requested By
0.0	mm/dd/yyyy	Initial Release	

[This page intentionally left blank]

FS1010-1 FINANCIAL REPORT CHECKLIST

For Fiscal Year _____

Financial Report	Date Submitted	Initials	Recipient
Quarterly Financial Reports			
SEC Quarterly Financial Report (10-Q)			SEC
State/Local Quarterly Report			
Exchange Quarterly Reports			
Annual Financial Reports			
SEC Annual Financial Report (10-K)			SEC
State/Local Annual Report			
Exchange Annual Reports			
Annual Report to Stockholders			
Financial Reports for Business Ops			

Comments:

[This page intentionally left blank]

FS1010-2 CEO/CFO CERTIFICATION STATEMENT

[Note: print on company letter head]

Statement Under Oath of Principal Executive Officer Regarding Facts and Circumstances Relating to Exchange Act Fillings

I, _____ , state and attest that
(CEO / CFO)

1. To the best of my knowledge, based upon a review of the covered reports, and, except as corrected or supplemented in a subsequent covered report:

    a. No covered report contained an untrue statement of a material fact as of the end of the period covered by such report (or in the case of a report on Form 8-K or definitive proxy materials as of the date of which it was filed); and

    b. No covered report omitted to state a material fact necessary to make the statements in the covered report, in light of the circumstances under which they were made, not misleading as of the end of the period covered by such report (or in the case of a report on Form 8-K or definitive proxy materials, as of the date of which it was filed).

2. I have reviewed the contents of this statement with the Company's Audit Committee.

3. In this statement under oath, each of the following, if filed on or before the date of this statement, is a "covered report":

    a. Company Report on Form 10-K for the year ended _____ ;
    (fiscal year end date)

    b. All reports on form 10-Q, all reports on Form 8-K and all definitive proxy materials filled with the Commission subsequent to the filling of the form 10-K identified above and

    c. Any amendments to any of the foregoing.

Name: [print CEO name]
Title: Chief Executive Officer
Date: mm / dd / year   [Notary Seal]

[This page intentionally left blank]

Document ID **FS1020**	Title **FINANCIAL STATEMENT ANALYSIS**	Print Date **mm/dd/yyyy**
Revision **0.0**	Prepared By **Preparer's Name / Title**	Date Prepared **mm/dd/yyyy**
Effective Date **mm/dd/yyyy**	Reviewed By **Reviewer's Name / Title**	Date Reviewed **mm/dd/yyyy**
	Approved By **Final Approver's Name / Title**	Date Approved **mm/dd/yyyy**

Policy: The Company shall analyze financial statements in order to understand, manage, and improve the Company's financial performance.

Purpose: To make information on financial statements more understandable and meaningful by:

- Rearranging and reordering for consistency and ease of use;

- Presenting financial objectives, forecasts, and historical performance; and

- Performing useful relationship calculations (e.g., total and relative increases/decreases, financial ratios, percentages).

Scope: This procedure applies to the Finance and Accounting departments.

Responsibilities: The CFO (Chief Financial Officer) is responsible for analyzing financial statements, and for preparing reports and recommendations to Top Management and the Board of Directors concerning financial performance.

Top Management and the Board of Directors are responsible for reviewing financial analysis and approving corrections or improvements to financial policies, objectives, or activities.

The Controller is responsible for providing the CFO with financial accounting statements at the end of each financial period.

Definitions: Financial Statements – Statements, typically created monthly, that give an overall picture of business operations and of financial condition.

Financial Analysis – To perform appropriate calculations and evaluations of information contained in financial statements in the form of historical trends, relationship ratios.

Financial or Accounting Period – The length of time businesses use for preparing and reviewing internal accounts to monitor business performance (e.g., weekly, monthly). The period used depends on the industry, business model, and business dynamics.

Procedure:

1.0   FINANCIAL STATEMENT ANALYSIS PLAN

1.1   The CFO shall conduct an analysis of the Company's financial statements at the end of every financial period, or as required by Top Management and the Board of Directors and/or in accordance with law. The financial analysis should include:

- Selected ratio calculations and evaluations for information on current or most recent financial statement.

- Trends of statement components (earning, expense, profit) over the recent financial periods and fiscal years, for example, the previous 2-10 fiscal years.

- Selected ratio analysis and ratio trends over the recent financial periods, fiscal year, and most recent 2-10 fiscal years, focusing on ratios important to the industry, business model, and financial objectives.

- Trends and ratios for the recent financial periods, fiscal year, and most recent 2-10 fiscal years in relation to typical industry benchmarks and standards.

1.2   The CFO shall produce a financial report and/or presentation (including narratives) for Top Management and the Board of Directors to explain in detail the results of the financial analysis, and recommend actions as necessary.

1.3   The CFO shall take action as approved by Top Management and the Board of Directors as a result of financial analysis in setting financial objectives and improving financial performance.

1.4   The CFO shall annually review the process of financial statement analysis and reporting, and improve the process as required.

2.0   COLLECT AND CALCULATE FINANCIAL DATA

2.1   The CFO shall receive the financial statements from the controller at the end of every financial period and the end of the fiscal year (or other financial periods as required).

2.2   The CFO shall list key ratios for analysis in Section I on the FS1020-1 FINANCIAL ANALYSIS PLAN. The particular ratios used for analysis should be consistent over time; the CFO shall present valid reason(s) for adding or dropping ratios used for analysis. Some ratios should be employed from each major category listed below, with emphasis placed on ratios and ratio categories believed to be critical or key indicators of performance according to the business model, industry segment, etc. Major ratio categories include the following:

- Profitability Ratios – A measure of success at generating profits (i.e. return on assets, return on equity, return on investment).

- Liquidity Ratios – A measure of the ability to meet short term obligations (i.e. current ratio, quick ratio, cash ratio).

- Asset Use Ratios – A measure of how effectively assets are used (i.e. sales to assets, sales to inventory, sales to working capital).

- Capitalization Ratios – A measure of the debt component (i.e. leverage on capital, long-term debt to capital, debt to equity).

2.3   The CFO shall complete the information on the FS1020-1 FINANCIAL ANALYSIS PLAN (See Figure 1) about ratios used that can provide valuable information about how the business is performing and areas of strengths and weaknesses, including:

- The actual formula being used (Formula)

- The resulting ratio calculation (Result)

- The target or objective for the ratio (Target)

- The industry average result for this ratio (Ind. Avg.)

- The ratio result for the best or top performers in the industry (Top Perf.)

- Any additional notes, including why the ratio is used and notes on result

A) Profitability Ratios

Ratio Name	Formula	Result	Target	Ind. Avg.	Top Perf.	Notes
1) Return on Assets	Net Income / Net Assets	15.4%	17%	16%	20%	Heavy investment in assets.
2)						
3)						
4)						
5)						
6)						

(Notes)

Figure 1 – Completing the Ratio Portion of Form FS1020-1

2.4   The CFO shall select (with advisement as required from Top Management or the Board of Directors) key components or elements of financial statements to track and plot over time (i.e. sales, expenses, debt) and list them in section II, III, and IV of FS1020-1, as well as the time range or history to be plotted (e.g., 2 year, 5 year).

2.5   The CFO shall collect the required data from financial statements for the following:

- Calculate ratios and percentages;

- Plot financial performance;

- Ratio and percentage calculations; and

- Create plots, charts, graphs, and tables representing information as needed.

3.0   FINANCIAL STATEMENT ANALYSIS AND REPORTING

3.1   The CFO shall review and evaluate the information compiled and calculated in Section 2.0, then note any meanings, interpretations, and explanations for the results in Section V of the FS1020-1 – FINANCIAL ANALYSIS PLAN.

3.2   The CFO shall prepare a report and/or presentation for Top Management and the Board of Directors on the results of the financial statement analysis. The report should include the following:

- Basic financial statement data and the results of financial statement analysis.

- Meanings, interpretations, and implications of analysis results.

- Meanings, interpretations, and implications of trends and results in light of historical data, forecasts, and current performance.

- Results and performance in light of financial objectives and business goals (including how targets or objectives were set, and why they were met, exceeded, or missed).

- Results and performance in light of industry or business segment benchmarks and standards (including source of benchmarks and how they were selected – see Reference section for sources of financial information by industry or business segment).

3.3   As part of the financial statement analysis report, the CFO shall recommend actions needed to improve financial performance.

3.4   Top Management and the Board of Directors shall review the financial statement analysis report and/or presentation, along with its recommendations for actions, and decide whether any specific actions need to be taken.

3.5   The CFO shall note and carry out the decisions by the Top Management and the Board of Directors.

4.0   IMPROVING THE FINANCIAL STATEMENT ANALYSIS PROCESS

4.1   The CFO shall annually review the process of financial statement analysis and its reporting. The CFO should consider the following:

- The success of previous financial statement analysis and reports at providing useful information about business performance for control and decision making

- The reports and presentations conveying the information in meaningful ways that aid Top Management and the Board of Directors in decision making

4.2   After reviewing the financial statement analysis process, the CFO shall improve the process as required.

Effectiveness Criteria:

- Conducting regular financial analysis and reporting analysis information to Top Management and the Board of Directors

- Using information and insight gained through financial analysis for decision making and management

Forms/Records:

- FS1020-1 FINANCIAL ANALYSIS PLAN

- Financial Statement Analysis Report

- Review Meeting Minutes and Reports

References:

A. Finance Policy Manual

- Section 5.4.3 – Financial Statement Analysis

B. Finance procedures

- FS1010 FINANCIAL REPORTING

Additional Resources:

A. www.Bizstats.com (free source of small business statistics and ratios)

B. www.Bizminer.com (fee-based source of business statistics and industry ratios)

C. www.Fintel.us (fee-based source of business statistics and industry ratios)

D. www.valusourcesoftware.com (fee-based source of business/industry ratios) E.

Dun & Bradstreet (source of business information; available on subscription basis); http://www.dnb.com.

Revision History:

Revision	Date	Description of Changes	Requested By
0.0	mm/dd/yyyy	Initial Release	

FS1020-1 FINANCIAL ANALYSIS PLAN

For Financial Period _____
Fiscal Year _____

I) Key Financial Ratios (list and perform ratio analysis)

A) Profitability Ratios

Ratio Name	Formula	Result	Target	Ind. Avg.	Top Perf.	Notes
1)						
2)						
3)						
4)						
5)						
6)						

B) Liquidity Ratios

Ratio Name	Formula	Result	Target	Ind. Avg.	Top Perf.	Notes
1)						
2)						
3)						
4)						
5)						
6)						

C) Asset Use Ratios

Ratio Name	Formula	Result	Target	Ind. Avg.	Top Perf.	Notes
1)						
2)						
3)						
4)						
5)						
6)						

D) Capitalization Ratios

Ratio Name	Formula	Result	Target	Ind. Avg.	Top Perf.	Notes
1)						
2)						
3)						
4)						
5)						
6)						

Comments:

_____

_____

II) Key Financial Plots (list historical/trend charts)

Name	Time Period	Notes
1)		
2)		
3)		
4)		
5)		
6)		

III) Key Ratio Financial Plots (list ratio historical/trend charts)

Name	Time Period	Notes
1)		
2)		
3)		
4)		
5)		
6)		

IV) Other Financial Items for Analysis or Plotting (list additional charts)

Name	Importance/Key	Notes
1)		
2)		
3)		
4)		
5)		
6)		

Comments:

_____

_____

_____

V) Interpretation of Analysis Results

A) Results of Historical Analysis (Trends)

_____

_____

_____

_____

_____

B) Results of Mathematical Analysis (Ratios, Percentages)

_____

_____

_____

_____

_____

C) Results of Performance Analysis (Business Objectives, Industry Benchmarks)

_____

_____

_____

_____

_____

D) General Comments/Overview on Analysis Results

_____

_____

_____

_____

_____

_____

_____

_____

_____

Completed by:

_____ Date _____

Approved By

_____ Date _____

Document ID **FS1030**	Title **FINANCIAL MANAGEMENT REVIEW**	Print Date **mm/dd/yyyy**
Revision **0.0**	Prepared By **Preparer's Name / Title**	Date Prepared **mm/dd/yyyy**
Effective Date **mm/dd/yyyy**	Reviewed By **Reviewer's Name / Title**	Date Reviewed **mm/dd/yyyy**
	Approved By **Final Approver's Name / Title**	Date Approved **mm/dd/yyyy**

Policy:
The Company shall develop clear communication between the CFO, CEO, Board of Directors, and other Top Management to achieve effective financial management, concerning financial goals, and objectives, strategies, and results, as well other financial information

Purpose:
To set a clear plan for meetings, reports, presentations, and other communication in order to set and document financial strategies and objectives, make financial decisions, and to convey financial results and analysis.

Scope:
This procedure applies to the Finance and Accounting departments.

Responsibilities:
The Chief Financial Officer (CFO) is responsible for arranging and chairing financial management meetings, and for preparing financial reports and presentations for scheduled financial management meetings.

The Chief Executive Officer (CEO), Top Management, and the Board of Directors are responsible for actively participating in the financial management process.

Definitions:
Financial Management- Involvement of upper level management in setting financial goals and objectives, setting financial processes, and conducting regular reviews.

Financial Statements – Statements, typically created monthly, that give an overall picture of business operations and of financial condition.

Financial Analysis – To perform appropriate calculations and evaluations of information contained in financial statements in the form of historical trends and relationship ratios.

Goals – Broad, general statements of the Company's direction and intention.

Objectives – Specific targets for the Company, departments, and/or individuals to reach within a specific time frame.

Strategies – Practices and actions employed by the Company in order to reach stated and implied goals and objectives.

Performance – The degree of success with which strategies are used to reach goals and objectives.

Procedure:

1.0   FINANCIAL MANAGEMENT PLAN

1.1   Many financial processes and procedures call for top level finance management, meaning that Top Management, and/or the Board of Directors to meet to develop and monitor financial goals, objectives, activities, and performance. These should be integrated and coordinated to the greatest degree possible into regular financial management meetings (see References).

1.2   The CFO shall establish a financial management plan for regularly meeting with Top Management and the Board of Directors to discuss and review aspects of financial management, including:

- Developing, monitoring, and reviewing financial goals, objectives, and strategies;

- Reporting and reviewing financial performance; and

- Communicating additional financial information to and from Top Management, the CEO, and the Board of Directors, or to other oversight group such as a strategy committee.

1.3   The financial management plan shall include the following:

- Frequency of financial management meetings (e.g., monthly, quarterly);

- Required and invited attendees to financial management meetings;

- Regular agenda items for financial management meetings; and

- Other agenda items for financial management meetings as required.

1.4   The CFO shall record adherence to that financial plan, and annually review the adherence and success of the financial management plan and improve it as required.

2.0   CONDUCTING FINANCIAL MANAGEMENT MEETINGS

2.1   The CFO shall list the meetings required to conduct financial management for the fiscal year in Section I of the FS1030-1 FINANCIAL MANAGEMENT PLAN.

2.2   The CFO shall list all members of the Board and Top Management to be invited to financial management meetings in Section II of the FS1030-1 FINANCIAL MANAGEMENT PLAN

2.3   The CFO shall create an agenda for each financial management meeting and list it in Section I of the FS1030-2 FINANCIAL MANAGEMENT MEETING AGENDA. Typical agenda items may include, but need not be limited to:

- Setting or adjusting overall financial goals, objectives, and strategies;

- Reviewing financial performance, financial statement analysis, and performance;

- Internal control, auditing, compliance, corrective action, and tax issues; and

- Plans and action items for maintaining or improving financial performance.

2.4   The CFO shall be responsible for creating all materials required for conducting financial management review meetings. Such materials can include, but are not limited to:

- Clearly stated goals, objectives, strategies, and actions;

- Financial Statements;

- Pro Forma Financial Statements (Forecasts) and Budgets; and

- Financial Statement analysis, as well as other reports and presentations that describe or detail financial performance (e.g., charts, graphs, tables).

2.5   The CFO shall conduct meetings as planned or scheduled, and record the date of meetings held on the FS1030-1 FINANCIAL MANAGEMENT PLAN.

2.6   The CFO shall and record results of meetings, such as decisions, general notes, required action items and assignments in the Minutes/Notes section of the FS1030-2 FINANCIAL MANAGEMENT MEETING AGENDA.

3.0   REVIEWING FINANCIAL MANAGEMENT

3.1   The CFO shall also annually review the execution of the FS1030-1 FINANCIAL MANAGEMENT PLAN to ensure:

- Meetings are occurring as planned and are properly attended;

- Meeting agendas allow for covering the required number of topics in sufficient amount of detail, and stay within the scope of financial management;

- Required materials (statements, reports, presentations) are prepared in a way that provides for informed financial management; and

- Results of financial review meetings are properly documented and acted upon.

3.2   The CFO shall annually review if the FS1030-1 FINANCIAL MANAGEMENT PLAN is leading to successful financial performance by evaluating execution of the following:

- Setting clear and realistic goals and objectives and then implementing plans and strategies that achieve them;

- Properly identifying and addressing financial concerns, risks, and issues; and

- Satisfactory compliance with applicable regulations and standards (reflected in audits, reporting).

4.0   IMPROVING FINANCIAL MANAGEMENT

The CFO shall revise the Financial Management procedure and/or its associated forms (i.e. FS1030-1 FINANCIAL MANAGEMENT PLAN) in order to improve financial performance (e.g., setting/achieving objectives, compliance, meeting schedule/agenda) as described in Sections 3.1 and 3.2, above, including:

- Altering (increasing/decreasing) meeting frequency and/or length;
- Altering meeting agendas and/or materials;
- Increasing or altering other financial-related communication; and
- Changing how financial performance is analyzed and decisions made.

Effectiveness Criteria:

- Regular financial management meetings with clear agendas are held and minutes/results of meetings are recorded.
- Clear financial goals, objectives, priorities, and strategies are established, and action plans developed to meet them.

Forms/Records:

- FS1030-1 FINANCIAL MANAGEMENT PLAN
- FS1030-2 FINANCIAL MANAGEMENT MEETING AGENDA
- Review Meeting Minutes and Reports
- Financial Statements
- Pro Forma Financial Statements
- Financial Statements Analysis reports and/or presentations

References:

A. Finance Policy Manual

- Section 5.4.4 – Financial Management Review

B. Finance procedures

- AC1040 EXTERNAL AUDITING
- AC1050 INTERNAL AUDITING
- AC1060 CORRECTIVE ACTION
- FA1000 FINANCIAL OBJECTIVES
- FS1000 FINANCIAL FORECASTING
- FS1010 FINANCIAL STATEMENT REPORTING
- FS1020 FINANCIAL STATEMENT ANALYSIS

Additional Resources:

A. Siegel, Levine, Qureshi, and Shim, <u>GAAP 2014: Handbook of Policies and Procedures</u>, CCH, Inc. (ISBN #978-0808035367.)

B. Sihler, Crawford, & Davis, <u>Smart Financial Management: The Essential Reference for the Successful Small Business</u>, Amacom Div., 2004. (ISBN #978-0814407899.)

Revision History:

Revision	Date	Description of Changes	Requested By
0.0	mm/dd/yyyy	Initial Release	

[This page intentionally left blank]

FS1030-1 FINANCIAL MANAGEMENT PLAN

I) Scheduled Financial Management Review Meetings

Meetings	Scheduled Date	Notices Sent on:	Place	Actual Date	Topics
Month 1)					
Month 2)					
Month 3)(Qtr 1)					
Month 4)					
Month 5)					
Month 6)(Qtr 2)					
Month 7)					
Month 8)					
Month 9)(Qtr 3)					
Month 10)					
Month 11)					
Month 12)(Qtr 4)(End of Year)					

Comments:

II) Financial Management Review Invitees

Name	Contact At	Notice for Meeting												Attended Meeting											
		1	2	3	4	5	6	7	8	9	10	11	12	1	2	3	4	5	6	7	8	9	10	11	12

FS1030-2 FINANCIAL MANAGEMENT MEETING AGENDA

Meeting (i.e., Month 1 or Qtr 1) _____

Meeting Date _____   Meeting Place_____

Meeting Start Time _____   Meeting End Time _____

I) Meeting Agenda

Agenda Item	Estimated Time	Actual Time	Notes
Action Item Review/General Review			
Financial Goals/Strategies			
Financial Objectives			
Financial Statements/Performance			
Financial Statement Analysis			
Financial Forecasting/Budget			
Audits/Audit Results			

Comments/Notes:

_____

_____

_____

_____

_____

II) Meeting Minutes & Action Items

Action Item	Assigned To:	Complete Date (Goal)	Complete Date (Actual)

Minutes/Notes:

_____

_____

_____

_____

_____

_____

_____

Completed by _____

Document ID **FS1040**	Title **FINANCIAL RESTATEMENTS**	Print Date **mm/dd/yyyy**
Revision **0.0**	Prepared By **Preparer's Name / Title**	Date Prepared **mm/dd/yyyy**
Effective Date **mm/dd/yyyy**	Reviewed By **Reviewer's Name / Title**	Date Reviewed **mm/dd/yyyy**
	Approved By **Final Approver's Name / Title**	Date Approved **mm/dd/yyyy**

Policy: The Company shall establish and follow appropriate standard procedures for handling errors discovered in published or submitted financial statements, including investigating and addressing sources of errors, preparing and submitting revised, corrected financial statements, properly announcing restatements, and preventing future errors.

Purpose: To ensure financial reporting errors are investigated and resolved in a timely manner, and that financial restatements (if required) are completed in accordance with legal and ethical requirements, in accordance with accepted accounting practices, and that proper notifications of restatements are made.

Scope: This procedure applies to the Finance and Accounting departments in restating financial statements due to errors resulting from:

- Mathematical mistakes;
- Misapplication of accounting principles;
- Other accounting errors;
- Improper oversight or control; or
- Misuse or misstatement of facts.

Responsibilities: The CFO (Chief Financial Officer) is responsible for overseeing investigations into reporting errors, preparing and submitting all financial restatements as required by law and by company policy, and for preparing press releases about restatements.

Top Management, the CEO (Chief Executive Officer), the Controller, and the Board of Directors are responsible for cooperating with inquiries into financial statement errors, and for reviewing and approving all financial restatements.

The Audit Team Leader is responsible for review and approval of root cause analysis and investigation results of material errors in financial statements.

Definitions: <u>Auditor</u> – A qualified accountant who inspects the accounting records and practices of a business or other organization.

<u>Audit Team</u> – Body formed by a company's Board of Directors to oversee internal and external audit operations. Sarbanes-Oxley (USA) requires that publicly traded companies form an Audit Team *from the Board of Directors.*

<u>Financial Statements</u> – Statements that give an overall picture of business operations and of financial condition.

<u>Financial Restatement</u> – When a company, either voluntarily or prompted by regulators or auditors, revises previous financial statements.

<u>Form 10-Q/A</u> – Form 10-Q is the form and instructions used for submitting *quarterly* financial reports to the SEC. "Q/A" is used when submitting a financial report that amends a previously submitted 10-Q.

<u>Form 10-K/A</u> – Form 10-K is the form and instructions used for submitting *annual* financial reports to the SEC. "K/A" indicates an amendment of a previously submitted 10-K.

<u>Generally Accepted Accounting Principles (GAAP)</u> - Standards, conventions, and rules (including creation of financial statements) followed by accountants in the USA and other countries. Established by the Financial Accounting Standards Board (FASB).

<u>Material</u> – Of real importance or great consequence; highly significant. According to the FASB, an omission or misstatement of an item in a financial report is material if, in light of the surrounding circumstances, the magnitude of the item is such that the judgment of a reasonable person relying on the report probably would have been changed or influenced by including or correcting that item.

<u>Securities and Exchange Commission (SEC)</u> - A government commission created by the Securities and Exchange Act of 1934 (USA) to regulate securities markets (stocks, bonds, derivatives, etc.) and protect investors.

Procedure:

1.0 FINANCIAL RESTATEMENT PLAN

1.1   The CFO shall follow the FS1040-1 FINANCIAL RESTATEMENT CHECKLIST when an error in a submitted financial statement error is discovered (by internal or external audit, or other means).

1.2   The CFO shall be responsible for investigating the source of the error, the nature and extent of the error, as well as implementing corrective action to ensure the error is corrected and not repeated in future statement preparation.

1.3   The CFO shall hold a discovery meeting with all affected parties, both internal and external, such as:

- Those discovering the financial statement error;

- Those who involved with the information or process that resulted in the error;

- Those investigating and/or resolving the error; and

- Members of Accounting and Finance Management and/or other management oversight (i.e. CEO, Board of Directors Audit Team Leader).

1.4   The CFO, along with the meeting attendees (see Section 1.3), shall discuss and make determinations (when possible) about the statement error, including the following:

- The source of the error;

- The category or type of error (i.e. revenue recognition, expense recognition, misclassification, assets, equity, inventory, reserves, taxes);

- The nature and extent of the error;

- The materiality of the financial statement errors. Material errors will require more attention and actions (including creating amended financial statements); and

- A list of required actions and the responsible party for carrying out the action (including investigations, reports, restatements, and restatement recipients).

1.5   The CFO shall, upon determination that the error is material, ensure the following actions are taken (as required):

- Prepare corrected financial statements (including explanation, description of errors, and reason for restatement);

- Determine the effect of the error on other statements, and if restating is required;

- Prepare and release public announcement of restatement(s) (i.e. press release);

- Review and re-conduct financial statement analysis on updated financial statements;

- Determine the effect of restatements on CEO and CFO performance bonuses if errors in statements were intentional or a result of misconduct; recalculate bonuses as needed and collect bonus overpayments (in accordance with the Sarbanes-Oxley Act);

- Submit revised financial statements and associated forms to government and private parties as necessary (i.e. SEC, state and local governments, creditors, investors); and

- Prepare for a formal or informal inquiry by the SEC (for public companies submitting amended statements).

1.6   The CFO shall form and oversee a qualified team to investigate the source and root cause of the error, as well as the extent and impact of the error (if these are not immediately determined in the discovery meeting). The team shall have three to five members and can be comprised of Company associates and/or external accounting and auditing experts. The CFO shall select members of the discovery team based on the following:

- The department or organizational segment that appears to be affiliated with the error (i.e. accounting, production, information systems, or sales departments);

- Accounting, finance, or auditing expertise; and

- Management and Board of Director roles (i.e. controller, Audit Team Leader).

1.7   The CFO shall be responsible for allocating the proper resources to investigate, resolve, and correct any discovered financial misstatement, including appropriate budget and internal/external personnel.

2.0   FINANCIAL RESTATEMENTS

2.1   The CFO shall ensure a thorough investigation is conducted into the statement error and the need for restating. The CFO shall set clear objectives for the investigation that align with the items listed in Section 1.4 above and ensure they are listed on the FS1040-1 FINANCIAL RESTATEMENT CHECKLIST.

2.2   The CFO shall be responsible for properly completing the actions listed on the FS1040-1 FINANCIAL RESTATEMENT CHECKLIST, in order to resolve errors and achieve the objectives listed in Section 1.4 above, including the following:

- Setting a required date for all actions to be complete;

- Noting the actual date of all actions completed;

- The person or department manager responsible for completing all actions; and

- Additional notes and comments as needed.

2.3   The CFO shall prepare a report to present at a restatement closing/review meeting that describes the following:

- The results of investigations into the error and required restatements (see Section 1.4), and results from other checklist activities (including materiality of the error);

- The risk of similar errors in past or future statements;

- Corrective and preventive actions; and

- Revised financial statements and statement analysis.

2.4   The CFO shall be responsible for completing or tracking restatement tasks, including financial re-statements in accordance to FS1010 FINANCIAL

REPORTING, and noting completion dates on the FS1040-1 FINANCIAL RESTATEMENT CHECKLIST.

2.5   The CFO and CEO shall review and approve all financial restatements prior to submission or release in accordance with the Sarbanes-Oxley Act.

3.0   REVIEWING THE FINANCIAL RESTATEMENT PROCESS

3.1   The CFO shall hold a closing/review meeting at the end of the financial restatement process to ensure the following:

- Investigation findings are clear and conclusive;

- Overall effectiveness of the investigation team;

- All actions (internal, external, and corrective) listed on the FS1040-1 FINANCIAL RESTATEMENT CHECKLIST are complete according to schedule;

- All required restatements and announcements are complete and submitted;

- Proper budget, schedule, and personnel for investigation and restating were allocated; and

- The status of any external investigation.

3.2   The CFO shall, after each financial restatement process, review the effectiveness of the FS1040-1 FINANCIAL RESTATEMENT CHECKLIST to ensure all the required (or potentially required) actions are correctly listed.

4.0   IMPROVING THE FINANCIAL RESTATEMENT PROCESS

4.1   The CFO shall, as a part of the financial restatement review meeting (see Section 3.1 above) or resulting from his or her own observations, modify the procedure and process as required, as well as the FS1040-1 FINANCIAL RESTATEMENT CHECKLIST, to improve the investigation of financial statement errors and financial restating.

4.2   After each use of the Financial Restatement procedure, the CFO shall review its performance and report to the Board of Directors' Audit Team (via written report or oral presentation) on the procedure's effectiveness and recommend improvements for ensuring:

- Investigative results;
- Restatements and restatement notifications complete (as required); and
- Corrective and preventive actions taken to prevent future statement errors.

Effectiveness Criteria:

- Meeting legal and ethical requirements for financial restatements
- Identification of root causes of errors in submitted financial statements
- Actions taken to correct existing errors and prevent future errors

Forms/Records:

- FS1040-1 FINANCIAL RESTATEMENTS CHECKLIST
- Required financial statement reports
- Meeting minutes and reports

References:

A. Finance Policy Manual

  - Section 5.4.5 – Financial Restatements

B. Finance procedures

  - FS1010 FINANCIAL REPORTING
  - AC1000 SARBANES-OXLEY COMPLIANCE
  - AC1060 CORRECTIVE ACTION
  - FS1010 FINANCIAL STATEMENT REPORTING

C. Bizmanualz® Accounting Policies and Procedures Manual, item #ABR31M (ISBN-10 #978-1-9315-9102-7).

  - G&A104 MANAGEMENT REPORTS
  - G&A105 PERIOD END REVIEW & CLOSING
  - G&A109 CONFIDENTIAL INFORMATION RELEASE

Additional Resources:

A. **SECURITIES EXCHANGE ACT OF 1934** (USA): Provides for the regulation of securities exchanges and of over-the counter markets operating in interstate and foreign commerce and through the mails, to prevent inequitable and unfair practices on such exchanges and markets. Text available at http://www.sec.gov/about/laws/sea34.pdf www.sec.gov/divisions/34act.shtml.

B. **SEC GENERAL RULES AND REGULATIONS** (12B CFR 240). Text available at http://ecfr.gpoaccess.gov/cgi/t/text/text-

idx?c=ecfr&sid=47b43cbb88844faad586861c05c81595&rgn=div5&view=text&n
ode=17:3.0.1.1.1&idno=17.

C. **SEC ACCOUNTING REGULATION S-X** (17 CFR 210). Available at
http://www.sec.gov/divisions/corpfin/ecfrlinks.shtml.

D. **SEC GENERAL REGULATION S-K** (17 CFR 229). Available at
http://www.sec.gov/divisions/corpfin/ecfrlinks.shtml.

E. **SEC GENERAL RULES FOR ELECTRONIC FILING REGULATION S-T**
(17 CFR 232). Available at http://www.sec.gov/divisions/corpfin/ecfrlinks.shtml.

F. **SARBANES-OXLEY ACT OF 2002** (USA). The Act (also known as "SOX")
was designed to protect investors by improving accuracy and reliability of
corporate disclosures.

G. **SEC REGULATION 14A SOLICITATION OF PROXIES** (14A CFR 240)

H. SEC Form 10-Q (quarterly financial report, filed with the SEC) – form and
instructions are available at http://www.sec.gov/about/forms/form10-q.pdf.

I. SEC Form 10-K (annual financial report) – form and instructions are available at
http://www.sec.gov/about/forms/form10-k.pdf.

J. SEC Form 8-K ("current report" companies must file with the SEC to announce
major events that shareholders should know about) – form and instructions are
available at http://www.sec.gov/about/forms/form8-k.pdf.

K. Siegel, Levine, Qureshi, and Shim, GAAP 2008: Handbook of Policies and
Procedures, CCH, Inc. (ISBN: 978-0808035367.)

L. FAS 154, Accounting Changes and Error Corrections, available at
http://www.fasb.org/pdf/fas154.pdf.

M. SEC webpage on Corporate Financial Reporting at
http://www.sec.gov/divisions/corpfin/cfreportingguidance.shtml

Revision History:

Revision	Date	Description of Changes	Requested By
0.0	mm/dd/yyyy	Initial Release	

FS1040-1 FINANCIAL RESTATEMENT CHECKLIST

Year _____

Restatement Action	Date Required	Date Complete	Assigned To	Notes
Determination/Investigation				
Discovery Meeting				
Investigation Team Assigned				
Investigation Budget/Schedule				
Investigation Complete				
Materiality Determined				
Corrective Actions				
Closing Meeting/Report				
Restating Financial Reports				
SEC Form 8-K (within 4 days of determination of materiality)				
SEC Form 10K/A (Amended)				
SEC Form 10Q/A (Amended)				
Annual Report to Stockholders				
Amended Reports to Investors				
Amended Reports to Creditors				
Amended Reports to State/Local				
Other Actions				
Press Release				
Internal Control Review				
Disciplinary/Legal Actions				
Performance Bonus Calculation				
Updated Financial Analysis				

Comments/Notes:

[This page intentionally left blank]

Document ID	Title	Print Date
FS1050	**FINANCIAL INFORMATION RELEASE**	**mm/dd/yyyy**
Revision	Prepared By	Date Prepared
0.0	**Preparer's Name / Title**	**mm/dd/yyyy**
Effective Date	Reviewed By	Date Reviewed
mm/dd/yyyy	**Reviewer's Name / Title**	**mm/dd/yyyy**
	Approved By	Date Approved
	Final Approver's Name / Title	**mm/dd/yyyy**

Policy: The Company shall control the release of financial information to third and outside parties.

Purpose: To establish the process for the CFO to approve the release of financial information to third and outside parties (creditors, vendors, customers) and for business operations as necessary.

Scope: This procedure applies to the Finance and Accounting departments.

Responsibilities: The CFO (Chief Financial Officer) is responsible for reviewing and approving requests for financial statements and any other proprietary, confidential, and/or sensitive financial information.

Definitions: Financial Statements – Statements, typically created quarterly, that give an overall picture of business operations and of the Company's financial condition.

Procedure:

FINANCIAL STATEMENT RELEASE PLAN

1.0 All requests for financial information shall be forwarded to the CFO. The CFO shall have sole authority to decide what information may be released according to the context and situation of the request, and shall direct the release of financial information or direct a denial response.

1.1 The CFO shall log each request for financial information during a given fiscal year, as well as note whether the request was fulfilled or denied, in the FS1050-2 FINANCIAL INFORMATION RELEASE LOG.

1.2 Those who request financial information shall typically receive a reply as soon as possible, and always within thirty days.

1.3 The CFO shall also consider using reporting or credit agencies for referring certain types of financial information requests, and if appropriate put referral processes in place.

FINANCIAL INFORMATION RELEASE

2.1 Upon receiving a phone or in-person request for financial information, the Accounting or Finance Department manager/employee shall complete a FS1050-1 FINANCIAL INFORMATION REQUEST, and forward the request to the CFO.

2.2 All letters and other written requests for financial information shall be forwarded to the CFO.

2.3   The CFO shall determine the appropriate response for each request, and enter each request in the FS1050-3 FINANCIAL INFORMATION RELEASE LOG, along with appropriate information, such as:

- Name of requester and date of request;

- The reason for the request (and possible referral to reporting agency – see Section 1.4 above);

- Whether the request is approved or denied with appropriate notes or reasons (particularly for denial);

- Contact information for providing financial information;

- The appropriate financial information to provide (i.e. most recent financial statements, most recent pro-forma statements, most recent annual financial statements) (also, see Section 2.5 below); and

- The types of financial statements to provide (i.e. Balance Sheet only, full set of Financial Statements, Summarized Statements).

2.4   The CFO shall verify that approved financial information is sent in a timely manner by noting the date financial information is sent on FS1050-2.

2.5   The CFO shall determine the most appropriate financial information/statement to provide. For example, a financial statement submitted to stakeholders such as banks should be accompanied by an opinion or comment from the company's Certified Public Accountant (CPA) prior to any formal presentation. (If no outside CPA review is obtained, the Financial Statements may be considered "pro forma" and result in requests for copies of completed tax returns). The CPA shall examine the financial statements and prepare a formal version to one of three standards:

- Compiled Financial Statement. The CPA is unable to make any assurances on the data or methods used to produce the financial statements. The CPA will re-cast the financial statements into a standard format (as per Generally Accepted Accounting Principles or GAAP) with a disclaimer that the statements are un-audited and the information is solely derived from the management of the business entity.

- Reviewed Financial Statement. The CPA is able to make some limited assurances that material changes are not required in order for the Financial Statements to be in conformity with GAAP. The CPA uses limited inquiry and some analytical procedures to ascertain the reasonableness of the statements. The information is then re-cast into a standard format with appropriate footnotes and a disclaimer that the statements are un-audited and only a limited inquiry has been made into the reasonableness of the information.

- Audited Financial Statement. The CPA provides assurance, through an opinion letter, that the financial statements are a fair representation of the financial position, results of operations, and cash flows of an entity. This opinion is given after a detailed review and verification of the accounting records and processes used to produce the data. Verification steps include various analytical procedures, client surveys, third party confirmation, and detailed accounting record reviews.

NOTE: Any irregularity found in the course of the CPA audit of the Company's financial statements could lead to a "qualified" opinion (something is inconsistent with GAAP) or an "adverse" opinion (calls into question the reliability of the information itself). An adverse opinion by a CPA indicates that there may be serious issues with the statements or the accounting system that produced them.

2.6   The CFO shall determine if the release of financial information to certain parties requires signing a *nondisclosure agreement* prior to release, and note this requirement on the FS1050-2 FINANCIAL INFORMATION RELEASE LOG by listing the date the nondisclosure request or form is sent in the appropriate column.

2.7   The CFO shall maintain all written financial information requests and completed FS1050-1 FINANCIAL INFORMATION REQUEST forms with the FS1050-2 FINANCIAL INFORMATION RELEASE LOG, in accordance with FA1040 RECORD CONTROL.

FINANCIAL INFORMATION RELEASE REVIEW

2.8   The CFO shall annually review and evaluate the process for releasing financial information and verify the following:

- All requests for financial information are forwarded in a timely manner.

- Release decisions are made and responses sent (either a release of information or a denial notice) in a timely manner.

- Appropriate type of financial information is provided to for approved requests.

2.9   The CFO shall improve the process, procedure, and forms associated with releasing financial information as needed to meet the goals listed in section 3.1 above.

Effectiveness Criteria:

- Timely responses to requests for financial information

- Appropriate financial information provided according to type of request and determination by CFO

Forms/Records:

- FS1050-1 FINANCIAL INFORMATION REQUEST

- FS1050-2 FINANCIAL INFORMATION RELEASE LOG

References:

    A. Finance Policy Manual

- Section 5.4.6 Release of Financial Information

    B. Finance procedures

- FS1010 FINANCIAL REPORTING
- FA1040 RECORD CONTROL

Additional Resources

- **FINANCIAL ACCOUNTING STANDARDS BOARD (FASB)**

   Since 1973, the Financial Accounting Standards Board (http://www.fasb.org/) has been the designated organization in the private sector for establishing standards of financial accounting and reporting. The FASB is officially recognized by the Securities and Exchange Commission (Financial Reporting Release No. 1, Section 101) and the American Institute of Certified Public Accountants (Rule 203, Rules of Professional Conduct, as amended May 1973 and May 1979). FASB pronouncements are the primary sources of generally accepted accounting principles, or "GAAP."

- **GENERALLY ACCEPTED ACCOUNTING PRINCIPLES (GAAP)**

   GAAP typically includes the most recent developments of all generally accepted accounting principles (GAAP) as derived or collected from various technical pronouncements. Sources include FASB statements, interpretations, technical bulletins and concepts; American Institute of CPAs (AICPA); Accounting Principles Board opinions, accounting research bulletins, and position statements; and Securities and Exchange (SEC) financial reporting releases.

- **INTERNATIONAL FINANCIAL REPORTING STANDARDS (IFRS)**

   ifrs.org/pages/default.aspx

Revision History:

Revision	Date	Description of Changes	Requested By
0.0	mm/dd/yyyy	Initial Release	

[This page intentionally left blank]

FS1050-1 FINANCIAL INFORMATION REQUEST

Company/Person making Request:		
Received by:		Date:

Reason for Requesting Financial Information:

Specific Information Requested:

Contact Information: (for requesting additional information and for sending financial statements)

CFO Use Only:

Approve?　　Y ☐　　N ☐

Notes: (Explain approval or denial):

CFO approves the release of the following financial information to this party:

Chief Financial Officer: _____ Date: _____

[This page intentionally left blank]

FS1050-2 FINANCIAL INFORMATION RELEASE LOG

For Fiscal Year

Party Requesting Information	Date	Reason	Approve /Deny	Non- Disclosure	Response Date	Notes	Contact Information

Comments:

[This page intentionally left blank]

Finance Policies and Procedures

Section 440

Internal Controls

Section 440
Internal Controls

Document ID **AC1000**	Title **SARBANES-OXLEY COMPLIANCE**	Print Date **mm/dd/yyyy**
Revision **0.0**	Prepared By **Preparer's Name / Title**	Date Prepared **mm/dd/yyyy**
Effective Date **mm/dd/yyyy**	Reviewed By **Reviewer's Name / Title**	Date Reviewed **mm/dd/yyyy**
	Approved By **Final Approver's Name / Title**	Date Approved **mm/dd/yyyy**
Applicable Standard: **Sarbanes-Oxley Act of 2002 (USA)**		

Policy: The Company shall comply with all requirements of the Sarbanes-Oxley Act of 2002.

Purpose: To list and assign Sarbanes-Oxley compliance requirements (e.g., develop adequate internal controls for financial reporting), measure and monitor (track) compliance, and note when key compliance items are complete.

Scope: This procedure applies to the Finance and Accounting departments, and to all departments that provide financial or accounting data to the finance and accounting departments.

Responsibilities: The CFO (Chief Financial Officer) is responsible for ensuring that the company is in compliance with the Sarbanes-Oxley Act of 2002. The CFO is also responsible for approving and signing all financial statements, financial reports, and tax returns.

The CEO (Chief Executive Officer) is responsible for approving and signing all financial statements, financial reports, and tax returns.

The Controller is responsible for assisting the CFO in preparation of financial statements.

Top Management is responsible for overseeing and verifying financial statement preparation, and for putting in place an internal control system as prescribed in Sections 302 and 404 of the Sarbanes-Oxley Act of 2002. Top Management shall also prepare an annual report on the effectiveness of the internal control system.

Department Managers are responsible for providing information necessary for preparing financial statements, and for assistance in developing and monitoring the system of internal controls needed to comply with the Sarbanes-Oxley Act of 2002.

The Audit Team Leader established by and of the board of directors, shall oversee the accounting and financial reporting processes and the audits of the financial statements of the Company.

Definitions: Blackout period – Period of up to sixty days, during which employees may not adjust the investments contained in their investment plans (e.g., 401-k); blackout periods often occur when the investment plan is undergoing significant changes.

Generally Accepted Accounting Principles (GAAP) - Standards, conventions, and rules followed by accountants practicing in the USA and established by the Financial Accounting Standards Board (FASB).

ICFR – Internal Control over Financial Reporting.

Public Company Accounting Oversight Board (PCAOB) – A private-sector, non-profit corporation established by SOX to oversee the auditors of public companies in order to protect the interests of investors and further the public interest in the preparation of informative, fair, and independent audit reports.

Sarbanes-Oxley Act of 2002 (SOX - USA) – Law designed to protect investors, in combination with other Securities regulations, by promoting ethical behavior by corporate officers and by improving the accuracy and reliability of corporate disclosures, particularly financial statements.

Securities Exchange Act of 1934 – Provides governance of securities transactions on the secondary market (after issue) and regulates the exchanges and broker-dealers in order to protect the investing public. All companies listed on stock exchanges must follow the requirements set forth in the Act.

Securities & Exchange Commission, The (SEC) – Government commission created by the Securities Exchange Act of 1934 to regulate the securities markets (e.g., stocks, bonds, derivatives) and protect investors.

Procedure:

1.0   SARBANES-OXLEY ACT – BACKGROUND

1.1   The Sarbanes-Oxley Act ("SOX") was developed in the aftermath of failures of companies like Enron and WorldCom; it further attempts to ensure ethical behavior of corporate officials and ensure that financial statements of companies that issue public stock (called "issuers in the act") are accurate and complete representations of the company's financial status. Existing and potential investors in a publicly trading company have a right to complete and accurate financial information.

1.2   SOX covers diverse and disparate areas of corporate accountability. Sections of SOX that do not directly impact the Company's compliance efforts include:

- The authorization and establishment of the PCAOB;

- Authorization and funding of studies on corporate accountability and fraud; and

- Increasing punishment for white collar crime.

1.3 Noteworthy areas of SOX that the Company must address in order to be compliant include:

- Forming an Audit Team, drawn from the Board of Directors, that oversees auditing activities and provides general accounting oversight;

- Using qualified auditors (auditing firms) that are free of other relationships with the Company or pose no other conflict of interest;

- The lead or overseeing auditor (audit lead) does not lead audits of the Company for more than five consecutive years;

- Creating, implementing, and maintaining a system of internal controls that ensures the completeness and *reasonable* accuracy of financial reporting;

- Top Management issuing an annual report on the effectiveness of the Company's internal control system and Top Management's attestation to the accuracy of financial reports; and

- Limits on stock trading by officers during "blackout periods" (section 306(a) of the Act).

1.4 This procedure focuses on the aspects of SOX listed in Section 1.3 that are material to the Company's compliance with SOX.

2.0 SOX AUDIT COMMITTEE PLAN

2.1 An Audit Team plan shall be completed at the start of each fiscal year by the Board of Directors with assistance from Top Management, in accordance with FA1060 – BOARD OF DIRECTORS' MEETINGS.

2.2 The Audit Team Plan shall address the following to comply with sections of SOX dealing with the formation and responsibilities of the Audit Team Leader:

- Establish an Audit Team from members of the Board of the Directors;

- At least one member of the Audit Team shall have expertise in accounting or finance;

- The Audit Team Leader shall ensure the Company uses Generally Accepted Accounting Procedures (GAAP);

- The Audit Team Leader shall pre-approve the use of all audit and non-audit financial services;

- The Audit Team Leader shall obtain and retain written audit reports and written minutes of audit discussions;

- The Audit Team members shall receive training on compliance issues such as GAAP, SOX, and the Securities and Exchange Commission Act of 1934 (particularly Section 10A);

- The Audit Team Leader shall ensure financial statements are prepared in accordance with GAAP; and

- The Audit Team Leader shall ensure policy and procedures are in place to receive and address anonymous concerns and complaints regarding accounting and financial practices from Company employees.

3.0   SOX AUDITOR PLAN

3.1   The CFO shall complete an Audit Plan at the start of each fiscal year for approval by the Audit Team Leader and the Board of Directors.

3.2   The Audit Plan shall address the following to comply with SOX sections dealing with the hiring and performance of auditors:

- Auditors shall be registered with the PCAOB;

- Auditors shall conform to quality control and ethics of the PCAOB;

- Financial or financial related services shall not be provided to the Company by the auditor or firms connected to the auditor;

- It shall be verified whether the auditor is being or has been investigated by the PCAOB, as well as the status or result of any investigation;

- Any company outside of the U.S. that provides any financial services to the Company shall comply with U.S. law; and

- A lead or reviewing auditor shall not provide auditing services for more than five consecutive years.

4.0   CORPORATE RESPONSIBILITY PLAN

4.1   The CFO shall complete a Corporate Financial Responsibility Plan at the start of each fiscal year and be approved by Top Management and the Board of Directors.

4.2   The Corporate Responsibility Plan shall address areas of compliance with SOX sections dealing with the lawful and ethical conduct of the Company executives and management specifically:

- Verify that no officer of the Company had been employed by the audit provider within the past year;

- Officers of the Company shall not apply influence to, or even appear to apply influence, to the auditors (such as conducting private or one-on-one meetings);

- Company officers and executives shall return, and clearly document such return, any performance pay, bonuses, or stock options based on financial statements that require restating;

- Company officers, executives, and managers shall not be allowed to trade, sell, buy, or transfer Company stock during designated employee blackout periods;

- All loans and other miscellaneous financial transactions between the Company and its officers and executives shall be transparent and fully disclosed and documented in accordance with TM1030 RELATED PARTY TRANSACTIONS;

- All officers, directors, and shareholders holding 10% of Company stock or more shall disclose in accordance with the Securities and Exchange Commission Act of 1934 Section 16; and

- A Code of Ethics shall be created for the CFO and other officers involved with financial operations, and placed in the policies and procedures manual; the CFO and other officers shall sign the Code of Ethics and the record maintained.

4.3   The Corporate Responsibility Plan must also create the Company's plan for complying with SOX requirements for dealing ethically with whistle blowing, legal cooperation, and other ethical issues such as:

- The CFO and Audit Team Leader shall create a procedure for properly publishing updated and/or restated financial information;

- The CFO shall ensure that no relationships between the Company and financial/securities analysts may be perceived as a conflict of interest;

- If the Company is required to appear before the SEC for any reason, a person of integrity and expertise shall appear;

- The CFO and Top Management shall ensure policies and procedures are in place to ensure employees can provide anonymous reports to company officers about the financial operations without fear of retribution;

- All officers, directors, managers, and supervisors shall be aware that it is illegal to retaliate against any employee who provides truthful information to law enforcement or to the SEC; and

- The CFO and Top Management shall set policies and procedures into place to prevent tampering with a record or impeding an official proceeding.

5.0   INTERNAL CONTROL SYSTEM PLAN

5.1   Top Management shall establish and maintain an internal control system to comply with requirements of Sarbanes-Oxley; in particular, sections 302 and 404. SOX presents no specifics on internal control, but subsequent publications and notices by the SEC use the COSO Framework (see Additional Resource "C") as an example or framework for an internal control system based on controlling material risks to the accurate reporting of financial information.

5.2   The COSO Framework presents an internal control system based on five principles:

- *Control Environment* – The tone of an organization providing discipline and structure; the foundation for all other components of internal control.

- *Risk Assessment* – The identification and analysis of relevant risks to achievement of the objectives, forming a basis for determining how the risks should be managed by internal controls (see AC1020 – RISK ASSESSMENT and AC1030 – RISK MANAGEMENT).

- ***Control Activities*** – The policies and procedures throughout the organization that help ensure management directives to address risks and to achieve the organization's objectives are carried out.

- ***Information and Communication*** – Information about internal and external events and operations must be communicated appropriately in the organization to make it possible to run and control the business.

- ***Monitoring*** – Accesses the quality of the system's performance over time through ongoing monitoring activities, separate evaluations, or a combination of the two (see AC1040 EXTERNAL AUDITING and AC1050 INTERNAL AUDITING).

5.3   The internal control system shall be established to ensure the CEO, CFO, and other signing officers of the annual report can have *a reasonable degree of confidence* that the report does not contain untrue statements, omit material facts, or is misleading.

5.4   Signing officers shall evaluate the internal control system 90 days prior to issuing financial statements, and include with the financial statements a report that describes the effectiveness of the internal control system (See FS1010 FINANCIAL REPORTING).

6.0   COMPLETING THE SOX CHECKLIST

6.1   The CFO shall use the AC1000-1 SARBANES-OXLEY COMPLIANCE CHECKLIST to track compliance activities carried out through executing the plans described in sections 2.0 through 5.0 above.

6.2   The CFO shall note the date of completed compliance action items on the AC1000-1 SARBANES-OXLEY COMPLIANCE CHECKLIST.

6.3   CFO shall verify the AC1000-1 SARBANES-OXLEY COMPLIANCE CHECKLIST is complete at least 30 days prior to the submission or release of annual financial statements in order to verify compliance.

7.0   IMPROVING SOX COMPLIANCE

7.1   Annually, after submission of financial reports, the CFO shall meet with Top Management, the Controller, and with key members or the Accounting, Finance, and other involved departments to review SOX compliance.

7.2   Key indicators of successful SOX compliance are the following:

- Audit reports with ***unqualified*** opinions;

- Timely completion of activities on the AC1000–1 SARBANES-OXLEY COMPLIANCE CHECKLIST;

- Audit Team Meeting Minutes with timely closing of action items; and

- Periodic review of accounting practices in light of GAAP.

7.3   The CFO (or their assignee) shall record minutes during SOX compliance review meetings, noting any discrepancies, problems, or issues in completing compliance items, including assigning action items for any issues requiring root cause analysis or other activities.

7.4   The CFO shall review the status of assigned action items sixty days after the SOX compliance review meetings, to ensure all outstanding action items are complete and accounted for.

7.5   The CFO shall take appropriate follow-up action for any outstanding or incomplete action item from the SOX compliance review meetings, in accordance with AC1060 CORRECTIVE ACTION.

Effectiveness Criteria:

- Timely compliance with all SOX requirements
- Accurate and complete financial statements

Forms/Records:

- AC1000-1 SARBANES-OXLEY COMPLIANCE CHECKLIST
- SOX Audit Team Plan
- SOX Audit Plan
- SOX Corporate Responsibility Plan
- Meeting minutes and reports

References:

A. Finance Policy Manual

- Section 5.5.1 – Sarbanes-Oxley Compliance

B. Finance Procedures

- AC1020 RISK ASSESSMENT
- AC1030 RISK MANAGEMENT
- AC1040 EXTERNAL AUDITING
- AC1050 INTERNAL AUDITING
- FS1010 FINANCIAL REPORTING
- TM1030 RELATED PARTY TRANSACTIONS

C. *Bizmanualz® Accounting Policies and Procedures Manual*, item #ABR31M.

D. **SECURITIES EXCHANGE ACT OF 1934** (USA). Provides for the regulation of securities exchanges and of over-the counter markets operating in interstate and foreign commerce and through the mails, to prevent inequitable and unfair practices on such exchanges and markets. Text available at http://www.sec.gov/about/laws/sea34.pdf.

E. **SARBANES-OXLEY ACT OF 2002** (USA). The Act (also known as "SOX") was designed to protect investors by improving accuracy and reliability of corporate disclosures. Information on the Sarbanes-Oxley Act can be found at:

- "Securities Lawyer's Deskbook," University of Cincinnati School of Law, © 1998-2011 – http://taft.law.uc.edu/CCL/SOact/toc.html

- Sarbanes-Oxley Act of 2002, U.S. Government Printing Office (GPO) –http://www.gpo.gov/fdsys/pkg/PLAW-107publ204/html/PLAW-107publ204.htm

- Public Company Accounting Oversight Board (PCAOB) website –http://pcaobus.org/Pages/default.aspx

F. **MARKETS IN FINANCIAL INSTRUMENTS DIRECTIVE** (MiFID – European Union). This Directive (law), sometimes considered a European Union counterpart of SOX, provides a harmonized regulatory regime for investment services across the 30 member states of the European Economic Area (the 27 Member States of the European Union plus Iceland, Norway and Liechtenstein). MiFID is a building block in the European Commission's (EC) Financial Services Action Plan, which governs how EU financial service markets operate. The main objectives of the Directive are to increase competition and consumer protection in investment services.

G. **FINANCIAL INSTRUMENTS AND EXCHANGE LAW** (Japan). Also known in some areas as "J-SOX," it differs from Sarbanes-Oxley in that there is a lower ratio of qualified-accountants-to-clients in Japan than in the USA; consequently, there is a greater reliance on automation in audits in Japan.

H. Other regulations around the world that are similar to Sarbanes-Oxley in nature or intent include:

- **CERTIFICATION OF DISCLOSURE IN ISSUERS' ANNUAL AND INTERIM FILINGS** (MI 52-109), Canada; and

- **CORPORATE LAW ECONOMIC REFORM PROGRAM (AUDIT REFORM & CORPORATE DISCLOSURE) ACT** (CLERP-9), Australia.

Additional Resources:

A. Siegel, Levine, Qureshi, and Shim, GAAP 2014: Handbook of Policies and Procedures, CCH, Inc. (ISBN: 978-0808035367.)

B. Holt, Michael F., Sarbanes-Oxley Act: Overview and Implementation Procedures, CIMA Publishing (2006).

C. The Committee of Sponsoring Organizations of the Treadway Commission (COSO) has several useful publications, including:

- Internal Control – Integrated Framework;

- Enterprise Risk Management – Integrated Framework; and

- Internal Control over Financial Reporting — Guidance for Smaller Public Companies.

These publications and others may be found through the COSO website, http://www.coso.org.

Revision History:

Revision	Date	Description of Changes	Requested By
0.0	mm/dd/yyyy	Initial Release	

[This page intentionally left blank]

AC1000-1 SARBANES-OXLEY COMPLIANCE CHECKLIST

For Fiscal Year _____

I) Audit Team Checklist

Action	Date Complete	Notes
Audit Team In Place		
Member w/Accounting/Finance Expertise		
AC Pre-approves Financial Services		
AC Received & Retained Audit Reports		
AC GAAP Training		
AC SEC Act of 1934 Training		
AC SOX Training		
AC Verifies Financial Statements Prepared in Accordance w/ GAAP		
Policies & Procedures in Place for Handling Anonymous Complaints		

II) Auditor Checklist

Action	Date Complete	Notes
Written Verification Auditors Are Registered w/ PCAOB		
Written Verification Auditors Conform with Quality Control and Ethics of PCAOB		
Auditors Have No Other Relationship w/ Company nor Provides Financial Services		
Verified Status/Result of Previous or Current PCAOB Investigations of Auditors		
All Companies Outside the U.S. that Provides Financial Services Comply w/ U. S. law		
Lead Auditor not Used for More than 5 Consecutive Years		

III) Corporate Responsibility Plan

Action	Date Complete	Notes
No Officer Employed by Auditor in Past Year		
All Dealings with Auditors are Open and Above Appearance of Impropriety		
All Officer/Executive Performance/Bonus Pay Based on Inaccurate Financial Statements Returned and Documented		
No Officer/Executive Trading Allowed During Blackout Periods		
All Loans and Financial Transactions with Officers/Executives Transparent and Clearly Documented		
All Officers/Executives/Shareholders holding 10% or More in Stock Discloses in Accordance with SEA Section 16		
Code of Ethics Signed by All Officers		
Procedure in Place for Re-stating Financial Reports		
No Conflicts in Interest Between Company and Financial Analysts		
A Qualified, Person of Integrity Designated to Appear at Any SEC Hearing		
Policies & Procedures in Place to Encourage Employees to Report Improper Financial Activities Without Retribution		
All Officers/Executives/Managers Aware That It Is Illegal to Retaliate Against any Employee Who Provides Truthful Information to the SEC or to a Law Enforcement Agency		
Policies and Procedures Are in Place to Prevent Tampering with an Investigation		
CEO and CFO are Responsible for Accuracy of Financial Statements		
CFO is Responsible for Accuracy of Tax Returns		

IV) Internal Control System Checklist

Action	Date Complete	Notes
Internal Control System Established		
Internal Control System Accounts for Needed Control Points as Prescribed by Risk Analysis/Management		
Top Management Prepared Report Stating Effectiveness of Internal Control System for Submission with Financial Statements		
Procedures in Place for Correcting and Improving Internal Control System Based on Audit Reports		

Comments:

CFO Approval:

_____ Date _____

CEO Approval:

_____ Date _____

[This page intentionally left blank]

Document ID **AC1010**	Title **SSAE 16 COMPLIANCE**	Print Date **mm/dd/yyyy**
Revision **0.0**	Prepared By **Preparer's Name / Title**	Date Prepared **mm/dd/yyyy**
Effective Date **mm/dd/yyyy**	Reviewed By **Reviewer's Name / Title**	Date Reviewed **mm/dd/yyyy**
	Approved By **Final Approver's Name / Title**	Date Approved **mm/dd/yyyy**
Applicable Standard: **Statement on Standards for Attestation Engagements (SSAE)** **#16** (formerly SAS 70)		

Policy: The Company shall ensure, with written verification, that third-party financial service providers comply with SSAE 16.[1]

Purpose: To ensure that SSAE 16 compliance status of third-party financial service providers is verified and on record; to save the Company from having to conduct an audit of each of its financial service providers.

Scope: This procedure applies to the Finance and Accounting Departments, and all departments that employ, use, or contract outside financial services (such as Payroll, Bookkeeping, and Data Processing).

Responsibilities: The CFO (Chief Financial Officer) is responsible for verifying that providers of financial services comply with SAS #70.

Department Managers are responsible for providing information to the CFO about financial service providers to their department.

Definitions: Third Party Financial Service Provider – Any external organization or company that provides financial related services to the Company for Company's financial or accounting operations (for example payroll, bookkeeping, accounting).

Statement on Auditing Standards No. 70 (SAS 70) – A recognized auditing standard developed by the American Institute of Certified Public Accountants (AICPA) for financial service providers. SAS 70 Certification represents that a service provider's control activities has been audited and will be able to provide a Service Auditor's Report on request. This report typically satisfies audit requirements for service providers.

Statement on Standards for Attestation Engagements #16 (SSAE 16) – SSAE 16 was drafted with the intention and purpose of updating the US service organization reporting standard so that it mirrors and complies with the new international service organization reporting standard, ISAE 3402. SSAE 16 also

---

[1] SSAE 16 effectively replaced SAS 70 as the authoritative guide for reporting on service organizations as of June 15, 2011.

establishes a new Attestation Standard called AT 801 which contains guidance for performing the service auditor's examination.

Many service organizations that previously had a SAS 70 service auditor's examination ("SAS 70 audit") performed converted to the new standard in 2011 and now have a SSAE 16 report instead - also referred to as a Service Organization Controls (SOC) 1 report.

Additional information on SSAE 16 and Service Organization Control reports can be viewed at http://www.aicpa.org/soc.

Procedure:

1.0   SSAE 16 COMPLIANCE PLAN

1.1   When a company's financial books and/or internal controls are audited, any financial service company providing financial services are also subject to the audit. This requirement would mean that financial service providers could constantly be audited. SSAE 16 Compliance avoids continual auditing of financial service providers.

1.2   The CFO is responsible for verifying that financial service providers comply with the SSAE 16 auditing standard.

1.3   The CFO shall, within 90 days prior to an external audit, ensure that a written request is sent to each financial service provider that asks for a statement in writing that they comply with SSAE 16 and can provide a Type I or Type II Service Auditor's Report upon request. A Type II shall be requested when the external audit will be of the complete system or of key financial areas or processes.

1.4   The CFO shall ensure that written responses from financial service providers are tracked on a checklist and that the checklist and written response is stored in the designated SSAE 16 File.

1.5   The CFO shall review the SSAE 16 compliance procedure with affected department managers and top management after each external audit.

2.0   CREATING AND COMPLETING A SSAE 16 COMPLIANCE CHECKLIST

2.1   The CFO shall ensure the creation of an AC1010-1 SSAE 16 COMPLIANCE CHECKLIST. The first section of the checklist shall consist of a list of Company departments and locations that may use financial service providers.

2.2   The CFO shall request a list of all financial service providers from each department listed in Section I of the AC1010-1 SSAE 16 COMPLIANCE CHECKLIST. The CFO and Controller shall coordinate in listing the financial service providers used by the Accounting and Finance Department.

2.3   The CFO shall record the following information on the AC1010-1 SSAE 16 COMPLIANCE CHECKLIST:

- The date each Department / location responds to the request; and

- The names, addresses, and contact information of the financial service providers listed by each responding Department or location.

2.4   The CFO shall follow-up as required with any department that does not respond to the request after 30 days until requested information is provided.

2.5   The CFO shall compare the list of submitted financial service providers with the Company's Approved Vendor list, verifying that all financial service providers are listed on the AC1010-1 SSAE 16 COMPLIANCE CHECKLIST, and add any providers not already listed.

2.6   The CFO shall send each financial services provider listed on form AC1010-1 a request for written verification that the service provider is SSAE 16-compliant and verify that they can provide a Service Auditor's Report upon request. On form AC1010-1, the CFO shall note:

- The date the request letter is sent;

- The type of report required (Type I or Type II);

- The date a reply is received from the service provider;

- Whether the reply indicates the service provider is SSAE 16-compliant and can provide the appropriate Service Auditor's Report; and

- That the report is dated no more than six months prior to the external audit.

2.7   The CFO shall follow-up with any finance service provider that does not respond after 30 days until a reply is received.

2.8   The CFO shall maintain the AC1010-1 SSAE 16 COMPLIANCE CHECKLIST, along with all written responses and correspondence from financial service providers, in a designated "SSAE 16 Compliance" file.

2.9   Form AC1010-1 shall be completed at least ten days prior to the scheduled external audit.

3.0   SSAE 16 COMPLIANCE CHECKLIST REVIEW

3.1   The CFO shall review form AC1010-1 ten days prior to an external audit to verify that all service providers on the checklist have replied that they are compliant and will provide a Service Auditor's Report on request.

3.2   The CFO shall send a written notice to any provider who has not responded or responded negatively (e.g., not compliant, SAR unavailable) that they will be subject to an audit by the Company's external auditor unless they respond immediately with a written notice that they are SSAE 16-compliant and can provide an SAR, if required.

3.3   Suggested controls identified in the SSAE 16 report should be cross-referenced to the Company's corresponding controls to ensure they are being appropriately implemented by the third-party service provider.

4.0   SSAE 16 COMPLIANCE CHECKLIST IMPROVEMENTS

4.1   The CFO shall meet with affected Department managers and key Finance and Accounting personnel, to review which financial service providers did not respond or responded negatively and discuss:

- The risks of continuing to use financial services organizations not in compliance with SSAE 16; and

- Whether to continue doing business with organizations that are not SSAE 16-compliant.

4.2   The CFO shall make improvements to the SSAE 16 Compliance process and checklist, as needed.

Effectiveness Criteria:

- The Company's financial service providers are SSAE 16-compliant

- A more efficient, less costly SSAE 16 audit process

Forms/Records:

- AC1010-1 SSAE 16 COMPLIANCE CHECKLIST

- Meeting minutes and reports

References:

A. Finance Policy Manual

- Section 5.5.2 SSAE 16 Compliance

B. Finance procedures

- None

Additional Resources:

A. "Service Organizations: Reporting on Controls at a Service Organization Relevant to User Entities' Internal Control over Financial Reporting Guide", AICPA – https://www.cpa2biz.com/AST/Main/CPA2BIZ_Primary/SOC/PRDOVR~PC-0127910/PC-0127910.jsp.

B. "Reporting on Controls at a Service Organization – SSAE No. 16", AICPA – https://www.cpa2biz.com/AST/Main/CPA2BIZ_Primary/AuditAttest/Standards/SSAEs/PRDOVR~PC-023035/PC-023035.jsp.

C. "Using a SOC 1 Report in a Financial Statement Audit", AICPA – https://www.cpa2biz.com/AST/Main/CPA2BIZ_Primary/AuditAttest/TopicSpecificGuidance/PRDOVR~PC-APASSAE/PC-APASSAE.jsp.

Revision History:

Revision	Date	Description of Changes	Requested By
0.0	mm/dd/yyyy	Initial Release	

[This page intentionally left blank]

AC1010-1 – SSAE 16 COMPLIANCE CHECKLIST

For Fiscal Year _____   Next Scheduled Audit_____

I) Departments that potentially use external financial services

Department	Date of Request for Providers	Date of Response	Date of 2nd Request

II) Financial Service Providers

Provider Company Name	Department Using Service	Date Added	Date Request Letter Sent	Date of Response	Date of 2nd Request	SSAE 16 Certified	Service Auditor's Report

Comments:

Approval:

_____ Date _____
                        Chief Financial Officer

Document ID AC1020	Title **RISK ASSESSMENT**	Print Date **mm/dd/yyyy**
Revision **0.0**	Prepared By **Preparer's Name / Title**	Date Prepared **mm/dd/yyyy**
Effective Date **mm/dd/yyyy**	Reviewed By **Reviewer's Name / Title**	Date Reviewed **mm/dd/yyyy**
	Approved By **Final Approver's Name / Title**	Date Approved **mm/dd/yyyy**

Policy: The Company shall periodically identify and assess risks to the business.

Purpose: To prioritize risks in order to manage them effectively and efficiently; to substantially decrease the opportunity for *material* weaknesses to go undetected.

Scope: This procedure pertains to the identification and assessment of risk.

Responsibilities: The Risk Manager is responsible for identifying and assessing risks.

The Risk Manager is responsible for directing the risk assessment and reporting the results of the assessment to the Board of Directors.

The Board of Directors is responsible for reviewing and approving the risk assessment prior to development of a Risk Management Plan (see AC1030 RISK MANAGEMENT).

Definitions: Hazard – Source of danger; specific situation that may influence the probability and/or extent of loss.

Material – *Relatively* significant or important in the context of the organization.

Risk – (n.) 1. A function of the likelihood of an event and its consequences (impact); 2. Possibility of loss or injury. (v.) Expose to hazard or danger; incur danger of.

Risk exposure –Numeric value assigned to a risk, allowing comparison of different risks, calculated as:

(Probability of threat) x *(Impact if threat materializes)* = *Risk exposure*

(e.g., 90% threat probability x 10% total loss probability = 0.09 risk exposure).

Risk matrix – Tool used to illustrate and prioritize risks.

Threat – Indication or source of *impending* danger; expression of *intent* to inflict evil, injury, or damage.

Procedure:

1.0   FORM A RISK MANAGEMENT COMMITTEE

1.1   The Company's CEO and CFO shall create a Risk Management Committee, to include:

- The Company Controller;
- The Compliance Officer;
- Legal counsel; and
- Potentially, various other Managers (e.g., A/P Manager).

The CEO and CFO shall appoint one member of the Committee to be the *Risk Manager*.

1.2   The Risk Management Committee shall meet periodically (annually, at a minimum) for the purpose of identifying and assessing financial hazards (threats) and to review the results of previous assessments.

2.0   IDENTIFY HAZARDS/THREATS

2.1   The Risk Management Committee shall identify financial statement elements (accounts) and list them in columns "A" through "C" of form AC1020-1 RISK ASSESSMENT / MANAGEMENT WORKSHEET, going into as much detail as needed (see Figure 1 for an example). A sample chart of accounts (AC1020-2 SAMPLE CHART OF ACCOUNTS) is listed at the end of this procedure to help with the first three columns. It is not designed to be, nor should it be, interpreted as an all-inclusive list; see Additional Resource "H" for more help.

Note: We recommend that the Company implement the Worksheet in the form of a spreadsheet or database.

A. CLASS	B. ACCT	C. SUB-ACCT	D. KEY THREAT	E. POSSIBLE CONSEQUENCES	F. IMPACT	G. LIKELI-HOOD	H. RISK	I. RANK
LIAB	Accts. Payable		Unauthorized payments	Could result in unfavorable and misstated financial results.	Medium	Medium	Medium	

Figure 1 – Section of Form AC1020-1

2.2   The Risk Management Committee shall list identified key financial reporting threats, or hazards, for each element listed in columns "A" through "C" and list those threats in column "D" of form AC1020-1. Key threats answer the question, "What threatens the effectiveness of the accounting/finance systems and, in turn, could compromise the continuing efficiency, profitability, and success of the Company's operations?"

2.3   The Risk Management Committee shall describe the *consequences* of a given threat, if it were to materialize, in column "E" of form AC1020-1. Possible consequences are negative outcomes; in other words, what *could* go wrong if the threat was real.

2.4   The Risk Management Committee may wish to implement the AC1020-3
        INTERNAL CONTROL CHECKLIST to help identify some of the Company's
        threats and weaknesses.

3.0   IDENTIFY THREAT IMPACT AND LIKELIHOOD

3.1   The Risk Management Committee shall determine the *potential impact* of each
        threat and indicate the *level* of impact[1] in column "F" of form AC1020-1 RISK
        ASSESSMENT/MANAGEMENT WORKSHEET. Threat impact should be
        determined individually *and* in the aggregate: a single threat occurrence might be
        considered as having little to no impact, but how frequently the threat occurs and
        whether it interacts with other threats can affect its impact on the Company.

3.2   The Committee should *use a combination of qualitative and quantitative methods*
        to assess impact. While quantitative methods (i.e., using dollar amounts,
        percentages, or ratios as thresholds) yield measurable results, relying *exclusively*
        on quantitative benchmarks to assess impact is inappropriate. In the words of the
        U.S. Securities and Exchange Commission (SEC), threats are not immaterial
        simply because they fall beneath a numerical threshold. The Committee shall
        consider the *type* of effect or consequence when assessing impact; for example:

        • An actual financial statement misstatement or error
        • An internal control deficiency caused by failure in design or operation
        • The degree of variance between an accounting estimate and the actual amount
        • Financial fraud committed by an employee for the purpose of enhancing the
          Company's reported financial position and operations results

3.3   The Committee shall estimate the *likelihood* that the threat will occur in the next
        reporting period (i.e., year) and record this ranking in column "G" of form
        AC1020-1. For some threats, likelihood is based on historical data; the
        Company's own (experience) is most appropriate. For other threats, industry or
        other benchmarks may be used.

4.0   DETERMINE RISK LEVELS

Impact	Low	Medium	High
High	Medium (3)	High (4)	Very High (5)
Medium	Low (2)	Medium (3)	High (4)
Low	Very Low (1)	Low (2)	Medium (3)

(Likelihood is indicated along the left side of the matrix)

Figure 2 – Risk Matrix

4.1   Risk is a function of the likelihood of a given threat and its potential impact (see
        Figure 2, "Risk Matrix"). For example, if a threat has a high likelihood of

---

[1] Impact and likelihood are ranked "low", "medium", or "high" in this text. The Company may use a
different scale, as appropriate.

occurrence but the potential impact of that threat on the Company is low, the Committee may classify it as a "medium" or "moderate" risk.

4.2 The Risk Management Committee shall assign a risk level to each threat and record that information in column "H" of form AC1020-1.

5.0 RANK THREATS

5.1 The Committee shall rank (sort) threats according to their risk level and other factors – since multiple threats could be assigned the same risk level – and record that ranking in column "I" of AC1020-1.

5.2 The Committee shall determine which and how many of the threats can be addressed within the coming fiscal year – these are its "priority threats" – and include this with the information on form AC1020-1 in its assessment, which it shall present (in summary and detail form) to the CFO.

6.0 RISK ASSESSMENT REVIEW

6.1 The CFO shall review the Risk Management Committee's assessment. If the CFO recommends revisions (e.g., disagrees with risk levels, rankings), the Committee shall make the appropriate revisions and resubmit the assessment.

6.2 When the CFO indicates his/her approval, the Committee shall complete the AC1020-1 RISK ASSESSMENT/MANAGEMENT WORKSHEET (fill in columns "J" through "L") in accordance with AC1030 RISK MANAGEMENT.

6.3 As the Company becomes aware of new threats, the CFO shall reconvene the Risk Management Committee for the purpose of assessing and prioritizing them in relation to threats already accounted for on AC1020-1.

6.4 On a periodic basis (annually, at a minimum), the Risk Management Committee shall review and reassess risks and risk rankings, to determine if the Company is working on controlling the "right" risks.

Effectiveness Criteria:

• Financial risks to the Company are identified, assessed, and appropriately prioritized

Forms:

- AC1020-1 RISK ASSESSMENT / MANAGEMENT WORKSHEET
- AC1020-2 SAMPLE CHART OF ACCOUNTS
- AC1020-3 INTERNAL CONTROL CHECKLIST

References:

A. CFO Manual

- Section 5.5.3 – Risk Assessment

B. Pertinent regulations

- 17 CFR 210, "Form and Content of and Requirements for Financial Statements, Securities Act of 1933, Securities Exchange Act of 1934, Public Utility Holding Company Act of 1935, Investment Company Act of 1940, Investment Advisers Act of 1940, and Energy Policy and Conservation Act of 1975" (USA). For details, see http://www.gpo.gov/fdsys/pkg/CFR-2002-title17-vol1/content-detail.html

- 17 CFR 240, "General Rules and Regulations, Securities Exchange Act of 1934."

- 17 CFR 241, "Interpretative Releases Relating to the Securities Exchange Act of 1934 and General Rules and Regulations Thereunder" (USA). For details of 240 and 241, see http://www.gpo.gov/fdsys/pkg/CFR-2004-title17-vol1/content-detail.html

- 1996 Amendment to the Capital Accord to Incorporate Market Risks (also known as the "1996 Market Risk Amendment" or "BIS 98"), Basel Accord I (last revised, 14 November 2005). This document is the main section of a three-part package of documents issued by the Basel Committee to amend the Capital Accord of July 1988 (Basel I) to take account of and set capital requirements for market risks. It describes two alternative approaches to the measurement of market risk, a standardized method (proposed by the Committee) and an internal models approach. More on this subject is at http://www.bis.org/publ/bcbs119.htm

Additional Resources:

A. ISP 31000:2009, "Risk Management – Principles and Guidelines," International Organization for Standardization (ISO) – http://www.iso.org/iso/iso31000.

B. "Risk Management Standard", Federation of European Risk Management Associations (FERMA), 2003.

FERMA adopted a Risk Management Standard, first published in the United Kingdom in 2002, which was the work of three risk management bodies – the private and public sector risk management associations (AIRMIC and ALARM) and the Institute of Risk Management (IRM), the profession's educational body. The FERMA Risk Management Standard sets out a strategic process that starts with an organization's overall objectives and aspirations, continues with the identification, evaluation, and mitigation of risk, and ends with the transfer of risk. Copies can be obtained at http://www.ferma.eu/risk-management/standards/risk-management-standard/.

C. "What Defines a Material Breach of Fixed Asset Accounting As It Relates to Sarbanes-Oxley Compliance Requirements?", Asset Management Resources, 2006 – http://www.assetmanagementresources.com/Sarbanes-Oxley/Material-Breach.aspx.

D. "Interal Control-Integrated Framework," COSO (May, 2013). Executive Summary at http://www.coso.org/documents/990025P_Executive_Summary_final_may20_e.pdf. The Framework and various tools may be purchased at http://www.coso.org/IC.htm.

E. "Management Risk," COBIT 5: A Business Framework for the Governance and Management of Enterprise IT, ISACA (2012) – http://www.isaca.org/COBIT/Pages/COBIT-5-Framework-product-page.aspx.

F. AICPA Guidance on Risk Assessment – http://www.aicpa.org/interestareas/frc/auditattest/pages/riskassessment.aspx

G. "An Audit of Internal Control over Financial Reporting That Is Integrated with an Audit of Financial Statements", proposed Auditing Standard #5, U.S. Public Company Accounting and Oversight Board (PCAOB), 2007.

H. Additional sample charts of accounts can be found at http://www.netmba.com/accounting/fin/accounts/chart/ and http://www.smallbusinessnotes.com/operating/finmgmt/financialstmts/cofa.html.

Revision History:

Revision	Date	Description of Changes	Requested By
0.0	mm/dd/yyyy	Initial Release	

AC1020-1 RISK ASSESSMENT / MANAGEMENT WORKSHEET

			RISK ASSESSMENT						RISK MANAGEMENT[2]			
A. CLASS	B. ACCT	C. SUB-ACCT	D. KEY THREAT	E. POSSIBLE CONSE-QUENCES	F. IMPACT	G. LIKELI-HOOD	H. RISK	I. RANK	J. MONITOR-ING	K. TARGETS	L. CONTROL MEASURES	

[2] See procedure AC1030, "Risk Management," for discussion of columns J - L.

[This page intentionally left blank]

AC1020-2 SAMPLE CHART OF ACCOUNTS

ASSETS CLASS

1100 - CASH AND MARKETABLE SECURITIES ACCOUNTS

1111 - Cash in Checking
Includes all cash held in the operating bank account. All withdrawals by check and deposits are recorded here. The reported balances are supported by a bank reconcilement prepared monthly.

1112 - Petty Cash
Includes the petty cash and change fund held by the cashier. This account is used only when a new fund is initiated or an existing fund is terminated.

1120 - Marketable Securities
Includes debt securities such as government and corporate bonds and equity securities such as common and preferred stock acquired with cash that is not immediately needed in operations.

1200 – RECEIVABLES

1210 - Notes Receivable
Formal short-term receivables documented by a promissory note and a provision for interest.

1220 - Accounts Receivable
Short-term receivables generated from sales and other activities.

1230 - Interest Receivable
Accrued interest receivable generated by notes and past-due accounts receivable.

1290 - Allowance for Uncollected Accounts
The estimated accrual for bad debts that will result from the current period's sales.

1300 - INVENTORY ACCOUNTS

1310 - Raw Materials
The cost assigned to goods and materials on hand and not in production.

1320 - Work in Process
The cost of the raw material on which production has been started but not completed, plus the cost of direct labor applied specifically to this material and a ratable share of manufacturing overhead costs.

1330 - Finished Goods
The costs identified with completed products on hand.

1500 - PREPAID EXPENSE ACCOUNTS

1510 - Prepaid Insurance
The current portion of insurance premiums paid that cover future periods.

1520 - Prepaid Taxes
Tax payments paid by the Company that relate to a future revenue period.

1530 - Deposits
Current deposits paid by the Company for future services or acquisitions such as trade show deposits, deposits on an equipment purchase, etc.

1600 - OTHER CURRENT ASSET ACCOUNTS

1700 - FIXED ASSET ACCOUNTS

1710 - Land
Represents the company's original cost for the purchase of real estate.

1720 - Buildings
The company's original cost for the purchase of buildings and structures.

1722 - Machinery and Equipment
The company's original cost for the purchase of machinery and equipment.

1724 - Furniture and Fixtures
Represents the company's original cost for the purchase of furniture and other accessory items.

1726 - Vehicles
The company's original cost for the purchase of automobiles and trucks.

1728 - Leasehold Improvements
The company's original cost for structural additions to leased premises.

1790 - ACCUMULATED DEPRECIATION ACCOUNTS
The cumulative depreciation expense recorded to date for all assets in a class.

1790 - Accumulated Depreciation, Buildings
1792 - Accumulated Depreciation, Machinery and Equipment
1794 - Accumulated Depreciation, Furniture and Fixtures
1796 - Accumulated Depreciation, Vehicles
1798 - Accumulated Depreciation, Leasehold Improvements

1800 - INTANGIBLE ASSET ACCOUNTS

1810 – Goodwill
Represents the excess cost over the fair market value of the identifiable assets of a business entity purchased by the company.

1820 - Patents
> The purchase price paid for the rights to a patent from an inventor. For internally developed products - the cost of securing or defending a patent such as attorney's fees. Does not include research and development costs such as labor, materials, consultants, etc. which are directly expensed.

1900 - OTHER ASSET ACCOUNTS

LIABILITIES CLASS

2100 - CURRENT LIABILITY ACCOUNTS

2110 - Notes Payable
> Obligations (written promissory notes) that will mature within one year.

2120 - Accounts Payable
> Balances owed for goods, supplies and services purchased on open account.

2130 - Wages and Salaries Payable
> The amount of wages or salaries earned for time worked but not yet paid as of the period being reported.

2135 - Long-Term Debt Due Within One Year
> The principal of long-term debt that will be repaid during the next year.

2140 - Interest Payable
> Represents the amount of interest accrued on debt obligations but not yet paid.

2150 - Dividends Payable
> Represents the amount of dividends declared or earned on stock investments but as not yet paid to the shareholder.

2160 - Payroll Taxes Payable
> Represents the amount of employee's payroll taxes withheld and employer's taxes due on employee's payroll that have not yet been deposited.

2170 - Property Taxes Payable
> Represents the accrual amount of property taxes to be assessed to the Company but not yet paid.

2190 - INCOME TAXES PAYABLE

2191 - Federal Income Taxes Payable
Represents the estimated accrual of federal taxes due on company earnings.

2192 - State Income Taxes Payable
Represents the estimated accrual amount of state taxes due on company earnings.

2300 - LONG-TERM LIABILITY ACCOUNTS
2310 - Bank Loan
Represents the amount of debt principal that is to be repaid after the next twelve month period.

2320 - Mortgage Payable
Represents the amount of debt principal that is to be repaid after the next twelve month period.

OWNERS' EQUITY CLASS

3100 - Common Stock
Represents the amount of the par value for investments in common stock of the company.

3200 - Preferred Stock
Represents the amount of investments in preferred stock of the company.

3300 - Paid-in-Capital in Excess of Par Value
Represents the excess amount paid for investment in common stock of the Company over the stated par value amount.

3400 - Treasury Stock
Represents the cost amount paid by the Company to repurchase stock from shareholders.

3900 - Retained Earnings
Represents the company's cumulative net profits and losses to date.

3910 - Dividends
Represents the amount of dividends declared during the current period.

SALES ACCOUNTS CLASS

4010 - Sales Product A
Represents the amount of net sales for this product line.

4011 - Sales Returns and Allowances Product A
Represents the amount for refunds given for returned or damaged merchandise.

4020 - Sales Product B
4021 - Sales Returns and Allowances Product B
4030 - Sales Product C
4031 - Sales Returns and Allowances Product C

COST OF SALES AND DEPARTMENTAL EXPENSE CLASS

5010 - Cost of Materials Product A
Represents the costs for materials used in the product.

5020 - Cost of Materials Product B
5030 - Cost of Materials Product C

5090 - Material Price Variance
Represents the differences between actual costs paid for materials and the standard costs used by the Company for pricing these materials.

NOTE: THE FOLLOWING ACCOUNTS ARE SET-UP FOR EACH DEPARTMENT WHEN APPLICABLE. ACCOUNTS ARE DESIGNATED AS FOLLOWS:

5XXX - Cost of Sales Accounts
6XXX - Administration Expense Accounts
7XXX - Sales Expense Accounts

X100 - Salaries
Represents the gross amount for labor costs.

X110 - Employer Taxes
Includes the employer's matching FICA and unemployment taxes.

X120 - Employee Benefits
Includes the portion of health insurance premiums paid by the company.

X200 - Telephone
Includes the costs for monthly line fees and long-distance charges.

X210 - Utilities
Includes the costs for electricity, natural gas, water, and sewer use.

X220 - Postage and Delivery
Includes the amounts for postal costs and delivery costs such as overnight services and messenger services.

X230 - Supplies and Small Equipment
Includes the costs for office and production supplies, tools and equipment type items that fall below the company's capitalization requirements.

X240 - Dues and Subscriptions
Includes amounts paid for membership in professional organizations and amounts paid for subscriptions to publications.

X250 - Travel
Includes the amounts paid for employee's business travel, such as airfare, lodging, rental cars, etc.

X260 - Meals and Entertainment
Includes the amounts paid to reimburse employees for meals while traveling on company business and entertainment incurred while conducting business with business prospects and customers.

X310 - Rent, Building
Includes leases payments for the company's office and manufacturing space.

X320 - Rent, Equipment
Includes amounts for lease payments for office and manufacturing equipment.

X330 - Repairs and Maintenance
Includes amounts for repairs, cleaning, and general maintenance of buildings, grounds, and equipment.

X340 - Depreciation
Represents the estimated amount of deterioration and depreciation of capital assets during the current period.

X350 - Amortization
Represents the scheduled amount of amortization of intangible assets during the current period.

X410 - Insurance
Represents the portion of insurance premiums paid for coverage of the current period for property, casualty and other business insurance.

X420 - Property Taxes
Represents the estimated amount of property taxes on buildings, properties and furniture and equipment for the current period.

X430 - Licenses
Includes amounts for business licenses and fees.

X510 - Consulting Services
This includes fees to non-employee individuals or firms for advisory services to the company.

X520 - Legal Fees
This includes all fees paid for attorneys, appraisers, notaries, court costs, document recording fees, and witnesses.

X530 - Accounting Fees
Includes costs to outside firms for auditing services and accounting advice.

X540 - Seminars and Conferences
This includes amounts incurred by employees attending outside seminar or conference programs.

X550 - Bank Fees
This includes amounts charge by banks to the Company for processing financial transactions. This does not include interest expense items.

X610 - Advertising and Promotions
This includes costs for camera and layout work, published advertisements, brochures, and trade show expenses.

X620 - Printing Costs
This includes amounts for printing, binding, and padding paid to outside print shops. This does not include items included in Advertising and Promotions.

OTHER EXPENSE ACCOUNTS CLASS

9110 - Interest Income
Includes interest income from cash and security investments.

9120 - Dividend Income
Represents dividend income from the company's security investments.

9190 - Miscellaneous Income
Includes minor income items not classified in the revenue accounts.

9210 - Interest Expense
Represents interest incurred by the Company for short-and long-term debts.

9220 - Penalties
Includes penalty items such as late payment or filing fees.

9290 - Miscellaneous Expense
Includes minor expense items not classified in the expenditure accounts.

AC1020-3 INTERNAL CONTROL CHECKLIST[3]

An effective internal control system enables the Company to manage significant risks and monitor the reliability and integrity of financial and operating information. It also ensures that the audit committee acts as a powerful and proactive agent for corporate self-regulation.

The Committee of Sponsoring Organizations (COSO) of the Treadway Commission developed the following questions to help senior executives and directors gain a better understanding of their organizations' control systems:

ETHICAL ENVIRONMENT

☐ Do board members and senior executives set a day-in, day-out example of high integrity and ethical behavior?

☐ Is there a written code of conduct for employees? Is it reinforced by training, top-down communications and periodic written statements of compliance from key employees?

☐ Are performance and incentive compensation targets reasonable and realistic, or do they create undue pressure for short-term results?

☐ Is it clear that fraudulent financial reporting at any level and in any form will not be tolerated?

☐ Are ethics woven into criteria used to evaluate individual and business unit performance?

☐ Does management react appropriately when receiving bad news from subordinates and business units?

☐ Does a process exist to resolve close ethical calls?

☐ Are business risks identified and candidly discussed with the board of directors?

RISK ASSESSMENT AND CONTROL ACTIVITIES

☐ Is relevant, reliable internal and external information timely identified, compiled and communicated to those positioned to act?

☐ Are risks identified and analyzed and actions taken to mitigate them?

☐ Are controls in place to ensure management decisions are properly carried out?

---

[3] Source: "Internal Control — Integrated Framework," COSO, 1993.

☐   Does management routinely monitor controls in the process of running the organizations operations?

☐   Are periodic, systematic evaluations of control systems conducted and documented?

AUDIT COMMITTEE EFFECTIVENESS

☐   Has the board recently reviewed the audit committee's written charter?

☐   Are audit committee members functioning independently of management?

☐   Do committee members possess an appropriate mix of operating and financial control expertise?

☐   Does the committee understand and monitor the broad organizational control environment?

☐   Does the committee oversee appropriateness, relevance and reliability of operational and financial reporting to the board, as well as to investors and other external users?

☐   Does the committee oversee existence of and compliance with ethical standards?

☐   Does the committee or full board have a meaningful but challenging relationship with independent and internal auditors, senior financial control executives, and key corporate and business unit operating executives?

INTERNAL AUDITING FUNCTION EFFECTIVENESS

☐   Does internal auditing have the support of top management, the audit committee, and the board of directors?

☐   Is the organizational relationship between internal auditing and senior executives appropriate?

☐   Does internal auditing have and use open lines of communication and private access to all senior officers and the audit committee?

☐   Is there an internal audit plan (reviewed by the audit committee) describing internal audit responsibility?

Document ID **AC1030**	Title **RISK MANAGEMENT**	Print Date **mm/dd/yyyy**
Revision **0.0**	Prepared By **Preparer's Name / Title**	Date Prepared **mm/dd/yyyy**
Effective Date **mm/dd/yyyy**	Reviewed By **Reviewer's Name / Title**	Date Reviewed **mm/dd/yyyy**
	Approved By **Final Approver's Name / Title**	Date Approved **mm/dd/yyyy**

Policy: The Company shall monitor and manage financial and other risks on an ongoing basis, to ensure they are addressed appropriately.

Purpose: Provide a framework (or "risk management system") for all levels of Company management (especially the CFO), which should enable, support, and promote:

- Awareness and understanding of real and significant risks and their impact;
- Exercising due diligence when making decisions;
- Exercise of appropriate duty of care;
- Innovation through taking *calculated* risks in pursuit of business opportunity and excellence; and
- Provision of assurance that risks are managed in accordance with their level of threat or exposure.

Scope: This procedure pertains to managing *financial* risks.

Responsibilities: The Risk Manager is responsible for conducting risk assessment and for identifying the most appropriate method(s) of managing financial risk (also see AC1020 RISK ASSESSMENT).

The Risk Manager is responsible for directing development of the risk management plan and reporting to the CEO and CFO.

The CEO (Chief Executive Officer) and CFO (Chief Financial Officer) are responsible for reviewing and approving the Risk Management Plan.

Definitions: Risk appetite – Amount of capital an individual or organization is willing to lose in order to generate a potential profit.

Risk management – Process of combining a risk assessment with decisions on how to address that risk. The Company can manage risk in one of four ways:

- **Avoid** the risk (e.g., discontinue a product, postpone expansion, sell a division);
- **Mitigate**, or reduce, the risk – take action to reduce the likelihood and/or impact of a given threat (e.g., install failure detection technology and auxiliary power source to reduce risk

of system down time);

- ***Transfer*** (share) the risk – reduce the likelihood or impact of a threat (e.g., buy insurance, pool risk, hedge, outsource); or
- ***Accept*** the risk – do nothing to affect the likelihood or impact of an event. If the threat materializes, the cost to implement risk controls will exceed the cost of repair/replacement.

Risk management system – Comprehensive framework for measuring, monitoring, and managing risk to (a) achieve an enterprise-wide view of the investment and risk profile, (b) increase return on risk, and (c) establish an appropriately focused risk culture.

Risk threshold – Amount/level of risk an organization is willing to bear in order to achieve a target rate of return.

Risk tolerance – Organization's ability to handle declines in the value of its portfolio.

Procedure:

1.0 DEVELOPING A RISK MANAGEMENT SYSTEM

1.1 For each "priority threat" identified by the Risk Management Committee and the CFO (see AC1020 RISK ASSESSMENT), the Committee shall identify and list possible *monitoring activities* in column "J" of form AC1020-1RISK ASSESSMENT AND MANAGEMENT WORKSHEET. Monitoring activities are a way to determine if threats are materializing (see examples in Figure 1.)

| | | | | RISK MANAGEMENT | | |
A. CLASS	B. ACCT	C. SUB-ACCT	D. KEY THREAT	J. MONITORING	K. TARGETS	L. CONTROL MEASURES
LIAB	Accts. Payable		Unauthorized payments	Match invoice with purchasing authority PO and proper budget code(s). Check cosigner reviews authorization. Supervisor reviews and initials log and A/P metrics. Amount of disbursement vs. number of signatures.	No unauthorized payments.	Require two signatures for payments over $1000. Segregate approval and signing duties.

Figure 1 – Section of Form AC1020-1

1.2 The Committee shall identify risk management targets and/or regulatory thresholds and list them in column "K" of form AC1020-1.

1.3 The Committee shall evaluate possible control measures – control measures should reduce the impact and/or the likelihood of threats – in light of:

- The *effect* the control should have on the likelihood and impact of the threat

- Whether controls are able to address multiple (vs. single) threats
- The *cost* to implement the control versus the *benefit* it may provide
- Opportunities with *potential* for significant benefits

The Committee shall identify and list preferred control measures in column "L" of form AC1020-1.

1.4   The Committee shall summarize its findings contained in form AC1020-1, work up a budget estimate and timeline for implementing the Risk Management Plan, and schedule a meeting to present the Risk Management Plan summary, details, and budget to the CEO and CFO.

1.5   On approval of the Plan, the Committee shall assign responsibility for implementation of control measures to the appropriate Accounting Managers (e.g., assign A/P control implementation to the A/P Manager).

2.0   IMPLEMENTING THE RISK MANAGEMENT SYSTEM

2.1   The various Accounting Managers shall implement assigned control measures in their respective Departments according to the timeline (schedule) prescribed in the Risk Management Plan. Accounting Managers shall report to the Committee periodically (e.g., weekly) on how implementation of controls is progressing.

2.2   Once control measures are in place, Accounting Managers shall monitor activities through the use of activity logs, account reconciliation, and other suitable methods. Managers shall report the results of control monitoring to the CFO periodically (e.g., weekly, biweekly).

3.0   EVALUATING THE RISK MANAGEMENT SYSTEM

3.1   The CFO shall ensure that an internal audit of finance is conducted periodically (annually, at a minimum) – or more frequently, if the desired control level has not been achieved – to evaluate, among other things, the effectiveness of the risk management controls that have been implemented, in accordance with AC1050 INTERNAL AUDITING.

3.2   As audit findings are brought to light and reviewed by the Risk Management Committee, any control found to be insufficient (a nonconformance) shall cause the Committee to initiate a corrective action, to be performed in accordance with AC1060 CORRECTIVE ACTION.

4.0   ADAPTING THE RISK MANAGEMENT SYSTEM

4.1   The Risk Management Committee shall review the Risk Management System semiannually, or as needed, to consider System improvements in response to such things as:

- Audit findings and timeliness of corrective actions;
- Changes to the business environment;
- Changes in the regulatory environment; and
- Changes within the Company.

4.2   The CFO shall review the Risk Management System annually, at a minimum, to verify that the System is working as expected and to ensure its continued suitability.

4.3   Where the Risk Management System is found in need of change, the Risk Management Committee shall reassess the System in accordance with AC1020 RISK ASSESSMENT.

Effectiveness Criteria:

- Financial risks to the Company are managed appropriately

- The Risk Management System is reviewed on a continuing basis for effectiveness and improved and adapted, as needed, to changing circumstances

Forms:

- AC1020-1 RISK ASSESSMENT AND MANAGEMENT WORKSHEET

References:

A. Finance Policy Manual

- Section 5.5.4 – Risk Management

B. Finance procedures

- AC1000 SARBANES-OXLEY COMPLIANCE

- AC1020 RISK ASSESSMENT

C. **SARBANES-OXLEY ACT OF 2002** (USA). The Act was designed to protect investors by improving the *accuracy and reliability* of corporate disclosures made pursuant to securities laws (e.g., Securities and Exchange Act of 1934).

Additional Resources:

A. ISP 31000:2009, "Risk Management – Principles and Guidelines," International Organization for Standardization (ISO) – http://www.iso.org/iso/iso31000.

B. "Risk Management Standard", Federation of European Risk Management Associations (FERMA), 2003.

FERMA adopted a Risk Management Standard originally published in the United Kingdom in 2002. The FERMA Risk Management Standard sets out a strategic process that starts with an organization's overall objectives and aspirations, continues with the identification, evaluation, and mitigation of risk, and ends with the transfer of risk.

C. "What Defines a Material Breach of Fixed Asset Accounting As It Relates to Sarbanes-Oxley Compliance Requirements?", Asset Management Resources, 2006 – http://www.assetmanagementresources.com/Sarbanes-Oxley/Material-Breach.aspx.

D. "Interal Control-Integrated Framework," COSO (May, 2013). Executive Summary at

http://www.coso.org/documents/990025P_Executive_Summary_final_may20_e.p
df. The Framework and various tools may be purchased at
http://www.coso.org/IC.htm.

E. "Management Risk," COBIT 5: A Business Framework for the Governance and
Management of Enterprise IT, ISACA (2012) –
http://www.isaca.org/COBIT/Pages/COBIT-5-Framework-product-page.aspx.

F. AICPA Guidance on Risk Assessment –
http://www.aicpa.org/interestareas/frc/auditattest/pages/riskassessment.aspx

G. "An Audit of Internal Control over Financial Reporting that is Integrated with an
Audit of Financial Statements" (Auditing Standard #5), U.S. Public Company
Accounting and Oversight Board (PCAOB), 2007.

H. "Basel II: The New Basel Capital Accord - Third Consultative Paper", Basel
Committee on Banking Supervision, April, 2003. The Basel II Accord is
designed to improve the capital adequacy framework for banks which, in turn, is
intended to foster a strong emphasis on risk management and encourage ongoing
improvements in banks' risk assessment capabilities.

Revision History:

Revision	Date	Description of Changes	Requested By
0.0	mm/dd/yyyy	Initial Release	

[This page intentionally left blank]

Document ID AC1040	Title **EXTERNAL AUDITING**	Print Date mm/dd/yyyy
Revision 0.0	Prepared By **Preparer's Name / Title**	Date Prepared mm/dd/yyyy
Effective Date mm/dd/yyyy	Reviewed By **Reviewer's Name / Title**	Date Reviewed mm/dd/yyyy
	Approved By **Final Approver's Name / Title**	Date Approved mm/dd/yyyy

Policy: The Company shall periodically undergo an external, or third-party, audit of its financial operations to determine if they conform to requirements and are achieving the desired results.

Purpose: To determine if the Company:

- Is presenting financial information in accordance with established criteria (such as accepted accounting practices, regulations);

- Is in compliance with specific requirements; and/or

- Has designed and implemented effective internal controls over financial reporting and/or safeguarding assets to achieve stated control objectives.

Scope: All of the Company's financial operations are subject to external audit.

Responsibilities: The Audit Team Leader is responsible for evaluating and selecting an External Auditor.

The CFO (Chief Financial Officer) is the main point of contact between the Company and the External Auditor and is responsible for coordinating Company audit activities and responses.

The External Auditor is responsible for preparing the Audit schedule and plan, conducting the Audit, keeping the Company informed of the audit's progress, and reporting audit findings and results to the Company.

All Employees are responsible for cooperating with External Auditors during the course of the audit and for taking appropriate actions, where required, to correct deficiencies/weaknesses found in the audit.

Definitions: Adverse opinion – Opinion of an external auditor that an organization's financial statements are so materially misstated or misleading that they do not fairly represent the entity's financial position or results of operations and cash flows and/or the entity's practices or controls are not in conformance with requirements (e.g., regulations).

Audit evidence – All information used by an auditor in arriving at conclusions on which the audit opinion is based. Audit evidence may be obtained from audit procedures performed during the course of the audit, the accounting records underlying financial statements, and possibly other sources (e.g., previous audits).

Audit opinion – Statement recorded by the external auditor in the audit report. An audit opinion can be qualified, unqualified, adverse, or it can be a disclaimer.

Disclaimer – Statement that the auditor is not expressing an opinion on the financial statements. A disclaimer of opinion is appropriate in such circumstances as when the auditor lacks independence (SAS 26), when sufficient competent evidential matter cannot be obtained (SAS 58), when there is substantial doubt about the entity's ability to survive (SAS 59), or in matters involving uncertainty (SAS 79).

External audit – Examination of a company's financial records and reports by an independent external auditor in order to verify that the company's financial reports are relevant, accurate, and complete.

Qualified opinion – Opinion of an external auditor that information presented in the Company's financial statements does not accurately reflect the Company's position; not as severe as an adverse opinion.

Unqualified opinion – Auditor's opinion that information presented in financial statements is reasonably accurate and reliable and/or that practices and controls conform to requirements; also called a "clean audit report."

Procedure:

1.0   EXTERNAL AUDITS – BACKGROUND

There are many reasons why companies have their books audited by outside firms, such as:

- Regulatory requirements (e.g., Sarbanes-Oxley);
- Lender requirements;
- Credibility that a third-party audit lends to the Company's financial statements;
- The discipline that external audits exert on the Company's reporting and controls;
- The external auditor's objectivity;
- Auditing expertise that does not exist within the company; and
- Receiving valuable recommendations for the company's operations.

2.0 PLANNING FOR AN EXTERNAL AUDIT

2.1   The Audit Team Leader shall choose a qualified Auditor to conduct the Company's third-party financial audits in accordance with AC1000 – SARBANES-OXLEY COMPLIANCE, as well as any Company's vendor evaluation or outsourcing policies. External Auditors are required to comply with professional and ethical standards and regulations (see "References" section). For example:

- No external auditor can be allowed to audit the same processes/controls for more than five consecutive years; and

- In some cases, external auditors may not render consulting services to their auditing clients.[1]

2.2   The External Auditor shall prepare the following documents in accordance with applicable standards and guidelines and submit them to the Audit Team Leader for review and approval *at least two weeks in advance* of the audit:[2]

- The audit schedule;

- An audit plan (including a statement of the auditor's responsibilities and estimated fees for doing the work); and

- A list of documents and records required.

2.3   The CFO shall contact owners of processes/controls to be audited to ensure that requested information and documents can be produced or obtained and to ensure that key employees associated with those processes/controls are available on the requested date(s). The Audit Team Leader should set a reasonable deadline for a response.

- If key employees are not available on the requested date(s), process owners should ascertain and convey alternative audit dates to the Audit Team Leader.

- The CFO shall have final discretionary authority over employees' availability.

2.4   The CFO shall notify the External Auditor in writing of the Company's acceptance of the Audit Schedule and Plan, as originally offered or with modifications. The CFO shall comply with reasonable requests for advance information; where such requests cannot be easily or immediately fulfilled, the CFO shall give the External Auditor an explanation.

3.0 SUPPORTING THE EXTERNAL AUDIT

3.1   The External Auditor shall begin the audit with an Opening Meeting with the CFO and key employees identified in the Audit Schedule. At this meeting, the CFO and key employees should be sure they understand the purpose of the audit and what is required of them. The External Auditor should address any questions

---

[1] Private organizations usually have more leeway than public ones, since relevant regulations are almost always directed at public companies.

[2] The amount of lead time should correspond to the Audit scope (i.e., greater audit scope = longer lead time).

or concerns the CFO or key employees bring up in the Opening Meeting before concluding it.

3.2   During the Audit, the CFO and key employees should make every effort to cooperate with the External Auditor. This includes being available at the scheduled date and time and responding to questions, requests for information, etc., to the best of their ability and within reason.

- If key employees have questions regarding the appropriateness of questions or requests from the External Auditor, they should contact the CFO for clarification

3.3   The External Auditor should provide periodic updates (once a day, at a minimum) on the Audit's progress to the CFO, in accordance with any agreement made prior to the start of the Audit, so that the CFO can address questions and concerns as they arise, rather than at the end of the Audit.

4.0   REVIEWING EXTERNAL AUDIT RESULTS

4.1   The External Auditor shall conclude the Audit with a Closing Meeting, attended by the CFO (and key employees, if needed or requested). In the Closing Meeting, the External Auditor shall give an overall audit opinion (e.g., qualified, unqualified, adverse, disclaimer) and review individual audit findings with the attendees.

4.2   As the audit results are discussed, if a qualified or adverse opinion is given, the CFO should list the identified material weaknesses in column "A" of form AC1040-1 CORRECTIVE ACTION PLAN. The External Auditor and the CFO should agree on a tentative time frame for the Company's response, subject to the Auditor's formal report.

4.3   The External Auditor shall submit a formal audit report, or "Letter to Management on Internal Controls," describing material weaknesses identified by the auditor in sufficient detail, to the Audit Team Leader and the CFO within the time frame agreed to at the Closing Meeting.

4.4   After receiving and reviewing the LMIC with the Audit Team Leader, the CFO shall delegate the investigation of potential corrective actions, noting the delegate in column "B" of form AC1040-1. The Committee shall ensure that the process owner and investigator are notified in writing.

4.5   The investigator shall determine the appropriate corrective action(s), estimate the resources needed and a target date for completing corrective actions, and list this information in columns "C" through "E" of form AC1040-1, respectively. The investigator shall return AC1040-1 to the CFO, who shall ensure that corrective actions are taken in accordance with AC1060 CORRECTIVE ACTION.

4.6   The CFO shall prepare the Management Response to the Auditor, using the information contained on AC1040-1, and submit this to the Audit Team Leader for review and approval. Upon the Audit Team Leader's approval, the CFO shall submit the Management Response to the Auditor.

4.7   External Audit and Corrective Action files shall be cross-referenced.

5.0   EXTERNAL AUDIT FOLLOW-UP

5.1   The External Auditor may be asked to conduct a follow-up visit – at a time agreed to by the Audit Team Leader – to verify that corrective actions taken in response to audit findings have been implemented *or* that suitable progress is being made. The Audit Team Leader shall ensure that the External Auditor can be shown that implemented corrective actions are having the desired effect.

5.2   A summary of External Audit activity, including audit results and corrective actions, shall be reported at the next Management Review Meeting (see FA1010 MANAGEMENT RESPONSIBILITY).

Effectiveness Criteria:

- Financial processes and controls conform to regulatory and standards requirements

- Material weaknesses are resolved in an effective, timely manner

- Number and types of deficiencies/weaknesses decrease over time

Forms:

- AC1040-1 CORRECTIVE ACTION PLAN

- External Audit file (incl. Letter to Management, objective evidence, audit schedules, Management Response)

References:

A. Finance Policy Manual

- Section 5.5.5 – External Auditing

B. Finance procedures

- FA1010 MANAGEMENT RESPONSIBILITY

- AC1060 CORRECTIVE ACTION

- AC1000 SOX COMPLIANCE

C. Audit of Internal Control over Financial Reporting that Is Integrated with an Audit of Financial Statements and Related Other Proposals (Auditing Standard #5), Public Company Accounting and Oversight Board (PCAOB-USA), 2007 – http://pcaobus.org/Standards/Auditing/Pages/Auditing_Standard_5.aspx.

D. Clarified Statements on Auditing Standards, AICPA (2013) – http://www.aicpa.org/Research/Standards/AuditAttest/Pages/clarifiedSAS.aspx.

E. Uniform Accountancy Act, 5th Edition, AICPA/NASBA (National Association of State Boards of Accountancy), July, 2007. This document, coauthored by AICPA and NASBA, is designed to advance the goal of uniformity, protect the public interest, and promote high professional standards within the accounting profession. The Act is designed as a guide for individual US states and territories when crafting their own legislation. Some states have adopted the Act with

modifications. The text of the Act can be found at
http://www.aicpa.org/advocacy/state/statecontactinfo/uaa/pages/default.aspx.

Additional Resources:

A. American Institute of Certified Public Accountants (AICPA) –
http://www.aicpa.org. The AICPA is the professional organization for U.S.
Certified Public Accountants. Its mission is to provide members with the
resources, information, and leadership that enable them to provide valuable
services in the highest professional manner to benefit the public as well as
employers and clients.

B. Information Systems Audit and Control Association (ISACA) –
http://www.isaca.org. ISACA began in 1967 in the USA as the EDP Auditors
Association. Today, ISACA has over 65,000 members worldwide, in more than
140 countries and covers a variety of professional IT-related positions, including
IS auditor, internal auditor, security professional, regulator, and chief information
officer.

C. National Association of State Boards of Accountancy (NASBA) –
http://www.nasba.org. NASBA serves as a forum for the 55 state and territorial
boards of accountancy in the US. NASBA's mission is to enhance the
effectiveness of state boards of accountancy. Its goals are to provide high quality,
effective programs and services; to identify, research, and analyze major current
and emerging issues affecting state boards of accountancy; to strengthen and
maintain communications with state boards to facilitate the exchange of ideas and
opinions; and to develop and foster relationships with organizations that impact
the regulation of public accounting.

D. Association of Chartered Certified Accountants (ACCA) –
http://www.accaglobal.com. ACCA is a UK-chartered accountancy body with a
global presence. It offers the Chartered Certified Accountant qualification
worldwide. It is one of the world's largest and fastest-growing accountancy
bodies with 115,345 members and 296,000 affiliates and students in 170
countries.

E. IT Standards, Guidelines, and Tools and Techniques for Audit and Assurance and
Control Professionals, ISACA, March 2010 – http://www.isaca.org/Knowledge-
Center/Standards/Documents/IT-Audit-Assurance-Guidance-1March2010.pdf

Revision History:

Revision	Date	Description of Changes	Requested By
0.0	mm/dd/yyyy	Initial Release	

[This page intentionally left blank]

AC1040-1 CORRECTIVE ACTION PLAN

A. Material Weakness	B. Investigation Assigned To	C. Corrective Action to be Taken	D. Resource Estimate	E. Target Date

[This page intentionally left blank]

Document ID	Title	Print Date
AC1050	**INTERNAL AUDITING**	**mm/dd/yyyy**
Revision	Prepared By	Date Prepared
0.0	**Preparer's Name / Title**	**mm/dd/yyyy**
Effective Date	Reviewed By	Date Reviewed
mm/dd/yyyy	**Reviewer's Name / Title**	**mm/dd/yyyy**
	Approved By	Date Approved
	Final Approver's Name / Title	**mm/dd/yyyy**
Applicable Standards: **IIA International Standards for the Professional Practice of Internal Auditing**		

Policy: The Company shall periodically conduct internal audits of its financial reporting and internal controls to determine if they conform to requirements and are achieving the desired results.

Purpose: To describe the Internal Audit process, intended to ensure that the Company complies with applicable standards and regulations pertaining to internal controls and financial reporting.

Scope: All financial/accounting operations are subject to periodic internal audits. Audit frequency and extent (scope) are determined by the complexity of the process/control, the risk of a deficiency or material weakness in that area and what impact that would have, and possibly other factors.

Responsibilities: The Audit Team Leader is responsible for managing the Internal Audit process, developing and managing the Internal Audit schedule (or cycle), supervising Audit Team members, and reporting the Audit Team Leader's findings to the Audit Team.

Internal auditors are responsible for conducting complete, detailed, and objective Internal Audits and reporting their findings to the Audit Team Leader.

The Audit Team Leader is responsible for reviewing and approving the Internal Audit Department's annual and long-range audit plans and activities, for reviewing significant findings and recommendations by Internal Audit, and for ensuring the adequacy of management's corrective actions.

The CFO (Chief Financial Officer) is responsible for ensuring that corrective actions are taken in a timely manner.

All Employees are responsible for cooperating with Internal Auditors in the course of the audit process and for taking appropriate actions, where required, to correct deficiencies found during the audit.

Definitions: Audit evidence – All information used by an auditor in arriving at conclusions on which the audit opinion is based. Audit evidence, which is cumulative in nature, includes audit evidence obtained from audit procedures performed during the course of the audit, information contained in accounting records underlying the financial statements, and possibly evidence obtained from other sources (e.g., previous audits, procedures).

Audit opinion – The part of the auditor's report in which the auditor expresses an opinion on the extent to which financial statements are materially misstated. The fact that it is an opinion and not a certification means the auditor is providing *reasonable* – not complete – assurance as to whether the financial statements are materially misstated.

Audit plan – Description or outline of the purpose, scope, objectives and activities of an audit.

Audit schedule – Annual plan of audits to be accomplished, areas to be audited, and participating auditors; also "audit cycle."

Audit scope – Refers to activities covered by an internal audit; includes such factors as the nature and extent of the audit subject (processes, controls, statements, etc.) and the time frame being audited.

Auditee – Organization, area, or function being audited.

Auditor – Individual who carries out an audit; one who is qualified and authorized to perform all or part of an audit.

Audit Team Leader – One who supervises an Audit Team (consisting of the Audit Team Leader and at least one other auditor) before and during an audit and for reports and corrective actions after the audit; someone qualified and authorized to manage and direct an audit.

Audit team – Consists of a Lead Auditor and at least one other Auditor; they conduct the Audit (the Lead Auditor supervises) and report on what they found.

Control deficiency – Gap in internal control that, by itself, does not affect the validity or integrity of the financial process or reporting; design or operation of a control that does not allow management or employees, in the normal course of performing their assigned functions, to prevent or detect misstatements on a timely basis.

Corrective action – Action taken to eliminate the cause of a defect, deficiency, nonconformity, or other undesirable situation and prevent its recurrence.

Material weakness – Significant deficiency or combination of significant deficiencies that results in more than a remote likelihood that a material misstatement will not be prevented or detected.

Misstatement – Incorrect financial statement information.

Objective evidence – Qualitative or quantitative information, records, or statements of fact supporting Internal Audit opinions.

Significant deficiency – Control deficiency or combination of control deficiencies that adversely affects the company's ability to initiate, record, process, or report external financial data reliably in accordance with generally accepted accounting principles, such that there is more than a remote likelihood that a misstatement that is more than inconsequential will not be prevented or detected.

Generally accepted accounting principles (GAAP) - Standards, conventions, and rules that U.S. accountants follow; established by the Financial Accounting Standards Board (FASB).

Procedure:

1.0 INTERNAL AUDIT BACKGROUND

1.1   The Audit Team shall choose an Audit Team Leader to manage the Company's Internal Audit program.

- The Audit Team Leader should have a working knowledge of auditing principles and techniques. They should be capable of organizing and directing audits, reporting audit opinions, and evaluating planned and implemented corrective actions;

- The Audit Team Leader should be familiar with GAAP and applicable audit standards and have Accounting experience;

- The Audit Team Leader should be qualified by an accepted qualification body;

- The Audit Team Leader should have participated in (a minimum number of) audits as a qualified auditor; and

- If the Company cannot justify the cost to have an Audit Team Leader on staff, the Board of Directors shall establish and maintain a relationship with a qualified provider of internal audit services, in accordance with the Company's Vendor Evaluation or Outsourcing procedure.

1.2   The Audit Team Leader shall prepare an Internal Audit Schedule (see AC1050-1 – AUDIT SCHEDULE for guidance) two to three months prior to the start of the next fiscal year and submit the Schedule to the Audit Team Leader for approval.

- The Audit Schedule will vary according to the size and complexity of processes and controls being audited. Similarly, audit frequency depends on the associated level of risk and other factors; where the risk of material misstatement is greater, processes/controls should be audited more frequently and thoroughly; and

- The Audit Schedule shall specify the processes/controls to be audited and the estimated time frame for each audit.

1.3   The Audit Team Leader shall select an Audit Team for each audit.

- The size of the Audit Team will vary according to the scope of the audit;

- Individual auditors must be competent and experienced. To be considered competent, Internal Auditors must be trained in auditing practices and the requirements of applicable standards and regulations (see "References"); and

- The Audit Team Leader should assign auditors according to their area and amount of expertise.

2.0 INTERNAL AUDIT PLANNING

2.1   The Audit Team Leader should review relevant audit requirements (e.g., regulatory, internal, standard/guideline related) before developing an Internal Audit plan. See the "References" section following this procedure.

2.2   The Audit Team Leader shall determine the *scope* of the Internal Audit – which statements, processes, and/or controls are to be audited – decide approximately *when* the audit should be conducted, and identify *key employees* (e.g., process owners) and provide this information to the Audit Team Leader at least a month in advance of the audit.[1]

2.3   The Audit Team Leader shall contact key employees to ensure their availability and to confirm availability of information needed for the audit (financial statements, source materials, corroborating documentation, etc.).

- The Audit Team Leader should give key employees at least two weeks – and possibly more – to gather the necessary information and prepare for the audit;

- Key employees should be notified *in writing* (by interoffice mail, e-mail, or both);

- Key employees may include or delegate tasks to subordinates. If this is done, it is up to key employees to ensure the availability of delegates;

- The Audit Team Leader shall make requests for information (which ledgers, reports, statements, etc., are needed) as specific as possible; and

- The Audit Team Leader and key employees should attempt to resolve scheduling conflicts in an appropriate manner. If the Audit Team Leader encounters difficulties (obstacles) in scheduling employees, he/she should bring this to the attention of the Audit Team so it can make a decision (to reschedule the audit or enforce availability, for instance).

2.4   While developing the Audit Plan, the Audit Team Leader should conduct at least one Audit Team meeting for the purpose of discussing the upcoming Internal Audit and reviewing previous audit reports, Corrective Action Requests (CAR), and other relevant documents.

- Audit Team members should prepare checklists for the processes, etc., they will be auditing (see AC1050-3 AUDIT CHECKLIST for guidance). While the sample checklist is general, audit checklists should be designed specifically to the activities and controls of each process to be audited;

---

[1] The lead time needed to plan and conduct an internal audit depends primarily on the audit scope.

- The Audit Team Leader may contribute to checklists based on their knowledge and experience. In fact, the Audit Team Leader should review individual Audit Checklists and add questions he/she believes are necessary to adequately evaluate controls/processes being audited; and

- Audit questions need not be limited to those on an individual's Audit Checklist. The Checklist is unlikely to be all-inclusive but it serves as a useful guide and Auditors should have some flexibility to address issues as they come up in the course of the audit.

2.5   The Audit Team Leader shall formalize the Audit Plan in accordance with AC1050-2 AUDIT PLAN and publish and distribute copies of the Audit Plan to the Audit Team, key employees, and Audit Team members at least two weeks in advance of the audit opening date. The formal Plan shall include, at a minimum:

- The purpose, scope, objectives, and criteria for the audit;

- Identification of specific processes and/or controls being audited;

- Audit dates and times;

- Audit Team members;

- Key employees; and

- A schedule and agenda for Opening and Closing Meetings and individual audit subjects.

3.0   CONDUCTING THE INTERNAL AUDIT

3.1   The Audit Team Leader should begin the audit with an Opening Meeting (see AC1050-2 AUDIT PLAN), to be attended by all employees identified in the plan. Other department employees may attend the Meeting, at the direction of department management.

- During the Opening Meeting, the Audit Team Leader introduces the Audit Team and explains the Audit Plan. The purpose, scope, objectives, and criteria of the audit are confirmed;

- Copies of the Audit Plan are distributed, if they have not been previously, and the Audit Schedule is confirmed;

- Questions from department employees will be answered to the degree the Audit Team is able to do so; and

- If there are any special concerns with the area to be audited (e.g., safety issues), it is the responsibility of the area manager to review special requirements with the Audit Team Leader.

3.2   The Audit Team Leader shall conduct the audit according to the planned schedule to the extent practicable, ensuring a thorough audit. The audit will consist of interviews, document reviews, observations of activities, and testing of internal controls. (NOTE: It is important to remain within the scope of the audit.)

- Internal Auditors must keep in mind that the purpose of the audit is to ensure that the Company's financial reporting is *reasonably* accurate, that internal controls are in place, and that those controls effectively minimize the risk of material misstatement.

- Auditing authorities (e.g., IIA, PCAOB) recommend that auditors take a "top-down, risk based" approach to auditing. The cost to comply with regulations (e.g., Sarbanes-Oxley) has been high relative to the benefits realized, mainly because companies tried to implement controls universally. Taking a risk-based approach, on the other hand, can significantly reduce compliance costs.

3.3 Each member of the Audit Team should keep detailed notes of all interviews, observations, and document reviews. Issues beyond the scope of the audit should be noted for follow-up.

3.4 The Audit Team Leader shall provide a periodic audit *progress report* to the Audit Team, indicating (at a minimum) which objectives have been accomplished and which have not and the difficulties that have been encountered, to date. The frequency and detail of these reports depends on the scope of the audit and they should be agreed to by the Audit Team Leader and the Audit Team.

3.5 When conducting interviews, Audit Team members should use the Audit Checklist (see AC1050-3 AUDIT CHECKLIST for guidance) to maintain focus and ensure completeness. There should be enough questions on the Checklist to enable a thorough evaluation of activities in the audited area; however, the Audit Team Leader must recognize that Auditors may not have time to ask all questions.

- Auditors should be flexible – when they find discrepancies, they should ask follow-up questions to clarify their understanding of the situation; and

- Auditors should probe for answers, especially with regard to open-ended questions.

3.6 When information presented is inadequate to demonstrate conformance with a requirement, the Auditor shall note this in the "Evidence" column of form AC1050-3. When information presented suggests or demonstrates a nonconformance, the Auditor shall write up a finding on form AC1050-4 AUDIT OPINION.

4.0 INTERNAL AUDIT REPORTING

4.1 At the conclusion of the auditing activity and prior to the Closing Meeting, the Audit Team shall meet in order to integrate findings, observations, general trends, and specific follow-up issues. During this "pre-closing" meeting, the team shall arrive at a conclusion on the degree to which audited processes/controls meet audit criteria and objectives:

- The strengths, weaknesses, and observations (not findings, but opportunities for improvement) noted by the entire Audit Team are collected and collated;

- Findings are identified and categorized according to their materiality and risk and *objective evidence* of each finding is identified;

- Forms AC1050-4 are collated, counted, and analyzed;

- Observations are identified; and

- Possible areas for disagreement are discussed and potential resolutions are developed.

4.2   Each audit should be concluded with a Closing Meeting, attended by essentially the same employees who attended the Opening Meeting. During the Closing Meeting, the Audit Team Leader shall present the overall audit opinion and a summary review of the Audit Team's findings and observations. The Closing Meeting should provide time for questions from the Audit Team and key employees.

4.3   At the Closing Meeting, the Audit Team Leader shall obtain a commitment from the Audit Team to reply to major findings by a specific date with corrective actions and a time frame for each. (See AC1060 CORRECTIVE ACTION.)

4.4   After the Closing Meeting, the Audit Team Leader shall prepare a final Audit Report (see AC1050-5 FINAL AUDIT REPORT for guidance), documenting in detail the audit conclusion, findings, and observations presented during the Closing Meeting, as well as the agreed upon reply deadline. (NOTE: Findings not presented in the Closing Meeting shall not be included in the Audit Report.)

4.5   Within two weeks of the Closing Meeting, the Audit Team Leader shall submit the final Audit Report to the Audit Team.

4.6   An Audit Team representative shall give a summary report of Internal Audit activity (including audit opinions, results, and corrective actions) at the next Management Review Meeting (see FA1010 MANAGEMENT RESPONSIBILITY).

5.0   INTERNAL AUDIT FOLLOW-UP

The Audit Team Leader may conduct a follow-up visit (or assign a member of the Audit Team), to take place at a time agreed to by the Audit Team Leader and the Manager of the affected process/control.

- The purpose of the follow-up visit is to verify that corrective actions in response to audit opinions have been implemented *or* that suitable progress toward their implementation has been made.

- Managers of audited processes/controls shall demonstrate that implemented corrective actions are achieving the desired effect.

Effectiveness Criteria:

- Financial processes and controls conform to requirements of applicable standards and statutes/regulations

- Internal audits conducted according to plan

- Closure of audit opinions

Forms:

- AC1050-1 AUDIT SCHEDULE

- AC1050-2 AUDIT PLAN

- AC1050-3 AUDIT CHECKLIST

- AC1050-4 AUDIT OPINION

- AC1050-5 FINAL AUDIT REPORT

- Internal Audit files (incl. Internal Audit reports, objective evidence that could not be included in the Audit Report, and audit schedules.)

References:

A. Finance Policy Manual

- Section 5.5.6 – Internal Auditing

B. Finance Procedures

- FA1000 MANAGEMENT RESPONSIBILITY

- AC1060 CORRECTIVE ACTION

C. International Standards for the Professional Practice of Internal Auditing, Institute of Internal Auditors (IIA). See https://na.theiia.org/standards-guidance/mandatory-guidance/Pages/Standards.aspx.

D. IIA Code of Ethics, Institute of Internal Auditors, 2000. See https://na.theiia.org/standards-guidance/mandatory-guidance/Pages/Code-of-Ethics.aspx.

E. Internal Audit Charter (version 1.0), Bank for International Settlements (BIS), March 20, 2003.

F. **PUBLIC COMPANY ACCOUNTING REFORM AND INVESTOR PROTECTION ACT OF 2002** (USA), also known as "Sarbanes-Oxley" or "SOX".

Section 301 of the Act, "Public Company Audit Teams", states that each member of a public company's audit committee *shall be* a member of the board of directors and shall otherwise be independent ("independent" meaning not receiving any consulting, advisory, or other compensatory fee other than for service on the board and not being affiliated with the company or any of its subsidiaries).

Additional Resources:

A. Institute of Internal Auditors (IIA) – http://www.theiia.org. Established in 1941, the IIA is an international professional association, headquartered in Altamonte Springs, Florida, USA. The IIA is the internal audit profession's global voice, recognized authority, acknowledged leader, chief advocate, and principal educator.

B. American Institute of Certified Public Accountants (AICPA) – http://www.aicpa.org. The AICPA is the professional organization for U.S. Certified Public Accountants. Its mission is to provide members with the resources, information, and leadership that enable them to provide valuable services in the highest professional manner to benefit the public as well as employers and clients.

C. Information Systems Audit and Control Association (ISACA) – http://www.isaca.org. ISACA began in 1967 in the USA as the EDP Auditors Association. Today, ISACA has over 65,000 members worldwide, in more than 140 countries and covers a variety of professional IT-related positions, including IS auditor, internal auditor, security professional, regulator, and chief information officer.

D. Audit of Internal Control over Financial Reporting that Is Integrated with an Audit of Financial Statements and Related Other Proposals (PCAOB Auditing Standard #5), July, 2007.

E. Generally Accepted Auditing Standards (GAAS), American Institute of Certified Public Accountants (AICPA) Statements on Auditing Standards (SAS) #95, 98, 102, 105, and 112 (June, 2006).

F. IT Standards, Guidelines, and Tools and Techniques for Audit and Assurance and Control Professionals – http://www.isaca.org/Knowledge-Center/Standards/Documents/IT-Audit-Assurance-Guidance-1March2010.pdf.

G. Audit Checklist for the Growing Business, US Small Business Administration (SBA), http://www.sba.gov/content/audit-program.

Revision History:

Revision	Date	Description of Changes	Requested By
0.0	mm/dd/yyyy	Initial Release	

AC1050-1 AUDIT SCHEDULE

Audit Scope	2007-08					
	Jan-Feb	Mar-Apr	May-Jun	Jul-Aug	Sep-Oct	Nov-Dec
• Processes A-F	Audit Plan[2] Assemble Audit Team	Audit[3]				
• Processes G-K		Audit Plan Audit Team	Audit			
• Processes L-P			Audit Plan Audit Team	Audit		
• Processes Q-V				Audit Plan Audit Team	Audit	
• Processes W-AB					Audit Plan Audit Team	Audit
• Processes AC-AG	Audit ('08)					Audit Plan ('08) Audit Team

APPROVAL

Audit Team Leader: _____ Date: _____

Audit Team Rep.: _____ Date: _____

CFO: _____ Date: _____

---

[2] "Audit Plan" and "Assemble Audit Team" are placed in the two-month period preceding the Audit for illustrative purposes only (to show that the Plan and Team must come before the Audit itself).

[3] Specific dates will be developed and mutually agreed upon by the Audit Team Leader and the Audit Team.

[This page intentionally left blank]

AC1050-2 AUDIT PLAN

Purpose: (e.g., to add credibility to management's assertions regarding the Company's financial statements)

Audit Scope: (i.e., which specific processes or controls are being audited)

Audit Objective(s): (e.g., gather; evaluate audit evidence of sufficient quantity and appropriate quality to form an audit opinion on the reliability of management's assertions in Company financial statements)

Audit Criteria:

- Regulatory requirements, where applicable
- Lenders' requirements, if applicable
- IIA and other applicable Standards
- Company Finance policies and internal requirements

Audit Date(s): (e.g., October 1 – 2, 2007; 8:00 a.m. – 4:00 p.m. each day)

Audit Team:

name	Audit Team Leader	name	Auditor 1
name	Auditor 2	name	

Key Auditee Employees:

name	Audit Team Chair	name	process owner
name	process owner	name	process owner

Audit Agenda: See following page(s)

AUDIT AGENDA

Date	Start Time	End Time	Activity	Audit Employees	Contact
October 1	8:00 am	8:30 am	Opening Meeting	all	Audit Team Chair & key auditees
	9:00 am	10:00 am	Audit process/control 1	Auditor 1	process owner (name & phone number)
	9:00 am	10:00 am	Audit process/control 2	Auditor 2	process owner
	9:00 am	10:00 am	Audit process/control 3	Audit Team Leader	process owner
	10:00 am	11:00 am	Audit process/control 4	Auditor 1	process owner
	10:00 am	11:00 am	Audit process/control 5	Auditor 2	process owner
	10:00 am	11:00 am	Audit process/control 6	Audit Team Leader	process owner
	11:00 am	12:00 pm	Audit process/control 7	Auditor 1	process owner
	11:00 am	12:00 pm	Audit process/control 8	Auditor 2	process owner
	12:00 pm	1:00 pm	Working lunch	all	n/a
	1:00 pm	2:30 pm	Audit process/control 9	Auditor 1	process owner
	1:00 pm	2:30 pm	Audit process/control 10	Auditor 2	process owner
	1:00 pm	2:30 pm	Audit process/control 11	Audit Team Leader	process owner
	2:30 pm	3:30 pm	Audit process/control 12	Auditor 1	process owner
	2:30 pm	3:30 pm	Audit process/control 13	Auditor 2	process owner
	2:30 pm	3:30 pm	Audit process/control 14	Audit Team Leader	process owner
	3:30 pm	4:00 pm	Audit review	all	n/a
October 2	8:00 am	9:30 am	Audit process/control 15	Auditor 1	process owner
	8:00 am	9:30 am	Audit process/control 16	Auditor 2	process owner

Date	Start Time	End Time	Activity	Audit Employees	Contact
October 2	8:00 am	9:30 am	Audit process/control 17	Audit Team Leader	process owner
	9:30 am	10:30 am	Audit process/control 18	Auditor 1	process owner
	9:30 am	10:30 am	Audit process/control 19	Auditor 2	process owner
	10:30 am	11:30 am	Audit review	all	n/a
	11:30 am	12:30 pm	Working lunch	all	n/a
	12:30 pm	2:30 pm	Gather & collate audit opinions	all	n/a
	2:30 pm	3:00 pm	Prepare findings for closing meeting	all	n/a
	3:00 pm	4:00 pm	Closing meeting	all	Audit Team Chair & key auditees

[This page intentionally left blank]

AC1050-3 AUDIT CHECKLIST[4]

Date _____

Audit # _____

Process/Control Audited _____   Process Mgr. _____

Audit Team Leader _____

	Evidence
I. General Bookkeeping / Accounting Practices	
A. The company has a bookkeeping system	
Single-entry	
Double-entry	
1. The owner (bookkeeper, etc.) prepares the Company's books	
a. Understands the "how" and "why"	
b. Prepares the financial statements	(ex., "produced statements dated xx/xx/xxxx")
2. The owner hires a bookkeeping service	
a. Understands financial statements	
b. Taxes are done by bookkeeping service	
c. Owner has compared cost of bookkeeper with that of CPA	
B. The company reconciles bank statements monthly	
C. The company keeps accurate income and expense statements and prepares statements monthly	
1. The owner understands the purpose of financial statements	
2. The owner compares monthly statements to identify trends	
3. The owner compares statements with industry averages	
4. The owner knows the current financial state of the company	
D. The company makes monthly deposits for federal withholding and Social Security taxes	
1. The owner understands Form 941	
2. The owner makes deposits on time to avoid penalties	
3. The owner provides W-2 information	
E. The company has a credit policy	

---

[4] Taken from US SBA "Audit Checklist for the Growing Business" (see Additional Resources).

	Evidence
1. The company ages the billing system monthly	
2. The company accesses late payment fees from customers	
3. The company writes off bad debts	
4. The company has good collection policies	
5. The company has a series of increasingly pointed letters to collect from late customers	
6. The company has a Visa, MasterCard, or other credit card system	
7. The company emphasizes cash discounts	
F. The company files all tax returns in a timely manner	
1. The owner considers tax implications of equipment early	
2. The owner considers "buy vs. lease" possibilities	
3. The owner considers possible advantages and disadvantages of incorporation / Subchapter S	
4. The company does not pay tax penalties (federal, state, local, sales)	
II. Financial Planning and Loan Proposals	
A. The company has adequate cash flow	
1. Renumbered cash receipts are monitored and accounted for	
2. Checks are deposited properly each day	
3. Customer invoicing is done promptly (ex., within two working days)	
4. Collections received within 60 days	
5. Accounts payable take advantage of cash discounts	
6. Disbursements are made by prenumbered check	
B. The company projects cash flow needs	
1. Payrolls are met without problems	
2. Money is set aside for expansion, emergencies, and opportunities	
3. Short-term financing is used when needed	
4. Line of credit is established with a bank	
C. The company understands the role of financial planning in today's highly competitive lending markets	
1. The owner's personal resume is prepared and current	
2. Personal financial statements have been prepared	
3. The business has a written business plan	

	Evidence
4. Source and use of funds statements exist for the past two years, with a projection for the next two years	
5. An accurate balance sheet exists for the past two years and includes a projection for the next two years	
6. The owner has a good working relationship with a banker	
7. There is a strong debt-to-equity ratio (1:2/1:1)	

Comments: _____

_____

_____

_____

_____

_____

_____

_____

_____

_____

_____

_____

_____

_____

_____

_____

_____

Acknowledgement:

Audit Team Leader: _____ Date: _____

Process Manager: _____ Date: _____

Names of other auditors: _____

_____

[This page intentionally left blank]

AC1050-4 AUDIT OPINION

To be completed by Lead Auditor				
Finding Number: _____ - _____ - _____ YYMMDD TYPE Sequence#				Major Minor
Auditor's No: _____ - _____ - _____ YYMMDD Auditor's Sequence# Initials				Major Minor

To be completed by Auditor

Referenced Standard or Regulation (incl. Std./Reg. name/ID, paragraph, clause, etc.):

Name, Description of Financial Statement/Document/Control:

Requirement:

Describe Deficiency/Weakness:

Objective Evidence:

Auditor:

_____	_____	_____
Name (print)	Signature	Date

Management Representative:

_____	_____	_____
Name (print)	Signature	Date

(Management Response on reverse)

Management Response:

AC1050-5 AUDIT REPORT

Report Date:

Audit Date(s):

Audit Scope: (identify processes, controls audited)

Audit Team:
- name   Audit Team Leader
- name   auditor
- name   auditor

Criteria:

Objective:

Audit Date(s):

Key Area Employees:
- name   area/title
- name   area/title
- name   area/title

Management Summary:

1) Overall Finding

We have conducted an audit of (name process/controls) and conclude that they are / are not generally in compliance with (name of standard/regulation, chapter/clause number) _____

2) Strengths

The (process) and its supporting systems are (well documented, thorough, well communicated, generally followed, etc.). Evidence shows that _____

3) Deficiencies / Weaknesses

The (process/control name) should be corrected (, could be improved, etc.) by _____

Some (controls, records) regarding (process) were found deficient because of _____

4) Obstacles Encountered

(e.g., "Key employees unavailable for scheduled interviews", "Key reports not provided")

Findings:

(List and describe deficiencies and weaknesses; note materiality; cite the part of the standard that applies; etc.)

Observations or Opportunities for Improvement:

(Areas/processes in conformance at the time of the audit but that could result in findings in a later audit if not addressed by the Company.)

Tentative Schedule for Corrective Action(s) and Follow-Up:

Other Comments:

Reviewed and Approved:

Audit Team Leader _____ Date: _____

Audit Team Rep. _____ Date: _____

CFO _____ Date: _____

Document ID **AC1060**	Title **CORRECTIVE ACTION**	Print Date **mm/dd/yyyy**
Revision **0.0**	Prepared By **Preparer's Name / Title**	Date Prepared **mm/dd/yyyy**
Effective Date **mm/dd/yyyy**	Reviewed By **Reviewer's Name / Title**	Date Reviewed **mm/dd/yyyy**
	Approved By **Final Approver's Name / Title**	Date Approved **mm/dd/yyyy**

Policy: The Company shall promptly take corrective action whenever it appears internal controls are inadequate or have been compromised in order to ensure the security of its financial systems.

Purpose: This procedure outlines the responsibilities and methods for identifying causes of nonconformities, initiating corrective action(s), and performing follow-up to ensure that the corrective action(s) have been effective in preventing the reason for the nonconformance.

Scope: This procedure applies to all causes of nonconformities relating to finance that are discovered during transaction processing or internal audits.

Responsibilities: The Controller is responsible for reporting on corrective actions taken at Management Review meetings and ensuring that this procedure is accurate, understood, and implemented effectively.

All Employees are responsible for identifying nonconforming conditions and initiating a Corrective Action, investigating and recording the cause of nonconforming conditions when assigned, and implementing corrective actions.

Definitions: CAR – Corrective action request.

Control Failure – Identified problem within the internal controls system.

NCR – Nonconformity (or nonconformance) report.

Nonconformity – Object or condition found not conforming to a standard or specification (regulatory, industry, customer, or Company); something that falls outside of identified critical limits. Also called "nonconformance."

Root cause – Most fundamental reason for the failure or inefficiency (the effect) of a process; effects can have more than one root cause.

Procedure:

1.0   NONCONFORMITY REPORTS

1.1   Any Finance employee observing an instance of control failure or failure of a process to comply with Generally Accepted Accounting Procedures (GAAP), other industry standards, or regulatory requirements should fill out and submit a form AC1060-1 NONCONFORMITY REPORT. A Nonconformity Report can also result from Internal Audit findings or an external auditor's Letter to Management on Internal Controls (see AC1040 EXTERNAL AUDITING and AC1050 INTERNAL AUDITING).

1.2   The AC1060-1 shall be filled out in the following manner:

- Briefly state the requirement, including a title and reference number, where appropriate;
- Describe the condition observed and where/how it deviates from the requirement; and
- Check the appropriate box to indicate whether or not a corrective action request (CAR) was also initiated.

NOTE 1: If an employee observes a nonconformity in an area *outside of his/her area of responsibility*, the employee should report the nonconformity to their Department manager, who should review the nonconformity report with the Manager of the affected Department and get *their* signature.

NOTE 2: It is every Finance employee's duty to report nonconformities when it appears to them that the effectiveness and integrity of the Company's financial systems and/or data could be compromised.

1.3   The Manager of the Department where the nonconformity was found shall sign the AC1060-1 and route it to the Controller for analysis and filing. Trends identified by the Controller through analysis of the NCR file should be reported to the CFO for review *as those trends are identified* (see FA1000 MANAGEMENT RESPONSIBILITY).

2.0   INITIATING CORRECTIVE ACTION

2.1   When the Controller determines that a corrective action is required, he/she shall fill out form AC1060-2 CORRECTIVE ACTION REQUEST and attach a copy of AC1060-1 and/or cross-reference that NCR. Every AC1060-2 must include a description of the problem, observation, or nonconformance, as well as when and where it was observed.

2.2   The Controller shall assign a CAR number to the request and enter that number in the AC1060-3 CORRECTIVE ACTION LOG, then forward a copy of the AC1060-2 CORRECTIVE ACTION REQUEST to the Manager of the responsible Department. The Controller shall keep the original AC1060-2 in the "Open Corrective Action" file.

2.3   The Department Manager shall assign responsibility for investigating and/or taking the necessary actions to correct and prevent the recurrence of the problem, providing the copy of form AC1060-2 to the assigned individual. The

Department Manager shall notify the Controller of the assignment, and the Controller shall note this on the original AC1060-2.

2.4   The Controller shall maintain and track the CAR's status on the AC1060-3 CORRECTIVE ACTION LOG.

3.0   INVESTIGATING THE CAUSE

3.1   The assigned individual, or investigator (section 2.3), shall investigate the nonconformity to determine the underlying, or root, cause or causes. Depending on the situation, the investigator may enlist the aid of other employees, forming an investigative team.

In investigating root cause, keep in mind - the *apparent* cause is rarely the *root* cause. It is often of value to identify the apparent cause and then identify contributing causes. Further analysis using this process can lead to the root cause of the problem.

3.2   The investigator shall record any observations, measurements, and results of the investigation on the AC1060-2 CORRECTIVE ACTION REQUEST.

4.0   TAKING CORRECTIVE ACTION

4.1   Following investigation of cause, the Department Manager (or an authorized delegate) shall review the results and consult with the investigator and appropriate employees to determine what corrective action(s) may be taken to eliminate the cause of the problem. The Department Manager shall record the corrective action to be taken on form AC1060-2.

4.2   The Department Manager shall set an action deadline (target date), based on the investigator's observations and the Department Manager's experience and judgment and record the date on form AC1060-2.

4.3   The Department Manager shall assign responsibility for implementing the corrective action(s) and note the assignment on form AC1060-2.

4.4   The Department Manager shall notify the Controller of the CAR's assignment, target date, person responsible, and change in status and the Controller shall update their copy of AC1060-2 and the AC1060-3 CORRECTIVE ACTION LOG accordingly.

5.0   PREVENTING RECURRENCE OF PROBLEMS

5.1   Actions will be taken to rectify and mitigate short-term problems, but the Controller and the affected department manager shall give consideration to preventing the problem from occurring again or similar potential problems from occurring in other areas, in accordance with GAAP and other relevant industry standards and guidelines. The Controller shall record their recommendation(s) for changes to internal procedures in the appropriate section of AC1060-2.

5.2   Upon completing the corrective action, the responsible individual will sign the AC1060-2 CORRECTIVE ACTION REQUEST and return it to the Controller for review and filing.

6.0   VERIFICATION AND CLOSURE

6.1   The Controller will review the corrective action(s) taken and determine the appropriate follow-up or verification required. (In the case of corrective actions taken in response to audit findings, verification and closure will be done in accordance with AC1050 INTERNAL AUDITING.) The verification shall be briefly described in the verification of implementation section of AC1060-2.

Note: To effectively gauge the effectiveness of some corrective actions, it may be necessary to allow a period of time (e.g., 1-2 weeks, months) for them to work, so their associated Corrective Action Requests may remain open for an indefinite period of time. The Controller should, therefore, review the AC1060-3 CORRECTIVE ACTION LOG and/or the Open Corrective Action file periodically (e.g., weekly) to verify the status of Corrective Actions.

6.2   When the Controller determines that the Corrective Action has been effective, he/she will sign and date the original AC1060-2 form and file it in the "Closed Corrective Actions" file with all other signed copies of the same form. Accordingly, the Controller shall update the Corrective Action's status in AC1060-3.

6.3   If the Controller determines that the Corrective Action was ineffective, he/she shall generate a new AC1060-2 CORRECTIVE ACTION REQUEST and cross-reference the new AC1060-2 in the Verification of Implementation section of the previous AC1060-2. Likewise, the new AC1060-2 shall reference the old AC1060-2 and the two CARs shall be cross-referenced in AC1060-3.

Effectiveness Criteria:

- Timeliness of corrective actions.

- No recurrence of the nonconformity.

Forms:

- AC1060-1 – NONCONFORMITY REPORT

- AC1060-2 – CORRECTIVE ACTION REQUEST

- AC1060-3 – CORRECTIVE ACTION LOG

References:

A. Finance Policy Manual

  - Section 5.5.7 – Corrective Action

Additional Resources:

A. "Root Cause Analysis", http://www.systems-thinking.org/rca/rootca.htm

B. Andersen, B., and Fagerhaug, T., <u>Root Cause Analysis: Simplified Tools and Techniques</u>, 2nd Edition, ASQ Quality Press (June, 2006). ISBN 978-0873896924.

C. Robitaille, D., <u>Root Cause Analysis – Basic Tools and Techniques</u>, Paton Press (August, 2004). ISBN 978-1932828023.

Revision History:

Revision	Date	Description of Changes	Requested By
0.0	mm/dd/yyyy	Initial Release	

[This page intentionally left blank]

AC1060-1 NONCONFORMITY REPORT

NCR Number:		
Issued To:	Issued By:	Issue Date:

Requirement (What is the requirement and why is the event/thing a nonconformity?)

Nonconformity (i.e., What is wrong?):   Major ☐ Minor ☐

Department/Location:

Management:

Action Taken:

CAR Issued? Y ☐   N ☐

If "Y", CAR #: _____

Department Manager: _____ Date: _____

Plant Manager: _____ Date: _____

[This page intentionally left blank]

AC1060-2 CORRECTIVE ACTION REQUEST

CAR NO. _____

TO (ORGANIZATION NAME, ADDRESS, PHONE NO.)	FROM
REQUEST DATE	REPLY DUE DATE
PRODUCT NAME	PRODUCT NO.
INSPECTION REPORT NO. OR NCR NO. (?)	PROGRAM OR PROJECT
DESCRIPTION OF CONDITION	
APPARENT CAUSE	
ACTUAL CAUSE	
ACTION TAKEN TO PREVENT RECURRENCE	
SIGNATURE	TITLE	DATE

Form AC1060-1

Page 1 of 2

AC1060 Corrective Action

DATE	NOTES

Form AC1060-1

AC1060 Corrective Action

AC1060-3 CORRECTIVE ACTION LOG

CAR #	DATE	LOCATION	DEPT	PROBLEM DESCRIPTION	PROB CATEGORY	CAR ORIGINA-TOR	REF PREV CAR #	DATE REPORTED	CA ASSGD TO	ACTION TAKEN	DATE RESOLVED

[This page intentionally left blank]

Finance Policies and Procedures

Section 500

Business Guide

Section 500

Business Guide

Starting and Managing a Business

Small Business Administration (SBA)
United States of America

[This page intentionally left blank]

Starting and Managing a Business

U. S. Small Business Administration
http://www.sba.gov/category/navigation-structure/starting-managing-business

Careful planning is fundamental to success. This SBA Small Business Planner includes information and resources that will help you at every stage of the business lifecycle.

[This page intentionally left blank]

I.   Starting a Business

A. Thinking About Starting a Business?

   1. Is Entrepreneurship For You?

   2. 20 Questions Before Starting

   3. 10 Steps to Starting a Business

   4. Understand Your Market

   5. Business Data and Statistics

   6. Business Types

   7. Find a Mentor or Counselor

   8. Ask Questions About Starting a Business

B. Create Your Business Plan

   1. Executive Summary

   2. Company Description

   3. Market Analysis

   4. Organization and Management

   5. Service or Product Line

   6. Marketing and Sales

   7. Funding Request

   8. Financial Projections

   9. Appendix

   10. How to Make Your Business Plan Stand Out

C. Choose Your Business Structure

D. Choose and Register Your Business

E. Obtain Business Licenses and Permits

F. Learn About Business Law and Regulations

G. Finance Your Business

H. Explore Loans, Grants, and Funding

I. Filing and Paying Taxes

J. Choose Your Location and Equipment

K. Hire and Retain Employees

II. Managing a Business

A. Leading Your Company
B. Growing Your Business
C. Exporting
D. Running a Business
E. Business Law and Regulations
F. Getting Out
G. Business Guides by Industry
H. Health Care
I. Forms

III. SBA Disclaimer of Endorsement

Any reference obtained from this server to a specific commercial product, process, or service does not constitute or imply an endorsement by SBA or the United States Government of the product, process, or service, or its producer or provider. The views and opinions expressed in any referenced document do not necessarily state or reflect those of the SBA or the United States Government.

IV. SBA Disclaimer of Liability

Neither SBA nor the United States Government nor any of their employees makes any warranty, express or implied (including warranties of merchantability and fitness for a particular purpose), or assumes any legal liability for the accuracy, completeness, or usefulness of any information in this document or on the SBA server or the links to servers on the Hot List (http://www.sba.gov/about-sba/sba_performance/open_government/about_the_sba_gov_website/disclaimer).

The information and links contained in this document are current as of 30 January 2007. The SBA's information changes from time to time, however, so that it is *strongly recommended* that you link to the SBA's website (http://www.sba.gov/index.html) to ensure that you have the most recent information.

[This page intentionally left blank]

Finance Policies and Procedures

Section 550

Job Descriptions

Section 550
Job Descriptions

Document ID JD0070	Title **BOARD MEMBER**	Print Date mm/dd/yyyy
Revision 0.0	Prepared By **Preparer's Name / Title**	Date Prepared mm/dd/yyyy
Effective Date mm/dd/yyyy	Reviewed By **Reviewer's Name / Title**	Date Reviewed mm/dd/yyyy
	Approved By **Final Approver's Name / Title**	Date Approved mm/dd/yyyy

SUMMARY OF FUNCTIONS

Each Member of the Board of Directors[1] acts in a position of trust for the community and is responsible for the effective governance of the organization.

ESSENTIAL DUTIES AND RESPONSIBILITIES

- Participate primarily in the organization's financial management process.
- Review and cast votes on stock offerings.
- Review and approve/disapprove of the organization's vision and mission statements and set forth the organization's direction.
- Review and vote on the organization's Strategic and Business Plans, as well as subordinate Plans (e.g., Marketing Plan, Technology Plan); ensure that the various Plans are in sync; ensure that the organization's Top Management effectively carries out these Plans.
- Approves the stakeholder analysis, as well as other inputs to the MP1070-1 – MARKETING PLAN, and ensures the Plan's effectiveness.
- Attend Board meetings and makes decisions regarding the Company's operations, as required.
- Authorize the raising of capital through bank loans.
- Oversee investigations into reporting errors; help prepare and submit all financial restatements as required by law and company policy; help prepare press releases about restatements.
- Reviews and accesses foreign exchange risks and policy options, and then sets the Company foreign exchange management policy.
- Reviews and approves all submitted financial reports, FA1000-1 FINANCIAL OBJECTIVES, the Capital Plan and any changes to the Plan, the Company's formal goals and objectives, the Finance department's continuity plan, and the RC1000-1 – BUSINESS PLAN.
- Reviews and approves the risk assessment/risk analysis prior to development of a Risk Management Plan (see procedure AC1030 – RISK MANAGEMENT).
- Reviews approved related party transactions and sets auditing or monitoring practices according to the requirements of each individual case.

---

[1] Where the organization is not large or complex enough to warrant a Board of Directors, the CEO/ President should consider having an informal group of advisors or business consultants.

- Reviews financial analysis and approves corrections or improvements to financial policies, objectives, or activities.
- Review and approve/disapprove of the organization's financial forecasts and forecasted financial statements.

ORGANIZATIONAL RELATIONSHIPS

Reports to the other members of the Board and to shareholders. Works in conjunction with other Board members and the organization's executive staff (President, Chief Finance Officer, etc.).

PROCEDURES

Procedure ID and Name	Policies & Procedures Manual
AC1020 Risk Assessment	Finance
FA1000 Financial Objectives	Finance
FA1020 Continuity Planning	Finance
FA1060 Board of Directors' Meetings	Finance
FS1000 Financial Forecasting	Finance
FS1010 Financial Reporting	Finance
FS1020 Financial Statement Analysis	Finance
FS1030 Financial Management Review	Finance
FS1040 Financial Restatements	Finance
ITAD101 Information Technology Management	Computer & Network (IT)
MP1010 Stakeholder Analysis	Sales and Marketing
MP1020 Vision and Mission	Sales and Marketing
MP1050 Goals and Objectives	Sales and Marketing
RC1000 Business Plan	Finance
RC1010 Capital Plan	Finance
RC1030 Bank Loans	Finance
RC1040 Stock Offerings	Finance
RC1050 Debt & Investment	Finance
TM1030 Related Party Transactions	Finance
TM1040 Foreign Exchange Management	Finance

QUALIFICATIONS

Prefer a candidate who currently holds (or recently held) an executive position with a firm having $2 million or more in revenue in the most recent fiscal year. Requires 10+ years of experience overseeing a company or companies in a related industry. Knowledge of, experience in field of finance is important.

The candidate must have a strong sense of and commitment to ethical behavior; the appearance of unethical or illegal behavior in the past is unacceptable.

Must be committed to the work of the organization. Require knowledge and skills in one or more areas of Board governance (e.g., policy, finance, programs, personnel). Must be willing to serve on at least one committee and actively participate. Require attendance at monthly Board meetings; a time commitment of about 5 hours per month (including Board preparation, meeting, and committee meeting time) is expected. Must also attend the organization's Annual General Meeting.

PHYSICAL DEMANDS

Ability to communicate orally with top management, advisors, and other board members is crucial. Regular use of the telephone and e-mail for communication is essential. Sitting for extended periods is common. Hearing and vision within normal ranges is essential for normal conversations, to receive ordinary information, and to prepare or inspect documents.

Activities require the ability to remain in a stationary position 50% of the time, occasionally move about inside the office to access files or office equipment, operate a computer and other office productivity machinery, such as a calculator, hand held devices, copy machine, and computer printer, and operate and monitor various medical equipment.

No heavy lifting is expected. Exertion of up to 10 lbs. of force occasionally may be required. Good manual dexterity for the use of common office equipment such as computer terminals, calculator, copiers, and FAX machines.

WORK ENVIRONMENT

The job is performed indoors in a traditional office setting. Activities include extended periods of sitting and extensive work at an office/conference desk, using a phone or computer.

REVISION HISTORY

Revision	Date	Description of Changes	Requested By
0.0	mm/dd/yyyy	Initial Release	

Document ID JD0140	Title **CHIEF EXECUTIVE OFFICER (CEO)**	Print Date mm/dd/yyyy
Revision **0.0**	Prepared By **Preparer's Name / Title**	Date Prepared mm/dd/yyyy
Effective Date mm/dd/yyyy	Reviewed By **Reviewer's Name / Title**	Date Reviewed mm/dd/yyyy
	Approved By **Final Approver's Name / Title**	Date Approved mm/dd/yyyy

SUMMARY OF FUNCTIONS

The Chief Executive Officer, or CEO, creates and communicates the organization's vision and mission and leads strategy development, implementation, and revision. The CEO also oversees development and implementation of the organization's strategic plan, helping formulate strategic objectives. To that end, the CEO must maintain an awareness of both the external and internal competitive landscape, opportunities for expansion, customers, markets, new industry developments and standards, and so forth.

The CEO leads a group of top executives, or "top management," including but not limited to the chief financial officer, chief operations officer, chief technology officer, and chief sales & marketing officer.

ESSENTIAL DUTIES AND RESPONSIBILITIES

- Actively participates in the financial management process.
- Approves and signs all financial statements, financial reports, and tax returns.
- Approves the Lead Management Plan, the MT1020-2 – PUBLIC RELATIONS PLAN, the Advertising Plan, the MP1070-1 – MARKETING PLAN, the MT1010-2 – INTERNET PLAN.
- Conducts strategic planning and sets the Strategic Objectives for the Company.
- Develops the Company's vision and mission statements, ensures that such statements are communicated to and understood by all employees, reviews the vision and mission statements, and ensures that changes are made to each, as needed.
- Ensures that the goals and objectives are appropriate for the Company, ensures that goals and objectives are communicated to employees, and monitors the Company's progress.
- Ensures the situational analysis is appropriate for developing marketing and sales strategies.
- Gives the final approval of all salary adjustments, changes in job titles, or job responsibilities.
- Oversees investigations into reporting errors, preparing and submitting all financial restatements as required by law and by company policy, and prepares press releases about restatements.
- Reviews and approves the Risk Management Plan, as well as financial forecasts and forecasted financial statements.

- Reviews the market analysis and uses the information to help shape the MP1070-1 – MARKETING PLAN.
- Selects a Strategy Team and ensures the Team has the necessary resources to develop/refine strategies.
- Selects a Strategy Team, ensures the Team has the necessary resources, monitors the Team's progress, and presents its findings to the Board of Directors.
- Signs all reported financial statements.

ORGANIZATIONAL RELATIONSHIPS

Reports directly to the organization's Board of Directors.

PROCEDURES

Procedure ID and Name	Policies & Procedures Manual
AC1000 Sarbanes-Oxley Compliance	Finance
AC1030 Risk Management	Finance
DEV105 Performance Appraisals	Human Resources
FS1000 Financial Forecasting	Finance
FS1010 Financial Reporting	Finance
FS1030 Financial Management Review	Finance
FS1040 Financial Restatements	Finance
ITAD101 Information Technology Management	Computer & Network (IT)
MP1000 Strategy Team	Sales & Marketing
MP1010 Stakeholder Analysis	Sales & Marketing
MP1020 Vision and Mission	Sales & Marketing
MP1030 Marketing Research and Analysis	Sales & Marketing
MP1040 Situational Analysis	Sales & Marketing
MP1050 Goals and Objectives	Sales & Marketing
MP1060 Marketing Strategy	Sales & Marketing
MP1070 Marketing Plan	Sales & Marketing
MT1000 Advertising	Sales & Marketing
MT1010 Internet Marketing	Sales & Marketing
MT1020 Public Relations	Sales & Marketing
MT1050 Lead Management	Sales & Marketing

QUALIFICATIONS

A bachelor's degree in business administration, finance, sales & marketing, engineering, or other suitable field is required.10+ years of experience in an officer's role (e.g., CFO, CMO) with a medium- to large-size company is also required. Must have demonstrated the ability to handle increasing levels of responsibility and to lead effectively.

Exceptional communication skills and the ability to work well with people are essential.

PHYSICAL DEMANDS

Ability to communicate orally with customers, vendors, management, and other co-workers is crucial. Regular use of the telephone and e-mail for communication is essential. Sitting for extended periods is common. Hearing and vision within normal ranges is essential for normal conversations, to receive ordinary information, and to prepare or inspect documents.

Activities require the ability to remain in a stationary position 50% of the time, occasionally move about inside the office to access files or office equipment, operate a computer and other office productivity machinery, such as a calculator, hand held devices, copy machine, and computer printer, and operate and monitor various medical equipment. Must be able to constantly position self to maintain equipment, including under tables and desks.

No heavy lifting is expected, though occasional exertion of up to 10 lbs. of force may be required. Good manual dexterity required for the use of computers, mobile devices, and other productivity technologies.

WORK ENVIRONMENT

The job is performed indoors in a traditional office setting. Extended periods of sitting and extensive work at a computer and phone are normal.

REVISION HISTORY

Revision	Date	Description of Changes	Requested By
0.0	mm/dd/yyyy	Initial Release	

[This page intentionally left blank]

Document ID	Title	Print Date
JD0150	**CHIEF FINANCIAL OFFICER (CFO)**	**mm/dd/yyyy**
Revision	Prepared By	Date Prepared
0.0	**Preparer's Name / Title**	**mm/dd/yyyy**
Effective Date	Reviewed By	Date Reviewed
mm/dd/yyyy	**Reviewer's Name / Title**	**mm/dd/yyyy**
	Approved By	Date Approved
	Final Approver's Name / Title	**mm/dd/yyyy**

SUMMARY OF FUNCTIONS

The CFO, or Chief Financial Officer, is ultimately responsible for the accuracy, completeness, and timeliness of the organization's financial reporting. The CFO helps establish and direct the organization's financial goals and objectives, its budget, and the Financial Plan. The CFO has primary responsibility for ensuring that internal controls are in place, enforced, and reviewed periodically for conformance to accounting and financial standards and applicable regulations.

ESSENTIAL DUTIES AND RESPONSIBILITIES

- Advises Top Management in the stock offering process, and executes the stock offering process.
- Analyzes financial statements, and prepares reports and recommendations to Top Management and the Board of Directors concerning financial performance.
- Annually creates a capital plan that aligns with overall business plans and strategies, and reviews the capital plan with Top Management and the Board of Directors.
- Annually reviews and updates related party transaction policies and procedures with Top Management and the Board of Directors; and reviews, approves, and discloses related party transactions, and annually distributes the Related Party Transaction Conflict of Interest Questionnaire.
- Approves all wire transfers over $10,000.
- Arranges and chairs financial management meetings, and prepares financial reports and presentations for scheduled financial management meetings.
- Assesses risks and exposure due to business conducted in foreign currency, prepares a report and recommendations for dealing with foreign currencies, and follows and executes the established foreign exchange management policy.
- Completes and gains the approval of FA1000-1 FINANCIAL OBJECTIVES, and oversees the financial health and financial performance of the Company, as well as a fiduciary responsibility to shareholders.
- Creates and reviews all period-end activities to ensure the period-end financial statements accurately reflect the results of the Company's activities, and is familiar with the specific software procedures for keeping the prior year open until all final closing adjustments have been made and approved.
- Directs the Finance Department in developing borrowing and financial plans to meet the needs of the Company's operations.

- Ensures development and implementation of a continuity plan for Finance and ensures that the continuity plan is in force; this includes ensuring that the plan is tested and verified periodically. In addition, the CFO reports to the CEO and the Board of Directors (or Advisory Board) on continuity plan test results and recommends improvements to the plan. (If the Company is large enough, the CFO may assign responsibilities to a continuity manager.)
- Ensures that corrective actions are taken in a timely manner and that the company is in compliance with the Sarbanes-Oxley Act of 2002, and approves and signs all financial statements, financial reports, and tax returns.
- Ensures that processes needed for the financial management system are established, implemented, and maintained, and reports to the CEO and Board of Directors (or Advisory Board) on the performance of the financial management system and reports any need for its improvement.
- Examines and certifies the annual summary of work-related injuries and illness report.
- Executes the valuation process, recording valuation plans, results, improvement plans, and provides all needed information for the valuation process.
- Is the main point of contact between the Company and the External Auditor and coordinates Company audit activities and responses.
- Manages banking relationships, the check signing authority process, and alerts all individuals and banks of any changes to authority.
- Oversees cash management processes to ensure proper cash availability and best practices in cash management, and completes the TM1010-1 CASH MANAGEMENT PLAN
- Oversees investigations into reporting errors, prepares and submits all financial restatements as required by law and by company policy, and prepares press releases about restatements.
- Oversees that regular shareholder meetings are conducted according the articles of incorporation, surplus funds investing and debt pay down, and the training and development plan to ensure that it supports the Company's objectives.
- Oversees the asset acquisition process and reviews the ROI Worksheet with the Capital Budget Committee.
- Oversees the Company's financial investment in inventories and assists in developing and reviewing the TM1020-1 INVENTORY MANAGEMENT PLAN.
- Oversees the selection of merchant accounts and conducts periodic reviews of merchant accounts.
- Oversees working capital and completes the TM1000-1 WORKING CAPITAL PLAN.
- Prepares and submits all financial statements as required by law and by company policy.
- Prepares forecasted financial statements, and prepares reports and recommendations to Top Management and the Board of Directors concerning forecasted financial statements.
- Reviews Accounts Payable material and adds his/her signature.

- Reviews and approves requests for financial statements and any other proprietary, confidential, and/or sensitive financial information, the Risk Management Plan, and all reconciliations.
- Reviews lease/buy considerations for capital equipment.
- Safeguards all company information and determines the appropriate level of detail for release.
- Sets and oversees the process of providing and/or receiving a Letter of Credit, and is responsible for all related bank communication and transactions.
- Signs all reported financial statements.
- Verifies that providers of financial services comply with SSAE 16.
- Writes off any accounts Receivable Account deemed not collectible.

ORGANIZATIONAL RELATIONSHIPS

Reports directly to the Chief Executive Officer and the organization's Board of Directors.

PROCEDURES

Procedure ID and Name	Policies & Procedures Manual
AC1000 Sarbanes-Oxley Compliance	Finance
AC1010 SAS 70 Compliance	Finance
AC1030 Risk Management	Finance
AC1040 External Auditing	Finance
AC1050 Internal Auditing	Finance
CMP101 Workplace Safety	HR
CSH104 Wire Transfers	Accounting
CSH105 Check Signing Authority	Accounting
CSH107 Bank Account Reconciliations	Accounting
DEV101 Development Management	HR
FA1000 Financial Objectives	Finance
FA1010 Management Responsibility	Finance
FA1020 Continuity Planning	Finance
FA1050 Annual Stockholders' Meetings	Finance
FS1000 Financial Forecasting	Finance
FS1010 Financial Reporting	Finance
FS1020 Financial Statement Analysis	Finance
FS1030 Financial Management Review	Finance
FS1040 Financial Restatements	Finance
FS1050 Financial Information Release	Finance

Procedure ID and Name	Policies & Procedures Manual
G&A105 Period-End Review & Closing	Accounting
G&A109 Release of Confidential Information	Accounting
PUR106 Accounts Payable and Cash Disbursement	Accounting
RC1010 Capital Plan	Finance
RC1020 Valuation	Finance
RC1030 Bank Loans	Finance
RC1040 Stock Offerings	Finance
RC1050 Debt & Investment	Finance
RC1060 Asset Acquisition	Finance
RC1070 Leasing	Finance
REV102 Point-Of-Sale Orders	Accounting
TM1000 Working Capital	Finance
TM1010 Cash Management	Finance
TM1020 Inventory Management	Finance
TM1030 Related Party Transactions	Finance
TM1040 Foreign Exchange Management	Finance
TM1050 Managing Bank Relationships	Finance
TM1060 Merchant Accounts	Finance
TM1070 Letters of Credit	Finance

QUALIFICATIONS

Must have 10+ years of experience as a financial executive and leader with industry experience. Must be a visionary and creative person with sound judgment and technical skills, analytical ability, and ability to focus and prioritize multiple – and sometimes competing – projects. High moral and ethical standards are required.

Must be well organized and efficient, decisive, intelligent, and able to articulate well; must possess outstanding communication skills and the ability to work well with people. Should be an outstanding educator, counselor, and mentor and a skilled negotiator.

A bachelor's degree in accounting, finance, business administration, economics, or other suitable field of study is required; a master's degree in finance, accounting, or business administration is preferred. Must be a Certified Public Accountant (Chartered Accountant).

PHYSICAL DEMANDS

Ability to communicate orally with customers, vendors, management, and other co-workers is crucial. Regular use of the telephone and e-mail for communication is essential. Sitting for extended periods is common. Hearing and vision within normal ranges is essential for normal conversations, to receive ordinary information and to prepare or inspect documents.

Activities require the ability to remain in a stationary position 50% of the time, occasionally move about inside the office to access files or office equipment, operate a computer and other office productivity machinery, such as a calculator, hand held devices, copy machine, and computer printer, and operate and monitor various medical equipment. Must be able to constantly position self to maintain equipment, including under tables and desks.

No heavy lifting is expected. Exertion of up to 10 lbs. of force occasionally may be required. Good manual dexterity for the use of common office equipment such as computer terminals, calculator, copiers, and FAX machines.

WORK ENVIRONMENT

The job is performed indoors in a traditional office setting. Activities include extended periods of sitting and extensive work at a computer and phone.

REVISION HISTORY

Revision	Date	Description of Changes	Requested By
0.0	mm/dd/yyyy	Initial Release	

[This page intentionally left blank]

Document ID	Title	Print Date
JD0210	**CONTROLLER**	**mm/dd/yyyy**
Revision	Prepared By	Date Prepared
0.0	**Preparer's Name / Title**	**mm/dd/yyyy**
Effective Date	Reviewed By	Date Reviewed
mm/dd/yyyy	**Reviewer's Name / Title**	**mm/dd/yyyy**
	Approved By	Date Approved
	Final Approver's Name / Title	**mm/dd/yyyy**

SUMMARY OF FUNCTIONS

Directs the accounting and control functions, reporting the results of operations, and provides chronological systems.

ESSENTIAL DUTIES AND RESPONSIBILITIES

- Develops and implements accounting policies, coordination of systems and procedures, and the preparation of operating data and special reports as required, including interim and year-end financial statements. Maintains company's system of accounts; keeps books and records on all company transactions and assets.
- Establishes, coordinate, and administers as an integral part of management, an adequate plan for the control of operations including, profit planning, programs for capital investing and financing, sales forecasts, expense budgets, and cost standards, together with necessary controls and procedures to effectuate the plan.
- In conjunction with the President and Vice President of Finance, coordinates, reviews, and endorses budget proposals and discusses proposed changes and significant changes.
- Compares performance with operating plans and standards, and reports and interprets the results of operations to all levels of management.
- Provides for the control and editing of all company orders, to insure conformity to established policies and procedures, and to facilitate data control and retrieval of records generated by these orders.
- Establishes and administers tax policies and procedures.
- Supervises or coordinates the preparation of reports to government agencies.
- Coordinates all matters of business between the company and its stock transfer agents and registrars.
- Provides other managers and departments with information required by them to carry out their assigned responsibilities.
- Assures protection for the assets of the business through internal control, internal auditing, and assuring proper insurance coverage.
- Assists Marketing in establishing and maintaining product pricing policies.
- Liaison between the company and legal counsel. Recommends appointment of independent auditors, overseeing their audit work.
- Provides advice on all matters to the Vice President of Finance and the President.

ORGANIZATIONAL RELATIONSHIPS

Reports to the Vice President of Finance. Supervises accounting staff and the Purchasing (Procurement) Manager.

PROCEDURES

Procedure ID and Name	Policies & Procedures Manual
AC1000 Sarbanes-Oxley Compliance	Finance
AC1060 Corrective Action	Finance
ADM101 Personnel Records	Human Resources
ADM103 Document Control	Human Resources
ADM106 Property & Access Control	Human Resources
ADM107 Separation	Human Resources
ADM109 Management Responsibility	Human Resources
CMP105 Health Insurance Portability Accountability	Human Resources
CMP108 Equal Employment Opportunity	Human Resources
COM101 Payroll	Human Resources
COM102 Paid & Unpaid Leave	Human Resources
COM103 Insurance Benefits	Human Resources
COM105 Employee Retirement Income Security	Human Resources
COM106 Consolidated Budget Reconciliation	Human Resources
CSH104 Wire Transfers	Accounting
CSH106 Check Requests	Accounting
CSH107 Bank Account Reconciliations	Accounting
FS1010 Financial Reporting	Finance
FS1020 Financial Statement Analysis	Finance
FS1040 Financial Restatements	Finance
G&A101 Chart of Accounts	Accounting
G&A102 Files and Records Management	Accounting
G&A106 Controlling Legal Costs	Accounting
G&A107 Taxes And Insurance	Accounting
G&A109 Release of Confidential Information	Accounting
G&A110 Document Control	Accounting
HRG101 Employee Hiring	Human Resources
INV101 Inventory Control	Accounting
INV102 Inventory Counts	Accounting

QUALIFICATIONS

A college degree is required with a major in accounting and a CPA designation preferred. Good communication skills and the ability to work well with people is essential. Good leadership skills are beneficial. Familiarity with common accounting and spreadsheet software applications is required.

PHYSICAL DEMANDS

Occasional travel by airplane and automobile in conducting business is necessary. Ability to communicate orally with board of directors, management, and other co-workers, both individually and in front of a group is crucial. Regular use of the telephone and e-mail for communication is essential.

Sitting for extended periods is common. Hearing and vision within normal ranges is essential for normal conversations, to receive ordinary information, and to prepare or inspect documents.

No heavy lifting is expected; exertion of up to 10 lbs. of force occasionally required. Good manual dexterity required for the use of common office equipment, such as computers, calculators, copiers, scanners, and fax machines.

Good reasoning ability is required to solve a wide range of business problems. Able to apply statistical calculations, analysis of variance, correlation techniques, and sampling theory as well as algebra, linear equations, and other analytics as required. Able to understand and utilize financial reports and legal documents to conduct business.

WORK ENVIRONMENT

The job is performed indoors in a traditional office setting. Activities include extended periods of sitting and extensive work at a computer monitor and/or calculator.

REVISION HISTORY

Revision	Date	Description of Changes	Requested By
0.0	mm/dd/yyyy	Initial Release	

[This page intentionally left blank]

Document ID	Title	Print Date
JD0330	**DOCUMENT MANAGER**	**mm/dd/yyyy**
Revision	Prepared By	Date Prepared
0.0	**Preparer's Name / Title**	**mm/dd/yyyy**
Effective Date	Reviewed By	Date Reviewed
mm/dd/yyyy	**Reviewer's Name / Title**	**mm/dd/yyyy**
	Approved By	Date Approved
	Final Approver's Name / Title	**mm/dd/yyyy**

SUMMARY OF FUNCTIONS

The document manager is responsible for control, security, accessibility, and timeliness of organizational documents that may be used by/useful to more than one employee, such as policies, procedures, guidelines, forms, templates, and training materials.

ESSENTIAL DUTIES AND RESPONSIBILITIES

- Develop the document management plan and update it, as needed.
- Manage organizational documentation through the document life cycle.
- Maintain organizational documents and the document management system.
- Identify and investigate the need for documents of various types.
- Ensure that organizational documents go through a documented and approved review-and-approval process before being stored.
- Ensure that internal controls are in place and are functional.
- Ensure the security, accessibility, and proper distribution of organizational documents.
- Help develop and enforce documentation design, review, and storage guidelines.
- With the IT security manager, assign/approve user privileges.
- Plan and conduct meetings and presentations related to document management.

ORGANIZATIONAL RELATIONSHIPS

Reports directly to the administrative services manager. Assists and works in conjunction with the IT staff to facilitate smooth operation of the document management system.

PROCEDURES

Procedure ID and Name	Policies & Procedures Manual
AD1000 Document Control	Sales and Marketing
AS1000 Document Control	AS 9100
AS1010 Quality Records	AS 9100
AS1090 Design Change	AS 9100
FA1030 Document Control	Finance
FS1000 Document Control	ISO 22000

Procedure ID and Name	Policies & Procedures Manual
ITAD103 IT Document Management	Computer & Network (IT)
QP1000 Document Control	ISO 9001 QMS
QP1010 Record Control	ISO 9001 QMS
QP1110 Design Change	ISO 9001 QMS

QUALIFICATIONS

A bachelor's degree in library science is required; an advanced degree (e.g., MLS, MA) is preferred. Experience in document management and document management systems or content management systems software is preferred. Must have experience conducting meetings and presentations.

PHYSICAL DEMANDS

Ability to communicate well with document users - orally and in writing - is crucial. Regular use of the telephone, email, and other means of communication is part of the job. Sitting for extended periods is common. Hearing and vision within normal ranges is essential for normal conversations, to receive ordinary information, and prepare or inspect documents.

The job mostly entails sitting at a workstation for extended periods, though you will occasionally move about the office to access files or office equipment, operate a computer and other office productivity devices (calculator, hand held devices, copier, printer, or fax), conduct meetings.

No heavy lifting is expected, though occasionally exerting up to 10 lbs. of force (carrying a laptop, tablet, or other device, for instance) may be required. Good manual dexterity (for the use of common office equipment such as computers, calculator, copiers, scanners, and fax machines) is helpful.

WORK ENVIRONMENT

The job is performed indoors in a traditional office setting. Activities include extended periods of sitting and extensive work at a computer, phone, and other mobile communication devices.

REVISION HISTORY

Revision	Date	Description of Changes	Requested By
0.0	mm/dd/yyyy	Initial Release	

[This page intentionally left blank]

Document ID **JD0390**	Title **EXTERNAL AUDITOR (INDEPENDENT AUDITOR)**	Print Date **mm/dd/yyyy**
Revision **0.0**	Prepared By **Preparer's Name / Title**	Date Prepared **mm/dd/yyyy**
Effective Date **mm/dd/yyyy**	Reviewed By **Reviewer's Name / Title**	Date Reviewed **mm/dd/yyyy**
	Approved By **Final Approver's Name / Title**	Date Approved **mm/dd/yyyy**

SUMMARY

The External Auditor[1] is hired by an organization to audit, or review in detail, its financial statements and related materials so as to inform investors and law enforcement authorities that the organization's financial statements are accurate, complete, current, and that financial controls are in force and in compliance.

ESSENTIAL DUTIES AND RESPONSIBILITIES

- Examine financial statements to be sure that they are accurate and in compliance with applicable standards (e.g., SAS, SSAE) and regulations (e.g., Sarbanes-Oxley)
- Inspect account books and accounting systems for efficiency and use of accepted accounting procedures (GAAP and/or IFRS)
- Assess financial operations and make best-practices recommendations to management

ORGANIZATIONAL RELATIONSHIPS

The independent auditor - or in the case of a team, the lead auditor - reports directly to the organization's Board of Directors.

PROCEDURES

Procedure ID and Name	Policies & Procedures Manual
AC1040 External Auditing	Finance

QUALIFICATIONS

A bachelor's degree in accounting or business administration is required. Seven years of experience as an accountant, with three or more in positions of increasing responsibility are also required. Must be a Certified Public Accountant (Chartered Accountant).

Excellent communication skills and the ability to work well with people at all levels are essential. Prior management experience is strongly preferred.

---

[1] More commonly referred to as an "Independent Auditor" by accounting and finance professionals.

Experience with SAP and/or JD Edwards software is crucial.

PHYSICAL DEMANDS

Ability to communicate orally with management and accountants is crucial. Regular use of phone and email for communication is essential. Hearing and vision correctable to within normal ranges is essential for normal conversations, receiving ordinary information, and preparing or inspecting documents.

The ability to remain in a stationary position roughly 50% of the time, as well as the ability to move about the office occasionally (accessing files/storage, office equipment, computers and other office productivity devices, attending meetings, etc.), is required.

Using a computer while sitting for extended periods is common. Must also be able to position self to maintain equipment, including under tables and desks.

No heavy lifting is expected, though occasional exertion of about 20 lbs. of force (e.g., carrying accounting books (G/L, etc.), laptops) may be required. Good manual dexterity required to use common office equipment (e.g., computers, mobile devices, calculators, copiers/scanners).

WORK ENVIRONMENT

The job is performed indoors in a traditional office setting. Extended periods of sitting while using a computer or other device are common.

REVISION HISTORY

Revision	Date	Description of Changes	Requested By
0.0	mm/dd/yyyy	Initial Release	

Document ID JD0410	Title **FINANCIAL MANAGER**	Print Date **mm/dd/yyyy**
Revision **0.0**	Prepared By **Preparer's Name / Title**	Date Prepared **mm/dd/yyyy**
Effective Date **mm/dd/yyyy**	Reviewed By **Reviewer's Name / Title**	Date Reviewed **mm/dd/yyyy**
	Approved By **Final Approver's Name / Title**	Date Approved **mm/dd/yyyy**

SUMMARY

The Financial Manager is responsible for the financial well-being of the organization. They develop strategies and plans for the organization's long-term financial objectives, produce financial reports, and direct investment activities.

ESSENTIAL DUTIES AND RESPONSIBILITIES

- Prepare financial statements, business activity reports, and financial forecasts.
- Ensure that the organization's financial records and recordkeeping methods are in compliance with applicable standards and regulations.
- Manage employees and contractors who are responsible for financial reporting and budgeting.
- Periodically review the organization's financial reports and identify opportunities for cost reduction.
- Analyze data and advise top management on how to maximize profits.
- Analyze market trends and identify opportunities for growth/expansion.
- Oversee organization's investments.
- Give final approval to expenditures greater than (*n* dollars).

ORGANIZATIONAL RELATIONSHIPS

Reports directly to the organization's President.

PROCEDURES

Procedure ID and Name	Policies & Procedures Manual
G&A108 Property Tax Assessments	Accounting
PUR101 Vendor Selection	Accounting
ITAD109 IT Outsourcing	Computer & Network (IT)
ITAM102 IT Asset Management	Computer & Network (IT)
ITAM103 IT Vendor Selection	Computer & Network (IT)
FA1010 Management Responsibility	Finance
FA1040 Record Control	Finance
FS1100 Supplier Evaluation	ISO 22000

QUALIFICATIONS

A bachelor's degree in finance, accounting, economics, or business administration is required. Five or more years' experience as a financial analyst is also required.

Must have demonstrated ability to lead a team of 6 or more. Good communication skills and the ability to work well with people with and without finance/accounting backgrounds are essential. Project management experience is a must.

Preference will be given to candidates with Certified Financial Analyst (CFA) designation.

PHYSICAL DEMANDS

Ability to communicate orally with top management, and coworkers is crucial. Regular use of phone and email for communication is essential. Hearing and vision correctable to within normal ranges is essential for normal conversations, receiving ordinary information, and preparing or inspecting documents.

The ability to remain in a stationary position roughly 50% of the time, as well as the ability to move about the office occasionally (accessing files/storage, office equipment, computers and other office productivity devices, attending meetings, etc.), is required.

Using a computer while sitting for extended periods is common. Must also be able to position self to maintain equipment, including under tables and desks.

No heavy lifting is expected, though occasional exertion of about 20 lbs. of force (e.g., picking up and carrying binders, laptops) may be required. Good manual dexterity required to use common office equipment (e.g., computers, mobile devices, calculators, copiers, scanners).

WORK ENVIRONMENT

The job is performed indoors in a traditional office setting. Extended periods of sitting while using a computer or other devices are common.

REVISION HISTORY

Revision	Date	Description of Changes	Requested By
0.0	mm/dd/yyyy	Initial Release	

Document ID	Title	Print Date
JD0560	**INTERNAL AUDIT TEAM LEADER**	**mm/dd/yyyy**
Revision	Prepared By	Date Prepared
0.0	**Preparer's Name / Title**	**mm/dd/yyyy**
Effective Date	Reviewed By	Date Reviewed
mm/dd/yyyy	**Reviewer's Name / Title**	**mm/dd/yyyy**
	Approved By	Date Approved
	Final Approver's Name / Title	**mm/dd/yyyy**

SUMMARY OF FUNCTIONS

The Audit Team Leader oversees a team of auditors for the duration of an internal audit

ESSENTIAL DUTIES AND RESPONSIBILITIES

- Oversee the accounting and financial reporting processes and the audits of the financial statements of the Company.
- Evaluate and select an External Auditor[1].
- Manage the Internal Audit process, develop and manage the Internal Audit schedule (or cycle), supervise Audit Team members, and report the Audit Team's findings to the Audit Committee.
- Review and approve of root cause analysis and investigate material errors in financial statements.
- Review and approve the Internal Audit Department's annual and long-range audit plans and activities, for reviewing significant findings and recommendations by Internal Audit and ensuring the adequacy of management's corrective actions.
- Conduct and supervise the IT Security audit; conduct opening and closing meetings for the audit; prepare and present the final audit report.

ORGANIZATIONAL RELATIONSHIPS

Reports directly to the IT Security Manager or Accounting Manager.

PROCEDURES

Procedure ID and Name	Policies & Procedures Manual
AC1000 Sarbanes-Oxley Compliance	Finance
AC1040 External Auditing	Finance
AC1050 Internal Auditing	Finance
FS1040 Financial Restatements	Finance
ITSD107 IT Security Audits	Computer & Network (IT)

---

[1] Also known as an "independent auditor" or a "third-party auditor."

QUALIFICATIONS

A high school diploma or GED plus 5 or more years of auditing experience is required; a bachelor's degree (in accounting, computer science, or other appropriate field of study) and 2+ years of auditing experience are acceptable, as well.

Good communication skills and the ability to work well with people are essential. 3+ years of experience with appropriate computer applications is beneficial. Project management experience is preferred.

PHYSICAL DEMANDS

Ability to communicate orally with customers, vendors, management, and coworkers is crucial. Regular use of the telephone and email for communication is essential. Sitting for extended periods is common. Hearing and vision within normal ranges is essential for normal conversations, to receive ordinary information, and to prepare or inspect documents.

Activities require the ability to remain in a stationary position 50% of the time, occasionally move about inside the office to access files or office equipment, operate a computer and other office productivity machinery, such as a calculator, hand held devices, copy machine, and computer printer, and operate and monitor various medical equipment. Must be able to constantly position self to maintain equipment, including under tables and desks.

No heavy lifting is expected. Exertion of up to 10 lbs. of force occasionally may be required. Good manual dexterity for the use of common office equipment such as computer terminals, calculator, copiers, and FAX machines.

WORK ENVIRONMENT

The job is performed indoors in a traditional office setting. Activities include extended periods of sitting and extensive work at a computer monitor and phone.

REVISION HISTORY

Revision	Date	Description of Changes	Requested By
0.0	mm/dd/yyyy	Initial Release	

Document ID **JD0570**	Title **INTERNAL AUDITOR-ACCOUNTING**	Print Date **mm/dd/yyyy**
Revision **0.0**	Prepared By **Preparer's Name / Title**	Date Prepared **mm/dd/yyyy**
Effective Date **mm/dd/yyyy**	Reviewed By **Reviewer's Name / Title**	Date Reviewed **mm/dd/yyyy**
	Approved By **Final Approver's Name / Title**	Date Approved **mm/dd/yyyy**

SUMMARY

The Internal Auditor periodically examines (audits) the organization's financial records to ensure they are accurate and up-to-date and that processes for generating and maintaining financial records and documents comply with applicable standards and regulations. They identify ways to improve processes for finding and eliminating waste and fraud.

Internal Auditors shall not audit their own work nor any work generated by their section, group, department, etc.

ESSENTIAL DUTIES AND RESPONSIBILITIES

- Examine financial statements to ensure accuracy, timeliness, and compliance with applicable standards and regulations.
- Inspect account books, statements, ledgers, and accounting systems for efficiency and use of accepted accounting procedures (GAAP, IFRS).
- Assess financial operations and make best-practices recommendations to management.

ORGANIZATIONAL RELATIONSHIPS

The Internal Auditor reports directly to the Audit Team leader for the duration of the internal audit.

PROCEDURES

Procedure ID and Name	Policies & Procedures Manual
AC1050 Internal Auditing	Finance

QUALIFICATIONS

A bachelor's degree in accounting or business administration is required, as is three (3) years' experience as an accountant. A Certified Public Accountant (Chartered Accountant) is desirable but not required. Must be an IIA-certified internal auditor or have equivalent work experience.

Excellent communication skills and the ability to work well with people at all levels are essential. Experience with SAP, JD Edwards software is crucial.

PHYSICAL DEMANDS

Ability to communicate orally with management and accountants is crucial. Regular use of phone and email for communication is essential. Hearing and vision correctable to within normal ranges is essential for normal conversations, receiving ordinary information, and preparing or inspecting documents.

The ability to remain in a stationary position roughly 50% of the time, as well as the ability to move about the office occasionally (accessing files/storage, office equipment, computers and other office productivity devices, attending meetings, etc.), is required.

Using a computer while sitting for extended periods is common. Must also be able to position self to maintain equipment, including under tables and desks.

No heavy lifting is expected, though occasional exertion of about 20 lbs. of force (e.g., carrying accounting books (G/L, etc.), laptops) may be required. Good manual dexterity required to use common office equipment (e.g., computers, mobile devices, calculators, copiers/scanners).

WORK ENVIRONMENT

The job is performed indoors in a traditional office setting. Extended periods of sitting while using a computer or other device are common.

REVISION HISTORY

Revision	Date	Description of Changes	Requested By
0.0	mm/dd/yyyy	Initial Release	

Document ID **JD1120**	Title **RISK MANAGER**	Print Date **mm/dd/yyyy**
Revision **0.0**	Prepared By **Preparer's Name / Title**	Date Prepared **mm/dd/yyyy**
Effective Date **mm/dd/yyyy**	Reviewed By **Reviewer's Name / Title**	Date Reviewed **mm/dd/yyyy**
	Approved By **Final Approver's Name / Title**	Date Approved **mm/dd/yyyy**

SUMMARY

The Risk Manager controls the organization's financial risk by employing various strategies to limit or offset the probability of a financial loss or exposure to financial uncertainty.

ESSENTIAL DUTIES AND RESPONSIBILITIES

- Design, implement, and manage an overall risk management plan that complies with customer, legal/regulatory, and the organization's requirements, as well as those of standards bodies (e.g., IASB, FASB).
- Manage the process of identifying and assessing the risks affecting the business.
- Educate and train leadership, staff, and business associates in the risk management program.
- Oversee, and in some areas implement, the plan of risk control actions, such as:
    a. Purchase of insurance and other risk financing options
    b. Health and safety measures
    c. Liaison with regulators
    d. Business continuity plans
    e. Corporate and department level standards and procedures
- Collect and analyze data with appropriate risk reporting, internally and externally.
- Manage claims and litigation; act as a liaison to insurance carriers and legal counsel.
- Develop and implement systems, policies, and procedures for the identification, collection, retention and analysis of risk related and compliance information.

ORGANIZATIONAL RELATIONSHIPS

Reports directly to the organization's Finance Manager. Works in conjunction with Financial, Physical Security, and IT Security management to facilitate risk management.

PROCEDURES

Procedure ID and Name	Policies & Procedures Manual
AC1020 Risk Assessment	Finance
AC1030 Risk Management	Finance

QUALIFICATIONS

A bachelor's degree in accounting or finance is required. Advanced training in risk analysis and management is also required, as is relevant certification in one or more areas (e.g., CPCU, ARM, CRC). 20 years combined business, insurance, and risk management or similar work experience is required. Must have knowledge of state and federal regulations and agencies, particularly with respect to risk assessment and management.

Require 10 years of financial operations, staff management experience; should have 10+ years multi-line claims experience in a carrier or 3rd-party administration environment.

PHYSICAL DEMANDS

Ability to communicate orally with customers, vendors, management, and coworkers is crucial. Regular use of phone and email for communication is essential. Hearing and vision correctable to within normal ranges is essential for normal conversations, receiving ordinary information, and preparing or inspecting documents.

The ability to remain in a stationary position roughly 50% of the time, as well as the ability to move about the office occasionally (accessing files/storage, office equipment, computers and other office productivity devices, attending meetings, etc.), is required.

Using a computer while sitting for extended periods is common. Must also be able to position self to maintain equipment, including under tables and desks.

No heavy lifting is expected, though occasional exertion of about 20 lbs. of force (e.g., picking up and carrying binders, laptops) may be required. Good manual dexterity required to use common office equipment (e.g., computers, mobile devices, calculators, copiers, scanners).

WORK ENVIRONMENT

The job is performed indoors in a traditional office setting. Extended periods of sitting while using a computer or other devices are common.

REVISION HISTORY

Revision	Date	Description of Changes	Requested By
0.0	mm/dd/yyyy	Initial Release	

Finance Policies and Procedures

Section 600

Index

Section 600
Index

B

D

INDEX   **SECTION/ID**   **Page**

E

F

INDEX   **SECTION/ID**   **Page**

<h2 style="text-align:center">J</h2>

<h2 style="text-align:center">K</h2>

<h2 style="text-align:center">L</h2>

S

INDEX	SECTION/ID	Page

X

Y

Z

[This page intentionally left blank]

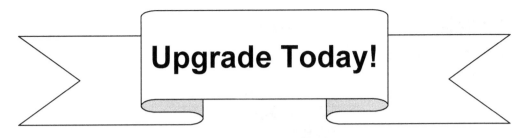

Upgrade Today!

Coupon Code HCB100

With this book from the *Professional's Ready-to-Use Procedure Series*, you've realized the benefits of prewritten procedures as a reference tool. Bizmanualz ® also publishes its policy-and-procedure manuals in easy-to-edit Microsoft Word files.

This Coupon code allows you to buy any one *editable* manual – or purchase one of our *bundles*, if you like – and deduct the cost of this book when you go to our website, http://www.bizmanualz.com.

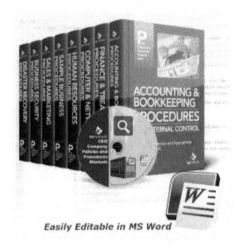

Easily Editable in MS Word

The above coupon code entitles you to **$100 off** the list price of any Bizmanualz policy and procedure manual. That's right! We're offering you the purchase price of this book as a discount on your purchase of any Bizmanualz Policies & Procedures manual.

Place your order online, by phone, or by fax. Be sure to use coupon code HCB100 when you place your order.

www.bizmanualz.com
(800) 466-9953, toll-free in the USA
(outside the USA, call 314-863-5079)
314-863-6571 (fax)

Policies and Procedures Manuals from Bizmanualz

Product details at www.bizmanualz.com
Free samples at www.bizmanualz.com/sample-policies-procedures

bizmanualz·
The Worlds #1 Business Process
Policies and Procedures Templates

Prewritten policies and procedures help you document your processes faster. No need to start from scratch! Our experts have done the research and writing, saving you time, money, and aggravation. Each manual contains a set of easily-**editable Microsoft Word** documents (available for download or on CD).

ABR31 Accounting Policies and Procedures

Protect your business assets with easily editable internal controls, policies, and procedures.

Includes over 3 dozen Accounting procedures for cash, inventory & assets, purchasing, revenue, and administration. Also contains an Accounting Policy Manual and Embezzlement Prevention guide.

ABR42 Finance Policies and Procedures

Quickly create a financial management system to manage risk, optimize returns, and establish effective internal controls.

Includes dozens of Finance procedures for administration, financial statements, internal controls, raising capital, and treasury management. Also includes a Finance Policy Manual and a business management guide.

ABR34 Computer & IT Policies and Procedures

Protect and control your IT assets with easily editable information technology policies and procedures.

Includes 40 procedures for IT administration, IT training and support, IT asset management, IT security and disaster recovery, and software development. Also includes an IT Policy Manual and IT security guide.

ABR44 Sales & Marketing Policies and Procedures

Drive customer satisfaction with improved strategies and tactics.

Includes over 30 Sales and Marketing procedures for planning and strategy, tactics, sales, administration, and product management. Also contains a Sales & Marketing Policy Manual and Internet Marketing guide.

ABR211 ISO 9001 QMS Policies and Procedures

Quickly create your own ISO 9001 quality management system with easily editable quality policies and procedures. Includes 30 quality procedures and a sample Quality Manual.

ABR41 Human Resources Policies and Procedures

Reduce exposure to employee liability issues with easily editable HR policies and procedures.

Includes 35 HR procedures for administration, hiring, compensation, payroll, development, and compliance. Also includes sample job descriptions, an HR Policy Manual, and an Employee Handbook.

A490 Business Policies and Procedures Sampler

Quickly create a total system of internal controls for key departments in your organization.

111 easily editable policies and procedures for a variety of everyday functional areas.

More Procedure Manuals from Bizmanualz

- Security Planning Policies & Procedures
- Disaster Recovery Policies & Procedures
- ISO22000 Food Safety Policies & Procedures
- AS9100 Aerospace Policies & Procedures
- Medical Office Policies & Procedures
- Banking Policies & Procedures
- Non-Profit Policies & Procedures
- Construction Policies & Procedures
- Software Development Policies & Procedures

Buy a Bundle, Save a Bundle!

Easily Editable in MS Word

Buy the 9-manual "CEO Management Procedures Series" or the 5-manual "CFO Management Series" and save *up to 40 percent*!

CPSIA information can be obtained
at www.ICGtesting.com
Printed in the USA
BVHW010827170919
R10295700002B/R102957PG557552BVX2B/2/P

9 781931 591041